CAPITALISM

is the only system geared to the life of a
rational being and the only *moral* politico-
economic system in history.

AYN RAND

and the Objectivists launch a major offensive in the name of a new morality. In one
fiery article after another they show that
capitalism is still an *unknown* ideal, threatened with destruction without a hearing,
"without any public knowledge of its principles, its nature, its history or its moral
meaning."

The political philosophy of Miss Rand's
bestselling novels is presented here in a
challenging new appraisal of our era, by
the "radicals for capitalism."

AYN RAND

CAPITALISM:
THE UNKNOWN IDEAL

With additional articles by
**NATHANIEL BRANDEN,
ALAN GREENSPAN,
and ROBERT HESSEN**

A SIGNET BOOK from
NEW AMERICAN LIBRARY
TIMES MIRROR

Library of Congress Catalog Card Number: 66-26772

This is a reprint of a hardcover edition published by The New
American Library, Inc.

 SIGNET TRADEMARK REG. U.S. PAT. OFF. AND FOREIGN COUNTRIES
REGISTERED TRADEMARK—MARCA REGISTRADA
HECHO EN CHICAGO, U.S.A.

SIGNET, SIGNET CLASSICS, MENTOR, PLUME AND MERIDIAN BOOKS
are published by The New American Library, Inc.,
1633 Broadway, New York, New York 10019

FIRST SIGNET PRINTING, NOVEMBER, 1967

11   12   13   14   15   16   17   18

PRINTED IN THE UNITED STATES OF AMERICA

CONTENTS

INTRODUCTION

This book is not a treatise on economics. It is a collection of essays on the *moral* aspects of capitalism.

Our approach can best be summarized by my statement in the first issue of *The Objectivist Newsletter* (January 1962):

"Objectivism is a philosophical movement; since politics is a branch of philosophy, Objectivism advocates certain political principles—specifically, those of laissez-faire capitalism—as the consequence and the ultimate practical application of its fundamental philosophical principles. It does not regard politics as a separate or primary goal, that is: as a goal that can be achieved without a wider ideological context.

"Politics is based on three other philosophical disciplines: metaphysics, epistemology and ethics—on a theory of man's nature and of man's relationship to existence. It is only on such a base that one can formulate a consistent political theory and achieve it in practice. . . . Objectivists are *not* 'conservatives.' We are *radicals for capitalism;* we are fighting for that philosophical base which capitalism did not have and without which it was doomed to perish."

I want to stress that our primary interest is not politics or economics as such, but *"man's nature and man's relationship to existence"*—and that we advocate capitalism because it is the only system geared to the life of a rational being.

In this respect, there is a fundamental difference between our approach and that of capitalism's classical defenders and modern apologists. With very few exceptions, they are responsible—by default—for capitalism's destruction. The default consisted of their inability or unwillingness to fight the battle where it had to be fought: on moral-philosophical grounds.

No politico-economic system in history has ever proved its value so eloquently or has benefited mankind so greatly as capitalism—and none has ever been attacked so savagely, viciously, and blindly. The flood of misinformation, misrepresentation, distortion, and outright falsehood about capitalism is such that the young people of today have no idea (and virtually no way of discovering any idea) of its actual nature. While archeologists are rummaging through the ruins of millennia for scraps of pottery and bits of bones, from which to reconstruct some information about prehistorical existence—the events of less than a century ago are hidden under a mound more impenetrable than the geological debris of winds, floods, and earthquakes: a mound of silence.

To obliterate the truth on such a large scale, to hide an open secret from the world, to hide—without any power of censorship, yet without any significant sound of protest—the fact that an ideal social system had once been almost within men's reach, cannot be done by any conspiracy of evildoers; it cannot be done except with the tacit compliance of those who know better.

By their silence—*by their evasion of the clash between capitalism and altruism*—it is capitalism's alleged champions who are responsible for the fact that capitalism is being destroyed without a hearing, without a trial, without any public knowledge of its principles, its nature, its history, or its moral meaning. It is being destroyed in the manner of a nightmare lynching—as if a blind, despair-crazed mob were burning a straw man, not knowing that the grotesquely deformed bundle of straw is hiding the living body of the ideal.

The method of capitalism's destruction rests on never letting the world discover *what* it is that is being destroyed—on never allowing it to be identified within the hearing of the young.

The purpose of this book is to identify it.

The guilt for the present state of the world rests on the shoulders of those who are over forty years old today (with a very few exceptions)—those who, when they spoke, said less than they knew and said it less clearly than the subject demanded.

This book is addressed to the young—in years or in spirit—who are not afraid to know and are not ready to give up.

What they have to discover, what all the efforts of capitalism's enemies are frantically aimed at hiding, is the fact that capitalism is not merely the "practical," but the only *moral* system in history. (See *Atlas Shrugged*.)

The political aspects of *Atlas Shrugged* are not its theme. Its theme is primarily ethical-epistemological: the role of the mind in man's existence—and politics, necessarily, is one of the theme's consequences. But the epistemological chaos of our age, fostered by modern philosophy, is such that many young readers find it difficult to translate abstractions into political principles and apply them to the evaluation of today's events. This present book may help them. It is a nonfiction footnote to *Atlas Shrugged*.

Since every political system rests on some theory of ethics, I suggest to those readers who are actually interested in understanding the nature of capitalism, that they read first *The Virtue of Selfishness*, a collection of essays on the Objectivist ethics, which is a necessary foundation for this present book. Since no political discussion can be meaningful or intelligible without a clear understanding of two crucial concepts: "rights" and "government"—yet these are the two most strenuously evaded in today's technique of obfuscation— I suggest that you begin this book by reading (or rereading) two essays from that earlier collection, which you will find here reprinted in the appendix: "Man's Rights" and "The Nature of Government."

Most of the essays in this book appeared originally in *The Objectivist Newsletter* (now, in magazine format, *The Objectivist*); others are based on lectures or papers, as indicated. Some of the essays cover, in brief summary, the answers to the most widely spread fallacies about the economics of capitalism. These essays appeared in the "Intellectual Ammunition Department" of *The Objectivist Newsletter* and were written in answer to questions from our readers. Those who are interested in studying political economy, will find, in the appendix, a recommended bibliography on that subject.

Now a word about the contributors to this book. Robert Hessen is presently completing his doctorate in history at Columbia University, and is teaching in Columbia's Graduate School of Business. Alan Greenspan is president of Townsend-Greenspan & Co., Inc., economic consultants.

—AYN RAND

New York, July 1966

P.S. Nathaniel Branden is no longer associated with me, with my philosophy or with *The Objectivist*.

A. R.

New York, November 1970

THEORY AND HISTORY

1. WHAT IS CAPITALISM?

BY AYN RAND

The disintegration of philosophy in the nineteenth century and its collapse in the twentieth have led to a similar, though much slower and less obvious, process in the course of modern science.

Today's frantic development in the field of technology has a quality reminiscent of the days preceding the economic crash of 1929: riding on the momentum of the past, on the unacknowledged remnants of an Aristotelian epistemology, it is a hectic, feverish expansion, heedless of the fact that its theoretical account is long since overdrawn—that in the field of scientific theory, unable to integrate or interpret their own data, scientists are abetting the resurgence of a primitive mysticism. In the humanities, however, the crash is past, the depression has set in, and the collapse of science is all but complete. •

The clearest evidence of it may be seen in such comparatively young sciences as psychology and political economy. In psychology, one may observe the attempt to study human behavior without reference to the fact that man is conscious. In political economy, one may observe the attempt to study and to devise social systems without reference to *man*.

It is philosophy that defines and establishes the epistemological criteria to guide human knowledge in general and specific sciences in particular. Political economy came into prominence in the nineteenth century, in the era of philosophy's post-Kantian disintegration, and no one rose to check its premises or to challenge its base. Implicitly, uncritically, and by default, political economy accepted as its axioms the fundamental tenets of collectivism.

The Objectivist Newsletter, November and December 1965.

Political economists—including the advocates of capitalism—defined their science as the study of the management or direction or organization or manipulation of a "community's" or a nation's "resources." The nature of these "resources" was not defined; their communal ownership was taken for granted—and the goal of political economy was assumed to be the study of how to utilize these "resources" for "the common good."

The fact that the principal "resource" involved was man himself, that he was an entity of a specific nature with specific capacities and requirements, was given the most superficial attention, if any. Man was regarded simply as one of the factors of production, along with land, forests, or mines—as one of the less significant factors, since more study was devoted to the influence and quality of these others than to *his* role or quality.

Political economy was, in effect, a science starting in midstream: it observed that men were producing and trading, it took for granted that they had always done so and always would—it accepted this fact as the given, requiring no further consideration—and it addressed itself to the problem of how to devise the best way for the "community" to dispose of human effort.

There were many reasons for this tribal view of man. The morality of altruism was one; the growing dominance of political statism among the intellectuals of the nineteenth century was another. Psychologically, the main reason was the soul-body dichotomy permeating European culture: material production was regarded as a demeaning task of a lower order, unrelated to the concerns of man's intellect, a task assigned to slaves or serfs since the beginning of recorded history. The institution of serfdom had lasted, in one form or another, till well into the nineteenth century; it was abolished, politically, only by the advent of capitalism; politically, but not intellectually.

The concept of man as a free, independent individual was profoundly alien to the culture of Europe. It was a tribal culture down to its roots; in European thinking, the tribe was the entity, the unit, and man was only one of its expendable cells. This applied to rulers and serfs alike: the rulers were believed to hold their privileges only by virtue of the services they rendered to the tribe, services regarded as of a noble order, namely, armed force or military defense. But a nobleman was as much chattel of the tribe as a serf: his life and property belonged to the king. It must be remembered that the institution of private property, in the full, legal meaning of the term, was brought into existence only by capitalism. In the pre-capitalist eras, private property existed *de facto*, but not *de jure*, *i.e.*, by custom and sufferance, not by right or by law. In law and in principle, all property belonged to the head of the tribe, the king, and was held only by his permission, which could be revoked at any time, at his pleasure. (The king could and did expropriate the estates of recalcitrant noblemen throughout the course of Europe's history.)

The American philosophy of the Rights of Man was never grasped fully by European intellectuals. Europe's predominant idea of emancipation consisted of changing the concept of man as a slave of the absolute state embodied by a king, to the concept of man as a slave of the absolute state embodied by "the people"—*i.e.*, switching from slavery to a tribal chief into slavery to the tribe. A non-tribal view of existence could not penetrate the mentalities that regarded the privilege of ruling material producers by physical force as a badge of nobility.

Thus Europe's thinkers did not notice the fact that during the nineteenth century, the galley slaves had been replaced by the inventors of steamboats, and the village blacksmiths by the owners of blast furnaces, and they went on thinking in such terms (such contradictions in terms) as "wage slavery" or "the antisocial selfishness of industrialists who take so much from society without giving anything in return"—on the unchallenged axiom that wealth is an anonymous, social, tribal product.

That notion has not been challenged to this day; it represents the implicit assumption and the base of contemporary political economy.

As an example of this view and its consequences, I shall cite the article on "Capitalism" in the *Encyclopaedia Britannica*. The article gives no definition of its subject; it opens as follows:

CAPITALISM, a term used to denote the economic system that has been dominant in the western world since the breakup of feudalism. Fundamental to any system called capitalist are the relations between private owners of nonpersonal means of production (land, mines, *industrial plants*, etc., collectively known as capital) [italics mine] and free but capitalless workers, who sell their labour services to employers. . . . The resulting wage bargains determine the proportion in which the total product of society will be shared between the class of labourers and the class of capitalist entrepreneurs.[1]

(I quote from Galt's speech in *Atlas Shrugged*, from a passage describing the tenets of collectivism: "An industrialist—blank-out—there is no such person. A factory is a 'natural resource,' like a tree, a rock or a mud-puddle.")

The success of capitalism is explained by the *Britannica* as follows:

> Productive use of the "social surplus" was the special virtue that enabled capitalism to outstrip all prior economic systems. Instead of building pyramids and cathedrals, those in command of the social surplus chose to invest in ships, warehouses, raw materials, finished goods and other material forms of wealth. The social surplus was thus converted into enlarged productive capacity.

This is said about a time when Europe's population subsisted in such poverty that child mortality approached fifty percent, and periodic famines wiped out the "surplus" *population* which the pre-capitalist economies were unable to feed. Yet, making no distinction between tax-expropriated and industrially produced wealth, the *Britannica* asserts that it was the *surplus wealth* of that time that the early capitalists "commanded" and "chose to invest"—and that this investment was the cause of the stupendous prosperity of the age that followed.

What is a "social surplus"? The article gives no definition or explanation. A "surplus" presupposes a norm; if subsistence on a chronic starvation level is above the implied norm, what is that norm? The article does not answer.

There is, of course, no such thing as a "social surplus." All wealth is produced by somebody and belongs to somebody. And "the special virtue that enabled capitalism to outstrip all prior economic systems" was *freedom* (a concept eloquently absent from the *Britannica's* account), which led, not to the expropriation, but to the *creation* of wealth.

I shall have more to say later about that disgraceful article (disgraceful on many counts, not the least of which is scholarship). At this point, I quoted it only as a succinct example of the tribal premise that underlies today's political economy. That premise is shared by the enemies and the champions of capitalism alike; it provides the former with a certain inner

[1] *Encyclopaedia Britannica*, 1964, Vol. IV, pp. 839–845.

consistency, and disarms the latter by a subtle, yet devastating aura of moral hypocrisy—as witness, their attempts to justify capitalism on the ground of "the common good" or "service to the consumer" or "the best allocation of resources." (*Whose* resources?)

If capitalism is to be understood, it is this *tribal premise* that has to be checked—and challenged.

Mankind is not an entity, an organism, or a coral bush. The entity involved in production and trade is *man*. It is with the study of man—not of the loose aggregate known as a "community"—that any science of the humanities has to begin.

This issue represents one of the epistemological differences between the humanities and the physical sciences, one of the causes of the former's well-earned inferiority complex in regard to the latter. A physical science would not permit itself (not yet, at least) to ignore or bypass the nature of its subject. Such an attempt would mean: a science of astronomy that gazed at the sky, but refused to study individual stars, planets, and satellites—or a science of medicine that studied disease, without any knowledge or criterion of health, and took, as its basic subject of study, a hospital as a whole, never focusing on individual patients.

A great deal may be learned about society by studying man; but this process cannot be reversed: nothing can be learned about man by studying society—by studying the inter-relationships of entities one has never identified or defined. Yet that is the methodology adopted by most political economists. Their attitude, in effect, amounts to the unstated, implicit postulate: "Man is that which fits economic equations." Since he obviously does not, this leads to the curious fact that in spite of the practical nature of their science, political economists are oddly unable to relate their abstractions to the concretes of actual existence.

It leads also to a baffling sort of double standard or double perspective in their way of viewing men and events: if they observe a shoemaker, they find no difficulty in concluding that he is working in order to make a living; but as political economists, on the tribal premise, they declare that his purpose (and duty) is to provide society with shoes. If they observe a panhandler on a street corner, they identify him as a bum; in political economy, he becomes "a sovereign consumer." If they hear the communist doctrine that all property should belong to the state, they reject it emphatically and feel, *sincerely*, that they would fight communism to the death; but in political economy, they speak of the government's duty to effect "a fair redistribution of wealth," and they speak of businessmen as the best, most efficient trustees of the nation's "natural resources."

This is what a basic premise (and philosophical negligence) will do; this is what the tribal premise has done.

To reject that premise and begin at the beginning—in one's approach to political economy and to the evaluation of various social systems—one must begin by identifying man's nature, *i.e.,* those essential characteristics which distinguish him from all other living species.

Man's essential characteristic is his rational faculty. Man's mind is his basic means of survival—his only means of gaining knowledge.

> Man cannot survive, as animals do, by the guidance of mere percepts. . . . He cannot provide for his simplest physical needs without a process of thought. He needs a process of thought to discover how to plant and grow his food or how to make weapons for hunting. His percepts might lead him to a cave, if one is available— but to build the simplest shelter, he needs a process of thought. No percepts and no "instincts" will tell him how to light a fire, how to weave cloth, how to forge tools, how to make a wheel, how to make an airplane, how to perform an appendectomy, how to produce an electric light bulb or an electronic tube or a cyclotron or a box of matches. Yet his life depends on such knowledge—and only a volitional act of his consciousness, a process of thought, can provide it.[2]

A process of thought is an enormously complex process of identification and integration, which only an individual mind can perform. There is no such thing as a collective brain. Men can learn from one another, but learning requires a process of thought on the part of every individual student. Men can cooperate in the discovery of new knowledge, but such cooperation requires the independent exercise of his rational faculty by every individual scientist. Man is the only living species that can transmit and expand his store of knowledge from generation to generation; but such transmission requires a process of thought on the part of the individual recipients. As witness, the breakdowns of civilization, the dark ages in the history of mankind's progress, when the accumulated knowledge of centuries vanished from the lives of men who were unable, unwilling, or forbidden to think.

[2] Ayn Rand, "The Objectivist Ethics," in *The Virtue of Selfishness.*

In order to sustain its life, every living species has to follow a certain course of action required by its nature. The action required to sustain human life is primarily intellectual: everything man needs has to be discovered by his mind and produced by his effort. Production is the application of reason to the problem of survival.

If some men do not choose to think, they can survive only by imitating and repeating a routine of work discovered by others—but those others had to discover it, or none would have survived. If some men do not choose to think or to work, they can survive (temporarily) only by looting the goods produced by others—but those others had to produce them, or none would have survived. Regardless of what choice is made, in this issue, by any man or by any number of men, regardless of what blind, irrational, or evil course they may choose to pursue—the fact remains that reason is man's means of survival and that men prosper or fail, survive or perish in proportion to the degree of their rationality.

Since knowledge, thinking, and rational action are properties of the individual, since the choice to exercise his rational faculty or not depends on the individual, man's survival requires that those who think be free of the interference of those who don't. Since men are neither omniscient nor infallible, they must be free to agree or disagree, to cooperate or to pursue their own independent course, each according to his own rational judgment. Freedom is the fundamental requirement of man's mind.

A rational mind does not work under compulsion; it does not subordinate its grasp of reality to anyone's orders, directives, or controls; it does not sacrifice its knowledge, its view of the truth, to anyone's opinions, threats, wishes, plans, or "welfare." Such a mind may be hampered by others, it may be silenced, proscribed, imprisoned, or destroyed; it cannot be forced; a gun is not an argument. (An example and symbol of this attitude is Galileo.)

It is from the work and the inviolate integrity of such minds—from the intransigent innovators—that all of mankind's knowledge and achievements have come. (See *The Fountainhead.*) It is to such minds that mankind owes its survival. (See *Atlas Shrugged.*)

The same principle applies to all men, on every level of ability and ambition. To the extent that a man is guided by his rational judgment, he acts in accordance with the requirements of his nature and, to that extent, succeeds in achieving a human form of survival and well-being; to the extent that he acts irrationally, he acts as his own destroyer.

The social recognition of man's rational nature—of the connection between his survival and his use of reason—is the concept of *individual rights*.

I shall remind you that "rights" are a moral principle defining and sanctioning a man's freedom of action in a social context, that they are derived from man's nature as a rational being and represent a necessary condition of his particular mode of survival. I shall remind you also that the right to life is the source of all rights, including the right to property.[8]

In regard to political economy, this last requires special emphasis: man has to work and produce in order to support his life. He has to support his life by his own effort and by the guidance of his own mind. If he cannot dispose of the product of his effort, he cannot dispose of his effort; if he cannot dispose of his effort, he cannot dispose of his life. Without property rights, no other rights can be practiced.

Now, bearing these facts in mind, consider the question of what social system is appropriate to man.

A social system is a set of moral-political-economic principles embodied in a society's laws, institutions, and government, which determine the relationships, the terms of association, among the men living in a given geographical area. It is obvious that these terms and relationships depend on an identification of man's nature, that they would be different if they pertain to a society of rational beings or to a colony of ants. It is obvious that they will be radically different if men deal with one another as free, independent individuals, on the premise that every man is an end in himself—or as members of a pack, each regarding the others as the means to *his* ends and to the ends of "the pack as a whole."

There are only two fundamental questions (or two aspects of the same question) that determine the nature of any social system: Does a social system recognize individual rights?— and: Does a social system ban physical force from human relationships? The answer to the second question is the practical implementation of the answer to the first.

Is man a sovereign individual who owns his person, his mind, his life, his work and its products—or is he the property of the tribe (the state, the society, the collective) that may dispose of him in any way it pleases, that may dictate his convictions, prescribe the course of his life, control his work and expropriate his products? Does man have the *right* to

---

[8] For a fuller discussion of rights, I refer you to my articles "Man's Rights" in the appendix, and "Collectivized 'Rights'" in *The Virtue of Selfishness*.

exist for his own sake—or is he born in bondage, as an indentured servant who must keep buying his life by serving the tribe but can never acquire it free and clear?

This is the first question to answer. The rest is consequences and practical implementations. The basic issue is only: Is man free?

In mankind's history, capitalism is the only system that answers: Yes.

Capitalism is a social system based on the recognition of individual rights, including property rights, in which all property is privately owned.

The recognition of individual rights entails the banishment of physical force from human relationships: basically, rights can be violated only by means of force. In a capitalist society, no man or group may *initiate* the use of physical force against others. The only function of the government, in such a society, is the task of protecting man's rights, *i.e.*, the task of protecting him from physical force; the government acts as the agent of man's right of self-defense, and may use force only in retaliation and only against those who initiate its use; thus the government is the means of placing the retaliatory use of force under *objective control.*[4]

It is the basic, metaphysical fact of man's nature—the connection between his survival and his use of reason—that capitalism recognizes and protects.

In a capitalist society, all human relationships are *voluntary*. Men are free to cooperate or not, to deal with one another or not, as their own individual judgments, convictions, and interests dictate. They can deal with one another only in terms of and by means of reason, *i.e.*, by means of discussion, persuasion, and *contractual* agreement, by voluntary choice to mutual benefit. The right to agree with others is not a problem in any society; it is *the right to disagree* that is crucial. It is the institution of private property that protects and implements the right to disagree—and thus keeps the road open to man's most valuable attribute (valuable personally, socially, and *objectively*): the creative mind.

This is the cardinal difference between capitalism and collectivism.

The power that determines the establishment, the changes, the evolution, and the destruction of social systems is philosophy. The role of chance, accident, or tradition, in this context, is the same as their role in the life of an individual: their power stands in inverse ratio to the power of a culture's

[4] For a fuller discussion of this subject, see my article "The Nature of Government" in the appendix.

(or an individual's) philosophical equipment, and grows as philosophy collapses. It is, therefore, by reference to philosophy that the character of a social system has to be defined and evaluated. Corresponding to the four branches of philosophy, the four keystones of capitalism are: metaphysically, the requirements of man's nature and survival—epistemologically, reason—ethically, individual rights—politically, freedom.

This, in substance, is the base of the proper approach to political economy and to an understanding of capitalism—not the tribal premise inherited from prehistorical traditions.

The "practical" justification of capitalism does not lie in the collectivist claim that it effects "the best allocation of national resources." Man is *not* a "national resource" and neither is his mind—and without the creative power of man's intelligence, raw materials remain just so many useless raw materials.

The *moral* justification of capitalism does not lie in the altruist claim that it represents the best way to achieve "the common good." It is true that capitalism does—if that catchphrase has any meaning—but this is merely a secondary consequence. The moral justification of capitalism lies in the fact that it is the only system consonant with man's rational nature, that it protects man's survival *qua* man, and that its ruling principle is: *justice*.

Every social system is based, explicitly or implicitly, on some theory of ethics. The tribal notion of "the common good" has served as the moral justification of most social systems—and of all tyrannies—in history. The degree of a society's enslavement or freedom corresponded to the degree to which that tribal slogan was invoked or ignored.

"The common good" (or "the public interest") is an undefined and undefinable concept: there is no such entity as "the tribe" or "the public"; the tribe (or the public or society) is only a number of individual men. Nothing can be good for the tribe as such; "good" and "value" pertain *only* to a living organism—to an individual living organism—not to a disembodied aggregate of relationships.

"The common good" is a meaningless concept, unless taken literally, in which case its only possible meaning is: the sum of the good of *all* the individual men involved. But in that case, the concept is meaningless as a moral criterion: it leaves open the question of what *is* the good of individual men and how does one determine it?

It is not, however, in its literal meaning that that concept is generally used. It is accepted precisely for its elastic, undefinable, mystical character which serves, not as a moral guide, but as an escape from morality. Since the good is not applicable to the disembodied, it becomes a moral blank check for those who attempt to embody it.

When "the common good" of a society is regarded as something apart from and superior to the individual good of its members, it means that the good of *some* men takes precedence over the good of others, with those others consigned to the status of sacrificial animals. It is tacitly assumed, in such cases, that "the common good" means "the good of the *majority*" as against the minority or the individual. Observe the significant fact that that assumption is *tacit:* even the most collectivized mentalities seem to sense the impossibility of justifying it morally. But "the good of the majority," too, is only a pretense and a delusion: since, in fact, the violation of an individual's rights means the abrogation of all rights, it delivers the helpless majority into the power of any gang that proclaims itself to be "the voice of society" and proceeds to rule by means of physical force, until deposed by another gang employing the same means.

If one begins by defining the good of individual men, one will accept as proper only a society in which that good is achieved and *achievable*. But if one begins by accepting "the common good" as an axiom and regarding individual good as its possible but not necessary consequence (not necessary in any particular case), one ends up with such a gruesome absurdity as Soviet Russia, a country professedly dedicated to "the common good," where, with the exception of a minuscule clique of rulers, the entire population has existed in subhuman misery for over two generations.

What makes the victims and, worse, the observers accept this and other similar historical atrocities, and still cling to the myth of "the common good"? The answer lies in philosophy—in philosophical theories on the nature of moral values.

There are, in essence, three schools of thought on the nature of the good: the intrinsic, the subjective, and the objective. The *intrinsic* theory holds that the good is inherent in certain things or actions as such, regardless of their context and consequences, regardless of any benefit or injury they may cause to the actors and subjects involved. It is a theory that divorces the concept of "good" from beneficiaries, and the concept of "value" from valuer and purpose—claiming that the good is good in, by, and of itself.

The *subjectivist* theory holds that the good bears no relation to the facts of reality, that it is the product of a man's consciousness, created by his feelings, desires, "intuitions," or whims, and that it is merely an "arbitrary postulate" or an "emotional commitment."

The intrinsic theory holds that the good resides in some sort of reality, independent of man's consciousness; the subjectivist theory holds that the good resides in man's consciousness, independent of reality.

The *objective* theory holds that the good is neither an attribute of "things in themselves" nor of man's emotional states, but *an evaluation* of the facts of reality by man's consciousness according to a rational standard of value. (Rational, in this context, means: derived from the facts of reality and validated by a process of reason.) The objective theory holds that *the good is an aspect of reality in relation to man*—and that it must be discovered, not invented, by man. Fundamental to an objective theory of values is the question: Of value to whom and for what? An objective theory does not permit context-dropping or "concept-stealing"; it does not permit the separation of "value" from "purpose," of the good from beneficiaries, and of man's actions from reason.

Of all the social systems in mankind's history, *capitalism is the only system based on an objective theory of values.*

The intrinsic theory and the subjectivist theory (or a mixture of both) are the necessary base of every dictatorship, tyranny, or variant of the absolute state. Whether they are held consciously or subconsciously—in the explicit form of a philosopher's treatise or in the implicit chaos of its echoes in an average man's feelings—these theories make it possible for a man to believe that the good is independent of man's mind and can be achieved by physical force.

If a man believes that the good is intrinsic in certain actions, he will not hesitate to force others to perform them. If he believes that the human benefit or injury caused by such actions is of no significance, he will regard a sea of blood as of no significance. If he believes that the beneficiaries of such actions are irrelevant (or interchangeable), he will regard wholesale slaughter as his moral duty in the service of a "higher" good. It is the intrinsic theory of values that produces a Robespierre, a Lenin, a Stalin, or a Hitler. It is not an accident that Eichmann was a Kantian.

If a man believes that the good is a matter of arbitrary, subjective choice, the issue of good or evil becomes, for him, an issue of: *my* feelings or *theirs?* No bridge, understanding, or communication is possible to him. Reason is the only means of communication among men, and an objectively perceivable reality is their only common frame of reference; when these are invalidated (*i.e.*, held to be irrelevant) in the field of morality, force becomes men's only way of dealing with one another. If the subjectivist wants to pursue some social ideal of his own, he feels morally entitled to force men "for their own good," since he *feels* that he is right and that there is nothing to oppose him but their misguided feelings.

Thus, in practice, the proponents of the intrinsic and the subjectivist schools meet and blend. (They blend in terms of their psycho-epistemology as well: by what means do the moralists of the intrinsic school discover their transcendental "good," if not by means of special, non-rational intuitions and revelations, *i.e.*, by means of their feelings?) It is doubtful whether anyone can hold either of these theories as an actual, if mistaken, conviction. But both serve as a rationalization of power-lust and of rule by brute force, unleashing the potential dictator and disarming his victims.

The objective theory of values is the only moral theory incompatible with rule by force. Capitalism is the only system based implicitly on an objective theory of values—and the historic tragedy is that this has never been made explicit.

If one knows that the good is *objective*—*i.e.*, determined by the nature of reality, but to be discovered by man's mind—one knows that an attempt to achieve the good by physical force is a monstrous contradiction which negates morality at its root by destroying man's capacity to recognize the good, *i.e.*, his capacity to value. Force invalidates and paralyzes a man's judgment, demanding that he act against it, thus rendering him morally impotent. A value which one is forced to accept at the price of surrendering one's mind, is not a value to anyone; the forcibly mindless can neither judge nor choose nor value. An attempt to achieve the good by force is like an attempt to provide a man with a picture gallery at the price of cutting out his eyes. Values cannot exist (cannot be valued) outside the full context of a man's life, needs, goals, and *knowledge*.

The objective view of values permeates the entire structure of a capitalist society.

The recognition of individual rights implies the recognition of the fact that the good is not an ineffable abstraction in some supernatural dimension, but a value pertaining to reality, to this earth, to the lives of individual human beings (note the right to the pursuit of happiness). It implies that the good cannot be divorced from beneficiaries, that men are not to be regarded as interchangeable, and that no man or tribe may attempt to achieve the good of some at the price of the immolation of others.

The free market represents the *social* application of an objective theory of values. Since values are to be discovered by man's mind, men must be free to discover them—to think, to study, to translate their knowledge into physical form, to offer their products for trade, to judge them, and to choose, be it material goods or ideas, a loaf of bread or a philosophical treatise. Since values are established contextually, every man must judge for himself, in the context of his own knowledge, goals, and interests. Since values are determined by the nature of reality, it is reality that serves as men's ultimate arbiter: if a man's judgment is right, the rewards are his; if it is wrong, he is his only victim.

It is in regard to a free market that the distinction between an intrinsic, subjective, and objective view of values is particularly important to understand. The market value of a product is *not* an intrinsic value, not a "value in itself" hanging in a vacuum. A free market never loses sight of the question: Of value *to whom?* And, within the broad field of objectivity, the market value of a product does not reflect its *philosophically objective* value, but only its *socially objective* value.

By "philosophically objective," I mean a value estimated from the standpoint of the best possible to man, *i.e.*, by the criterion of the most rational mind possessing the greatest knowledge, in a given category, in a given period, and in a defined context (nothing can be estimated in an undefined context). For instance, it can be rationally proved that the airplane is *objectively* of immeasurably greater value to man (to *man at his best*) than the bicycle—and that the works of Victor Hugo are *objectively* of immeasurably greater value than true-confession magazines. But if a given man's intellectual potential can barely manage to enjoy true confessions, there is no reason why his meager earnings, the product of *his* effort, should be spent on books he cannot read—or on subsidizing the airplane industry, if his own transportation needs do not extend beyond the range of a bicycle. (Nor is there any reason why the rest of mankind should be held down to the level of his literary taste, his engineering capacity, and his income. Values are not determined by fiat nor by majority vote.)

Just as the number of its adherents is not a proof of an idea's truth or falsehood, of an art work's merit or demerit, of a product's efficacy or inefficacy—so the free-market value of goods or services does not necessarily represent their philosophically objective value, but only their *socially objective* value, *i.e.*, the sum of the individual judgments of all the men involved in trade at a given time, the sum of what *they* valued, each in the context of his own life.

Thus, a manufacturer of lipstick may well make a greater fortune than a manufacturer of microscopes—even though it can be rationally demonstrated that microscopes are scientifically more valuable than lipstick. But—valuable *to whom?*

A microscope is of no value to a little stenographer struggling to make a living; a lipstick is; a lipstick, to her, may mean the difference between self-confidence and self-doubt, between glamour and drudgery.

This does not mean, however, that the values ruling a free market are *subjective.* If the stenographer spends all her money on cosmetics and has none left to pay for the use of a microscope (for a visit to the doctor) *when she needs it,* she learns a better method of budgeting her income; the free market serves as her teacher: she has no way to penalize others for her mistakes. If she budgets rationally, the microscope is always available to serve her own specific needs *and no more,* as far as she is concerned: she is not taxed to support an entire hospital, a research laboratory, or a space ship's journey to the moon. Within her own productive power, she does pay a part of the cost of scientific achievements, *when and as she needs them.* She has no "social duty," her own life is her only responsibility—and the only thing that a capitalist system requires of her is the thing that *nature* requires: rationality, *i.e.,* that she live and act to the best of her own judgment.

Within every category of goods and services offered on a free market, it is the purveyor of the best product at the cheapest price who wins the greatest financial rewards *in that field*—not automatically nor immediately nor by fiat, but by virtue of the free market, which teaches every participant to look for the *objective* best within the category of his own competence, and penalizes those who act on irrational considerations.

Now observe that a free market does not level men down to some common denominator—that the intellectual criteria of the majority do not rule a free market or a free society— and that the exceptional men, the innovators, the intellectual giants, are not held down by the majority. In fact, it is the members of this exceptional minority who lift the whole of a free society to the level of their own achievements, while rising further and ever further.

A free market is a *continuous process* that cannot be held still, an upward process that demands the best (the most rational) of every man and rewards him accordingly. While the majority have barely assimilated the value of the automobile, the creative minority introduces the airplane. The majority learn by demonstration, the minority is free to demonstrate. The "philosophically objective" value of a new product serves as the teacher for those who are willing to exercise their rational faculty, each to the extent of his ability. Those who are unwilling remain unrewarded—as well as those who aspire to more than their ability produces. The stagnant, the irrational, the subjectivist have no power to stop their betters.

(The small minority of adults who are *unable* rather than unwilling to work, have to rely on voluntary charity; misfortune is not a claim to slave labor; there is no such thing as the *right* to consume, control, and destroy those without whom one would be unable to survive. As to depressions and mass unemployment, they are not caused by the free market, but by government interference into the economy.)

The mental parasites—the imitators who attempt to cater to what they think is the public's known taste—are constantly being beaten by the innovators whose products raise the public's knowledge and taste to ever higher levels. It is in this sense that the free market is ruled, not by the consumers, but by the producers. The most successful ones are those who discover new fields of production, fields which had not been known to exist.

A given product may not be appreciated at once, particularly if it is too radical an innovation; but, barring irrelevant accidents, it wins in the long run. It is in this sense that the free market is not ruled by the intellectual criteria of the majority, which prevail only at and for any given moment; the free market is ruled by those who are able to see and plan long-range—and the better the mind, the longer the range.

The economic value of a man's work is determined, on a free market, by a single principle: by the voluntary consent of those who are willing to trade him their work or products in return. This is the moral meaning of the law of supply and demand; it represents the total rejection of two vicious doctrines: the tribal premise and altruism. It represents the recognition of the fact that man is not the property nor the servant of the tribe, that *a man works in order to support his own life*—as, by his nature, he must—that he has to be guided by his own rational self-interest, and if he wants to trade with others, he cannot expect sacrificial victims, *i.e.*, he cannot expect to receive values without trading commensurate values in return. The sole criterion of what is commensurate, in this context, is the free, voluntary, uncoerced judgment of the traders.

The tribal mentalities attack this principle from two seemingly opposite sides: they claim that the free market is "unfair" both to the genius and to the average man. The first objection is usually expressed by a question such as: "Why should Elvis Presley make more money than Einstein?" The answer is: Because men work in order to support and enjoy their own lives—and if many men find value in Elvis Presley, they are entitled to spend their money on their own pleasure. Presley's fortune is not taken from those who do not care for his work (I am one of them) nor from Einstein—nor does he stand in Einstein's way—nor does Einstein lack proper recognition and support in a free society, on an appropriate intellectual level.

As to the second objection, the claim that a man of average ability suffers an "unfair" disadvantage on a free market—

Look past the range of the moment, you who cry that you fear to compete with men of superior intelligence, that their mind is a threat to your livelihood, that the strong leave no chance to the weak in a market of voluntary trade. . . . When you live in a rational society, where men are free to trade, you receive an incalculable bonus: the material value of your work is determined not only by your effort, but by the effort of the best productive minds who exist in the world around you. . . .

The machine, the frozen form of a living intelligence, is the power that expands the potential of your life by raising the productivity of your time. . . . Every man is free to rise as far as he's able or willing, but it's only the degree to which he thinks that determines the degree to which he'll rise. Physical labor as such can extend no further than the range of the moment. The man who does no more than physical labor, consumes the material value-equivalent of his own contribution to the process of production, and leaves no further value, neither for himself nor others. But the man who produces an idea in any field of rational endeavor—the man who discovers new knowledge—is the permanent benefactor of humanity. . . . It is only the value of an idea that can be shared with unlimited numbers of men, making all sharers richer at no one's sacrifice or loss, raising the productive capacity of whatever labor they perform. . . .

In proportion to the mental energy he spent, the man who creates a new invention receives but a small percentage of his value in terms of material payment, no matter what fortune he makes, no matter what millions he earns. But the man who works as a janitor in the factory producing that invention, receives an enormous payment in proportion to the mental effort that his job requires of *him.* And the same is true of all men between, on all levels of ambition and ability. The man at the top of the intellectual pyramid contributes the most to all those below him, but gets nothing except his material payment, receiving no intellectual bonus from others to add to the value of his time. The man at the bottom who, left to himself, would starve in his hopeless ineptitude, contributes nothing to those above him, but receives the bonus of all of their brains. Such is the nature of the "competition" between the strong and the weak of the intellect. Such is the pattern of "exploitation" for which you have damned the strong. (*Atlas Shrugged*)

And such is the relationship of capitalism to man's mind and to man's survival.

The magnificent progress achieved by capitalism in a brief span of time—the spectacular improvement in the conditions of man's existence on earth—is a matter of historical record. It is not to be hidden, evaded, or explained away by all the propaganda of capitalism's enemies. But what needs special emphasis is the fact that this progress was achieved by *non-sacrificial* means.

Progress cannot be achieved by forced privations, by squeezing a "social surplus" out of starving victims. Progress can come only out of *individual surplus, i.e.,* from the work, the energy, the creative over-abundance of those men whose ability produces more than their personal consumption requires, those who are intellectually and financially able to seek the new, to improve on the known, to move forward. In a capitalist society, where such men are free to function and to take their own risks, progress is not a matter of sacrificing to some distant future, it is part of the living present, it is the normal and natural, it is achieved as and while men live—and *enjoy*—their lives.

Now consider the alternative—the tribal society, where all men throw their efforts, values, ambitions, and goals into a tribal pool or common pot, then wait hungrily at its rim, while the leader of a clique of cooks stirs it with a bayonet in one hand and a blank check on all their lives in the other.

The most consistent example of such a system is the Union of Soviet Socialist Republics.

Half a century ago, the Soviet rulers commanded their subjects to be patient, bear privations, and make sacrifices for the sake of "industrializing" the country, promising that this was only temporary, that industrialization would bring them abundance, and Soviet progress would surpass the capitalistic West.

Today, Soviet Russia is still unable to feed her people— while the rulers scramble to copy, borrow, or steal the technological achievements of the West. Industrialization is not a static goal; it is a dynamic process with a rapid rate of obsolescence. So the wretched serfs of a planned tribal economy, who starved while waiting for electric generators and tractors, are now starving while waiting for atomic power and interplanetary travel. Thus, in a "people's state," the progress of science is a threat to the people, and every advance is taken out of the people's shrinking hides.

This was not the history of capitalism.

America's abundance was not created by public sacrifices to "the common good," but by the productive genius of free men who pursued their own personal interests and the making of their own private fortunes. They did not starve the people to pay for America's industrialization. They gave the people better jobs, higher wages, and cheaper goods with every new machine they invented, with every scientific discovery or technological advance—and thus the whole country was moving forward and profiting, not suffering, every step of the way.

Do not, however, make the error of reversing cause and effect: the good of the country was made possible precisely by the fact that it was not forced on anyone as a moral goal or duty; it was merely an effect; the cause was a man's right to pursue his own good. It is this right—not its consequences —that represents the moral justification of capitalism.

But this right is incompatible with the intrinsic or the subjectivist theory of values, with the altruist morality and the tribal premise. It is obvious which human attribute one rejects when one rejects objectivity; and, in view of capitalism's record, it is obvious against which human attribute the altruist morality and the tribal premise stand united: against man's mind, against intelligence—particularly against intelligence applied to the problems of human survival, *i.e.*, productive ability.

While altruism seeks to rob intelligence of its rewards, by asserting that the moral duty of the competent is to serve the incompetent and sacrifice themselves to anyone's need—the tribal premise goes a step further: it denies the existence of intelligence and of its role in the production of wealth.

It is morally obscene to regard wealth as an anonymous, tribal product and to talk about "redistributing" it. The view that wealth is the result of some undifferentiated, collective process, that we all did something and it's impossible to tell who did what, therefore some sort of equalitarian "distribution" is necessary—might have been appropriate in a primordial jungle with a savage horde moving boulders by crude physical labor (though even there someone had to initiate and organize the moving). To hold that view in an industrial society—where individual achievements are a matter of public record—is so crass an evasion that even to give it the benefit of the doubt is an obscenity.

Anyone who has ever been an employer or an employee, or has observed men working, or has done an honest day's work himself, knows the crucial role of ability, of intelligence, of a focused, competent mind—in any and all lines of work, from the lowest to the highest. He knows that ability or the lack of it (whether the lack is actual or volitional) makes a difference of life-or-death in any productive process. The evidence is so overwhelming—theoretically and practically, logically and "empirically," in the events of history and in anyone's own daily grind—that no one can claim ignorance of it. Mistakes of this size are not made innocently.

When great industrialists made fortunes on a *free* market (*i.e.*, without the use of force, without government assistance or interference), they *created* new wealth—they did not take it from those who had *not* created it. If you doubt it, take a look at the "total social product"—and the standard of living—of those countries where such men are not permitted to exist.

Observe how seldom and how inadequately the issue of human intelligence is discussed in the writings of the tribal-statist-altruist theoreticians. Observe how carefully today's advocates of a mixed economy avoid and evade any mention of intelligence or ability in their approach to politico-economic issues, in their claims, demands, and pressure-group warfare over the looting of "the total social product."

It is often asked: Why was capitalism destroyed in spite of its incomparably beneficent record? The answer lies in the fact that the lifeline feeding any social system is a culture's dominant philosophy and that capitalism never had a philosophical base. It was the last and (theoretically) incomplete product of an Aristotelian influence. As a resurgent tide of mysticism engulfed philosophy in the nineteenth century, capitalism was left in an intellectual vacuum, its lifeline cut. Neither its moral nature nor even its political principles had ever been fully understood or defined. Its alleged defenders regarded it as compatible with government controls (*i.e.,* government interference into the economy), ignoring the meaning and implications of the concept of laissez-faire. Thus, what existed in practice, in the nineteenth century, was not pure capitalism, but variously mixed economies. Since controls necessitate and breed further controls, it was the statist element of the mixtures that wrecked them; it was the free, capitalist element that took the blame.

Capitalism could not survive in a culture dominated by mysticism and altruism, by the soul-body dichotomy and the tribal premise. No social system (and no human institution or activity of any kind) can survive without a moral base. On the basis of the altruist morality, capitalism had to be—and was—damned from the start.[5]

For those who do not fully understand the role of philosophy in politico-economic issues, I offer—as the clearest example of today's intellectual state—some further quotations from the *Encyclopaedia Britannica's* article on capitalism.

> Few observers are inclined to find fault with capitalism as an engine of production. Criticism usually proceeds either from *moral* or *cultural* disapproval of certain features of the capitalist system, or from the short-run vicissitudes (crises and depressions) with which long-run improvement is interspersed. [Italics mine.]

The "crises and depressions" were caused by government interference, not by the capitalist system. But what was the nature of the "moral or cultural disapproval"? The article does not tell us explicitly, but gives one eloquent indication:

> Such as they were, however, both tendencies and realizations [of capitalism] bear the unmistakable stamp of the businessman's interests and still more the businessman's type of mind. Moreover it was not only policy but the philosophy of national and individual life, the scheme of cultural values, that bore that stamp. Its materialistic utilitarianism, its naive confidence in prog-

---

[5] For a discussion of the philosophers' default in regard to capitalism, see the title essay in my book *For the New Intellectual.*

ress of a certain type, its actual achievements in the field of pure and applied science, the temper of its artistic creations, may all be traced to *the spirit of rationalism* that emanates from the businessman's office. [Italics mine.]

The author of the article, who is not "naive" enough to believe in a capitalistic (or *rational*) type of progress, holds, apparently, a different belief:

At the end of the middle ages western Europe stood about where many underdeveloped countries stand in the 20th century. [This means that the culture of the Renaissance was about the equivalent of today's Congo; or else, it means that people's intellectual development has nothing to do with economics.] In underdeveloped economies the difficult task of statesmanship is to get under way a cumulative process of economic development, for once a certain momentum is attained, further advances appear to follow more or less automatically.

Some such notion underlies every theory of a planned economy. It is on some such "sophisticated" belief that two generations of Russians have perished, waiting for *automatic* progress.

The classical economists attempted a tribal justification of capitalism on the ground that it provides the best "allocation" of a community's "resources." Here are their chickens coming home to roost:

The market theory of resource allocation within the private sector is the central theme of classical economics. The criterion for allocation between the public and private sectors is formally the same as in any other resource allocation, namely that the community should receive equal satisfaction from a marginal increment of resources used in the public and private spheres. . . . Many economists have asserted that there is substantial, perhaps overwhelming, evidence that total welfare in capitalist United States, for example, would be increased by a reallocation of resources to the public sector—more schoolrooms and fewer shopping centers, more public libraries and fewer automobiles, more hospitals and fewer bowling alleys.

This means that some men must toil all their lives without adequate transportation (automobiles), without an adequate number of places to buy the goods they need (shopping centers), without the pleasures of relaxation (bowling alleys) —in order that other men may be provided with schools, libraries, and hospitals.

If you want to see the ultimate results and full meaning of the tribal view of wealth—the total obliteration of the distinction between private action and government action, between production and force, the total obliteration of the concept of "rights," of an individual human being's reality, and its replacement by a view of men as interchangeable beasts of burden or "factors of production"—study the following:

> Capitalism has a bias against the public sector for two reasons. First, all products and income accrue [?] initially to the private sector while resources reach the public sector through the painful process of taxation. Public needs are met only by sufferance of consumers in their role as taxpayers [what about *producers?*], whose political representatives are acutely conscious of their constituents' tender feelings [!] about taxation. That people know better than governments what to do with their income is a notion more appealing than the contrary one, that people get more for their tax money than for other types of spending. [By what theory of values? By whose judgment?] . . .
>
> Second, the pressure of private business to sell leads to the formidable array of devices of modern salesmanship which influence consumer choice and bias consumer values toward private consumption . . . [This means that your desire to spend the money you earn rather than have it taken away from you, is a mere *bias.*] Hence, much private expenditure goes for wants that are not very urgent in any fundamental sense. [Urgent—to whom? Which wants are "fundamental," beyond a cave, a bearskin, and a chunk of raw meat?] The corollary is that many public needs are neglected because these superficial private wants, artificially generated, compete successfully for the same resources. [*Whose* resources?] . . .
>
> A comparison of resource allocation to the public and private sectors under capitalism and under socialist collectivism is illuminating. [It is.] In a collective economy all resources operate in the public sector and are available for education, defense, health, welfare, and other public needs without any transfer through taxation. Private consumption is restricted to the claims that are *permitted* [by whom?] against the *social product,* much as public services in a capitalist economy

are limited to the claims permitted against the private sector. [Italics mine.] In a collective economy public needs enjoy the same sort of built-in priority that private consumption enjoys in a capitalist economy. In the Soviet Union teachers are plentiful, but automobiles are scarce, whereas the opposite condition prevails in the United States.

Here is the conclusion of that article:

Predictions concerning the survival of capitalism are, in part, a matter of definition. One sees everywhere in capitalist countries a shifting of economic activity from the private to the public sphere. . . . At the same time [after World War II] private consumption appeared destined to increase in communist countries. [Such as the consumption of wheat?] The two economic systems seemed to be drawing closer together by changes converging from both directions. Yet significant differences in the economic structures still existed. It seemed reasonable to assume that the society which invested more in people would advance more rapidly and inherit the future. In this important respect capitalism, in the eyes of some economists, labours under a fundamental but not inescapable disadvantage in competition with collectivism.

The collectivization of Soviet agriculture was achieved by means of a government-planned famine—planned and carried out deliberately to force peasants into collective farms; Soviet Russia's enemies claim that fifteen million peasants died in that famine; the Soviet government admits the death of seven million.

At the end of World War II, Soviet Russia's enemies claimed that thirty million people were doing forced labor in Soviet concentration camps (and were dying of planned malnutrition, human lives being cheaper than food); Soviet Russia's apologists admit to the figure of twelve million people.

This is what the *Encyclopaedia Britannica* refers to as "investment in people."

In a culture where such a statement is made with intellectual impunity and with an aura of moral righteousness, the guiltiest men are not the collectivists; the guiltiest men are those who, lacking the courage to challenge mysticism or altruism, attempt to bypass the issues of reason and morality and to defend the only rational and moral system in mankind's history—capitalism—on any grounds other than rational and moral.

2. THE ROOTS OF WAR

BY AYN RAND

It is said that nuclear weapons have made wars too horrible to contemplate. Yet every nation on earth feels, in helpless terror, that such a war might come.

The overwhelming majority of mankind—the people who die on the battlefields or starve and perish among the ruins—do not want war. They never wanted it. Yet wars have kept erupting throughout the centuries, like a long trail of blood underscoring mankind's history.

Men are afraid that war might come because they know, consciously or subconsciously, that they have never rejected the doctrine which causes wars, which has caused the wars of the past and can do it again—the doctrine that it is right or practical or necessary for men to achieve their goals by means of *physical force* (by *initiating* the use of force against other men) and that some sort of "good" can justify it. It is the doctrine that force is a proper or unavoidable part of human existence and human societies.

Observe one of the ugliest characteristics of today's world: the mixture of frantic war preparations with hysterical peace propaganda, and the fact that *both come from the same source*—from the same political philosophy. The bankrupt, yet still dominant, political philosophy of our age is *statism*.

Observe the nature of today's alleged peace movements. Professing love and concern for the survival of mankind, they keep screaming that the nuclear-weapons race should be stopped, that armed force should be abolished as a means of settling disputes among nations, and that war should be outlawed in the name of humanity. Yet these same peace movements do not oppose dictatorships; the political views of their members range through all shades of the statist spectrum, from welfare statism to socialism to fascism to communism. This means that they are opposed to the use of

The Objectivist, June 1966.

coercion by one nation against another, but not by the government of a nation against its own citizens; it means that they are opposed to the use of force against *armed* adversaries, but not against the *disarmed*.

Consider the plunder, the destruction, the starvation, the brutality, the slave-labor camps, the torture chambers, the wholesale slaughter perpetrated by dictatorships. Yet *this* is what today's alleged peace-lovers are willing to advocate or tolerate—in the name of love for humanity.

It is obvious that the ideological root of statism (or collectivism) is the *tribal premise* of primordial savages who, unable to conceive of individual rights, believed that the tribe is a supreme, omnipotent ruler, that it owns the lives of its members and may sacrifice them whenever it pleases to whatever it deems to be its own "good." Unable to conceive of any social principles, save the rule of brute force, they believed that the tribe's wishes are limited only by its physical power and that other tribes are its natural prey, to be conquered, looted, enslaved, or annihilated. The history of all primitive peoples is a succession of tribal wars and intertribal slaughter. That this savage ideology now rules nations armed with nuclear weapons, should give pause to anyone concerned with mankind's survival.

Statism is a system of institutionalized violence and perpetual civil war. It leaves men no choice but to fight to seize political power—to rob or be robbed, to kill or be killed. When brute force is the only criterion of social conduct, and unresisting surrender to destruction is the only alternative, even the lowest of men, even an animal—even a cornered rat—will fight. There can be no peace within an enslaved nation.

The bloodiest conflicts of history were not wars between nations, but *civil wars* between men of the same nation, who could find no peaceful recourse to law, principle, or justice. Observe that the history of all absolute states is punctuated by bloody uprisings—by violent eruptions of blind despair, without ideology, program, or goals—which were usually put down by ruthless extermination.

In a full dictatorship, statism's chronic "cold" civil war takes the form of bloody purges, when one gang deposes another—as in Nazi Germany or Soviet Russia. In a mixed economy, it takes the form of pressure-group warfare, each group fighting for legislation to extort its own advantages by force from all other groups.

The degree of statism in a country's political system, is the degree to which it breaks up the country into rival gangs and sets men against one another. When individual rights are abrogated, there is no way to determine who is entitled to what; there is no way to determine the justice of anyone's claims, desires, or interests. The criterion, therefore, reverts to the tribal concept of: one's wishes are limited only by the power of one's gang. In order to survive under such a system, men have no choice but to fear, hate, and destroy one another; it is a system of underground plotting, of secret conspiracies, of deals, favors, betrayals, and sudden, bloody coups.

It is not a system conducive to brotherhood, security, cooperation, and peace.

Statism—in fact and in principle—is nothing more than gang rule. A dictatorship is a gang devoted to looting the effort of the productive citizens of its own country. When a statist ruler exhausts his own country's economy, he attacks his neighbors. It is his only means of postponing internal collapse and prolonging his rule. A country that violates the rights of its own citizens, will not respect the rights of its neighbors. Those who do not recognize individual rights, will not recognize the rights of nations: a nation is only a number of individuals.

Statism *needs* war; a free country does not. Statism survives by looting; a free country survives by production.

Observe that the major wars of history were started by the more controlled economies of the time against the freer ones. For instance, World War I was started by monarchist Germany and Czarist Russia, who dragged in their freer allies. World War II was started by the alliance of Nazi Germany with Soviet Russia and their joint attack on Poland.

Observe that in World War II, both Germany and Russia seized and dismantled entire factories in conquered countries, to ship them home—while the freest of the mixed economies, the semi-capitalistic United States, sent billions worth of lend-lease equipment, including entire factories, to its allies.[1]

Germany and Russia needed war; the United States did not and gained nothing. (In fact, the United States lost, economically, even though it won the war: it was left with an enormous national debt, augmented by the grotesquely futile policy of supporting former allies and enemies to this day.) Yet it is capitalism that today's peace-lovers oppose and statism that they advocate—in the name of peace.

[1] For a detailed, documented account of the full extent of Russia's looting, see Werner Keller, *East Minus West = Zero*, New York: G. P. Putnam's Sons, 1962.

Laissez-faire capitalism is the only social system based on the recognition of individual rights and, therefore, the only system that bans force from social relationships. By the nature of its basic principles and interests, it is the only system fundamentally opposed to war.

Men who are free to produce, have no incentive to loot; they have nothing to gain from war and a great deal to lose. Ideologically, the principle of individual rights does not permit a man to seek his own livelihood at the point of a gun, inside or outside his country. Economically, wars cost money; in a free economy, where wealth is privately owned, the costs of war come out of the income of private citizens—there is no overblown public treasury to hide that fact—and a citizen cannot hope to recoup his own financial losses (such as taxes or business dislocations or property destruction) by winning the war. Thus his own economic interests are on the side of peace.

In a statist economy, where wealth is "publicly owned," a citizen has no economic interests to protect by preserving peace—he is only a drop in the common bucket—while war gives him the (fallacious) hope of larger handouts from his masters. Ideologically, he is trained to regard men as sacrificial animals; he is one himself; he can have no concept of why foreigners should not be sacrificed on the same public altar for the benefit of the same state.

The trader and the warrior have been fundamental antagonists throughout history. Trade does not flourish on battlefields, factories do not produce under bombardments, profits do not grow on rubble. Capitalism is a society of *traders*—for which it has been denounced by every would-be gunman who regards trade as "selfish" and conquest as "noble."

Let those who are actually concerned with peace observe that *capitalism gave mankind the longest period of peace in history*—a period during which there were no wars involving the entire civilized world—from the end of the Napoleonic wars in 1815 to the outbreak of World War I in 1914.

It must be remembered that the political systems of the nineteenth century were not pure capitalism, but mixed economies. The element of freedom, however, was dominant; it was as close to a century of capitalism as mankind has come. But the element of statism kept growing throughout the nineteenth century, and by the time it blasted the world in 1914, the governments involved were dominated by statist policies.

Just as, in domestic affairs, all the evils caused by statism and government controls were blamed on capitalism and the free market—so, in foreign affairs, all the evils of statist policies were blamed on and ascribed to capitalism. Such myths as "capitalistic imperialism," "war-profiteering," or the notion that capitalism has to win "markets" by military conquest are examples of the superficiality or the unscrupulousness of statist commentators and historians.

The essence of capitalism's foreign policy is *free trade*—i.e., the abolition of trade barriers, of protective tariffs, of special privileges—the opening of the world's trade routes to free international exchange and competition among the private citizens of all countries dealing directly with one another. During the nineteenth century, it was free trade that liberated the world, undercutting and wrecking the remnants of feudalism and the statist tyranny of absolute monarchies.

> As with Rome, the world accepted the British empire because it opened world channels of energy for commerce in general. Though repressive (status) government was still imposed to a considerable degree on Ireland with very bad results, on the whole England's invisible exports were law and free trade. Practically speaking, while England ruled the seas any man of any nation could go anywhere, taking his goods and money with him, in safety.[2]

As in the case of Rome, when the repressive element of England's mixed economy grew to become her dominant policy and turned her to statism, her empire fell apart. It was not military force that had held it together.

Capitalism wins and holds its markets by free competition, at home and abroad. A market conquered by war can be of value (temporarily) only to those advocates of a mixed economy who seek to close it to international competition, impose restrictive regulations, and thus acquire special privileges by force. The same type of businessmen who sought special advantages by government action in their own countries, sought special markets by government action abroad. At whose expense? At the expense of the overwhelming majority of businessmen who paid the taxes for such ventures, but gained nothing. Who justified such policies and sold them to the public? The statist intellectuals who manufac-

---

[2] Isabel Paterson, *The God of the Machine*, Caldwell, Idaho: The Caxton Printers, 1964, p. 121. Originally published by G. P. Putnam's Sons, New York, 1943.

tured such doctrines as "the public interest" or "national prestige" or "manifest destiny."

The actual war profiteers of all mixed economies were and are of that type: men with political pull who acquire fortunes by government favor, during or after a war—*fortunes which they could not have acquired on a free market.*

Remember that private citizens—whether rich or poor, whether businessmen or workers—have no power to start a war. That power is the exclusive prerogative of a government. Which type of government is more likely to plunge a country into war: a government of limited powers, bound by constitutional restrictions—or an unlimited government, open to the pressure of any group with warlike interests or ideologies, a government able to command armies to march at the whim of a single chief executive?

Yet it is not a limited government that today's peace-lovers are advocating.

(Needless to say, unilateral pacifism is merely an invitation to aggression. Just as an individual has the right of self-defense, so has a free country if attacked. But this does not give its government the right to draft men into military service—which is the most blatantly statist violation of a man's right to his own life. There is no contradiction between the moral and the practical: a volunteer army is the most efficient army, as many military authorities have testified. A free country has never lacked volunteers when attacked by a foreign aggressor. But not many men would volunteer for such ventures as Korea or Vietnam. Without drafted armies, the foreign policies of statist or mixed economies would not be possible.)

So long as a country is even semi-free, its mixed-economy profiteers are not the source of its warlike influences or policies, and are not the primary cause of its involvement in war. They are merely political scavengers cashing-in on a public trend. The primary cause of that trend is the mixed-economy intellectuals.

Observe the link between statism and militarism in the intellectual history of the nineteenth and twentieth centuries. Just as the destruction of capitalism and the rise of the totalitarian state were not caused by business or labor or any economic interests, but by the dominant statist ideology of the intellectuals—so the resurgence of the doctrines of military conquest and armed crusades for political "ideals" were the product of the same intellectuals' belief that "the good" is to be achieved by force.

The rise of a spirit of nationalistic imperialism in the

United States did not come from the right, but from the left, not from big-business interests, but from the collectivist reformers who influenced the policies of Theodore Roosevelt and Woodrow Wilson. For a history of these influences, see *The Decline of American Liberalism* by Arthur A. Ekiroh, Jr.[3]

> In such instances [writes Professor Ekirch] as the progressives' increasing acceptance of compulsory military training and of the white man's burden, there were obvious reminders of the paternalism of much of their economic reform legislation. Imperialism, according to a recent student of American foreign policy, was a revolt against many of the values of traditional liberalism. "The spirit of imperialism was an exaltation of duty above rights, of collective welfare above individual self-interest, the heroic values as opposed to materialism, action instead of logic, the natural impulse rather than the pallid intellect."[4]

In regard to Woodrow Wilson, Professor Ekirch writes:

> Wilson no doubt would have preferred the growth of United States foreign trade to come about as a result of free international competition, but he found it easy with his ideas of moralism and duty to rationalize direct American intervention as a means of safeguarding the national interest.[5]

And: "He [Wilson] seemed to feel that the United States had a mission to spread its institutions—which he conceived as liberal and democratic—to the more benighted areas of the world."[6] It was not the advocates of capitalism who helped Wilson to whip up a reluctant, peace-loving nation into the hysteria of a military crusade—it was the "liberal" magazine *The New Republic*. Its editor, Herbert Croly, used such arguments as: "The American nation needs the tonic of a serious moral adventure."

Just as Wilson, a "liberal" reformer, led the United States into World War I, "to make the world safe for democracy"—so Franklin D. Roosevelt, another "liberal" reformer, led it into World War II, in the name of the "Four Freedoms." In both cases, the "conservatives"—and the big-business interests—were overwhelmingly opposed to war but were silenced. In the case of World War II, they were smeared as "isolationists," "reactionaries," and "America-First'ers."

World War I led, not to "democracy," but to the creation of three dictatorships: Soviet Russia, Fascist Italy, Nazi Germany. World War II led, not to "Four Freedoms," but to the surrender of one-third of the world's population into communist slavery.

If peace were the goal of today's intellectuals, a failure of that magnitude—and the evidence of unspeakable suffering on so large a scale—would make them pause and check their statist premises. Instead, blind to everything but their hatred for capitalism, they are now asserting that "poverty breeds wars" (and justifying war by sympathizing with a "material greed" of that kind). But the question is: *what breeds poverty?* If you look at the world of today and if you look back at history, you will see the answer: the degree of a country's freedom is the degree of its prosperity.

Another current catch-phrase is the complaint that the nations of the world are divided into the "haves" and the "have-nots." Observe that the "haves" are those who have freedom, and that it is freedom that the "have-nots" have not.

If men want to oppose war, it is *statism* that they must oppose. So long as they hold the tribal notion that the individual is sacrificial fodder for the collective, that some men have the right to rule others by force, and that some (any) alleged "good" can justify it—there can be no peace *within* a nation and no peace among nations.

It is true that nuclear weapons have made wars too horrible to contemplate. But it makes no difference to a man whether he is killed by a nuclear bomb or a dynamite bomb or an old-fashioned club. Nor does the number of other victims or the scale of the destruction make any difference to him. And there is something obscene in the attitude of those who regard horror as a matter of numbers, who are willing to send a small group of youths to die for the tribe, but scream against the danger to the tribe itself—and more: who are willing to condone the slaughter of defenseless victims, but march in protest against wars between the well-armed.

So long as men are subjugated by force, they will fight back and use any weapons available. If a man is led to a Nazi gas chamber or a Soviet firing squad, with no voices raised to defend him, would he feel any love or concern for the survival of mankind? Or would he be more justified in feeling that a cannibalistic mankind, which tolerates dictatorships, does not deserve to survive?

If nuclear weapons are a dreadful threat and mankind cannot afford war any longer, then *mankind cannot afford statism any longer.* Let no man of good will take it upon his conscience to advocate the rule of force—outside or *inside* his own country. Let all those who are actually concerned with peace—those who do love *man* and do care about his survival—realize that if war is ever to be outlawed, it is *the use of force* that has to be outlawed.

3. AMERICA'S PERSECUTED MINORITY: BIG BUSINESS

BY AYN RAND

If a small group of men were always regarded as guilty, in any clash with any other group, regardless of the issues or circumstances involved, would you call it persecution? If this group were always made to pay for the sins, errors, or failures of any other group, would you call *that* persecution? If this group had to live under a silent reign of terror, under special laws, from which all other people were immune, laws which the accused could not grasp or define in advance and which the accuser could interpret in any way he pleased—would you call *that* persecution? If this group were penalized, not for its faults, but for its virtues, not for its incompetence, but for its ability, not for its failures, but for its achievements, and the greater the achievement, the greater the penalty—would you call *that* persecution?

If your answer is "yes"—then ask yourself what sort of monstrous injustice you are condoning, supporting, or perpetrating. That group is the American businessmen.

The defense of minority rights is acclaimed today, virtually by everyone, as a moral principle of a high order. But this principle, which forbids discrimination, is applied by most of the "liberal" intellectuals in a *discriminatory* manner: it is applied only to racial or religious minorities. It is not applied to that small, exploited, denounced, defenseless minority which consists of businessmen.

Yet every ugly, brutal aspect of injustice toward racial or religious minorities is being practiced toward businessmen. For instance, consider the evil of condemning some men and absolving others, without a hearing, regardless of the facts. Today's "liberals" consider a businessman guilty in any con-

Lecture given at The Ford Hall Forum, Boston, on December 17, 1961, and at Columbia University on February 15, 1962. Published by Nathaniel Branden Institute, New York, 1962.

flict with a labor union, regardless of the facts or issues involved, and boast that they will not cross a picket line "right or wrong." Consider the evil of judging people by a double standard and of denying to some the rights granted to others. Today's "liberals" recognize the workers' (the majority's) right to their livelihood (their wages), but deny the businessmen's (the minority's) right to *their* livelihood (their profits). If workers struggle for higher wages, this is hailed as "social gains"; if businessmen struggle for higher profits, this is damned as "selfish greed." If the workers' standard of living is low, the "liberals" blame it on the businessmen; but if the businessmen attempt to improve their economic efficacy, to expand their markets, and to enlarge the financial returns of their enterprises, thus making higher wages and lower prices possible, the same "liberals" denounce it as "commercialism." If a non-commercial foundation—*i.e.,* a group which did not have to *earn* its funds—sponsors a television show, advocating its particular views, the "liberals" hail it as "enlightenment," "education," "art," and "public service"; if a businessman sponsors a television show and wants it to reflect *his* views, the "liberals" scream, calling it "censorship," "pressure," and "dictatorial rule." When three locals of the International Brotherhood of Teamsters deprived New York City of its milk supply for fifteen days—no moral indignation or condemnation was heard from the "liberal" quarters; but just imagine what would happen if *businessmen* stopped that milk supply for one hour—and how swiftly they would be struck down by that legalized lynching or pogrom known as "trust-busting."

Whenever, in any era, culture, or society, you encounter the phenomenon of prejudice, injustice, persecution, and blind, unreasoning hatred directed at some minority group— look for the gang that has something to gain from that persecution, look for those who have a vested interest in the destruction of these particular sacrificial victims. Invariably, you will find that the persecuted minority serves as a scapegoat for some movement that does not want the nature of its own goals to be known. Every movement that seeks to enslave a country, every dictatorship or potential dictatorship, needs some minority group as a scapegoat which it can blame for the nation's troubles and use as a justification of its own demands for dictatorial powers. In Soviet Russia, the scapegoat was the bourgeoisie; in Nazi Germany, it was the Jewish people; in America, it is the businessmen.

America has not yet reached the stage of a dictatorship. But, paving the way to it, for many decades past, the businessmen have served as the scapegoat for *statist* movements of all kinds: communist, fascist, or welfare. For whose sins and evils did the businessmen take the blame? For the sins and evils of the bureaucrats.

A disastrous intellectual package-deal, put over on us by the theoreticians of statism, is the equation of *economic* power with *political* power. You have heard it expressed in such bromides as: "A hungry man is not free," or "It makes no difference to a worker whether he takes orders from a businessman or from a bureaucrat." Most people accept these equivocations—and yet they know that the poorest laborer in America is freer and more secure than the richest commissar in Soviet Russia. What is the basic, the essential, the crucial principle that differentiates freedom from slavery? It is the principle of voluntary action *versus* physical coercion or compulsion.

The difference between political power and any other kind of social "power," between a government and any private organization, is the fact that *a government holds a legal monopoly on the use of physical force*. This distinction is so important and so seldom recognized today that I must urge you to keep it in mind. Let me repeat it: *a government holds a legal monopoly on the use of physical force*.

No individual or private group or private organization has the legal power to initiate the use of physical force against other individuals or groups and to compel them to act against their own voluntary choice. Only a government holds that power. The nature of governmental action is: *coercive* action. The nature of political power is: the power to force obedience under threat of physical injury—the threat of property expropriation, imprisonment, or death.

Foggy metaphors, sloppy images, unfocused poetry, and equivocations—such as "A hungry man is not free"—do not alter the fact that *only* political power is the power of physical coercion and that freedom, in a political context, has only one meaning: *the absence of physical coercion*.

The only proper function of the government of a free country is to act as an agency which protects the individual's rights, *i.e.*, which protects the individual from physical violence. Such a government does not have the right to *initiate* the use of physical force against anyone—a right which the individual does not possess and, therefore, cannot delegate to any agency. But the individual does possess the right of self-defense and *that* is the right which he delegates to the government, for the purpose of an orderly, legally defined enforcement. A proper government has the right to use

physical force *only* in retaliation and *only* against those who
initiate its use. The proper functions of a government are:
the police, to protect men from criminals; the military forces,
to protect men from foreign invaders; and the law courts,
to protect men's property and contracts from breach by force
or fraud, and to settle disputes among men according to
objectively defined laws.

These, implicitly, were the political principles on which the
Constitution of the United States was based; implicitly, but
not explicitly. There were contradictions in the Constitution,
which allowed the statists to gain an entering wedge, to
enlarge the breach, and, gradually, to wreck the structure.

A statist is a man who believes that some men have the
right to force, coerce, enslave, rob, and murder others. To be
put into practice, this belief has to be implemented by the
political doctrine that the government—the state—has the
right to *initiate* the use of physical force against its citizens.
How often force is to be used, against whom, to what extent,
for what purpose and for whose benefit, are irrelevant questions. The basic principle and the ultimate results of all statist
doctrines are the same: dictatorship and destruction. The rest
is only a matter of time.

Now let us consider the question of economic power.

What is economic power? It is the power to produce and
to trade what one has produced. In a free economy, where
no man or group of men can use physical coercion against
anyone, economic power can be achieved only by *voluntary*
means: by the voluntary choice and agreement of all those
who participate in the process of production and trade. In a
free market, all prices, wages, and profits are determined—
not by the arbitrary whim of the rich or of the poor, not by
anyone's "greed" or by anyone's need—but by the law of
supply and demand. The mechanism of a free market reflects
and sums up all the economic choices and decisions made by
all the participants. Men trade their goods or services by
mutual consent to mutual advantage, according to their own
independent, uncoerced judgment. A man can grow rich only
if he is able to offer better *values*--better products or services, at a lower price—than others are able to offer.

Wealth, in a free market, is achieved by a free, general,
"democratic" vote—by the sales and the purchases of every
individual who takes part in the economic life of the country.
Whenever you buy one product rather than another, you are
voting for the success of some manufacturer. And, in this
type of voting, every man votes only on those matters which
he is qualified to judge: on his own preferences, interests, and

needs. No one has the power to decide for others or to substitute *his* judgment for theirs; no one has the power to appoint himself "the voice of the public" and to leave the public voiceless and disfranchised.

Now let me define the difference between economic power and political power: economic power is exercised by means of a *positive*, by offering men a reward, an incentive, a payment, a value; political power is exercised by means of a *negative*, by the threat of punishment, injury, imprisonment, destruction. The businessman's tool is *values;* the bureaucrat's tool is *fear*.

America's industrial progress, in the short span of a century and a half, has acquired the character of a legend: it has never been equaled anywhere on earth, in any period of history. The American businessmen, as a class, have demonstrated the greatest productive genius and the most spectacular achievements ever recorded in the economic history of mankind. What reward did they receive from our culture and its intellectuals? The position of a hated, persecuted minority. The position of a scapegoat for the evils of the bureaucrats.

A system of pure, unregulated laissez-faire capitalism has never yet existed anywhere. What did exist were only so-called mixed economies, which means: a mixture, in varying degrees, of freedom and controls, of voluntary choice and government coercion, of capitalism and statism. America was the freest country on earth, but elements of statism were present in her economy from the start. These elements kept growing, under the influence of her intellectuals who were predominantly committed to the philosophy of statism. The intellectuals—the ideologists, the interpreters, the assessors of public events—were tempted by the opportunity to seize political power, relinquished by all other social groups, and to establish their own versions of a "good" society at the point of a gun, *i.e.*, by means of legalized physical coercion. They denounced the free businessmen as exponents of "selfish greed" and glorified the bureaucrats as "public servants." In evaluating social problems, they kept damning "economic power" and exonerating political power, thus switching the burden of guilt from the politicians to the businessmen.

All the evils, abuses, and iniquities, popularly ascribed to businessmen and to capitalism, were not caused by an unregulated economy or by a free market, but by government intervention into the economy. The giants of American industry—such as James Jerome Hill or Commodore Vanderbilt or Andrew Carnegie or J. P. Morgan—were self-made men who earned their fortunes by personal ability, by free trade on a free market. But there existed another kind of businessmen, the products of a mixed economy, the men with political pull, who made fortunes by means of special privileges granted to them by the government, such men as the Big Four of the Central Pacific Railroad. It was the political power behind their activities—the power of forced, unearned, economically unjustified privileges—that caused dislocations in the country's economy, hardships, depressions, and mounting public protests. But it was the free market and the free businessmen that took the blame. Every calamitous consequence of government controls was used as a justification for the extension of the controls and of the government's power over the economy.

If I were asked to choose the date which marks the turning point on the road to the ultimate destruction of American industry, and the most infamous piece of legislation in American history, I would choose the year 1890 and the Sherman Act—which began that grotesque, irrational, malignant growth of unenforceable, uncompliable, unjudicable contradictions known as the antitrust laws.

Under the antitrust laws, a man becomes a criminal from the moment he goes into business, no matter what he does. If he complies with one of these laws, he faces criminal prosecution under several others. For instance, if he charges prices which some bureaucrats judge as too high, he can be prosecuted for monopoly, or, rather, for a successful "intent to monopolize"; if he charges prices lower than those of his competitors, he can be prosecuted for "unfair competition" or "restraint of trade"; and if he charges the same prices as his competitors, he can be prosecuted for "collusion" or "conspiracy."

I recommend to your attention an excellent book entitled *The Antitrust Laws of the U.S.A.* by A. D. Neale.[1] It is a scholarly, dispassionate, objective study; the author, a British civil servant, is not a champion of free enterprise; as far as one can tell, he may probably be classified as a "liberal." But he does not confuse facts with interpretations, he keeps them severely apart; and the facts he presents are a horror story.

Mr. Neale points out that the prohibition of "restraint of trade" is the essence of antitrust—and that no exact definition of what constitutes "restraint of trade" can be given.

[1] A. D. Neale, *The Antitrust Laws of the United States of America: A Study of Competition Enforced by Law,* Cambridge, England: Cambridge University Press, 1960.

Thus no one can tell what the law forbids or permits one to do; the interpretation of these laws is left entirely up to the courts. A businessman or his lawyer has to study the whole body of the so-called case law—the whole record of court cases, precedents, and decisions—in order to get even a generalized idea of the current meaning of these laws; except that the precedents may be upset and the decisions reversed tomorrow or next week or next year. "The courts in the United States have been engaged ever since 1890 in deciding case by case exactly what the law proscribes. No broad definition can really unlock the meaning of the statute . . ."[2]

This means that a businessman has no way of knowing in advance whether the action he takes is legal or illegal, whether he is guilty or innocent. It means that a businessman has to live under the threat of a sudden, unpredictable disaster, taking the risk of losing everything he owns or being sentenced to jail, with his career, his reputation, his property, his fortune, the achievement of his whole lifetime left at the mercy of any ambitious young bureaucrat who, for any reason, public or private, may choose to start proceedings against him.

Retroactive (or *ex post facto*) law—*i.e.*, a law that punishes a man for an action which was not legally defined as a crime at the time he committed it—is rejected by and contrary to the entire tradition of Anglo-Saxon jurisprudence. It is a form of persecution practiced only in dictatorships and forbidden by every civilized code of law. It is specifically forbidden by the United States Constitution. It is not supposed to exist in the United States and it is not applied to anyone—except to businessmen. A case in which a man cannot know until he is convicted whether the action he took in the past was legal or illegal, is certainly a case of retroactive law.

I recommend to you a brilliant little book entitled *Ten Thousand Commandments* by Harold Fleming.[3] It is written for the layman and presents—in clear, simple, logical terms, with a wealth of detailed, documented evidence—such a picture of the antitrust laws that "nightmare" is too feeble a word to describe it.

> One of the hazards [writes Mr. Fleming] that sales managers must now take into account is that some policy followed today in the light of the best legal opinion may next year be reinterpreted as illegal. In

[2] *Ibid.*, p. 13.
[3] *Ten Thousand Commandments: A Story of the Antitrust Laws*, New York: Prentice-Hall, 1951.

such case the crime and the penalty may be retroactive. . . . Another kind of hazard consists in the possibility of treble damage suits, also possibly retroactive. Firms which, with the best of intentions, run afoul of the law on one of the above counts, are open to treble damage suits under the antitrust laws, even though their offense was a course of conduct that everyone considered, at the time, quite legal as well as ethical, but that a subsequent reinterpretation of the law found to be illegal.[4]

What do businessmen say about it? In a speech entitled "Guilty Before Trial" (May 18, 1950), Benjamin F. Fairless, then President of United States Steel Corporation, said:

Gentlemen, I don't have to tell you that if we persist in that kind of a system of law—and if we enforce it impartially against all offenders—virtually every business in America, big and small, is going to have to be run from Atlanta, Sing Sing, Leavenworth, or Alcatraz.

The legal treatment accorded to actual criminals is much superior to that accorded to businessmen. The criminal's rights are protected by objective laws, objective procedures, objective rules of evidence. A criminal is presumed to be innocent until he is proved guilty. Only businessmen—the producers, the providers, the supporters, the Atlases who carry our whole economy on their shoulders—are regarded as guilty by nature and are required to prove their innocence, without any definable criteria of innocence or proof, and are left at the mercy of the whim, the favor, or the malice of any publicity-seeking politician, any scheming statist, any envious mediocrity who might chance to work his way into a bureaucratic job and who feels a yen to do some trust-busting.

The better or more honorable kind of government officials have repeatedly protested against the non-objective nature of the antitrust laws. In the same speech, Mr. Fairless quotes a statement made by Lowell Mason, who was then a member of the Federal Trade Commission:

American business is being harrassed, bled, and even blackjacked under a preposterous crazyquilt system of laws, many of which are unintelligible, unenforceable

[4] *Ibid.,* pp. 16–17.

and unfair. There is such a welter of laws governing interstate commerce that the Government literally can find some charge to bring against any concern it chooses to prosecute. I say that this system is an outrage.

Further, Mr. Fairless quotes a comment written by Supreme Court Justice Jackson when he was the head of the Antitrust Division of the Department of Justice:

It is impossible for a lawyer to determine what business conduct will be pronounced lawful by the Courts. This situation is embarrassing to businessmen wishing to obey the law and to Government officials attempting to enforce it.

That embarrassment, however, is not shared by all members of the government. Mr. Fleming's book quotes the following statement made by Emanuel Celler, Chairman of the House Judiciary Committee, at a symposium of the New York State Bar Association, in January 1950:

I want to make it clear that I would vigorously oppose any antitrust laws that attempted to particularize violations, giving bills of particulars to replace general principles. The law must remain fluid, allowing for a dynamic society.[5]

I want to make it clear that *"fluid law"* is a euphemism for *"arbitrary power"*—that "fluidity" is the chief characteristic of the law under any dictatorship—and that the sort of *"dynamic society"* whose laws are so fluid that they flood and drown the country may be seen in Nazi Germany or Soviet Russia.

The tragic irony of that whole issue is the fact that the antitrust laws were created and, to this day, are supported by the so-called "conservatives," by the alleged defenders of free enterprise. This is a grim proof of the fact that capitalism has never had any proper, philosophical defenders—and a measure of the extent to which its alleged champions lacked any political principles, any knowledge of economics, and any understanding of the nature of political power. The concept of *free* competition *enforced* by law is a grotesque contradiction in terms. It means: forcing people to be free at the point

---

[5] *Ibid.*, p. 22.

of a gun. It means: protecting people's freedom by the arbitrary rule of unanswerable bureaucratic edicts.

What were the historical causes that led to the passage of the Sherman Act? I quote from the book by Mr. Neale:

> The impetus behind the movement for the earliest legislation gathered strength during the 1870's and the 1880's. . . . After the Civil War the railways with their privileges, charters, and subsidies became the main objects of suspicion and hostility. Many bodies with revealing names like "The National Anti-Monopoly Cheap Freight Railway League" sprang up.[6]

This is an eloquent example of the businessmen serving as scapegoat, taking the blame for the sins of the politicians. It was the politically granted privileges—the charters and subsidies of the railroads—that people rebelled against; it was these privileges that had placed the railroads of the West outside the reach of competition and had given them a monopolistic power, with all its consequent abuses. But the remedy, written into law by a *Republican* Congress, consisted of destroying the businessmen's freedom and of extending the power of political controls over the economy.

If you wish to observe the real American tragedy, compare the ideological motivation of the antitrust laws to their actual results. I quote from Mr. Neale's book:

> It seems likely that American distrust of all sources of unchecked power is a more deep-rooted and persistent motive behind the antitrust policy than any economic belief or any radical political trend. This distrust may be seen in many spheres of American life . . . It is expressed in the theories of "checks and balances" and of "separation of powers." In the United States the fact that some men possess power over the activities and fortunes of others is sometimes recognized as inevitable but never accepted as satisfactory. It is always hoped that any particular holder of power, *whether political or economic,* will be subject to the threat of encroachment by other authorities. . . . [Italics mine.]
>
> At one with this basic motivation of antitrust is its reliance on legal process and judicial remedy rather than on administrative regulation. The famous prescription of the Massachusetts Bill of Rights—"to the end it may be a government of laws and not of men"—is a favourite American quotation and an essential one for understanding antitrust. Without this factor it would be

[6] Neale, p. 23.

impossible to explain the degree of acceptance—so astonishing to those outside the United States—that is accorded to the antitrust policy by those interests, especially "big business" interests, which are frequently and expensively subject to its discipline.[7]

Here is the tragedy of what happens to human intentions without a clearly defined philosophical theory to guide their practical implementation. The first free society in history destroyed its freedom—in the name of protecting freedom. The failure to differentiate between *political* and *economic* power allowed men to suppose that coercion could be a proper "balance" to production, that both were activities of the same order which could serve as a "check" on each other, that the "authority" of a businessman and the "authority" of a bureaucrat were interchangeable rivals for the same social function. Seeking "a government of laws and not of men," the advocates of antitrust delivered the entire American economy into the power of as arbitrary a government of men as any dictatorship could hope to establish.

In the absence of any rational criteria of judgment, people attempted to judge the immensely complex issues of a free market by so superficial a standard as *"bigness."* You hear it to this day: *"big* business," *"big* government," or *"big* labor" are denounced as threats to society, with no concern for the nature, source, or function of the "bigness," as if *size* as such were evil. This type of reasoning would mean that a *"big"* genius, like Edison, and a *"big"* gangster, like Stalin, were equal malefactors: one flooded the world with immeasurable values and the other with incalculable slaughter, but both did it on a very *big* scale. I doubt whether anyone would care to equate these two—yet *this* is the precise difference between big business and big government. The sole means by which a government can grow big is physical force; the sole means by which a business can grow big, in a free economy, is productive achievement.

The only actual factor required for the existence of free competition is: the unhampered, unobstructed operation of the mechanism of a free market. The only action which a government can take to protect free competition is: *Laissez-faire!*—which, in free translation, means: *Hands off!* But the antitrust laws established exactly opposite conditions—and achieved the exact opposite of the results they had been intended to achieve.

There is no way to legislate competition; there are no

[7] *Ibid.*, pp. 422–423.

standards by which one could define who should compete with whom, how many competitors should exist in any given field, what should be their relative strength or their so-called "relevant markets," what prices they should charge, what methods of competition are "fair" or "unfair." None of these can be answered, because *these* precisely are the questions that can be answered only by the mechanism of a free market.

With no principles, standards, or criteria to guide it, the antitrust case law is the record of seventy years of sophistry, casuistry, and hair-splitting, as absurd and as removed from any contact with reality as the debates of medieval scholastics. With only this difference: the scholastics had better reasons for the questions they raised—and no specific human lives or fortunes hung on the outcome of their debates.

Let me give you a few examples of antitrust cases. In the case of *Associated Press v. United States* of 1945, the Associated Press was found guilty, because its bylaws restricted its membership and made it very difficult for newly established newspapers to join. I quote from Mr. Neale's book:

> It was argued in defense of the Associated Press that there were other news agencies from which new entrants might draw their news. . . . The Court held that . . . Associated Press was collectively organized to secure competitive advantages for members over non-members have built up a facility . . . for themselves; though the non-members were not necessarily prevented altogether from competing. [The Associated Press news service was considered so important a facility that] by keeping it exclusive to themselves the members of the association impose a real hardship on *would-be competitors*. . . . It is no defense that the members have built up a facility . . . for themselves; new entrants must still be allowed to share it on reasonable terms *unless it is practicable* for them to compete without it. [Italics mine.][8]

Whose *rights* are here being violated? And whose *whim* is being implemented by the power of the law? What qualifies one to be "a would-be competitor"? If I decided to start competing with General Motors tomorrow, what part of their facilities would they have to share with me in order to make it "practicable" for me to compete with them?

In the case of *Milgram v. Loew's*, of 1951, the consistent refusal of the major distributors of motion pictures to grant

[8] *Ibid.*, pp. 70—71.

first-runs to a drive-in theater was held to be a proof of *collusion.* Each company had obviously valid reasons for its refusal, and the defense argued that each had made its own independent decision without knowing the decisions of the others. But the Court ruled that "consciously parallel business practices" are sufficient proof of conspiracy and that "further proof of actual agreement among the defendants is unnecessary." The Court of Appeals upheld this decision, suggesting that evidence of parallel action should transfer the burden of proof to the defendants "to explain away the inference of joint action," which they had not, apparently, explained away.

Consider for a moment the implications of *this* case. If three businessmen reach independently the same blatantly obvious business decision—do they then have to prove that they did *not* conspire? Or if two businessmen observe an intelligent business policy originated by the third—should they refrain from adopting it, for fear of a conspiracy charge? Or if they do adopt it, should he then find himself dragged into court and charged with conspiracy, on the ground of the actions taken by two men he had never heard of? And how, then, is he "to explain away" his presumed guilt and prove himself innocent?

In the case of patents, the antitrust laws seem to respect a patent owner's right—so long as he is alone in using his patent and does not share it with anyone else. But if he decides not to engage in a patent war with a competitor who holds patents of the same general category—if they both decide to abandon that alleged "dog-eat-dog" policy of which businessmen are so often accused—if they decide to pool their patents and to license them to a few other manufacturers of their own choice—*then* the antitrust laws crack down on them both. The penalties, in such patent-pool cases, involve compulsory licensing of the patents to any and all comers—or the outright confiscation of the patents.

I quote from Mr. Neale's book:

> The compulsory licensing of patents—even valid patents lawfully acquired through the research efforts of the company's own employees—is intended not as punishment but as a way in which rival companies may be brought into the market. . . . In the *I.C.I. and duPont* case of 1952, for example, Judge Ryan . . . ordered the compulsory licensing of their existing patents in the fields to which their restrictive agreements applied and improvement patents but not new patents in these fields. In this case an auxiliary remedy was awarded

which has become common in recent years. Both I.C.I. and duPont were ordered to provide applicants, at a reasonable charge, with technical manuals which would show in detail how the patents were practiced.[9]

This, mind you, is not regarded as "punitive"!

Whose mind, ability, achievement, and rights are here sacrificed—and for *whose* unearned benefit?

The most shocking court decision in this grim progression (up to, but not including, the year 1961) was written—as one would almost expect—by a distinguished "conservative," Judge Learned Hand. The victim was ALCOA. The case was *United States v. Aluminum Company of America* of 1945.

Under the antitrust laws, monopoly, as such, is not illegal; what *is* illegal is the "intent to monopolize." To find ALCOA guilty, Judge Learned Hand had to find evidence that ALCOA had taken aggressive action to exclude competitors from its market. Here is the kind of evidence which he found and on which he based the ruling that has blocked the energy of one of America's greatest industrial concerns. I quote from Judge Hand's opinion:

> It was not inevitable that it [ALCOA] should always anticipate increases in the demand for ingot and be prepared to supply them. Nothing compelled it to keep doubling and redoubling its capacity before others entered the field. It insists that it never excluded competitors; but we can think of no more effective exclusion than progressively to embrace each new opportunity as it opened, and to face every newcomer with new capacity already geared into a great organization, having the advantage of experience, trade connections and the elite of personnel.[10]

Here, the meaning and purpose of the antitrust laws come blatantly and explicitly into the open, the only meaning and purpose these laws *could* have, whether their authors intended it or not: the penalizing of ability for being ability, the penalizing of success for being success, and the sacrifice of productive genius to the demands of envious mediocrity.

If such a principle were applied to all productive activity, if a man of intelligence were forbidden "to embrace each new opportunity as it opened," for fear of discouraging some coward or fool who might wish to compete with him, it

[9] *Ibid.*, p. 410.
[10] *Ibid.*, p. 114.

would mean that none of us, in any profession, should venture forward, or rise, or improve, because any form of personal progress—be it a typist's greater speed, or an artist's greater canvas, or a doctor's greater percentage of cures—can discourage the kind of newcomers who haven't yet started, but who expect to start competing at the top.

As a small, but crowning touch, I will quote Mr. Neale's footnote to his account of the ALCOA case:

> It is of some interest to note that the main ground on which economic writers have condemned the aluminum monopoly has been precisely that ALCOA consistently failed to embrace opportunities for expansion and so underestimated the demand for the metal that the United States was woefully short of productive capacity at the outset of both world wars.[11]

Now I will ask you to bear in mind the nature, the essence, and the record of the antitrust laws, when I mention the ultimate climax which makes the rest of that sordid record seem insignificant: the *General Electric* case of 1961.

The list of the accused in that case reads like a roll call of honor of the electrical-equipment industry: General Electric, Westinghouse, Allis-Chalmers, and twenty-six other, smaller companies. Their crime was that they had provided you with all the matchless benefits and comforts of the electrical age, from bread toasters to power generators. It is for *this* crime that they were punished—because they could not have provided any of it, nor remained in business, without breaking the antitrust laws.

The charge against them was that they had made secret agreements to fix the prices of their products and to rig bids. But without such agreements, the larger companies could have set their prices so low that the smaller ones would have been unable to match them and would have gone out of business, whereupon the larger companies would have faced prosecution, under these same antitrust laws, for "intent to monopolize."

I quote from an article by Richard Austin Smith entitled "The Incredible Electrical Conspiracy," in *Fortune* (April and May 1961): "If G.E. were to drive for 50 per cent of the market, even strong companies like I-T-E Circuit Breaker might be mortally wounded." This same article shows that the price-fixing agreements did not benefit General Electric,

[11] *Ibid.*

that they worked to its disadvantage, that General Electric was, in effect, "the sucker" and that its executives knew it, wanted to leave the "conspiracy," but had no choice (by reason of antitrust and other government regulations).

The best evidence of the fact that the antitrust laws were a major factor in forcing the "conspiracy" upon the electrical industry, can be seen in the aftermath of that case—in the issue of the "consent decree." When General Electric announced that it now intended to charge the lowest prices possible, it was the smaller companies and the government, the Antitrust Division, who objected.

Mr. Smith's article mentions the fact that the meetings of the "conspirators" started as a result of the O.P.A. During the war, the prices of electrical equipment were *fixed by the government,* and the executives of the electrical industry held meetings to discuss a common policy. They continued this practice, after the O.P.A. was abolished.

By what conceivable standard can the policy of price-fixing be a crime, when practiced by businessmen, but a public benefit, when practiced by the government? There are many industries, in peacetime—trucking, for instance—whose prices are fixed by the government. If price-fixing is harmful to competition, to industry, to production, to consumers, to the whole economy, and to the "public interest"—as the advocates of the antitrust laws have claimed—then how can that same harmful policy become beneficial in the hands of the government? Since there is no rational answer to this question, I suggest that you question the economic knowledge, the purpose, and the motives of the champions of antitrust.

The electrical companies offered no defense to the charge of "conspiracy." They pleaded *"nolo contendere,"* which means: *"no contest."* They did it, because the antitrust laws place so deadly a danger in the path of any attempt to defend oneself that defense becomes virtually impossible. These laws provide that a company convicted of an antitrust violation can be sued for *treble damages* by any customer who might claim that he was injured. In a case of so large a scale as the electrical industry case, such treble damage suits could, conceivably, wipe all the defendants out of existence. With that kind of threat hanging over him, who can or will take the risk of offering a defense in a court where there are no objective laws, no objective standards of guilt or innocence, no objective way to estimate one's chances?

Try to project what clamor of indignation and what protests would be heard publicly all around us, if some other group of men, some other minority group, were subjected to a trial in which *defense* was made impossible—or in which the laws prescribed that the more serious the offense, the more dangerous the defense. Certainly the opposite is true in regard to actual criminals: the more serious the crime, the greater the precautions and protections prescribed by the law to give the defendant a chance and the benefit of every doubt. It is only businessmen who have to come to court, bound and gagged.

Now what started the government's investigation of the electrical industry? Mr. Smith's article states that the investigation was started because of complaints by T.V.A. and *demands* by Senator Kefauver. This was in 1959, under Eisenhower's *Republican* Administration. I quote from *Time* of February 17, 1961:

> Often the Government has a hard time gathering evidence in antitrust cases, but this time it got a break. In October 1959, four Ohio businessmen were sentenced to jail after pleading *nolo contendere* in an antitrust case. (One of them committed suicide on the way to jail.) This news sent a chill through the electrical-equipment executives under investigation, and some agreed to testify about their colleagues under the security of immunity. With the evidence gathered from them (most are still with their companies), the Government sewed up its case.

It is not gangsters, racketeers, or dope peddlers that are here being discussed in such terms, but *businessmen*—the productive, creative, efficient, competent members of society. Yet the antitrust laws, *now,* in this new phase, are apparently aimed at transforming business into an underworld, with informers, stool pigeons, double-crossers, special "deals," and all the rest of the atmosphere of *The Untouchables.*

Seven executives of the electrical industry were sentenced to jail. We shall never know what went on behind the scenes of this case or in the negotiations between the companies and the government. Were *these seven* responsible for the alleged "conspiracy"? If it be guilt, were they guiltier than others? Who "informed" on them—and why? Were they framed? Were they double-crossed? Whose purposes, ambitions, or goals were served by their immolation? We do not know. Under a set-up such as the antitrust laws have created, there is no way to know.

When these seven men, who could not defend themselves, came into the courtroom to hear their sentences, their lawyers addressed the judge with pleas for mercy. I quote from the same story in *Time:* "First before the court came the lawyer for ... a vice president of Westinghouse, to plead for mercy. His client, said the lawyer, was a vestryman of St. John's Episcopal Church in Sharon, Pa. and a benefactor of charities for crippled children." Another defendant's lawyer pleaded that his client was "the director of a boy's club in Schenectady, N.Y. and the chairman of a campaign to build a new Jesuit seminary in Lenox, Mass."

It was not these men's achievements or their productive ability or their executive talent or their intelligence or their *rights* that their lawyers found it necessary to cite—but their altruistic "service" to the "welfare of the needy." The *needy* had a right to welfare—but those who produced and provided it, had not. The welfare and the rights of the producers were not regarded as worthy of consideration or recognition. *This* is the most damning indictment of the present state of our culture.

The final touch on that whole gruesome farce was Judge Ganey's statement. He said: "What is really at stake here is the survival of the kind of economy under which America has grown to greatness, the free-enterprise system." He said it, while delivering the most staggering blow that the free-enterprise system had ever sustained, while sentencing to jail seven of its best representatives and thus declaring that the very class of men who brought America to greatness—the businessmen—are now to be treated, by their nature and profession, as criminals. In the person of these seven men, it is the free-enterprise system that he was sentencing.

These seven men were martyrs. They were treated as sacrificial animals—they were *human sacrifices,* as truly and more cruelly than the human sacrifices offered by prehistorical savages in the jungle.

If you care about justice to minority groups, remember that businessmen are a small minority—a *very small* minority, compared to the total of all the uncivilized hordes on earth. Remember how much you owe to this minority—and what disgraceful persecution it is enduring. Remember also that the smallest minority on earth is the individual. Those who deny individual rights, cannot claim to be defenders of minorities.

What should we do about it? We should demand a re-examination and revision of the entire issue of antitrust. We should challenge its philosophical, political, economic, and *moral* base. We should have a Civil Liberties Union—for businessmen. The repeal of the antitrust laws should be our ultimate goal; it will require a long intellectual and political struggle; but, in the meantime and as a first step, we should demand that the jail-penalty provisions of these laws be abolished. It is bad enough if men have to suffer financial penalties, such as fines, under laws which everyone concedes to be non-objective, contradictory, and undefinable, since no two jurists can agree on their meaning and application; it is obscene to impose prison sentences under laws of so controversial a nature. We should put an end to the outrage of sending men to jail for breaking unintelligible laws which they cannot avoid breaking.

Businessmen are the one group that distinguishes capitalism and the American way of life from the totalitarian statism that is swallowing the rest of the world. All the other social groups—workers, farmers, professional men, scientists, soldiers—exist under dictatorships, even though they exist in chains, in terror, in misery, and in progressive self-destruction. *But there is no such group as businessmen under a dictatorship.* Their place is taken by armed thugs: by bureaucrats and commissars. Businessmen are the symbol of a free society—the symbol of America. If and when they perish, civilization will perish. But if you wish to fight for freedom, you must begin by fighting for its unrewarded, unrecognized, unacknowledged, yet best representatives—the American businessmen.

4. ANTITRUST

BY ALAN GREENSPAN

The world of antitrust is reminiscent of Alice's Wonderland: everything seemingly is, yet apparently isn't, simultaneously. It is a world in which competition is lauded as the basic axiom and guiding principle, yet "too much" competition is condemned as "cutthroat." It is a world in which actions designed to limit competition are branded as criminal when taken by businessmen, yet praised as "enlightened" when initiated by the government. It is a world in which the law is so vague that businessmen have no way of knowing whether specific actions will be declared illegal until they hear the judge's verdict—after the fact.

In view of the confusion, contradictions, and legalistic hairsplitting which characterize the realm of antitrust, I submit that the entire antitrust system must be opened for review. It is necessary to ascertain and to estimate: (a) the historical roots of the antitrust laws, and (b) the economic theories upon which these laws were based.

Americans have always feared the concentration of arbitrary power in the hands of politicians. Prior to the Civil War, few attributed such power to businessmen. It was recognized that government officials had the legal power to compel obedience by the use of physical force—and that businessmen had no such power. A businessman needed customers. He had to appeal to their self-interest.

This appraisal of the issue changed rapidly in the immediate aftermath of the Civil War, particularly with the coming of the railroad age. Outwardly, the railroads did not have the backing of legal force. But to the farmers of the West, the railroads seemed to hold the arbitrary power previously ascribed solely to the government. The railroads appeared

Based on a paper given at the Antitrust Seminar of the National Association of Business Economists, Cleveland, September 25, 1961. Published by Nathaniel Branden Institute, New York, 1962.

unhampered by the laws of competition. They seemed able to charge rates calculated to keep the farmers in seed grain—no higher, no lower. The farmers' protest took the form of the National Grange movement, the organization responsible for the passage of the Interstate Commerce Act of 1887.

The industrial giants, such as Rockefeller's Standard Oil Trust, which were rising during this period, were also alleged to be immune from competition, from the law of supply and demand. The public reaction against the trusts culminated in the Sherman Act of 1890.

It was claimed then—as it is still claimed today—that business, if left free, would necessarily develop into an institution vested with arbitrary power. Is this assertion valid? Did the post-Civil War period give birth to a new form of arbitrary power? Or did the government remain the source of such power, with business merely providing a new avenue through which it could be exercised? This is the crucial historical question.

The railroads developed in the East, prior to the Civil War, in stiff competition with one another as well as with the older forms of transportation—barges, riverboats, and wagons. By the 1860's there arose a political clamor demanding that the railroads move west and tie California to the nation: national prestige was held to be at stake. But the traffic volume outside of the populous East was insufficient to draw commercial transportation westward. The potential profit did not warrant the heavy cost of investment in transportation facilities. In the name of "public policy" it was, therefore, decided to subsidize the railroads in their move to the West.

Between 1863 and 1867, close to one hundred million acres of public lands were granted to the railroads. Since these grants were made to individual roads, no competing railroads could vie for traffic in the same area in the West. Meanwhile, the alternative forms of competition (wagons, riverboats, etc.) could not afford to challenge the railroads in the West. Thus, with the aid of the federal government, a segment of the railroad industry was able to "break free" from the competitive bounds which had prevailed in the East.

As might be expected, the subsidies attracted the kind of promoters who always exist on the fringe of the business community and who are constantly seeking an "easy deal." Many of the new western railroads were shabbily built: they were not constructed to carry traffic, but to acquire land grants.

The western railroads were true monopolies in the textbook sense of the word. They could, and did, behave with an aura of arbitrary power. But that power was not derived from a free market. It stemmed from governmental subsidies and governmental restrictions.[1]

When, ultimately, western traffic increased to levels which could support other profit-making transportation carriers, the railroads' monopolistic power was soon undercut. In spite of their initial privileges, they were unable to withstand the pressure of free competition.

In the meantime, however, an ominous turning point had taken place in our economic history: the Interstate Commerce Act of 1887.

That Act was not necessitated by the "evils" of the free market. Like subsequent legislation controlling business, the Act was an attempt to remedy the economic distortions which prior government interventions had created, but which were blamed on the free market. The Interstate Commerce Act, in turn, produced new distortions in the structure and finances of the railroads. Today, it is proposed that these distortions be corrected by means of further subsidies. The railroads are on the verge of final collapse, yet no one challenges the original misdiagnosis to discover—and correct —the actual cause of their illness.

To interpret the railroad history of the nineteenth century as "proof" of the failure of a free market, is a disastrous error. The same error—which persists to this day—was the nineteenth century's fear of the "trusts."

The most formidable of the "trusts" was Standard Oil. Nevertheless, at the time of the passage of the Sherman Act, a pre-automotive period, the entire petroleum industry amounted to less than one percent of the Gross National Product and was barely one-third as large as the shoe industry. It was not the absolute size of the trusts, but their dominance within their own industries that gave rise to apprehension. What the observers failed to grasp, however, was the fact that the control by Standard Oil, at the turn of the century, of more than eighty percent of refining capacity made economic sense and accelerated the growth of the American economy.

Such control yielded obvious gains in efficiency, through the integration of divergent refining, marketing, and pipeline operations; it also made the raising of capital easier and

[1] I am indebted to Ayn Rand for her identification of this principle. See her "Notes on the History of American Free Enterprise" (chapter 7).

cheaper. Trusts came into existence because they were the most efficient units in those industries which, being relatively new, were too small to support more than one large company.

Historically, the general development of industry has taken the following course: an industry begins with a few small firms; in time, many of them merge; this increases efficiency and augments profits. As the market expands, new firms enter the field, thus cutting down the share of the market held by the dominant firm. This has been the pattern in steel, oil, aluminum, containers, and numerous other major industries.

The observable tendency of an industry's dominant companies eventually to lose part of their share of the market, is not caused by antitrust legislation, but by the fact that it is difficult to prevent new firms from entering the field when the demand for a certain product increases. Texaco and Gulf, for example, would have grown into large firms even if the original Standard Oil Trust had not been dissolved. Similarly, the United States Steel Corporation's dominance of the steel industry half a century ago would have been eroded with or without the Sherman Act.

It takes extraordinary skill to hold more than fifty percent of a large industry's market in a free economy. It requires unusual productive ability, unfailing business judgment, unrelenting effort at the continuous improvement of one's product and technique. The rare company which is able to retain its share of the market year after year and decade after decade does so by means of productive efficiency—and deserves praise, not condemnation.

The Sherman Act may be understandable when viewed as a projection of the nineteenth century's fear and economic ignorance. But it is utter nonsense in the context of today's economic knowledge. The seventy additional years of observing industrial development should have taught us something.

If the attempts to justify our antitrust statutes on historical grounds are erroneous and rest on a misinterpretation of history, the attempts to justify them on theoretical grounds come from a still more fundamental misconception.

In the early days of the United States, Americans enjoyed a large measure of economic freedom. Each individual was free to produce what he chose, and sell to whomever he chose, at a price mutually agreed upon. If two competitors concluded that it was to their mutual self-interest to set joint price policies, they were free to do so. If a customer requested a rebate in exchange for his business, a firm (usually a railroad) could comply or deny as it saw fit. According to classical economics, which had a profound influence on the nineteenth century, competition would keep the economy in balance.

But while many theories of the classical economists—such as their description of the working of a free economy—were valid, their concept of competition was ambiguous and led to confusion in the minds of their followers. It was understood to mean that competition consists merely of producing and selling the maximum possible, like a robot, passively accepting the market price as a law of nature, never making any attempt to influence the conditions of the market.

The businessmen of the latter half of the nineeenth century, however, aggressively attempted to affect the conditions of their markets by advertising, varying production rates, and bargaining on price with suppliers and customers.

Many observers assumed that these activities were incompatible with the classical theory. They concluded that competition was no longer working effectively. In the sense in which they understood competition, it had never worked or existed, except possibly in some isolated agricultural markets. But in a meaningful sense of the word, competition did, and does, exist—in the nineteenth century as well as today.

"Competition" is an active, not a passive, noun. It applies to the entire sphere of economic activity, not merely to production, but also to trade; it implies the necessity of taking action to affect the conditions of the market in one's own favor.

The error of the nineteenth-century observers was that they restricted a wide abstraction—competition—to a narrow set of particulars, to the "passive" competition projected by their own interpretation of classical economics. As a result, they concluded that the alleged "failure" of this fictitious "passive competition" negated the entire theoretical structure of classical economics, including the demonstration of the fact that laissez-faire is the most efficient and productive of all possible economic systems. They concluded that a free market, by its nature, leads to its own destruction—and they came to the grotesque contradiction of attempting to preserve the freedom of the market by government controls, *i.e.*, to preserve the benefits of laissez-faire by abrogating it.

The crucial question which they failed to ask is whether "active" competition does inevitably lead to the establishment of coercive monopolies, as they supposed—or whether a laissez-faire economy of "active" competition has a built-in regulator that protects and preserves it. That is the question which we must now examine.

A "coercive monopoly" is a business concern that can set its prices and production policies independent of the market, with immunity from competition, from the law of supply and demand. An economy dominated by such monopolies would be rigid and stagnant.

The necessary precondition of a coercive monopoly is closed entry—the barring of all competing producers from a given field. This can be accomplished only by an act of government intervention, in the form of special regulations, subsidies, or franchises. Without government assistance, it is impossible for a would-be monopolist to set and maintain his prices and production policies independent of the rest of the economy. For if he attempted to set his prices and production at a level that would yield profits to new entrants significantly above those available in other fields, competitors would be sure to invade his industry.

The ultimate regulator of competition in a free economy is *the capital market*. So long as capital is free to flow, it will tend to seek those areas which offer the maximum rate of return.

The potential investor of capital does not merely consider the actual rate of return earned by companies within a specific industry. His decision concerning where to invest depends on what he himself could earn in that particular line. The existing profit rates within an industry are calculated in terms of existing costs. He has to consider the fact that a new entrant might not be able to achieve at once as low a cost structure as that of experienced producers.

Therefore, the existence of a free capital market does not guarantee that a monopolist who enjoys high profits will necessarily and immediately find himself confronted by competition. What it does guarantee is that a monopolist whose high profits are caused by *high prices*, rather than *low costs*, will soon meet competition originated by the capital market.

The capital market acts as a regulator of prices, not necessarily of profits. It leaves an individual producer free to earn as much as he can by lowering his costs and by increasing his efficiency relative to others. Thus, it constitutes the mechanism that generates greater incentives to increased productivity and leads, as a consequence, to a rising standard of living.

The history of the Aluminum Company of America prior

to World War II illustrates the process. Envisaging its self-interest and long-term profitability in terms of a growing market, ALCOA kept the price of primary aluminum at a level compatible with the maximum expansion of its market. At such a price level, however, profits were forthcoming only by means of tremendous efforts to step up efficiency and productivity.

ALCOA was a monopoly—the only producer of primary aluminum—but it was not a coercive monopoly, *i.e.*, it could not set its price and production policies independent of the competitive world. In fact, only because the company stressed cost-cutting and efficiency, rather than raising prices, was it able to maintain its position as sole producer of primary aluminum for so long. Had ALCOA attempted to increase its profits by raising prices, it soon would have found itself competing with new entrants in the primary aluminum business.

In analyzing the competitive processes of a laissez-faire economy, one must recognize that capital outlays (investments in new plant and equipment either by existing producers or new entrants) are not determined solely by current profits. An investment is made or not made depending upon the estimated *discounted* present worth of expected future profits. Consequently, the issue of whether or not a new competitor will enter a hitherto monopolistic industry, is determined by his expected future returns.

The present worth of the discounted expected future profits of a given industry is represented by the market price of the common stock of the companies in that industry.[2] If the price of a particular company's stock (or an average for a particular industry) rises, the move implies a higher present worth for expected future earnings.

Statistical evidence demonstrates the correlation between stock prices and capital outlays, not only for industry as a whole, but also within major industry groups.[3] Moreover, the time between the fluctuations of stock prices and the corresponding fluctuations of capital expenditures is rather short, a fact which implies that the process of relating new capital investments to profit expectations is relatively fast. If

[2] Alan Greenspan, "Stock Prices and Capital Evaluation." Paper delivered before a joint session of the American Statistical Association and the American Finance Association on December 27, 1959.

[3] For a detailed analysis of this correlation, see Alan Greenspan, "Business Investment Decisions and Full Employment Models," American Statistical Association, 1961 Proceedings of the Business and Economic Statistics Section.

such a correlation works as well as it does, considering today's governmental impediments to the free movement of capital, one must conclude that in a completely free market the process would be much more efficient.

The churning of a nation's capital, in a fully free economy, would be continuously pushing capital into profitable areas— and this would effectively control the competitive price and production policies of business firms, making a coercive monopoly impossible to maintain. It is only in a so-called mixed economy that a coercive monopoly can flourish, protected from the discipline of the capital markets by franchises, subsidies, and special privileges from governmental regulators.

To sum up: The entire structure of antitrust statutes in this country is a jumble of economic irrationality and ignorance. It is the product: (a) of a gross misinterpretation of history, and (b) of rather naive, and certainly unrealistic, economic theories.

As a last resort, some people argue that at least the antitrust laws haven't done any harm. They assert that even though the competitive process itself inhibits coercive monopolies, there is no harm in making doubly sure by declaring certain economic actions to be illegal.

But the very existence of those undefinable statutes and contradictory case law inhibits businessmen from undertaking what would otherwise be sound productive ventures. No one will ever know what new products, processes, machines, and cost-saving mergers failed to come into existence, killed by the Sherman Act before they were born. No one can ever compute the price that all of us have paid for that Act which, by inducing less effective use of capital, has kept our standard of living lower than would otherwise have been possible.

No speculation, however, is required to assess the injustice and the damage to the careers, reputations, and lives of business executives jailed under the antitrust laws.

Those who allege that the purpose of the antitrust laws is to protect competition, enterprise, and efficiency, need to be reminded of the following quotation from Judge Learned Hand's indictment of ALCOA's so-called monopolistic practices.

It was not inevitable that it should always anticipate increases in the demand for ingot and be prepared to supply them. Nothing compelled it to keep doubling and redoubling its capacity before others entered the field. It insists that it never excluded competitors; but we can think of no more effective exclusion than progressively to embrace each new opportunity as it opened, and to face every newcomer with new capacity already geared into a great organization, having the advantage of experience, trade connections and the elite of personnel.

ALCOA is being condemned for being too successful, too efficient, and too good a competitor. Whatever damage the antitrust laws may have done to our economy, whatever distortions of the structure of the nation's capital they may have created, these are less disastrous than the fact that the effective purpose, the hidden intent, and the actual practice of the antitrust laws in the United States have led to the condemnation of the productive and efficient members of our society *because* they are productive and efficient.

5. COMMON FALLACIES ABOUT CAPITALISM

BY NATHANIEL BRANDEN

MONOPOLIES

IN A SOCIETY OF LAISSEZ-FAIRE CAPITALISM, WHAT WOULD
PREVENT THE FORMATION OF POWERFUL MONOPOLIES ABLE TO
GAIN CONTROL OVER THE ENTIRE ECONOMY?

One of the worst fallacies in the field of economics—
propagated by Karl Marx and accepted by almost everyone
today, including many businessmen—is the notion that the
development of monopolies is an inescapable and intrinsic
result of the operation of a free, unregulated economy. In
fact, the exact opposite is true. It is a free market that makes
monopolies impossible.

It is imperative that one be clear and specific in one's
definition of "monopoly." When people speak, in an economic or political context, of the dangers and evils of monopoly,
what they mean is a *coercive* monopoly—*i.e.*, exclusive control of a given field of production which is closed to and
exempt from competition, so that those controlling the field
are able to set arbitrary production policies and charge
arbitrary prices, independent of the market, immune from
the law of supply and demand. Such a monopoly, it is
important to note, entails more than the *absence* of competition; it entails the *impossibility* of competition. That is a
coercive monopoly's characteristic attribute, which is essential to any condemnation of such a monopoly.

In the entire history of capitalism, no one has been able to

These articles appeared originally in the "Intellectual Ammunition
Department" of *The Objectivist Newsletter*. They are brief answers to
the economic questions most frequently asked by readers—questions that
reflect the most widely spread misconceptions about capitalism.

establish a coercive monopoly by means of competition on a free market. There is only one way to forbid entry into a given field of production: by *law*. Every coercive monopoly that exists or has ever existed—in the United States, in Europe, or anywhere else in the world—*was created and made possible only by an act of government:* by special franchises, licenses, subsidies, by *legislative* actions which granted special privileges (*not* obtainable on a free market) to a man or a group of men, and forbade all others to enter that particular field.

A coercive monopoly is not the result of laissez-faire; it can result only from the *abrogation* of laissez-faire and from the introduction of the *opposite* principle—the principle of *statism.*

In this country, a utility company is a coercive monopoly: the government grants it a franchise for an exclusive territory, and no one else is allowed to engage in that service in that territory; a would-be competitor, attempting to sell electric power, would be stopped by law. A telephone company is a coercive monopoly. As recently as World War II, the government ordered the two then existing telegraph companies, Western Union and Postal Telegraph, to merge into one monopoly.

In the comparatively free days of American capitalism, in the late-nineteenth–early-twentieth century, there were many attempts to "corner the market" on various commodities (such as cotton and wheat, to mention two famous examples)—then close the field to competition and gather huge profits by selling at exorbitant prices. All such attempts failed. The men who tried it were compelled to give up—or go bankrupt. They were defeated, not by legislative action, but by the action of the free market.

The question is often asked: What if a large, rich company kept buying out its smaller competitors or kept forcing them out of business by means of undercutting prices and selling at a loss—would it not be able to gain control of a given field and then start charging high prices and be free to stagnate with no fear of competition? The answer is: No, it could not be done. If a company assumed heavy losses in order to drive out competitors, then began to charge high prices to regain what it had lost, this would serve as an incentive for new competitors to enter the field and take advantage of the high profitability, without any losses to recoup. The new competitors would force prices down to the market level. The large company would have to abandon its attempt to establish monopoly prices—or go bankrupt, fighting off the competitors that its own policies would attract.

It is a matter of historical fact that no "price war" has ever succeeded in establishing a monopoly or in maintaining prices *above* the market level, outside the law of supply and demand. ("Price wars" *have*, however, acted as spurs to the economic efficiency of competing companies—and have thereby resulted in enormous benefits to the public, in terms of better products at lower prices.)

In considering this issue, people frequently ignore the crucial role of the capital market in a free economy. As Alan Greenspan observes in his article "Antitrust"[1]: If entry into a given field of production is not impeded by government regulations, franchises, or subsidies, "the ultimate regulator of competition in a free economy is *the capital market*. So long as capital is free to flow, it will tend to seek those areas which offer the maximum rate of return." Investors are constantly seeking the most profitable uses of their capital. If, therefore, some field of production is seen to be highly profitable (particularly when the profitability is due to high prices rather than to low costs), businessmen and investors necessarily will be attracted to that field; and, as the supply of the product in question is increased relative to the demand for it, prices fall accordingly. "The capital market," writes Mr. Greenspan, "acts as a regulator of prices, not necessarily of profits. It leaves an individual producer free to earn as much as he can by lowering his costs and by increasing his efficiency relative to others. Thus it constitutes the mechanism that generates greater incentives to increased productivity and leads, as a consequence, to a rising standard of living."

The free market does not permit inefficiency or stagnation—with economic impunity—in any field of production. Consider, for instance, a well-known incident in the history of the American automobile industry. There was a period when Henry Ford's Model-T held an enormous part of the automobile market. But when Ford's company attempted to stagnate and to resist stylistic changes—"You can have any color of the Model-T you want, so long as it's black"—General Motors, with its more attractively styled Chevrolet, cut into a major segment of Ford's market. And the Ford Company was compelled to change its policies in order to compete. One will find examples of this principle in the history of virtually every industry.

Now if one considers the only kind of monopoly that *can* exist under capitalism, a *non*-coercive monopoly, one will see

[1] See chapter 4.

that its prices and production policies are not independent of the wider market in which it operates, but are fully bound by the law of supply and demand; that there is no particular reason for or value in retaining the designation of "monopoly" when one uses it in a non-coercive sense; and that there are no rational grounds on which to condemn such "monopolies."

For instance, if a small town has only one drugstore, which is barely able to survive, the owner might be described as enjoying a "monopoly"—except that no one would think of using the term in this context. There is no economic need or market for a second drugstore, there is not enough trade to support it. But if that town grew, its one drugstore would have no way, no power, to prevent other drugstores from being opened.

It is often thought that the field of mining is particularly vulnerable to the establishment of monopolies, since the materials extracted from the earth exist in limited quantity and since, it is believed, some firm might gain control of all the sources of some raw material. But observe that International Nickel of Canada produces more than two-thirds of the world's nickel—yet it does *not* charge monopoly prices. It prices its product *as though* it had a great many competitors —and the truth is that it *does* have a great many competitors. Nickel (in the form of alloy and stainless steels) is competing with aluminum and a variety of other materials. The seldom recognized principle involved in such cases is that no single product, commodity, or material is or can be indispensable to an economy *regardless of price*. A commodity can be only *relatively* preferable to other commodities. For example, when the price of bituminous coal rose (which was due to John L. Lewis' forcing an economically unjustified wage raise), this was instrumental in bringing about a large-scale conversion to the use of oil and gas in many industries. The free market is its own protector.

Now if a company were able to gain and hold a non-coercive monopoly, if it were able to win all the customers in a given field, not by special government-granted privileges, but by sheer productive efficiency—by its ability to keep its costs low and/or to offer a better product than any competitor could—there would be no grounds on which to condemn such a monopoly. On the contrary, the company that achieved it would deserve the highest praise and esteem.

No one can morally claim the *right* to compete in a given field if he cannot match the productive efficiency of those with whom he hopes to compete. There is no reason why people should buy inferior products at higher prices in order to maintain less efficient companies in business. Under capitalism, any man or company that can surpass competitors is free to do so. It is in this manner that the free market rewards ability and works for the benefit of everyone—except those who seek the undeserved.

A bromide commonly cited in this connection by capitalism's opponents is the story of the old corner grocer who is driven out of business by the big chain store. What is the clear implication of their protest? It is that the people who live in the neighborhood of the old grocer have to continue buying from him, even though a chain store could give them better service at lower prices and thereby let them save money. Thus both the owners of the chain store and the people in the neighborhood are to be penalized—in order to protect the stagnation of the old grocer. *By what right?* If that grocer is unable to compete with the chain store, then, properly, he has no choice but to move elsewhere or go into another line of business or seek employment from the chain store. Capitalism, by its nature, entails a constant process of motion, of growth, of progress; no one has a *vested right* to a position if others can do better than he can.

When people denounce the free market as "cruel," the fact they are decrying is that the market is ruled by a single moral principle: *justice*. And *that* is the root of their hatred for capitalism.

There is only one kind of monopoly that men may rightfully condemn—the only kind for which the designation of "monopoly" is economically significant: a *coercive* monopoly. (Observe that in the *non*-coercive meaning of the term, *every* man may be described as a "monopolist"—since he is the exclusive owner of his effort and product. But *this* is not regarded as evil—except by socialists.)

In the issue of monopolies, as in so many other issues, capitalism is commonly blamed for the evils perpetrated by its destroyers: it is not free trade on a free market that creates coercive monopolies, but government legislation, government action, government controls. If men are concerned about the evils of monopolies, let them identify the actual villain in the picture and the actual cause of the evils: government intervention into the economy. Let them recognize that there is only one way to destroy monopolies: by the separation of State and Economics—that is, by instituting the principle that the government may not abridge the freedom of production and trade.

(JUNE 1962.)

DEPRESSIONS

ARE PERIODIC DEPRESSIONS INEVITABLE IN A SYSTEM OF LAISSEZ-FAIRE CAPITALISM?

It is characteristic of the enemies of capitalism that they denounce it for evils which are, in fact, the result not of capitalism but of statism: evils which result from and are made possible only by government intervention in the economy.

I have discussed a flagrant example of this policy: the charge that capitalism leads to the establishment of coercive monopolies. The most notorious instance of this policy is the claim that capitalism, by its nature, inevitably leads to periodic depressions.

Statists repeatedly assert that depressions (the phenomenon of the so-called business cycle, of "boom and bust") are inherent in laissez-faire, and that the great crash of 1929 was the final proof of the failure of an unregulated, free-market economy. What is the truth of the matter?

A depression is a large-scale decline in production and trade; it is characterized by a sharp drop in productive output, in investment, in employment, and in the value of capital assets (plants, machinery, etc.). Normal business fluctuations, or a temporary decline in the rate of industrial expansion, do not constitute a depression. A depression is a nation-wide contraction of business activity—and a general decline in the value of capital assets—of major proportions.

There is nothing in the nature of a free-market economy to cause such an event. The popular explanations of depression as caused by "over-production," "under-consumption," monopolies, labor-saving devices, maldistribution, excessive accumulations of wealth, etc., have been exploded as fallacies many times.[2]

Readjustments of economic activity, shifts of capital and

[2] See, in this connection, Carl Snyder, *Capitalism the Creator,* New York: The Macmillan Company, 1940.

labor from one industry to another, due to changing conditions, occur constantly under capitalism. This is entailed in the process of motion, growth, and progress that characterizes capitalism. But there always exists the possibility of profitable endeavor in one field or another, there is always the need and demand for goods, and all that can change is the kind of goods it becomes most profitable to produce.

In any one industry, it is possible for supply to exceed demand, in the context of all the other existing demands. In such a case, there is a drop in prices, in profitableness, in investment, and in employment in that particular industry; capital and labor tend to flow elsewhere, seeking more rewarding uses. Such an industry undergoes a period of stagnation, as a result of unjustified, that is, uneconomic, unprofitable, unproductive investment.

In a free economy that functions on a gold standard, such unproductive investment is severely limited; unjustified speculation does not rise, unchecked, until it engulfs an entire nation. In a free economy, the supply of money and credit needed to finance business ventures is determined by *objective* economic factors. It is the banking system that acts as the guardian of economic stability. The principles governing money supply operate to forbid large-scale unjustified investment.

Most businesses finance their undertakings, at least in part, by means of bank loans. Banks function as an investment clearing house, investing the savings of their customers in those enterprises which promise to be most successful. Banks do not have unlimited funds to loan; they are limited in the credit they can extend by the amount of their gold reserves. In order to remain successful, to make profits and thus attract the savings of investors, banks must make their loans judiciously: they must seek out those ventures which they judge to be most sound and potentially profitable.

If, in a period of increasing speculation, banks are confronted with an inordinate number of requests for loans, then, in response to the shrinking availability of money, they (a) raise their interest rates, and (b) scrutinize more severely the ventures for which loans are requested, setting more exacting standards of what constitutes a justifiable investment. As a consequence, funds are more difficult to obtain, and there is a temporary curtailment and contraction of business investment. Businessmen are often unable to borrow the funds they desire and have to reduce plans for expansion. The purchase of common stocks, which reflects the investors' estimates of the future earnings of companies, is similarly curtailed; overvalued stocks fall in price. Businesses engaged in uneconomic ventures, now unable to obtain additional credit, are obliged to close their doors; a further waste of productive factors is stopped and economic errors are liquidated.

At worst, the economy may experience a mild recession, *i.e.*, a slight general decline in investment and production. In an unregulated economy, readjustments occur quite swiftly, and then production and investment begin to rise again. The temporary recession is not harmful but beneficial; it represents an economic system in the process of correcting its errors, of curtailing disease and returning to health.

The impact of such a recession may be significantly felt in a few industries, but it does not wreck an entire economy. A nation-wide depression, such as occurred in the United States in the thirties, would not have been possible in a fully free society. It was made possible only by government intervention in the economy—more specifically, by government manipulation of the money supply.

The government's policy consisted, in essence, of anesthetizing the regulators, inherent in a free banking system, that prevent runaway speculation and consequent economic collapse.

All government intervention in the economy is based on the belief that economic laws need not operate, that principles of cause and effect can be suspended, that everything in existence is "flexible" and "malleable," except a bureaucrat's whim, which is omnipotent; reality, logic, and economics must not be allowed to get in the way.

This was the implicit premise that led to the establishment, in 1913, of the Federal Reserve System—an institution with control (through complex and often indirect means) over the individual banks throughout the country. The Federal Reserve undertook to free individual banks from the "limitations" imposed on them by the amount of their own individual reserves, to free them from the laws of the market—and to arrogate to government officials the right to decide how much credit they wished to make available at what times.

A "cheap money" policy was the guiding idea and goal of these officials. Banks were no longer to be limited in making loans by the amount of their gold reserves. Interest rates were no longer to rise in response to increasing speculation and increasing demands for funds. Credit was to remain readily available—until and unless the Federal Reserve decided otherwise.[3]

The government argued that by taking control of money and credit out of the hands of private bankers, and by contracting or expanding credit at will, guided by considerations other than those influencing the "selfish" bankers, it could—in conjunction with other interventionist policies—so control investment as to guarantee a state of virtually constant prosperity. Many bureaucrats believed that the government could keep the economy in a state of unending boom.

To borrow an invaluable metaphor from Alan Greenspan: if, under laissez-faire, the banking system and the principles controlling the availability of funds act as a fuse that prevents a blowout in the economy—then the government, through the Federal Reserve System, *put a penny in the fuse-box*. The result was the explosion known as the Crash of 1929.

Throughout most of the 1920's, the government compelled banks to keep interest rates artificially and uneconomically low. As a consequence, money was poured into every sort of speculative venture. By 1928, the warning signals of danger were clearly apparent: unjustified investment was rampant and stocks were increasingly overvalued. The government chose to ignore these danger signals.

A free banking system would have been compelled, by economic necessity, to put the brakes on this process of runaway speculation. Credit and investment, in such a case, would be drastically curtailed; the banks which made unprofitable investments, the enterprises which proved unproductive, and those who dealt with them, would suffer—but that would be all; the country as a whole would not be dragged down. However, the "anarchy" of a free banking system had been abandoned—in favor of "enlightened" government planning.

The boom and the wild speculation—which had preceded every major depression—were allowed to rise unchecked, involving, in a widening network of malinvestments and miscalculations, the entire economic structure of the nation. People were investing in virtually everything and making fortunes overnight—*on paper*. Profits were calculated on

[3] See Benjamin M. Anderson, *Economics and the Public Welfare*, Princeton, New Jersey: D. Van Nostrand Co., 1949. This is the best financial and economic history of the United States from 1914 through 1946.

hysterically exaggerated appraisals of the future earnings of companies. Credit was extended with promiscuous abandon, on the premise that somehow the goods would be there to back it up. It was like the policy of a man who passes out rubber checks, counting on the hope that he will somehow find a way to obtain the necessary money and to deposit it in the bank before anyone presents his checks for collection.

But A is A—and reality is not infinitely elastic. In 1929, the country's economic and financial structure had become impossibly precarious. By the time the government finally and frantically raised the interest rates, it was too late. It is doubtful whether anyone can state with certainty what events first set off the panic—and it does not matter: the crash had become inevitable; any number of events could have pulled the trigger. But when the news of the first bank and commercial failures began to spread, uncertainty swept across the country in widening waves of terror. People began to sell their stocks, hoping to get out of the market with their gains, or to obtain the money they suddenly needed to pay bank loans that were being called in—and other people, seeing this, apprehensively began to sell *their* stocks—and, virtually overnight, an avalanche hurled the stock market downward, prices collapsed, securities became worthless, loans were called in, many of which could not be paid, the value of capital assets plummeted sickeningly, fortunes were wiped out, and, by 1932, business activity had come almost to a halt. The law of causality had avenged itself.

Such, in essence, was the nature and cause of the 1929 depression.

It provides one of the most eloquent illustrations of the disastrous consequences of a "planned" economy. In a free economy, when an individual businessman makes an error of economic judgment, *he* (and perhaps those who immediately deal with him) suffers the consequences; in a controlled economy, when a central planner makes an error of economic judgment, the whole country suffers the consequences.

But it was not the Federal Reserve, it was not government intervention that took the blame for the 1929 depression—it was capitalism. Freedom—cried statists of every breed and sect—had had its chance and had failed. The voices of the few thinkers who pointed to the real cause of the evil were drowned out in the denunciations of businessmen, of the profit motive, of capitalism.

Had men chosen to understand the cause of the crash, the country would have been spared much of the agony that followed. The depression was prolonged for tragically unnecessary years by the same evil that had caused it: government controls and regulations.

Contrary to popular misconception, controls and regulations began long before the New Deal; in the 1920's, the mixed economy was already an established fact of American life. But the trend toward statism began to move faster under the Hoover Administration—and, with the advent of Roosevelt's New Deal, it accelerated at an unprecedented rate. The economic adjustments needed to bring the depression to an end were prevented from taking place—by the imposition of strangling controls, increased taxes, and labor legislation. This last had the effect of forcing wage rates to unjustifiably high levels, thus raising the businessman's costs at precisely the time when costs needed to be lowered, if investment and production were to revive.

The National Industrial Recovery Act, the Wagner Act, and the abandonment of the gold standard (with the government's subsequent plunge into inflation and an orgy of deficit spending) were only three of the many disastrous measures enacted by the New Deal for the avowed purpose of pulling the country out of the depression; all had the opposite effect.

As Alan Greenspan points out in "Stock Prices and Capital Evaluation,"[4] the obstacle to business recovery did not consist exclusively of the specific New Deal legislation passed; more harmful still was the general atmosphere of *uncertainty* engendered by the Administration. Men had no way to know what law or regulation would descend on their heads at any moment; they had no way to know what sudden shifts of direction government policy might take; they had no way to plan long-range.

To act and produce, businessmen require *knowledge,* the possibility of rational calculation, not "faith" and "hope"—above all, not "faith" and "hope" concerning the unpredictable twistings within a bureaucrat's head.

Such advances as business was able to achieve under the New Deal collapsed in 1937—as a result of an intensification of uncertainty regarding what the government might choose to do next. Unemployment rose to more than ten million and business activity fell almost to the low point of 1932, the worst year of the depression.

---

[4] Paper delivered before a joint session of the American Statistical Association and the American Finance Association on December 27, 1959.

It is part of the official New Deal mythology that Roosevelt "got us out of the depression." How was the problem of the depression finally "solved"? By the favorite expedient of all statists in times of emergency: a war.

The depression precipitated by the stock market crash of 1929 was not the first in American history—though it was incomparably more severe than any that had preceded it. If one studies the earlier depressions, the same basic cause and common denominator will be found: in one form or another, by one means or another, government manipulation of the money supply. It is typical of the manner in which interventionism grows that the Federal Reserve System was instituted as a proposed antidote against those earlier depressions— which were themselves products of monetary manipulation by the government.

The financial mechanism of an economy is the sensitive center, the living heart, of business activity. In no other area can government intervention produce quite such disastrous consequences. For a general discussion of the business cycle and its relation to government manipulation of the money supply, see Ludwig von Mises, *Human Action.*[5]

One of the most striking facts of history is men's failure to learn from it. For further details, see the policies of the present Administration.

(AUGUST 1962.)

THE ROLE OF LABOR UNIONS

DO LABOR UNIONS RAISE THE GENERAL STANDARD OF LIVING?

One of the most widespread delusions of our age is the belief that the American worker owes his high standard of living to unions and to "humanitarian" labor legislation. This belief is contradicted by the most fundamental facts and principles of economics—facts and principles which are systematically evaded by labor leaders, legislators, and intellectuals of the statist persuasion.

A country's standard of living, including the wages of its workers, depends on the productivity of labor; high productivity depends on machines, inventions, and capital investment; which depend on the creative ingenuity of individual

[5] New Haven, Connecticut: Yale University Press, 1949.

men; which requires, for its exercise, a politico-economic system that protects the individual's rights and freedom.

The productive value of physical labor as such is low. If the worker of today produces more than the worker of fifty years ago, it is not because the former exerts more physical effort; quite the contrary: the physical effort required of him is far less. The productive value of his effort has been multiplied many times by the tools and machines with which he works; they are crucial in determining the economic worth of his services. To illustrate this principle: consider what would be a man's economic reward, on a desert island, for pushing his finger the distance of half an inch; then consider the wages paid, for pushing a button, to an elevator operator in New York City. It is not muscles that make the difference.

As Ludwig von Mises observes:

> American wages are higher than wages in other countries because the capital invested per head of the worker is greater and the plants are thereby in the position to use the most efficient tools and machines. What is called the American way of life is the result of the fact that the United States has put fewer obstacles in the way of saving and capital accumulation than other nations. The economic backwardness of such countries as India consists precisely in the fact that their policies hinder both the accumulation of capital and the investment of foreign capital. As the capital required is lacking, the Indian enterprises are prevented from employing sufficient quantities of modern equipment, are therefore producing much less per man hour and can only afford to pay wage rates which, compared with American wage rates, appear as shockingly low.[6]

In a free-market economy, employers must bid competitively for the services of workers, just as they must bid competitively for all the other factors of production. If an employer attempts to pay wages which are lower than his workers can obtain elsewhere, he will lose his workers and thus will be compelled to change his policy or go out of business. If, other things being equal, an employer pays wages which are above the market level, his higher costs will put him at a competitive disadvantage in the sale of his products, and again he will be compelled to change his policy or go out of business. Employers do not lower wages because

[6] Ludwig von Mises, *Planning for Freedom*, 2nd edition, South Holland, Illinois: Libertarian Press, 1962, pp. 151–152.

they are cruel, nor raise wages because they are kind. Wages are not determined by the employer's *whim*. Wages are the prices paid for human labor and, like all other prices in a free economy, are determined by the law of supply and demand.

Since the start of the Industrial Revolution and capitalism, wage rates have risen steadily—as an inevitable economic consequence of rising capital accumulation, technological progress, and industrial expansion. As capitalism created countless new markets, so it created an ever-widening market for labor: it multiplied the number and kinds of jobs available, increased the demand and competition for the worker's services, and thus drove wage rates upward.

It was the *economic self-interest* of employers that led them to raise wages and shorten working hours—not the pressure of labor unions. The eight-hour day was established in most American industries long before unions acquired any significant size or economic power. At a time when his competitors were paying their workers between two and three dollars a day, Henry Ford offered five dollars a day, thereby attracting the most efficient labor force in the country, and thus raising his own production and profits. In the 1920's, when the labor movement in France and Germany was far more dominant than in the United States, the standard of living of the American worker was greatly superior. It was the consequence of economic *freedom*.

Needless to say, men have a right to organize into unions, provided they do so voluntarily, that is, provided no one is *forced* to join. Unions can have value as fraternal organizations, or as a means of keeping members informed of current market conditions, or as a means of bargaining more effectively with employers—particularly in small, isolated communities. It may happen that an individual employer is paying wages that, in the overall market context, are too low; in such a case, a strike, or the threat of a strike, can compel him to change his policy, since he will discover that he cannot obtain an adequate labor force at the wages he offers. However, the belief that unions can cause a *general* rise in the standard of living, is a myth.

Today, the labor market is no longer free. Unions enjoy a unique, near-monopolistic power over many aspects of the economy. This has been achieved through legislation which has forced men to join unions, whether they wished to or not, and forced employers to deal with these unions, whether they wished to or not. As a consequence, wage rates in many industries are no longer determined by a free market; unions

have been able to force wages substantially above their
normal market level. These are the "social gains" for which
unions are usually given credit. In fact, however, the result of
their policy has been (a) a curtailment of production, (b)
widespread unemployment, and (c) the penalizing of workers
in other industries, as well as the rest of the population.

(a) With the rise of wage rates to inordinately high
levels, production costs are such that cutbacks in production
are often necessary, new undertakings become too expensive,
and growth is hindered. At the increased costs, marginal
producers—those who have been barely able to compete in
the market—find themselves unable to remain in business.
The overall result: goods and services that would have been
produced are not brought into existence.

(b) As a result of the high wage rates, employers can
afford to hire fewer workers; as a result of curtailed production, employers need fewer workers. Thus, one group of
workers obtains unjustifiably high wages at the expense of
other workers who are unable to find jobs at all. This—in
conjunction with minimum wage laws—is the cause of widespread unemployment. *Unemployment is the inevitable result
of forcing wage rates above their free-market level.* In a free
economy, in which neither employers nor workers are subject
to coercion, wage rates always tend toward the level at which
all those who seek employment will be able to obtain it. In a
frozen, controlled economy, this process is blocked. As a
result of allegedly "pro-labor" legislation and of the monopolistic power that labor unions enjoy, unemployed workers are
not free to compete in the labor market by offering their
services for less than the prevailing wage rates; employers are
not free to hire them. In the case of strikes, if unemployed
workers attempted to obtain the jobs vacated by union
strikers, by offering to work for a lower wage, they often
would be subjected to threats and physical violence at the
hands of union members. These facts are as notorious as they
are evaded in most current discussions of the unemployment
problem—particularly by government officials.

(c) When market conditions are such that producers
whose labor costs have risen, cannot raise the prices of the
goods they sell, a curtailment of production results, as indicated above; and the general population accordingly suffers a
loss of potential goods and services. (The notion that producers can "absorb" such wage increases, by "taking them
out of profits," without a detriment to future production, is
worse than economically naive; it is profits that make future
production possible; the amount of profits that go, not into

investment, but into the producer's personal consumption, is negligible in the overall economic context.) To the extent that market conditions *do* allow, producers whose labor costs have risen are obliged to raise the prices of their goods. Then, workers in other industries find that their living costs have gone up, that they must now pay higher prices for the goods they purchase. Then, they in turn demand a raise in *their* industries, which leads to new price rises, which leads to new wage increases, etc. (Union leaders typically express indignation whenever prices are raised; the only prices they consider it moral to raise are the prices paid for labor, *i.e.*, wages.) Non-unionized workers, and the rest of the population generally, face this same steady rise in their living costs; they are made to subsidize the unjustifiably high wages of union workers—and are the unacknowledged victims of the unions' "social gains." And one observes the spectacle of bricklayers receiving two or even three times the salary of office workers and professors.

It cannot be sufficiently emphasized that it is not unionism as such but government controls and regulations which make this state of affairs possible. In a free, unregulated economy, in a market from which coercion is barred, no economic group can acquire the power so to victimize the rest of the population. The solution does not lie in new legislation directed against unions, but in the repeal of the legislation that made the present evil possible.

The inability of unions to achieve real, widespread raises in wage rates—to raise the standard of living generally—is in part obscured by the phenomenon of inflation. As a consequence of the government's policy of deficit spending and credit expansion, the purchasing power of the monetary unit, the dollar, has diminished drastically across the years. *Nominal* wage rates have increased considerably more than *real* wage rates, that is, wages measured in terms of actual purchasing power.

What has further served to obscure this issue is the fact that real wage rates *have* risen considerably since the start of the century. In spite of destructive and increasing governmental restraints on the freedom of production and trade, major advances in science, technology, and capital accumulation have been made and have raised the general standard of living. It should be added that these advances are less than would have occurred in a fully free economy and, as controls continue to tighten, such advances become slower and rarer.

It is relevant to consider against what obstacles businessmen have had to fight and to go on producing—when one hears labor leaders proclaiming, in indignant tones, the workers' right to a "larger share" of the "national product." To paraphrase John Galt: A larger share—*provided by whom?* Blank out.

Economic progress, like every other form of progress, has only one ultimate source: man's *mind*—and can exist only to the extent that man is free to translate his thought into action.

Let anyone who believes that a high standard of living is the achievement of labor unions and government controls, ask himself the following question: If one had a "time machine" and transported the united labor chieftains of America, plus three million government bureaucrats, back to the tenth century—would *they* be able to provide the medieval serf with electric light, refrigerators, automobiles, and television sets? When one grasps that they would *not,* one should identify who and what made these things possible.[7]

Postscript: After completing the above, I noticed an article in *The New York Times* of September 8 that is too *apropos* to let pass without acknowledgment. The article, entitled "10 U.A.W. Leaders Find Unions Are Losing Members' Loyalty," by Damon Stetson, reports that executives of the United Automobile Workers met to discuss the problem of workers' increasing lack of loyalty to union leadership and union solidarity. One U.A.W. official is quoted as declaring: "How can we get greater loyalty from the individual to the union? All the things we fought for, the corporation is now giving the workers. What we have to find are other things the workers want which the employer is not willing to give him, and we have to develop our program around these things as reasons for belonging to the union."

Is any comment necessary?

(NOVEMBER 1963.)

---

[7] For excellent, more detailed discussions of these issues, see Ludwig von Mises, *Planning for Freedom,* especially the chapter entitled "Wages, Unemployment and Inflation," and Henry Hazlitt, *Economics in One Lesson* (New York: Harper and Brothers, 1946), especially the chapters entitled "Minimum Wage Laws" and "Do Unions Really Raise Wages?"

PUBLIC EDUCATION

SHOULD EDUCATION BE COMPULSORY AND TAX-SUPPORTED, AS
IT IS TODAY?

The answer to this question becomes evident if one makes
the question more concrete and specific, as follows: Should
the government be permitted to remove children forcibly
from their homes, with or without the parents' consent, and
subject the children to educational training and procedures of
which the parents may or may not approve? Should citizens
have their wealth expropriated to support an educational
system which they may or may not sanction, and to pay for
the education of children who are not their own? To anyone
who understands and is consistently committed to the principle of individual rights, the answer is clearly: *No.*

There are no moral grounds whatever for the claim that
education is the prerogative of the State—or for the claim
that it is proper to expropriate the wealth of some men for
the unearned benefit of others.

The doctrine that education should be controlled by the
State is consistent with the Nazi or communist theory of
government. It is not consistent with the American theory of
government.

The totalitarian implications of State education (preposterously described as "free education") have in part been obscured by the fact that in America, unlike Nazi Germany or
Soviet Russia, private schools are legally tolerated. Such
schools, however, exist not by right but only by *permission.*

Further, the facts remain that: (a) most parents are
effectively compelled to send their children to State schools,
since they are taxed to support these schools and cannot afford
to pay the additional fees required to send their children to
private schools; (b) the *standards* of education, controlling *all*
schools, are prescribed by the State; (c) the growing trend
in American education is for the government to exert wider
and wider control over every aspect of education.

As an example of this last: when many parents, who
objected to the pictographic method of teaching schoolchil-
dren to read, undertook to teach their children at home by

the phonetic method—a proposal was made *legally to forbid* parents to do so. What is the implication of this, if not that the child's mind belongs to the State?

When the State assumes *financial* control of education, it is logically appropriate that the State should progressively assume control of the *content* of education—since the State has the responsibility of judging whether or not its funds are being used "satisfactorily." But when a government enters the sphere of *ideas,* when it presumes to prescribe in issues concerning intellectual *content,* that is the death of a free society.

To quote Isabel Paterson in *The God of the Machine:*

> Educational texts are necessarily selective, in subject matter, language, and point of view. Where teaching is conducted by private schools, there will be a considerable variation in different schools; the parents must judge what they want their children taught, by the curriculum offered. Then each must strive for objective truth. . . . Nowhere will there be any inducement to teach the "supremacy of the state" as a compulsory philosophy. But every politically controlled educational system will inculcate the doctrine of state supremacy sooner or later, whether as the divine right of kings, or the "will of the people" in "democracy." Once that doctrine has been accepted, it becomes an almost superhuman task to break the stranglehold of the political power over the life of the citizen. It has had his body, property, and mind in its clutches from infancy.[8]

The disgracefully low level of education in America today is the predictable result of a State-controlled school system. Schooling, to a marked extent, has become a status symbol and a ritual. More and more people are entering college— and fewer and fewer people are emerging properly educated. Our educational system is like a vast bureaucracy, a vast civil service, in which the trend is toward a policy of considering everything about a teacher's qualifications (such as the number of his publications) *except his teaching ability;* and of considering everything about a student's qualifications (such as his "social adaptability") *except his intellectual competence.*

The solution is to *bring the field of education into the marketplace.*

[8] Caldwell, Idaho: The Caxton Printers, 1964, pp. 271–272. Originally published by G. P. Putnam's Sons, New York, 1943.

There is an urgent *economic need* for education. When educational institutions have to compete with one another in the quality of the training they offer—when they have to compete for the value that will be attached to the diplomas they issue—educational standards will necessarily rise. When they have to compete for the services of the best teachers, the teachers who will attract the greatest number of students, then the caliber of teaching—and of teachers' salaries—will necessarily rise. (Today, the most talented teachers often abandon their profession and enter private industry, where they know their efforts will be better rewarded.) When the economic principles that have resulted in the superlative efficiency of American industry are permitted to operate in the field of education, the result will be a revolution, in the direction of unprecedented educational development and growth.

Education should be liberated from the control or intervention of government, and turned over to *profit-making* private enterprise, not because education is unimportant, but because education is so *crucially important*.

What must be challenged is the prevalent belief that education is some sort of "natural right"—in effect, a free gift of nature. There *are* no such free gifts. But it is in the interests of statism to foster this delusion—in order to throw a smokescreen over the issue of whose freedom must be sacrificed to pay for such "free gifts."

As a result of the fact that education has been tax-supported for such a long time, most people find it difficult to project an alternative. Yet there is nothing unique about education that distinguishes it from the many other human needs which are filled by private enterprise. If, for many years, the government had undertaken to provide all the citizens with shoes (on the grounds that shoes are an urgent necessity), and if someone were subsequently to propose that this field should be turned over to private enterprise, he would doubtless be told indignantly: "What! Do you want everyone except the rich to walk around barefoot?"

But the shoe industry is doing its job with immeasurably greater competence than public education is doing *its* job.

To quote Isabel Paterson once more:

The most vindictive resentment may be expected from the pedagogic profession for any suggestion that they should be dislodged from their dictatorial position; it will be expressed mainly in epithets, such as "reactionary," at the mildest. Nevertheless, the question to put to any teacher moved to such indignation is: Do you think nobody would *willingly* entrust his children to you and pay you for teaching them? Why do you have to extort your fees and collect your pupils by compulsion?[9]

(JUNE 1963.)

INHERITED WEALTH

DOES INHERITED WEALTH GIVE SOME INDIVIDUALS AN UNFAIR ADVANTAGE IN A COMPETITIVE ECONOMY?

In considering the issue of inherited wealth, one must begin by recognizing that the crucial right involved is not that of the heir but of the original *producer* of the wealth. The right of property is the right of use and disposal; just as the man who produces wealth has the right to use it and dispose of it in his lifetime, so he has the right to choose who shall be its recipient after his death. No one else is entitled to make that choice. It is irrelevant, therefore, in this context, to consider the worthiness or unworthiness of any particular heir; his is not the basic right at stake; when people denounce inherited wealth, it is the *right of the producer* that they, in fact, are attacking.

It has been argued that, since the heir did not work to produce the wealth, he has no inherent right to it; that is true: the heir's is a *derived* right; the only *primary* right is the producer's. But if the future heir has no moral claim to the wealth, except by the producer's choice, *neither has anyone else*—certainly not the government or "the public."

In a *free* economy, inherited wealth is not an impediment or a threat to those who do not possess it. Wealth, it is necessary to remember, is not a static, limited quantity that can only be divided or looted; wealth is produced; its potential quantity is virtually unlimited.

If an heir is worthy of his money, *i.e.*, if he uses it productively, he brings more wealth into existence, he raises the general standard of living—and, to that extent, he makes the road to the top easier for any talented newcomer. The greater the amount of wealth, of industrial development, in existence, the higher the economic rewards (in wages and profits) and *the wider the market for ability*—for new ideas, products and services.

[9] *Ibid.*, p. 274.

The *less* the wealth in existence, the longer and harder the struggle for everyone. In the beginning years of an industrial economy, wages are low; there is little market yet for unusual ability. But with every succeeding generation, as capital accumulation increases, the economic demand for men of ability rises. The existing industrial establishments desperately need such men; they have no choice but to bid ever higher wages for such men's services—and thus *to train their own future competitors*—so that the time required for a talented newcomer to accumulate his own fortune and establish his own business grows continually shorter.

If the heir is not worthy of his money, the only person threatened by it is himself. A free, competitive economy is a constant process of improvement, innovation, progress; it does not tolerate stagnation. If an heir who lacks ability acquires a fortune and a great industrial establishment from his successful father, he will not be able to maintain it for long; he will not be equal to the competition. In a free economy, where bureaucrats and legislators would not have the power to sell or grant economic favors, all of the heir's money would not be able to buy him protection for his incompetence; he would have to be good at his work or lose his customers to companies run by men of superior ability. There is nothing as vulnerable as a large, mismanaged company that competes with small, efficient ones.

The personal luxuries or drunken parties that the incompetent heir may enjoy on his father's money, are of no *economic* significance. In business, he would not be able to stand in the way of talented competitors or serve as an impediment to men of ability. He would find no automatic security anywhere.

At the turn of the century, there was a popular phrase that is very eloquent with regard to the foregoing: "From shirtsleeves to shirtsleeves in three generations." If a self-made man rose by ability and left his business to unworthy heirs, his grandson went back to the shirtsleeves of obscure employment. (He did *not* end up with the governorship of a state.)

It is a *mixed* economy—such as the semi-socialist or semi-fascist variety we have today—that protects the non-productive rich by freezing a society on a given level of development, by freezing people into classes and castes and making it increasingly more difficult for men to rise or fall or move from one caste to another; so that whoever inherited a fortune before the freeze, can keep it with little fear of competition, like an heir in a feudal society.

It is significant how many heirs of great industrial fortunes, the second- and third-generation millionaires, are welfare statists, clamoring for more and more controls. The target and victims of these controls are the men of ability who, in a free economy, would displace these heirs; the men with whom the heirs would be unable to compete.

As Ludwig von Mises writes in *Human Action:*

> Today taxes often absorb the greater part of the new-comer's "excessive" profits. He cannot accumulate capital; he cannot expand his own business; he will never become big business and a match for the vested interests. The old firms do not need to fear his competition; they are sheltered by the tax collector. They may with impunity indulge in routine, . . . It is true, the income tax prevents them, too, from accumulating new capital. But what is more important for them is that it prevents the dangerous newcomer from accumulating any capital. They are virtually privileged by the tax system. In this sense progressive taxation checks economic progress and makes for rigidity. . . .
>
> The interventionists complain that big business is getting rigid and bureaucratic and that it is no longer possible for competent newcomers to challenge the vested interests of the old rich families. However, as far as their complaints are justified, they complain about things which are merely the result of their own policies.[10]

(JUNE 1963.)

CAPITALISM'S PRACTICALITY

IS THERE ANY VALIDITY TO THE CLAIM THAT LAISSEZ-FAIRE CAPITALISM BECOMES LESS PRACTICABLE AS SOCIETY BECOMES MORE COMPLEX?

This claim is the sort of collectivist bromide that "liberals" repeat ritualistically, without any attempt to prove or substantiate it. To examine it, is to perceive its absurdity.

The same condition of freedom that is necessary in order to *attain* a high level of industrial development—a high level of "complexity"—is necessary in order to *keep* it. To say that

[10] pp. 804–805.

a society has become more complex, merely means that more men live in the same geographical area and deal with one another, that they engage in a greater volume of trading, and in a greater number and diversity of productive activities. There is nothing in these facts which conceivably could justify the abandonment of economic freedom in favor of government "planning."

On the contrary: the more "complex" an economy, the greater the number of choices and decisions that have to be made—and, therefore, the more blatantly impracticable it becomes for this process to be taken over by a central government authority. If there are degrees of irrationality, it would be more plausible to imagine that a primitive, pre-industrial economy could be managed, non-disastrously, by the state; but the notion of running a scientific, highly industrialized society with slave labor, is barbaric in the ignorance it reveals.

Observe that the same type of persons who espouse this doctrine, also declare that the under-developed nations of the world are not suited for economic freedom, that their primitive level of development makes socialism imperative. Thus, they simultaneously argue that a country should not be permitted freedom because it is too *un*developed economically—and that a country should not be permitted freedom because it is too *highly* developed economically.

Both positions are crude rationalizations on the part of statist mentalities who have never grasped what makes industrial civilization possible.

(NOVEMBER 1963.)

6. GOLD AND ECONOMIC FREEDOM

BY ALAN GREENSPAN

An almost hysterical antagonism toward the gold standard is one issue which unites statists of all persuasions. They seem to sense—perhaps more clearly and subtly than many consistent defenders of laissez-faire—that gold and economic freedom are inseparable, that the gold standard is an instrument of laissez-faire and that each implies and requires the other.

In order to understand the source of their antagonism, it is necessary first to understand the specific role of gold in a free society.

Money is the common denominator of all economic transactions. It is that commodity which serves as a medium of exchange, is universally acceptable to all participants in an exchange economy as payment for their goods or services, and can, therefore, be used as a standard of market value and as a store of value, *i.e.*, as a means of saving.

The existence of such a commodity is a precondition of a division of labor economy. If men did not have some commodity of objective value which was generally acceptable as money, they would have to resort to primitive barter or be forced to live on self-sufficient farms and forgo the inestimable advantages of specialization. If men had no means to store value, *i.e.*, to save, neither long-range planning nor exchange would be possible.

What medium of exchange will be acceptable to all participants in an economy is not determined arbitrarily. First, the medium of exchange should be durable. In a primitive society of meager wealth, wheat might be sufficiently durable to serve as a medium, since all exchanges would occur only during and immediately after the harvest, leaving no value-surplus to store. But where store-of-value considerations are important, as they are in richer, more civilized societies, the

The Objectivist, July 1966.

medium of exchange must be a durable commodity, usually a metal. A metal is generally chosen because it is homogeneous and divisible: every unit is the same as every other and it can be blended or formed in any quantity. Precious jewels, for example, are neither homogeneous nor divisible.

More important, the commodity chosen as a medium must be a luxury. Human desires for luxuries are unlimited and, therefore, luxury goods are always in demand and will always be acceptable. Wheat is a luxury in underfed civilizations, but not in a prosperous society. Cigarettes ordinarily would not serve as money, but they did in post-World War II Europe where they were considered a luxury. The term "luxury good" implies scarcity and high unit value. Having a high unit value, such a good is easily portable; for instance, an ounce of gold is worth a half-ton of pig iron.

In the early stages of a developing money economy, several media of exchange might be used, since a wide variety of commodities would fulfill the foregoing conditions. However, one of the commodities will gradually displace all others, by being more widely acceptable. Preferences on what to hold as a store of value, will shift to the most widely acceptable commodity, which, in turn, will make it still more acceptable. The shift is progressive until that commodity becomes the sole medium of exchange. The use of a single medium is highly advantageous for the same reasons that a money economy is superior to a barter economy: it makes exchanges possible on an incalculably wider scale.

Whether the single medium is gold, silver, seashells, cattle, or tobacco is optional, depending on the context and development of a given economy. In fact, all have been employed, at various times, as media of exchange. Even in the present century, two major commodities, gold and silver, have been used as international media of exchange, with gold becoming the predominant one. Gold, having both artistic and functional uses and being relatively scarce, has always been considered a luxury good. It is durable, portable, homogeneous, divisible, and, therefore, has significant advantages over all other media of exchange. Since the beginning of World War I, it has been virtually the sole international standard of exchange.

If all goods and services were to be paid for in gold, large payments would be difficult to execute, and this would tend to limit the extent of a society's division of labor and specialization. Thus a logical extension of the creation of a medium of exchange, is the development of a banking system and credit instruments (bank notes and deposits) which act as a substitute for, but are convertible into, gold.

A free banking system based on gold is able to extend credit and thus to create bank notes (currency) and deposits, according to the production requirements of the economy. Individual owners of gold are induced, by payments of interest, to deposit their gold in a bank (against which they can draw checks). But since it is rarely the case that all depositors want to withdraw all their gold at the same time, the banker need keep only a fraction of his total deposits in gold as reserves. This enables the banker to loan out more than the amount of his gold deposits (which means that he holds claims to gold rather than gold as security for his deposits). But the amount of loans which he can afford to make is not arbitrary: he has to gauge it in relation to his reserves and to the status of his investments.

When banks loan money to finance productive and profitable endeavors, the loans are paid off rapidly and bank credit continues to be generally available. But when the business ventures financed by bank credit are less profitable and slow to pay off, bankers soon find that their loans outstanding are excessive relative to their gold reserves, and they begin to curtail new lending, usually by charging higher interest rates. This tends to restrict the financing of new ventures and requires the existing borrowers to improve their profitability before they can obtain credit for further expansion. Thus, under the gold standard, a free banking system stands as the protector of an economy's stability and balanced growth.

When gold is accepted as the medium of exchange by most or all nations, an unhampered free international gold standard serves to foster a world-wide division of labor and the broadest international trade. Even though the units of exchange (the dollar, the pound, the franc, etc.) differ from country to country, when all are defined in terms of gold the economies of the different countries act as one—so long as there are no restraints on trade or on the movement of capital. Credit, interest rates, and prices tend to follow similar patterns in all countries. For example, if banks in one country extend credit too liberally, interest rates in that country will tend to fall, inducing depositors to shift their gold to higher-interest paying banks in other countries. This will immediately cause a shortage of bank reserves in the "easy money" country, inducing tighter credit standards and a return to competitively higher interest rates again.

A fully free banking system and fully consistent gold standard have not as yet been achieved. But prior to World

War I, the banking system in the United States (and in most of the world) was based on gold, and even though governments intervened occasionally, banking was more free than controlled. Periodically, as a result of overly rapid credit expansion, banks became loaned up to the limit of their gold reserves, interest rates rose sharply, new credit was cut off, and the economy went into a sharp, but short-lived recession. (Compared with the depressions of 1920 and 1932, the pre-World War I business declines were mild indeed.) It was limited gold reserves that stopped the unbalanced expansions of business activity, before they could develop into the post-World War I type of disaster. The readjustment periods were short and the economies quickly re-established a sound basis to resume expansion.

But the process of cure was misdiagnosed as the disease: if shortage of bank reserves was causing a business decline—argued economic interventionists—why not find a way of supplying increased reserves to the banks so they never need be short! If banks can continue to loan money indefinitely—it was claimed—there need never be any slumps in business. And so the Federal Reserve System was organized in 1913. It consisted of twelve regional Federal Reserve banks nominally owned by private bankers, but in fact government sponsored, controlled, and supported. Credit extended by these banks is in practice (though not legally) backed by the taxing power of the federal government. Technically, we remained on the gold standard; individuals were still free to own gold, and gold continued to be used as bank reserves. But now, in addition to gold, credit extended by the Federal Reserve banks ("paper" reserves) could serve as legal tender to pay depositors.

When business in the United States underwent a mild contraction in 1927, the Federal Reserve created more paper reserves in the hope of forestalling any possible bank reserve shortage. More disastrous, however, was the Federal Reserve's attempt to assist Great Britain who had been losing gold to us because the Bank of England refused to allow interest rates to rise when market forces dictated (it was politically unpalatable). The reasoning of the authorities involved was as follows: if the Federal Reserve pumped excessive paper reserves into American banks, interest rates in the United States would fall to a level comparable with those in Great Britain; this would act to stop Britain's gold loss and avoid the political embarrassment of having to raise interest rates.

The "Fed" succeeded: it stopped the gold loss, but it

nearly destroyed the economies of the world, in the process. The excess credit which the Fed pumped into the economy spilled over into the stock market—triggering a fantastic speculative boom. Belatedly, Federal Reserve officials attempted to sop up the excess reserves and finally succeeded in braking the boom. But it was too late: by 1929 the speculative imbalances had become so overwhelming that the attempt precipitated a sharp retrenching and a consequent demoralizing of business confidence. As a result, the American economy collapsed. Great Britain fared even worse, and rather than absorb the full consequences of her previous folly, she abandoned the gold standard completely in 1931, tearing asunder what remained of the fabric of confidence and inducing a world-wide series of bank failures. The world economies plunged into the Great Depression of the 1930's.

With a logic reminiscent of a generation earlier, statists argued that the gold standard was largely to blame for the credit debacle which led to the Great Depression. If the gold standard had not existed, they argued, Britain's abandonment of gold payments in 1931 would not have caused the failure of banks all over the world. (The irony was that since 1913, we had been, not on a gold standard, but on what may be termed "a *mixed* gold standard"; yet it is gold that took the blame.)

But the opposition to the gold standard in any form—from a growing number of welfare-state advocates—was prompted by a much subtler insight: the realization that the gold standard is incompatible with chronic deficit spending (the hallmark of the welfare state). Stripped of its academic jargon, the welfare state is nothing more than a mechanism by which governments confiscate the wealth of the productive members of a society to support a wide variety of welfare schemes. A substantial part of the confiscation is effected by taxation. But the welfare statists were quick to recognize that if they wished to retain political power, the amount of taxation had to be limited and they had to resort to programs of massive deficit spending, *i.e.*, they had to borrow money, by issuing government bonds, to finance welfare expenditures on a large scale.

Under a gold standard, the amount of credit that an economy can support is determined by the economy's tangible assets, since every credit instrument is ultimately a claim on some tangible asset. But government bonds are not backed by tangible wealth, only by the government's promise to pay out of future tax revenues, and cannot easily be absorbed by the financial markets. A large volume of new government bonds can be sold to the public only at progressively higher interest rates. Thus, government deficit spending under a gold standard is severely limited.

The abandonment of the gold standard made it possible for the welfare statists *to use the banking system* as a means to an unlimited expansion of credit. They have created paper reserves in the form of government bonds which—through a complex series of steps—the banks accept in place of tangible assets and treat as if they were an actual deposit, *i.e.*, as the equivalent of what was formerly a deposit of gold. The holder of a government bond or of a bank deposit created by paper reserves believes that he has a valid claim on a real asset. But the fact is that there are now more claims outstanding than real assets.

The law of supply and demand is not to be conned. As the supply of money (of claims) increases relative to the supply of tangible assets in the economy, prices must eventually rise. Thus the earnings saved by the productive members of the society lose value in terms of goods. When the economy's books are finally balanced, one finds that this loss in value represents the goods purchased by the government for welfare or other purposes with the money proceeds of the government bonds financed by bank credit expansion.

In the absence of the gold standard, there is no way to protect savings from confiscation through inflation. There is no safe store of value. If there were, the government would have to make its holding illegal, as was done in the case of gold. If everyone decided, for example, to convert all his bank deposits to silver or copper or any other good, and thereafter declined to accept checks as payment for goods, bank deposits would lose their purchasing power and government-created bank credit would be worthless as a claim on goods. The financial policy of the welfare state requires that there be no way for the owners of wealth to protect themselves.

This is the shabby secret of the welfare statists' tirades against gold. Deficit spending is simply a scheme for the "hidden" confiscation of wealth. Gold stands in the way of this insidious process. It stands as a protector of property rights. If one grasps this, one has no difficulty in understanding the statists' antagonism toward the gold standard.

7. NOTES ON THE HISTORY OF AMERICAN FREE ENTERPRISE

BY AYN RAND

If a detailed, factual study were made of all those instances in the history of American industry which have been used by the statists as an indictment of free enterprise and as an argument in favor of a government-controlled economy, it would be found that the actions blamed on businessmen were caused, necessitated, and made possible *only* by government intervention in business. The evils, popularly ascribed to big industrialists, were not the result of an unregulated industry, but of government power over industry. The villain in the picture was not the businessman, but the legislator, not free enterprise, but government controls.

Businessmen were the victims, yet the victims have taken the blame (and are still taking it), while the guilty parties have used their own guilt as an argument for the extension of their power, for wider and wider opportunities to commit the same crime on a greater and greater scale. Public opinion has been so misinformed about the true facts that we have now reached the stage where, as a cure for the country's problems, people are asking for more and more of the poison which made them sick in the first place.

As illustration, I will list below some examples which I have found in the course of my research into the history of just one industry—the American railroads.

One of the statists' arguments in favor of government controls, is the notion that American railroads were built mainly through the financial help of the government and would have been impossible without it. Actually, government help to the railroads amounted to ten percent of the cost of all the railroads in the country—and the consequences of this help have been disastrous to the railroads. I quote from *The Story of American Railroads* by Stewart H. Holbrook:

Published by Nathaniel Branden Institute, New York, 1959.

In a little more than two decades, three transcontinental railroads were built with government help. All three wound up in bankruptcy courts. And thus, when James Jerome Hill said he was going to build a line from the Great Lakes to Puget Sound, without government cash or land grant, even his close friends thought him mad. But his Great Northern arrived at Puget Sound without a penny of federal help, nor did it fail. It was an achievement to shame the much-touted construction of the Erie Canal.[1]

The degree of government help received by any one railroad, stood in direct proportion to that railroad's troubles and failures. The railroads with the worst histories of scandal, double-dealing, and bankruptcy were the ones that had received the greatest amount of help from the government. The railroads that did best and never went through bankruptcy were the ones that had neither received nor asked for government help. There may be exceptions to this rule, but in all my reading on railroads I have not found one yet.

It is generally believed that in the period when railroads first began to be built in this country, there was a great deal of useless "over-building," a great many lines which were started and abandoned after being proved worthless and ruining those involved. The statists often use this period as an example of "the unplanned chaos" of free enterprise. The truth is that most (and perhaps all) of the useless railroads were built, not by men who intended to build a railroad for profit, but by speculators with political pull, who started these ventures for the sole purpose of obtaining money from the government.

There were many forms of government help for these projects, such as federal land grants, subsidies, state bonds, municipal bonds, etc. A great many speculators started railroad projects as a quick means to get some government cash, with no concern for the future or the commercial possibilities of their railroads. They went through the motions of laying so many miles of shoddy rail, anywhere at all, without inquiring whether the locations they selected had any need for a railroad or any economic future. Some of those men collected the cash and vanished, never starting any railroad at all. This is the source of the popular impression that the origin of American railroads was a period of wild, unscrupulous speculation. But the railroads of this period which were planned and built by businessmen for a proper, private,

[1] New York: Crown Publishers, 1947, pp. 8–9.

commercial purpose were the ones that survived, prospered, and proved unusual foresight in the choice of their locations.

Among our major railroads, the most scandalous histories were those of the Union Pacific and the Central Pacific (now called Southern Pacific). These were the two lines built with a federal government subsidy. The Union Pacific collapsed into bankruptcy soon after its construction, with what was, perhaps, the most disgraceful scandal in the history of any railroad; the scandal involved official corruption. The road did not become properly organized and managed until it was taken over by a private capitalist, Edward H. Harriman.

The Central Pacific—which was built by the "Big Four" of California, on federal subsidies—was the railroad which was guilty of all the evils popularly held against railroads. For almost thirty years, the Central Pacific controlled California, held a monopoly, and permitted no competitor to enter the state. It charged disastrous rates, changed them every year, and took virtually the entire profit of the California farmers or shippers, who had no other railroad to turn to. What made this possible? It was done through the power of the California legislature. The Big Four controlled the legislature and held the state closed to competitors by legal restrictions— such as, for instance, a legislative act which gave the Big Four exclusive control of the entire coastline of California and forbade any other railroad to enter any port. During these thirty years, many attempts were made by private interests to build competing railroads in California and break the monopoly of the Central Pacific. These attempts were defeated—not by methods of free trade and free competition, but by *legislative action*.

This thirty-year monopoly of the Big Four and the practices in which they engaged are always cited as an example of the evils of big business and free enterprise. Yet the Big Four were not free enterprisers; they were not businessmen who had achieved power by means of unregulated trade. They were typical representatives of what is now called a mixed economy. They achieved power by legislative intervention in business; none of their abuses would have been possible in a free, unregulated economy.

The same Central Pacific is notorious for a land deal which led to the dispossession of farmers and to bloody riots in the late 1870's. This is the incident which served as the basis for the anti-business novel, *The Octopus*, by Frank Norris, the incident which caused great public indignation and led to hatred of all railroads and of all big business. But this deal involved land given to the Big Four by the government—and the subsequent injustice was made possible only by legislative and judicial assistance. Yet it was not government intervention in business that took the blame, it was business.[2]

At the other side of the scale, the railroad that had the cleanest history, was most efficiently built in the most difficult circumstances, and was responsible, single-handed, for the development of the entire American Northwest, was the Great Northern, built by J. J. Hill without any federal help whatever. Yet Hill was persecuted by the government all his life—under the Sherman Act, for being a monopolist (!).

The worst injustice has been done by popular misconception to Commodore Vanderbilt of the New York Central. He is always referred to as "an old pirate," "a monster of Wall Street," etc., and always denounced for the alleged ruthlessness of his Wall Street activities. But here is the actual story. When Vanderbilt began to organize several small, obscure railroads into what was to become the New York Central system, he had to obtain a franchise from the City Council to permit his railroad, the New York and Harlem, to enter New York City. The Council was known to be corrupt, and if one wanted a franchise, one had to pay for it, which Vanderbilt did. (Should he be blamed for this, or does the blame rest on the fact that the government held an arbitrary, unanswerable power in the matter and Vanderbilt had no choice?) The stock of his company went up, once it was known that his railroad had permission to enter the city. A little while later, the Council suddenly revoked the franchise—and the Vanderbilt stock began to fall. The aldermen (who had taken Vanderbilt's money), together with a clique of speculators, were selling the Vanderbilt stock short. Vanderbilt fought them and saved his railroad. His ruthlessness consisted of buying his stock as fast as it was being dumped on the market, and thus preventing its price from crashing down to the level that the short-sellers needed. He risked everything he owned in this battle, but he won. The clique and the aldermen went broke.

And, as if this were not enough, the same trick was repeated again a little later, this time involving the New York State Legislature. Vanderbilt needed an act of the legislature to permit him to consolidate the two railroads which he owned. Again, he had to pay the legislators for a promise to

---

[2] For a good factual history of the Central Pacific, see Oscar Lewis, *The Big Four*, New York: Alfred A. Knopf, 1938.

pass the necessary bill. The stock of his company went up, the legislators started selling it short and denied Vanderbilt the promised legislation. He had to go through the same Wall Street battle again, he took on a frightening responsibility, he risked everything he owned plus millions borrowed from friends, but he won and ruined the Albany statesmen. "We busted the whole legislature," he said, "and some of the honorable members had to go home without paying their board bills."

Nothing is said or known nowadays about the details of this story, and it is viciously ironic that Vanderbilt is now used as one of the examples of the evils of free enterprise by those who advocate government controls. The Albany statesmen are forgotten and Vanderbilt is made to be a villain. If you now ask people just what was evil about Vanderbilt, they will answer: "Why, he did something cruel in Wall Street and ruined a lot of people."[8]

The best illustration of the general confusion on the subject of business and government can be found in Holbrook's *The Story of American Railroads*. On page 231, Mr. Holbrook writes:

> Almost from the first, too, the railroads had to undergo the harassments of politicians and their catchpoles, or to pay blackmail in one way or another. The method was almost sure-fire; the politico, usually a member of a state legislature, thought up some law or regulation that would be costly or awkward to the railroads in his state. He then put this into the form of a bill, talked loudly about it, about how it must pass if the sovereign people were to be protected against the monster railroad, and then waited for some hireling of the railroad to dissuade him by a method as old as man. There is record of as many as thirty-five bills that would harass railroads being introduced at one sitting of one legislature.

And the same Mr. Holbrook in the same book just four pages later (pages 235–236) writes:

> In short, by 1870, to pick an arbitrary date, railroads had become, as only too many orators of the day

[8] For details of this story, see David Marshall, *Grand Central*, New York: McGraw-Hill (Whittlesey House), 1946, pp. 60–64, and Alvin F. Harlow, *The Road of the Century*, New York: Creative Age Press, 1947, pp. 166–173.

pointed out, a law unto themselves. They had bought United States senators and congressmen, just as they bought rails and locomotives—with cash. They owned whole legislatures, and often the state courts. . . . To call the roads of 1870 corrupt is none too strong a term.

The connection between these two statements and the conclusion to be drawn from them has, apparently, never occurred to Mr. Holbrook. It is the railroads that he blames and calls "corrupt." Yet what could the railroads do, except try to "own whole legislatures," if these legislatures held the power of life or death over them? What could the railroads do, except resort to bribery, if they wished to exist at all? Who was to blame and who was "corrupt"—the businessmen who had to pay "protection money" for the right to remain in business—or the politicians who held the power to sell that right?

Still another popular accusation against big business is the idea that selfish, private interests restrain and delay progress, when they are threatened with a new invention that might destroy their market. No private interest could or ever has done this, except with government help. The early history of the railroads is a good illustration. The railroads were violently opposed by the owners of canals and steamship companies, who were doing most of the transportation at the time. A great number of laws, regulations, and restrictions were passed by various legislatures, at the instigation of the canal interests, in an attempt to hamper and stop the development of the railroads. This was done in the name of the "public welfare" (!). When the first railroad bridge was built across the Mississippi, the river steamship interests brought suit against its builder, and the court ordered the bridge destroyed as a "material obstruction and a nuisance." The Supreme Court reversed the ruling, by a narrow margin, and allowed the bridge to stand.[4] Ask yourself what the fate of the entire industrial development of the United States would have been, if that narrow margin had been different—and what is the fate of all economic progress when it is left, not to objective demonstration, but to the arbitrary decision of a few men armed with political power.

It is important to note that the railroad owners did not start in business by corrupting the government. They had to

[4] See Frank H. Spearman, *The Strategy of Great Railroads,* New York: Scribner's, 1904, pp. 273–276.

turn to the practice of bribing legislators only in self-protection. The first and best builders of railroads were free enterprisers who took great risks on their own, with private capital and no government help. It was only when they demonstrated to the country that the new industry held a promise of tremendous wealth that the speculators and the legislators rushed into the game to milk the new giant for all it was worth. It was only when the legislatures began the blackmail of threatening to pass disastrous and impossible regulations that the railroad owners had to turn to bribery.

It is significant that the best of the railroad builders, those who started out with private funds, did not bribe legislatures to throttle competitors nor to obtain any kind of special legal advantage or privilege. They made their fortunes by their own personal ability—and if they resorted to bribery at all, like Commodore Vanderbilt, it was only to buy the removal of some artificial restriction, such as a permission to consolidate. They did not pay to *get* something from the legislature, but only to get the legislature out of their way. But the builders who started out with government help, such as the Big Four of the Central Pacific, were the ones who used the government for special advantages and owed their fortunes to legislation more than to personal ability. This is the inevitable result of any kind or degree of mixed economy. It is only with the help of government regulations that a man of lesser ability can destroy his better competitors—and he is the only type of man who runs to government for economic help.

It is not a matter of accidental personalities, of "dishonest businessmen" or "dishonest legislators." The dishonesty is inherent in and created by the system. So long as a government holds the power of economic control, it will necessarily create a special "elite," an "aristocracy of pull," it will attract the corrupt type of politician into the legislature, it will work to the advantage of the dishonest businessman, and will penalize and, eventually, destroy the honest and the able.

The examples quoted are only a few of the more obvious ones; there is a great number of others, all demonstrating the same point. These were taken from the history of a single industry. One can well imagine what one would discover if one went through the history of other American industries in similar detail.

It is time to clarify in the public mind the pernicious confusion which was created by Marxism and which most people have unthinkingly accepted: the notion that economic controls are the proper function of government, that government is a tool of economic class interests, and that the issue is only which particular class or pressure group shall be served by the government. Most people believe that free enterprise is a controlled economy allegedly serving the interests of the industrialists—as opposed to the welfare state, which is a controlled economy allegedly serving the interests of the workers. The idea or possibility of an *uncontrolled economy* has been entirely forgotten and is now being deliberately ignored. Most people would see no difference between businessmen such as J. J. Hill of the Great Northern and businessmen such as the Big Four of the Central Pacific. Most people would simply dismiss the difference by saying that businessmen are crooks who will always corrupt the government and that the solution is to let the government be corrupted by labor unions.

The issue is not between pro-business controls and pro-labor controls, but between controls and freedom. It is not the Big Four against the welfare state, but the Big Four and the welfare state on one side—against J. J. Hill and every honest worker on the other. Government control of the economy, no matter in whose behalf, has been the source of all the evils in our industrial history—and the solution is laissez-faire capitalism, *i.e.*, the abolition of any and all forms of government intervention in production and trade, the separation of State and Economics, in the same way and for the same reasons as the separation of Church and State.

8. THE EFFECTS OF THE INDUSTRIAL REVOLUTION ON WOMEN AND CHILDREN

BY ROBERT HESSEN

CHILD LABOR AND

THE INDUSTRIAL REVOLUTION

The least understood and most widely misrepresented aspect of the history of capitalism is child labor.

One cannot evaluate the phenomenon of child labor in England during the Industrial Revolution of the late eighteenth and early nineteenth century, unless one realizes that the introduction of the factory system offered a livelihood, a means of survival, to tens of thousands of children who would not have lived to be youths in the pre-capitalistic eras.

The factory system led to a rise in the general standard of living, to rapidly falling urban death rates and decreasing infant mortality—and produced an unprecedented population explosion.

In 1750, England's population was six million; it was nine million in 1800 and twelve million in 1820, a rate of increase without precedent in any era. The age distribution of the population shifted enormously; the proportion of children and youths increased sharply. "The proportion of those born in London dying before five years of age" fell from 74.5 percent in 1730–49 to 31.8 percent in 1810–29.[1] Children who hitherto would have died in infancy now had a chance for survival.

Both the rising population and the rising life expectancy

The Objectivist Newsletter, April and November 1962.

[1] Mabel C. Buer, *Health, Wealth and Population in the Early Days of the Industrial Revolution, 1760–1815*, London: George Routledge & Sons, 1926, p. 30.

give the lie to the claims of socialist and fascist critics of capitalism that the conditions of the laboring classes were progressively deteriorating during the Industrial Revolution.

One is both morally unjust and ignorant of history if one blames capitalism for the condition of children during the Industrial Revolution, since, in fact, capitalism brought an enormous improvement over their condition in the preceding age. The source of that injustice was ill-informed, emotional novelists and poets, like Dickens and Mrs. Browning; fanciful medievalists, like Southey; political tract writers posturing as economic historians, like Engels and Marx. All of them painted a vague, rosy picture of a lost "golden age" of the working classes, which, allegedly, was destroyed by the Industrial Revolution. Historians have not supported their assertions. Investigation and common sense have deglamorized the pre-factory system of domestic industry. In that system, the worker made a costly initial investment, or paid heavy rentals, for a loom or frame, and bore most of the speculative risks involved. His diet was drab and meager, and even subsistence often depended on whether work could be found for his wife and children. There was nothing romantic or enviable about a family living and working together in a badly lighted, improperly ventilated, and poorly constructed cottage.

How did children thrive before the Industrial Revolution? In 1697, John Locke wrote a report for the Board of Trade on the problem of poverty and poor-relief. Locke estimated that a laboring man and his wife in good health could support no more than two children, and he recommended that *all children over three years of age* should be taught to earn their living at working schools for spinning and knitting, where they would be given food. "What they can have at home, from their parents," wrote Locke, "is seldom more than bread and water, and that very scantily too."

Professor Ludwig von Mises reminds us:

The factory owners did not have the power to compel anybody to take a factory job. They could only hire people who were ready to work for the wages offered to them. Low as these wage rates were, they were nonetheless much more than these paupers could earn in any other field open to them. It is a distortion of facts to say that the factories carried off the housewives from the nurseries and the kitchen and the children from their play. These women had nothing to cook

with and to feed their children. These children were
destitute and starving. Their only refuge was the factory. It saved them, in the strict sense of the term, from
death by starvation.[2]

Factory children went to work at the insistence of their
parents. The children's hours of labor were very long, but the
work was often quite easy—usually just attending a spinning
or weaving machine and retying threads when they broke. It
was not on behalf of such children that the agitation for
factory legislation began. The first child labor law in England
(1788) regulated the hours and conditions of labor of the
miserable children who worked as chimney sweeps—a dirty,
dangerous job which long antedated the Industrial Revolution, and which was not connected with factories. The first
Act which applied to factory children was passed to protect
those who had been sent into virtual slavery by the parish
authorities, *a government body:* they were deserted or or-
phaned pauper children who were legally under the custody
of the poor-law officials in the parish, and who were bound
by these officials into long terms of unpaid apprenticeship in
return for a bare subsistence.

Conditions of employment and sanitation are acknowledged to have been best in the larger and newer factories. As
successive Factory Acts, between 1819 and 1846, placed
greater and greater restrictions on the employment of children and adolescents, the owners of the larger factories,
which were more easily and frequently subject to visitation
and scrutiny by the factory inspectors, increasingly chose to
dismiss children from employment rather than be subjected
to elaborate, arbitrary, and ever-changing regulations on how
they might run a factory which employed children. The result
of legislative intervention was that these dismissed children,
who needed to work in order to survive, were forced to seek
jobs in smaller, older, and more out-of-the-way factories,
where the conditions of employment, sanitation, and safety
were markedly inferior. Those who could not find new jobs
were reduced to the status of their counterparts a hundred
years before, that is, to irregular agricultural labor, or worse—
in the words of Professor von Mises—to "infest the country
as vagabonds, beggars, tramps, robbers and prostitutes."

Child labor was not ended by legislative fiat; child labor
ended when it became economically unnecessary for children
to earn wages in order to survive—when the income of their

---

[2] Ludwig von Mises, *Human Action*, New Haven, Connecticut: Yale
University Press, 1949, p. 615.

arents became sufficient to support them. The emancipators nd benefactors of those children were not legislators or actory inspectors, but manufacturers and financiers. Their fforts and investments in machinery led to a rise in real vages, to a growing abundance of goods at lower prices, and o an incomparable improvement in the general standard of iving.

The proper answer to the critics of the Industrial Revolu-ion is given by Professor T. S. Ashton:

> There are today on the plains of India and China men and women, plague-ridden and hungry, living lives little better, to outward appearance, than those of the cattle that toil with them by day and share their places of sleep by night. Such Asiatic standards, and such un-mechanized horrors, are the lot of those who increase their numbers without passing through an industrial revolution.[3]

Let me add that the Industrial Revolution and its conse-quent prosperity were the achievement of capitalism and cannot be achieved under any other politico-economic system. As proof, I offer you the spectacle of Soviet Russia which combines industrialization—and famine.

WOMEN AND THE
INDUSTRIAL REVOLUTION

To condemn capitalism one must first misrepresent its history. The notion that industrial capitalism led to nothing but misery and degradation for women is an article of faith among critics of capitalism. It is as prevalent as the view that children were victimized and exploited by the Industrial Revolution—and it is as false.

Let us examine the source of this view. To appreciate the benefits that capitalism brought to women, one must compare their status under capitalism with their condition in the preceding centuries. But the nineteenth-century critics of cap-italism did not do this; instead, they distorted and falsified history, glamorizing the past and disparaging everything mod-ern by contrast.

[3] T. S. Ashton, *The Industrial Revolution, 1760–1830,* London: Oxford University Press, 1948, p. 161.

For instance, Richard Oastler, one of the most fanatical nineteenth-century enemies of capitalism, claimed that everyone was better off spiritually and materially in the Middle Ages than in the early nineteenth century. Describing medieval England, Oastler rhapsodized about the lost golden age: "Oh, what a beautiful ship was England once! She was well built, well manned, well provisioned, well rigged! All were then merry, cheerful and happy on board."

This was said of centuries in which "the bulk of the population were peasants in a servile condition, bound by status, not free to change their mode of life or to move from their birthplace"⁴—when people had only the promise of happiness in the life beyond the grave to succor them against decimating plagues, recurring famines and at best half-filled stomachs—when people lived in homes so infested with dirt and vermin that one historian's verdict about these cottages is: "From a health point of view the only thing to be said in their favor was that they burnt down very easily!"⁵

Oastler represented the viewpoint of the medievalists. The socialists, who agreed with them, were equally inaccurate historians.

For example, describing the conditions of the masses in the pre-industrial seventeenth and early eighteenth centuries, Friedrich Engels alleged: "The workers vegetated throughout a passably comfortable existence, leading a righteous and peaceful life in all piety and probity; and their material position was far better off than their successors."

This was written of an age characterized by staggeringly high mortality rates, especially among children—crowded towns and villages untouched by sanitation—notoriously high gin consumption. The working-class diet consisted mainly of oatmeal, milk, cheese, and beer; while bread, potatoes, coffee, tea, sugar, and meat were still expensive luxuries. Bathing was infrequent and laundering a rarity because soap was so costly, and clothing—which had to last a decade or generation—would not last if washed too often.

The most rapid change wrought by the Industrial Revolution was the shifting of textile production out of the home and into the factory. Under the previous system, called "domestic industry," the spinning and weaving was done in the workers's own home with the aid of his wife and children. When technological advances caused the shifting of textile

---

⁴ Buer, p. 250.
⁵ *Ibid.*, p. 88.

production into factories, this led, said one critic of capitalism, "to the breakup of the home as a social unit."[6]

Mrs. Neff writes approvingly that "under the system of domestic industry the parents and the children had worked together, the father the autocratic head, pocketing the family earnings and directing their expenditure." Her tone turns to condemnation when she recounts: "But under the factory system the members of the family all had their own earnings, they worked in separate departments of the mill, coming home only for food and sleep. The home was little but a shelter."

The factories were held responsible, by such critics, for every social problem of that age, including promiscuity, infidelity, and prostitution. Implicit in the condemnation of women working in the factories was the notion that a woman's place is in the home and that her only proper role is to keep house for her husband and to rear his children. The factories were blamed simultaneously for removing girls from the watchful restraints of their parents and for encouraging early marriages; and later, for fostering maternal negligence and incompetent housekeeping, as well as for encouraging lack of female subordination and the desire for luxuries.

It is a damning indictment of the pre-factory system to consider what kind of "luxuries" the Industrial Revolution brought within reach of the working-class budget. Women sought such luxuries as shoes instead of clogs, hats instead of shawls, "delicacies" (like coffee, tea, and sugar) instead of "plain food."

Critics denounced the increasing habit of wearing ready-made clothes, and they viewed the replacement of wools and linens by inexpensive cottons as a sign of growing poverty. Women were condemned for not making by hand that which they could buy more cheaply, thanks to the revolution in textile production. Dresses no longer had to last a decade— women no longer had to wear coarse petticoats until they disintegrated from dirt and age; cheap cotton dresses and undergarments were a revolution in personal hygiene.

The two most prevalent nineteenth-century explanations of why women worked in the factories were: (a) that their "husbands preferred to remain home idle, supported by their wives," and (b) that the factory system "displaced adult men and imposed on women 'the duty and burden of supporting their husbands and families.'" These charges are examined in

[6] Wanda Neff, *Victorian Working Women*, New York: Columbia University Press, 1920, p. 51.

Wives and Mothers in Victorian Industry, a definitive study by Dr. Margaret Hewitt of the University of Exeter. Her conclusion is: "Neither of these assumptions proves to have any statistical foundation whatsoever."[7]

In fact, women worked in the factories for far more conventional reasons. Dr. Hewitt enumerates them: many women worked because "their husbands' wages were insufficient to keep the home going"; others were widowed or deserted; others were barren, or had grown-up children; some had husbands who were unemployed, or employed in seasonal jobs; and a few chose to work in order to earn money for extra comforts in the home, although their husbands' wages were sufficient to cover necessities.[8]

What the factory system offered these women was—*not* misery and degradation—but a means of survival, of economic independence, of rising above the barest subsistence. Harsh as nineteenth-century factory conditions were, compared to twentieth-century conditions, women increasingly preferred work in the factories to any other alternatives open to them, such as domestic service, or back-breaking work in agricultural gangs, or working as haulers and pullers in the mines; moreover, if a woman could support herself, she was not driven into early marriage.

Even Professor Trevelyan, who persistently disparaged the factories and extolled "the good old days," admitted:

> . . . the women who went to work in the factories though they lost some of the best things in life [Trevelyan does not explain what he means], gained independence. . . . The money they earned was their own. The factory hand acquired an economic position personal to herself, which in the course of time other women came to envy.

And Trevelyan concluded: "The working class home often became more comfortable, quiet and sanitary by ceasing to be a miniature factory.[9]

Critics of the factory system still try to argue that the domestic spinners or weavers could have a creator's pride in their work, which they lost by becoming mere cogs in a huge industrial complex. Dr. Dorothy George easily demolishes this thesis: "It seems unlikely that the average weaver, toiling

[7] London: Rockliff, 1958, p. 190.

[8] *Ibid.,* pp. 192, 194.

[9] George M. Trevelyan, *English Social History,* New York and London: Longmans, Green & Company, 1942, p. 487.

hour after hour throwing the shuttle backwards and forwards on work which was monotonous and exhausting, had the reactions which would satisfy a modern enthusiast for peasant arts."[10]

Finally, it was charged that factory work made women too concerned with material comforts at the expense of spiritual considerations.

The misery in which women lived before capitalism, might have made them cherish the New Testament injunction: "Love not the world, nor the things that are in the world." But the productive splendor of capitalism vanquished that view. Today, the foremost champions of that viewpoint are Professor Galbraith and the austerity-preachers behind the Iron Curtain.

---

[10] M. Dorothy George, *England in Transition: Life and Work in the Eighteenth Century,* London: Penguin, 1953, p. 139.

9. THE ASSAULT ON INTEGRITY

BY ALAN GREENSPAN

Protection of the consumer against "dishonest and unscrupulous business practices" has become a cardinal ingredient of welfare statism. Left to their own devices, it is alleged, businessmen would attempt to sell unsafe food and drugs, fraudulent securities, and shoddy buildings. Thus, it is argued, the Pure Food and Drug Administration, the Securities and Exchange Commission, and the numerous building regulatory agencies are indispensable if the consumer is to be protected from the "greed" of the businessman.

But it is precisely the "greed" of the businessman or, more appropriately, his profit-seeking, which is the unexcelled protector of the consumer.

What collectivists refuse to recognize is that it is in the self-interest of every businessman to have a reputation for honest dealings and a quality product. Since the market value of a going business is measured by its money-making potential, reputation or "good will" is as much an asset as its physical plant and equipment. For many a drug company, the value of its reputation, as reflected in the salability of its brand name, is often its major asset. The loss of reputation through the sale of a shoddy or dangerous product would sharply reduce the market value of the drug company, though its physical resources would remain intact. The market value of a brokerage firm is even more closely tied to its good-will assets. Securities worth hundreds of millions of dollars are traded every day over the telephone. The slightest doubt as to the trustworthiness of a broker's word or commitment would put him out of business overnight.

Reputation, in an unregulated economy, is thus a major competitive tool. Builders who have acquired a reputation for top quality construction take the market away from their less scrupulous or less conscientious competitors. The most reputable securities dealers get the bulk of the commission business. Drug manufacturers and food processors vie with one another to make their brand names synonymous with fine quality.

Physicians have to be just as scrupulous in judging the quality of the drugs they prescribe. They, too, are in business and compete for trustworthiness. Even the corner grocer is involved: he cannot afford to sell unhealthy foods if he wants to make money. In fact, in one way or another, every producer and distributor of goods or services is caught up in the competition for reputation.

It requires years of consistently excellent performance to acquire a reputation and to establish it as a financial asset. Thereafter, a still greater effort is required to maintain it: a company cannot afford to risk its years of investment by letting down its standards of quality for one moment or one inferior product; nor would it be tempted by any potential "quick killing." Newcomers entering the field cannot compete immediately with the established, reputable companies, and have to spend years working on a more modest scale in order to earn an equal reputation. Thus the incentive to scrupulous performance operates on all levels of a given field of production. It is a built-in safeguard of a free enterprise system and the only real protection of consumers against business dishonesty.

Government regulation is not an alternative means of protecting the consumer. It does not build quality into goods, or accuracy into information. Its sole "contribution" is to substitute force and fear for incentive as the "protector" of the consumer. The euphemisms of government press releases to the contrary notwithstanding, the basis of regulation is armed force. At the bottom of the endless pile of paper work which characterizes all regulation lies a gun. What are the results?

To paraphrase Gresham's Law: bad "protection" drives out good. The attempt to protect the consumer by force undercuts the protection he gets from incentive. First, it undercuts the value of reputation by placing the reputable company on the same basis as the unknown, the newcomer, or the fly-by-nighter. It declares, in effect, that all are equally suspect and that years of evidence to the contrary do not free a man from that suspicion. Second, it grants an automatic (though, in fact, unachievable) guarantee of safety to the products of any company that complies with its arbitrarily set minimum standards. The value of a reputation rested on the fact that it was necessary for the consumers to exercise judgment in the choice of the goods and services they purchased. The government's "guarantee" undermines this necessity; it declares to the consumers, in effect, that no choice or judgment is required—and that a company's record, its years of achievement, is irrelevant.

The minimum standards, which are the basis of regulation, gradually tend to become the maximums as well. If the building codes set minimum standards of construction, a builder does not get very much competitive advantage by exceeding those standards and, accordingly, he tends to meet only the minimums. If minimum specifications are set for vitamins, there is little profit in producing something of above-average quality. Gradually, even the attempt to maintain minimum standards becomes impossible, since the draining of incentives to improve quality ultimately undermines even the minimums.

The guiding purpose of the government regulator is to prevent rather than to create something. He gets no credit if a new miraculous drug is discovered by drug company scientists; he does if he bans thalidomide. Such emphasis on the negative sets the framework under which even the most conscientious regulators must operate. The result is a growing body of restrictive legislation on drug experimentation, testing, and distribution. As in all research, it is impossible to add restrictions to the development of new drugs without simultaneously cutting off the secondary rewards of such research—the improvement of existing drugs. Quality improvement and innovation are inseparable.

Building codes are supposed to protect the public. But by being forced to adhere to standards of construction long after they have been surpassed by new technological discoveries, builders divert their efforts to maintaining the old rather than adopting new and safer techniques of construction.

Regulation—which is based on force and fear—undermines the moral base of business dealings. It becomes cheaper to bribe a building inspector than to meet his standards of construction. A fly-by-night securities operator can quickly meet all the S.E.C. requirements, gain the inference of respectability, and proceed to fleece the public. In an unregulated economy, the operator would have had to spend a number of years in reputable dealings before he could earn a position of trust sufficient to induce a number of investors to place funds with him.

Protection of the consumer by regulation is thus illusory. Rather than isolating the consumer from the dishonest businessman, it is gradually destroying the only reliable protection the consumer has: competition for reputation.

While the consumer is thus endangered, the major victim of "protective" regulation is the producer: the businessman. Regulation which acts to destroy the competition of businessmen for reputation undermines the market value of the good will which businessmen have built up over the years. It is an act of expropriation of wealth created by integrity. Since the value of a business—its wealth—rests on its ability to make money, the acts of a government seizing a company's plant or devaluing its reputation are in the same category: both are acts of expropriation.

Moreover, "protective" legislation falls in the category of preventive law. Businessmen are being subjected to governmental coercion *prior* to the commission of any crime. In a free economy, the government may step in only when a fraud has been perpetrated, or a demonstrable damage has been done to a consumer; in such cases the only protection required is that of criminal law.

Government regulations do not eliminate potentially dishonest individuals, but merely make their activities harder to detect or easier to hush up. Furthermore, the possibility of individual dishonesty applies to government employees fully as much as to any other group of men. There is nothing to guarantee the superior judgment, knowledge, and integrity of an inspector or a bureaucrat—and the deadly consequences of entrusting him with arbitrary power are obvious.

The hallmark of collectivists is their deep-rooted distrust of freedom and of the free-market processes; but it is their advocacy of so-called "consumer protection" that exposes the nature of their basic premises with particular clarity. By preferring force and fear to incentive and reward as a means of human motivation, they confess their view of man as a mindless brute functioning on the range of the moment, whose actual self-interest lies in "flying-by-night" and making "quick kills." They confess their ignorance of the role of intelligence in the production process, of the wide intellectual context and long-range vision required to maintain a modern industry. They confess their inability to grasp the crucial importance of the moral values which are the motive power of capitalism. Capitalism is based on self-interest and self-esteem; it holds integrity and trustworthiness as cardinal virtues and makes them pay off in the marketplace, thus demanding that men survive by means of virtues, not of vices. It is this superlatively moral system that the welfare statists propose to improve upon by means of preventive law, snooping bureaucrats, and the chronic goad of fear.

10. THE PROPERTY STATUS OF AIRWAVES

BY AYN RAND

Any material element or resource which, in order to become of use or value to men, requires the application of human knowledge and effort, should be private property—by the right of those who apply the knowledge and effort.

This is particularly true of broadcasting frequencies or waves, because they are produced by human action and do not exist without it. What exists in nature is only the potential and the space through which those waves must travel.

Just as two trains cannot travel on the same section of track at the same time, so two broadcasts cannot use the same frequency at the same time in the same area without "jamming" each other. There is no difference in principle between the ownership of land and the ownership of airways. The only issue is the task of defining the application of property rights to this particular sphere. It is on this task that the American government has failed dismally, with incalculably disastrous consequences.

There is no essential difference between a broadcast and a concert: the former merely transmits sounds over a longer distance and requires more complex technical equipment. No one would venture to claim that a pianist may own his fingers and his piano, but the space inside the concert hall—through which the sound waves he produces travel—is "public property" and, therefore, he has no right to give a concert without a license from the government. Yet this is the absurdity foisted on our broadcasting industry.

The chief argument in support of the notion that broadcasting frequencies should be "public property" has been stated succinctly by Justice Frankfurter: "[Radio] facilities are limited; they are not available to all who may wish to use them; the radio spectrum simply is not large enough to accommodate everybody. There is a fixed natural limitation upon the number of stations that can operate without interfering with one another."

The fallacy of this argument is obvious. The number of broadcasting frequencies *is* limited; so is the number of concert halls; so is the amount of oil or wheat or diamonds; so is the acreage of land on the surface of the globe. There is no material element or value that exists in *unlimited* quantity. And if a "wish" to use a certain "facility" is the criterion of the right to use it, then the universe is simply not large enough to accommodate all those who harbor wishes for the unearned.

It is the proper task of the government to protect individual rights and, as part of it, to formulate the laws by which these rights are to be implemented and adjudicated. It is the government's responsibility to define the application of individual rights to a given sphere of activity—to *define* (*i.e.,* to identify), *not* to create, invent, donate, or expropriate. The question of defining the application of property rights has arisen frequently, in the wake of major scientific discoveries or inventions, such as the question of oil rights, vertical space rights, etc. In most cases, the American government was guided by the proper principle: it sought to protect all the individual rights involved, *not* to abrogate them.

A notable example of the proper method of establishing private ownership from scratch, in a previously ownerless area, is the Homestead Act of 1862, by which the government opened the western frontier for settlement and turned "public land" over to private owners. The government offered a 160-acre farm to any adult citizen who would settle on it and cultivate it for five years, after which it would become his property. Although that land was originally regarded, in law, as "public property," the method of its allocation, *in fact,* followed the proper principle (*in fact,* but not in explicit ideological intention). The citizens did not have to *pay* the government as if it were an owner; ownership began with *them,* and they earned it by the method which is the source and root of the concept of "property": by working on unused material resources, by turning a wilderness into a civilized settlement. Thus, the government, in this case, was acting not as the owner but as the *custodian* of ownerless resources who defines objectively impartial rules by which potential owners may acquire them.

This should have been the principle and pattern of the allocation of broadcasting frequencies.

As soon as it became apparent that radio broadcasting had opened a new realm of material resources which, in the absence of legal definitions, would become a wilderness of clashing individual claims, the government should have promulgated the equivalent of a Homestead Act of the airways—an act defining private property rights in the new realm, establishing the rule that the user of a radio frequency would own it after he had operated a station for a certain number of years, and allocating all frequencies by the rule of priority, *i.e.*, "first come, first served."

Bear in mind that the development of commerical radio took many years of struggle and experimentation, and that the goldrush of the "wishers" did not start until the pioneers—who had taken the risks of venturing into the unknown—had built it into a bright promise of great commercial value. By what right, code, or standard was anyone entitled to that value except the men who had created it?

If the government had adhered to the principle of private property rights, and the pioneers' ownership had been legally established, then a latecomer who wished to acquire a radio station would have had to *buy* it from one of the original owners (as is the case with every other type of property). The fact that the number of available frequencies was limited would have served, not to entrench the original owners, but to threaten their hold, if they did not make the best economic use of their property (which is what free competition does to every other type of property). With a limited supply and a growing demand, competition would have driven the market value of a radio (and later, TV) station so high that only the most competent men could have afforded to buy it or to keep it; a man, unable to make a profit, could not have long afforded to waste so valuable a property. Who, on a free market, determines the economic success or failure of an enterprise? The *public* (the public as a sum of individual producers, viewers, and listeners, each making his own decisions—*not* as a single, helpless, disembodied *collective* with a few bureaucrats posturing as the spokesmen of its will on earth).

Contrary to the "argument from scarcity," if you want to make a "limited" resource available to the whole people, make it private property and throw it on a free, open market.

The "argument from scarcity," incidentally, is outdated, even in its literal meaning: with the discovery of ultra-high frequencies, there are more broadcasting channels available today than prospective applicants willing to pioneer in their development. As usual, the "wishers" seek, not to create, but to take over the rewards and advantages created by others.

The history of the collectivization of radio and television demonstrates, in condensed form, in a kind of microcosm, the process and the causes of capitalism's destruction. It is an eloquent illustration of the fact that capitalism is perishing by the philosophical default of its alleged defenders.

Collectivists frequently cite the early years of radio as an example of the failure of free enterprise. In those years, when broadcasters had no property rights in radio, no legal protection or recourse, the airways were a chaotic no man's land where anyone could use any frequency he pleased and jam anyone else. Some professional broadcasters tried to divide their frequencies by private agreements, which they could not enforce on others; nor could they fight the interference of stray, maliciously mischievous amateurs. This state of affairs was used, then and now, to urge and justify government control of radio.

This is an instance of capitalism taking the blame for the evils of its enemies.

The chaos of the airways was an example, not of free enterprise, but of *anarchy*. It was caused, not by private property rights, but by their absence. It demonstrated why capitalism is incompatible with anarchism, why men do need a government and what is a government's proper function. What was needed was *legality*, not *controls*.

What was imposed was worse than controls: outright nationalization. By a gradual, uncontested process—by ideological default—it was taken for granted that the airways belong to "the people" and are "public property."

If you want to know the intellectual state of the time, I will ask you to guess the political ideology of the author of the following quotation:

> Radio communication is not to be considered as merely a business carried on for private gain, for private advertisement, or for entertainment of the curious. It is a public concern impressed with the public trust and to be considered primarily from the standpoint of public interest in the same extent and upon the basis of the same general principles as our other public utilities.

No, this was not said by a business-hating collectivist eager to establish the supremacy of the "public interest" over "private gain"; it was not said by a socialist planner nor by a communist conspirator; it was said by Herbert Hoover, then Secretary of Commerce, in 1924.

It was Hoover who fought for government control of radio and, as Secretary of Commerce, made repeated attempts to extend government power beyond the limits set by the legislation of the time, attempts to attach detailed conditions to radio licenses, which he had no legal authority to do and which were repeatedly negated by the courts. It was Hoover's influence that was largely responsible for that tombstone of the radio (and the then unborn television) industry known as the Act of 1927, which established the Federal Radio Commission with all of its autocratic, discretionary, undefined, and undefinable powers. (That Act—with minor revisions and amendments, including the Act of 1934 that changed the Federal Radio Commission into the Federal Communications Commission—is still, in all essential respects, the basic legal document ruling the broadcasting industry today.)

"What we are doing," said F.C.C. Chairman Newton N. Minow in 1962, "did not begin with the New Frontier." He was right.

The Act of 1927 did not confine the government to the role of a traffic policeman of the air who protects the rights of broadcasters from technical interference (which is all that was needed and all that a government should properly do). It established service to the "public interest, convenience, or necessity" as the criterion by which the Federal Radio Commission was to judge applicants for broadcasting licenses and accept or reject them. Since there is no such thing as the "public interest" (other than the sum of the individual interests of individual citizens), since that collectivist catch-phrase has never been and can never be defined, it amounted to a blank check on totalitarian power over the broadcasting industry, granted to whatever bureaucrats happened to be appointed to the Commission.

"The public interest"—that intellectual knife of collectivism's sacrificial guillotine, which the operators of broadcasting stations have to test by placing their heads on the block every three years—was not raised over their heads by capitalism's enemies, but by their own leaders.

It was the so-called "conservatives"—including some of the pioneers, some of the broadcasting industry's executives who, today, are complaining and protesting—who ran to the government for regulations and controls, who cheered the notion of "public property" and service to the "public interest," and thus planted the seeds of which Mr. Minow and Mr. Henry are merely the logical, consistent flowers. The broadcasting industry was enslaved with the sanction of the victims—but they were not fully innocent victims.

Many businessmen, of the mixed-economy persuasion, resent the actual nature of capitalism; they believe that it is safer to hold a position, not by right, but by favor; they dread the competition of a free market and they feel that a bureaucrat's friendship is much easier to win. Pull, not merit, is their form of "social security." They believe that they will always succeed at courting, pressuring, or bribing a bureaucrat, who is "a good fellow" they can "get along with" and who will protect them from that merciless stranger: the abler competitor.

Consider the special privileges to be found in the status of a certified servant of the "public interest" and a licensed user of "public property." Not only does it place a man outside the reach of economic competition, but it also spares him the responsibility and *the costs* entailed in private property. It grants him *gratuitously* the use of a broadcasting frequency for which he would have had to pay an enormous price on a free market and would not have been able to keep for long, if he sent forth through the air the kind of unconscionable trash he is sending forth today.

Such are the vested interests made possible by the doctrine of the "public interest"—and such are the beneficiaries of any form, version, or degree of the doctrine of "public property."

Now observe the practical demonstration of the fact that without property rights, no other rights are possible. If censorship and the suppression of free speech ever get established in this country, they will have originated in radio and television.

The Act of 1927 granted to a government Commission total power over the professional fate of broadcasters, with the "public interest" as the criterion of judgment—and, simultaneously, forbade the Commission to censor radio programs. From the start, and progressively louder through the years, many voices have been pointing out that this is a contradiction impossible to practice. If a commissioner has to judge which applicant for a broadcastng license will best serve the "public interest," how can he judge it without judging the content, nature, and value of the programs the applicants have offered or will offer?

If capitalism had had any proper intellectual defenders, it is they who should have been loudest in opposing a contradiction of that kind. But such was not the case: it was the *statists* who seized upon it, not in defense of free speech, but in support of the Commission's *"right"* to censor programs. And, so long as the criterion of the "public interest" stood unchallenged, logic was on the side of the statists.

The result was what it had to be (illustrating once more the power of basic principles): by gradual, unobtrusive, progressively accelerating steps, the Commission enlarged its control over the content of radio and television programs—leading to the open threats and ultimatums of Mr. Minow, who merely made explicit what had been known implicitly for many years. No, the Commission did not censor specific programs: it merely took cognizance of program content at license-renewal time. What was established was worse than open censorship (which could be knocked out in a court of law): it was the unprovable, intangible, insidious *censorship-by-displeasure*—the usual, and only, result of any non-objective legislation.[1]

All media of communication influence one another. It is impossible to compute the extent to which the gray, docile, fear-ridden, appeasement-minded mediocrity of so powerful a medium as television has contributed to the demoralization of our culture.

Nor can the freedom of one medium of communication be destroyed without affecting all the others. When censorship of radio and television becomes fully accepted, as a *fait accompli*, it will not be long before all the other media—books, magazines, newspapers, lectures—follow suit, unobtrusively, unofficially, and by the same method: overtly, in the name of the "public interest"; covertly, for fear of government reprisals. (This process is taking place already.)

So much for the relationship of "human" rights to property rights.

Since "public property" is a collectivist fiction, since the public as a whole can neither use nor dispose of its "property," that "property" will always be taken over by some political "elite," by a small clique which will then rule the public—a public of literal, dispossessed proletarians.

If you want to gauge a collectivist theory's distance from reality, ask yourself: by what inconceivable standard can it be claimed that the broadcasting airways are the property of some illiterate sharecropper who will never be able to grasp the concept of electronics, or of some hillbilly whose engi-

---

[1] See my articles "Have Gun, Will Nudge" and "Vast Quicksands" in *The Objectivist Newsletter*, March 1962 and July 1963. For a graphic report on the state of the television industry, see Edith Efron's articles "TV: The Timid Giant" and "Why the Timid Giant Treads Softly" in *TV Guide*, May 18 and August 10, 1963.

neering capacity is not quite sufficient to cope with a corn-liquor still—and that broadcasting, the product of an incalculable amount of scientific genius, is to be ruled by the will of such owners?

Remember that *this literally* is the alleged principle at the base of the entire legal structure of our broadcasting industry.

There is only one solution to this problem, and it has to start at the base; nothing less will do. The airways should be turned over to private ownership. The only way to do it now is to sell radio and television frequencies to the highest bidders (by an objectively defined, open, impartial process)—and thus put an end to the gruesome fiction of "public property."

Such a reform cannot be accomplished overnight; it will take a long struggle; but that is the ultimate goal which the advocates of capitalism should bear in mind. That is the only way to correct the disastrous, atavistic error made by capitalism's alleged defenders.

I say "atavistic," because it took many centuries before primitive, nomadic tribes of savages reached the concept of private property—specifically, *land* property, which marked the beginning of civilization. It is a tragic irony that in the presence of a new realm opened by a gigantic achievement of science, our political and intellectual leaders reverted to the mentality of primitive nomads and, unable to conceive of property rights, declared the new realm to be a tribal hunting ground.

The breach between man's scientific achievements and his ideological development is growing wider every day. It is time to realize that men cannot keep this up much longer if they continue to retrogress to ideological savagery with every step of scientific progress.

11. PATENTS AND COPYRIGHTS

BY AYN RAND

Patents and copyrights are the legal implementation of the base of all property rights: a man's right to the product of his mind.

Every type of productive work involves a combination of mental and physical effort: of thought and of physical action to translate that thought into a material form. The proportion of these two elements varies in different types of work. At the lowest end of the scale, the mental effort required to perform unskilled manual labor is minimal. At the other end, what the patent and copyright laws acknowledge is the paramount role of mental effort in the production of material values; these laws protect the mind's contribution in its purest form: the origination of an *idea*. The subject of patents and copyrights is *intellectual* property.

An idea as such cannot be protected until it has been given a material form. An invention has to be embodied in a physical model before it can be patented; a story has to be written or printed. But what the patent or copyright protects is not the physical object as such, but the *idea* which it embodies. By forbidding an unauthorized reproduction of the object, the law declares, in effect, that the physical labor of copying is not the source of the object's value, that that value is created by the originator of the idea and may not be used without his consent; thus the law establishes the property right of a mind to that which it has brought into existence.

It is important to note, in this connection, that a *discovery* cannot be patented, only an *invention*. A scientific or philosophical discovery, which identifies a law of nature, a principle or a fact of reality not previously known, cannot be the exclusive property of the discoverer because: (a) he did not *create* it, and (b) if he cares to make his discovery public, claiming it to be true, he cannot demand that men continue to pursue or practice falsehoods except by his permission. He

The Objectivist Newsletter, May 1964.

can copyright the book in which he presents his discovery and he *can* demand that his authorship of the discovery be acknowledged, that no other man appropriate or plagiarize the credit for it—but he cannot copyright *theoretical* knowledge. Patents and copyrights pertain only to the *practical* application of knowledge, to the creation of a specific object which did not exist in nature—an object which, in the case of patents, *may* never have existed without its particular originator; and in the case of copyrights, *would* never have existed.

The government does not "grant" a patent or copyright, in the sense of a gift, privilege, or favor; the government merely *secures* it—*i.e.*, the government certifies the origination of an idea and protects its owner's exclusive right of use and disposal. A man is not forced to apply for a patent or copyright; he may give his idea away, if he so chooses; but if he wishes to exercise his property right, the government will protect it, as it protects all other rights. A patent or copyright represents the formal equivalent of registering a property deed or title. The patent or copyright notice on a physical object represents a public statement of the conditions on which the inventor or author is willing to sell his product: for the purchaser's use, but *not* for commercial reproduction.

The right to intellectual property cannot be exercised in perpetuity. Intellectual property represents a claim, not on material objects, but on the idea they embody, which means: not merely on existing wealth, but on wealth yet to be produced—a claim to payment for the inventor's or author's work. No debt can be extended into infinity.

Material property represents a static amount of wealth already produced. It can be left to heirs, but it cannot remain in their effortless possession in perpetuity: the heirs can consume it or must *earn* its continued possession by their own productive work. The greater the value of the property, the greater the effort demanded of the heir. In a free, competitive society, no one could long retain the ownership of a factory or of a tract of land without exercising a commensurate effort.

But intellectual property cannot be consumed. If it were held in perpetuity, it would lead to the opposite of the very principle on which it is based: it would lead, not to the earned reward of achievement, but to the unearned support of parasitism. It would become a cumulative lien on the production of unborn generations, which would ultimately paralyze them. Consider what would happen if, in producing an automobile, we had to pay royalties to the descendants of all the inventors involved, starting with the inventor of the wheel and on up. Apart from the impossibility of keeping such records, consider the accidental status of such descendants and the unreality of their unearned claims.

The inheritance of material property represents a dynamic claim on a static amount of wealth; the inheritance of intellectual property represents a static claim on a dynamic process of production.

Intellectual achievement, *in fact,* cannot be transferred, just as intelligence, ability, or any other personal virtue cannot be transferred. All that can be transferred is the material results of an achievement, in the form of actually produced wealth. By the very nature of the right on which intellectual property is based—a man's right to the product of his mind—that right ends with him. He cannot dispose of that which he cannot know or judge: the yet-unproduced, indirect, potential results of his achievement four generations—or four centuries—later.

It is in this issue that our somewhat collectivistic terminology might be misleading: on the expiration of a patent or copyright, the intellectual property involved does not become "public property" (though it is labeled as "in the public domain"); it ceases to exist *qua* property. And if the invention or the book continues to be manufactured, the benefit of that former property does not go to the "public," it goes to the only rightful heirs: to the producers, to those who exercise the effort of embodying that idea in new material forms and thus keeping it alive.

Since intellectual property rights cannot be exercised in perpetuity, the question of their time limit is an enormously complex issue. If they were restricted to the originator's life-span, it would destroy their value by making long-term contractual agreements impossible: if an inventor died a month after his invention were placed on the market, it could ruin the manufacturer who may have invested a fortune in its production. Under such conditions, investors would be unable to take a long-range risk; the more revolutionary or important an invention, the less would be its chance of finding financial backers. Therefore, the law has to define a period of time which would protect the rights and interests of all those involved.

In the case of copyrights, the most rational solution is Great Britain's Copyright Act of 1911, which established the copyright of books, paintings, movies, etc. for the lifetime of the author and fifty years thereafter.

In the case of patents, the issue is much more complex. A

patented invention often tends to hamper or restrict further research and development in a given area of science. Many patents cover overlapping areas. The difficulty lies in defining the inventor's specific rights without including more than he can properly claim, in the form of indirect consequences or yet-undiscovered implications. A lifetime patent could become an unjustifiable barrier to the development of knowledge beyond the inventor's potential power or actual achievement. The legal problem is to set a time limit which would secure for the inventor the fullest possible benefit of his invention without infringing the right of others to pursue independent research. As in many other legal issues, that time limit has to be determined by the principle of defining and protecting all the individual rights involved.

As an objection to the patent laws, some people cite the fact that two inventors may work independently for years on the same invention, but one will beat the other to the patent office by an hour or a day and will acquire an exclusive monopoly, while the loser's work will then be totally wasted. This type of objection is based on the error of equating the potential with the actual. The fact that a man *might* have been first, does not alter the fact that he *wasn't*. Since the issue is one of commercial rights, the loser in a case of that kind has to accept the fact that in seeking to trade with others he must face the possibility of a competitor winning the race, which is true of all types of competition.

Today, patents are the special target of the collectivists' attacks—directly and indirectly, through such issues as the proposed abolition of trademarks, brand names, etc. While the so-called "conservatives" look at those attacks indifferently or, at times, approvingly, the collectivists seem to realize that patents are the heart and core of property rights, and that once they are destroyed, the destruction of all other rights will follow automatically, as a brief postscript.

The present state of our patent system is a nightmare. The inventors' rights are being infringed, eroded, chipped, gnawed, and violated in so many ways, under cover of so many non-objective statutes, that industrialists are beginning to rely on secrecy to protect valuable inventions which they are afraid to patent. (Consider the treatment accorded to patents under the antitrust laws, as just one example out of many.)

Those who observe the spectacle of the progressive collapse of patents—the spectacle of mediocrity scrambling to cash-in on the achievements of genius—and who understand its implications, will understand why in the closing paragraphs of Chapter VII, Part II, of *Atlas Shrugged,* one of the guiltiest men is the passenger who said: "Why should Rearden be the only one permitted to manufacture Rearden Metal?"

2. THEORY AND PRACTICE

BY AYN RAND

THE MAN-HATERS

Few errors are as naive and suicidal as the attempts of the "conservatives" to justify capitalism on altruist-collectivist grounds.

Many people believe that altruism means kindness, benevolence, or respect for the rights of others. But it means the exact opposite: it teaches self-sacrifice, as well as the sacrifice of others, to any unspecified "public need"; it regards man as a sacrificial animal.

Believing that collectivists are motivated by an authentic concern for the welfare of mankind, capitalism's alleged defenders assure its enemies that capitalism is the practical road to the socialists' goal, the best means to the same end, the best "servant" of public needs.

Then they wonder why they fail—and why the bloody muck of socialization keeps oozing forward over the face of the globe.

They fail, because no one's welfare can be achieved by anyone's sacrifice—and because man's welfare is not the socialists' goal. It is not for its alleged flaws that the altruist-collectivists hate capitalism, but for its virtues.

If you doubt it, consider a few examples.

Many collectivist historians criticize the Constitution of the United States on the ground that its authors were rich landowners who, allegedly, were motivated, not by any political ideals, but only by their own "selfish" economic interests.

This, of course, is not true. But it is true that capitalism does not require the sacrifice of anyone's interests. And what is significant here is the nature of the morality behind the collectivists' argument.

These two articles appeared originally in Ayn Rand's column in the *Los Angeles Times*, 1962.

Prior to the American Revolution, through centuries of feudalism and monarchy, the interests of the rich lay in the expropriation, enslavement, and misery of the rest of the people. A society, therefore, where the interests of the rich require general freedom, unrestricted productiveness, and the protection of individual rights, should have been hailed as an ideal system by anyone whose goal is man's well-being.

But that is not the collectivists' goal.

A similar criticism is voiced by collectivist ideologists about the American Civil War. The North, they claim disparagingly, was motivated, not by self-sacrificial concern for the plight of the slaves, but by the "selfish" economic interests of capitalism—which requires a free labor market.

This last clause is true. Capitalism cannot work with slave labor. It was the agrarian, feudal South that maintained slavery. It was the industrial, capitalistic North that wiped it out—as capitalism wiped out slavery and serfdom in the whole civilized world of the nineteenth century.

What greater virtue can one ascribe to a social system than the fact that it leaves no possibility for any man to serve his own interests by enslaving other men? What nobler system could be desired by anyone whose goal is man's well-being?

But that is not the collectivists' goal.

Capitalism has created the highest standard of living ever known on earth. The evidence is incontrovertible. The contrast between West and East Berlin is the latest demonstration, like a laboratory experiment for all to see. Yet those who are loudest in proclaiming their desire to eliminate poverty are loudest in denouncing capitalism. Man's well-being is not their goal.

The "under-developed" nations are an alleged problem to the world. Most of them are destitute. Some, like Brazil, loot (or nationalize) the property of foreign investors; others, like the Congo, slaughter foreigners, including women and children; after which, all of them scream for foreign help, for technicians and money. It is only the indecency of altruistic doctrines that permits them to hope to get away with it.

If those nations were taught to establish capitalism, with full protection of property rights, their problems would vanish. Men who could afford it, would invest private capital in the development of natural resources, expecting to earn profits. They would bring the technicians, the funds, the civilizing influence, and the employment which those nations need. Everyone would profit, at no one's expense or sacrifice.

But this would be "selfish" and, therefore, evil—according

o the altruists' code. Instead, they prefer to seize men's earnings—through taxation—and pour them down any foreign drain, and watch our own economic growth slow down year by year.

Next time you refuse yourself some necessity you can't afford or some small luxury which would have made the difference between pleasure and drudgery—ask yourself what part of your money has gone to pay for a crumbling road in Cambodia or for the support of those "selfless" little altruists of the Peace Corps, who play the role of big shots in the jungle, at taxpayers' expense.

If you wish to stop it, you must begin by realizing that altruism is not a doctrine of love, but of hatred for man.

Collectivism does not preach sacrifice as a temporary means to some desirable end. Sacrifice is its end—sacrifice as a way of life. It is man's independence, success, prosperity, and happiness that collectivists wish to destroy.

Observe the snarling, hysterical hatred with which they greet any suggestion that sacrifice is not necessary, that a non-sacrificial society is possible to men, that it is the only society able to achieve man's well-being.

If capitalism had never existed, any honest humanitarian should have been struggling to invent it. But when you see men struggling to evade its existence, to misrepresent its nature, and to destroy its last remnants—you may be sure that whatever their motives, love for man is not one of them.

BLIND CHAOS

There is an important political lesson to be learned from the current events in Algeria.

President Kennedy has been waging an ideological war against ideology. He has been stating repeatedly that political philosophy is useless and that "sophistication" consists of acting on the expediency of the moment.

On July 31, he declared to a group of Brazilian students that there are no rules or principles governing "the means of providing progress" and that any political system is as good as any other, including socialism, as long as it represents "a free choice" of the people.

On August 31, just one month later, history—like a well-constructed play—gave him an eloquent answer. The people

of Algiers marched through the streets of the city, in despe
ate protest against the new threat of civil war, shouting: "W
want peace! We want a government!"

How are they to go about getting it?

Through the years of civil war, they had been united, no
by any political philosophy, but only by a racial issue. The
were fighting, not for any program, but only against Frenc
rule. When they won their independence, they fell apart—
into rival tribes and armed "willayas" fighting one another.

The New York Times (September 2, 1962) described it a
"a bitter scramble for power among the men who wer
expected to lead the country." But to lead it—where? In th
absence of political principles, the issue of government is a
issue of seizing power and ruling by brute force.

The people of Algeria and their various tribal chieftains
who represent the majority that fought the war agains
France, are being taken over by a well-organized minority
that did not appear on the scene until after the victory. Tha
minority is led by Ben Bella and was armed by Sovie
Russia.

A majority without an ideology is a helpless mob, to be
taken over by anyone.

Now consider the meaning of Mr. Kennedy's advice to the
Brazilians and to the world. It was not the political philosophy of the United States that he was enunciating, but the
principle of unlimited majority rule—the doctrine that the
majority may choose anything it wishes, that anything done by
the majority is right and practical, because its will is omnipotent.

This means that the majority may vote away the rights of
a minority—and dispose of an individual's life, liberty, and
property, until such time, if ever, as he is able to gather his
own majority gang. This, somehow, will guarantee political
freedom.

But wishing won't make it so—neither for an individual
nor for a nation. Political freedom requires much more than
the people's wish. It requires an enormously complex knowledge of political theory and of how to implement it in
practice.

It took centuries of intellectual, philosophical development
to achieve political freedom. It was a long struggle, stretching
from Aristotle to John Locke to the Founding Fathers. The
system they established was not based on unlimited majority
rule, but on its opposite: on individual rights, which were not
to be alienated by majority vote or minority plotting. The
individual was not left at the mercy of his neighbors or his

aders: the Constitutional system of checks and balances as scientifically devised to protect him from both.

This was the great American achievement—and if concern or the actual welfare of other nations were our present leaders' motive, this is what we should have been teaching the world.

Instead, we are deluding the ignorant and the semi-savage by telling them that no political knowledge is necessary—that our system is only a matter of subjective preference—that any prehistorical form of tribal tyranny, gang rule, and slaughter will do just as well, with our sanction and support.

It is thus that we encourage the spectacle of Algerian workers marching through the streets and shouting the demand: "Work, not blood!"—without knowing what great knowledge and virtue are required to achieve it.

In the same way, in 1917, the Russian peasants were demanding: "Land and Freedom!" But Lenin and Stalin is what they got.

In 1933, the Germans were demanding: "Room to live!" But what they got was Hitler.

In 1793, the French were shouting: "Liberty, Equality, Fraternity!" What they got was Napoleon.

In 1776, the Americans were proclaiming "The Rights of Man"—and, led by political philosophers, they achieved it.

No revolution, no matter how justified, and no movement, no matter how popular, has ever succeeded without a political philosophy to guide it, to set its direction and goal.

The United States—history's magnificent example of a country created by political theorists—has abandoned its own philosophy and is falling apart. As a nation, we are splintering into warring tribes which—only by the fading momentum of a civilized tradition—are called "economic pressure groups," at present. As opposition to our growing statism, we have nothing but the futile "willayas" of the so-called "conservatives," who are fighting, not for any political principles, but only against the "liberals."

Embittered by Algeria's collapse into chaos, one of her leaders remarked: "We used to laugh at the Congolese; now it goes for us."

And it goes for us, as well.

13. LET US ALONE!

BY AYN RAND

Since "economic growth" is today's great problem, and our present Administration is promising to "stimulate" it—to achieve general prosperity by ever wider government controls, while spending an unproduced wealth—I wonder how many people know the origin of the term laissez-faire?

France, in the seventeenth century, was an absolute monarchy. Her system has been described as "absolutism limited by chaos." The king held total power over everyone's life, work, and property—and only the corruption of government officials gave people an unofficial margin of freedom.

Louis XIV was an archetypical despot: a pretentious mediocrity with grandiose ambitions. His reign is regarded as one of the brilliant periods of French history: he provided the country with a "national goal," in the form of long and successful wars; he established France as the leading power and the cultural center of Europe. But "national goals" cost money. The fiscal policies of his government led to a chronic state of crisis, solved by the immemorial expedient of draining the country through ever-increasing taxation.

Colbert, chief adviser of Louis XIV, was one of the early modern statists. He believed that government regulations can create national prosperity and that higher tax revenues can be obtained only from the country's "economic growth"; so he devoted himself to seeking "a general increase in wealth by the encouragement of industry." The encouragement consisted of imposing countless government controls and minute regulations that choked business activity; the result was dismal failure.

Colbert was not an enemy of business; no more than is our present Administration. Colbert was eager to help fatten the sacrificial victims—and on one historic occasion, he asked a group of manufacturers what he could do for industry. A

Based on a column in the *Los Angeles Times*, August 1962.

manufacturer named Legendre answered: *"Laissez-nous faire!"* ("Let us alone!")

Apparently, the French businessmen of the seventeenth century had more courage than their American counterparts of the twentieth, and a better understanding of economics. They knew that government "help" to business is just as disastrous as government persecution, and that the only way a government can be of service to national prosperity is by keeping its hands off.

To say that that which was true in the seventeenth century cannot possibly be true today, because we travel in jet planes while they traveled in horse carts—is like saying that we do not need food, as men did in the past, because we are wearing trenchcoats and slacks, instead of powdered wigs and hoop skirts. It is that sort of concrete-bound superficiality—or inability to grasp principles, to distinguish the essential from the non-essential—that blinds people to the fact that the economic crisis of our day is the oldest and stalest one in history.

Consider the essentials. If government controls could achieve nothing but paralysis, starvation, and collapse in a pre-industrial age, what happens when one imposes controls on a highly industrialized economy? Which is easier for bureaucrats to regulate: the operation of hand looms and hand forges—or the operation of steel mills, aircraft plants, and electronics concerns? Who is more likely to work under coercion: a horde of brutalized men doing unskilled manual labor—or the incalculable number of individual men of creative genius required to build and to maintain an industrial civilization? And if government controls fail even with the first, what depth of evasion permits modern statists to hope that they can succeed with the second?

The statists' epistemological method consists of endless debates about single, concrete, out-of-context, range-of-the-moment issues, never allowing them to be integrated into a sum, never referring to basic principles or ultimate consequences—and thus inducing a state of intellectual disintegration in their followers. The purpose of that verbal fog is to conceal the evasion of two fundamentals: (a) that production and prosperity are the product of men's intelligence, and (b) that government power is the power of coercion by physical force.

Once these two facts are acknowledged, the conclusion to be drawn is inevitable: that intelligence does not work under coercion, that man's mind will not function at the point of a gun.

This is the essential issue to consider; all other considerations are trivial details by comparison.

The details of a country's economy are as varied as the many cultures and societies that have existed. But all of mankind's history is the practical demonstration of the same basic principle, no matter what the variants of form: the degree of human prosperity, achievement, and progress is a direct function and corollary of the degree of political freedom. As witness: ancient Greece, the Renaissance, the nineteenth century.

In our own age, the difference between West Germany and East Germany is so eloquent a demonstration of the efficacy of a (comparatively) free economy versus a controlled economy that no further discussion is necessary. And no theorist can deserve serious consideration if he evades the existence of that contrast, leaving its implications unanswered, its causes unidentified, and its lesson unlearned.

Now consider the fate of England, "the peaceful experiment in socialism," the example of a country that committed suicide by vote: there was no violence, no bloodshed, no terror, merely the throttling process of "democratically" imposed government controls—but observe the present cries about England's "brain drain," about the fact that the best and ablest men, particularly the scientists and engineers, are deserting England and running to whatever small remnant of freedom they can find anywhere in today's world.

Remember that the Berlin wall was erected to stop a similar "brain drain" from East Germany; remember that after forty-five years of a totally controlled economy, Soviet Russia, who possesses some of the best agricultural land in the world, is unable to feed her population and has to import wheat from semi-capitalist America; read *East Minus West = Zero* by Werner Keller,[1] for a graphic (and unrefuted) picture of the Soviet economy's impotence—and *then,* judge the issue of freedom versus controls.

Regardless of the purpose for which one intends to use it, wealth must first be produced. As far as economics is concerned, there is no difference between the motives of Colbert and of President Johnson. Both wanted to achieve national prosperity. Whether the wealth extorted by taxation is drained for the unearned benefit of Louis XIV or for the unearned benefit of the "underprivileged" makes no difference to the economic productivity of a nation. Whether one is chained for a "noble" purpose or an ignoble one, for the

[1] New York: G. P. Putnam's Sons, 1962.

benefit of the poor or the rich, for the sake of somebody's "need" or somebody's "greed"—when one is chained, one cannot produce.

There is no difference in the ultimate fate of all chained economies, regardless of any alleged justifications for the chains.

Consider some of these justifications:

The creation of "consumer demand"? It would be interesting to compute how many housewives with relief checks would equal the "consumer demands" provided by Madame de Maintenon and her numerous colleagues.

A "fair" distribution of wealth? The privileged favorites of Louis XIV did not enjoy so unfair an advantage over other people as do our "aristocrats of pull," the actual and potential variants of Billie Sol Estes or Bobby Baker.

The requirements of the "national interest"? If there is such a thing as a "national interest," achieved by sacrificing the rights and the interests of individuals, then Louis XIV acquitted himself superlatively. The greater part of his extravagance was not "selfish": he did build France up into a major international power—and wrecked her economy. (Which means: he achieved "prestige" among other totalitarian rulers—at the price of the welfare, the future, and the lives of his own subjects.)

The furtherance of our "cultural" or "spiritual" progress? It is doubtful that a government-subsidized theater project will ever produce an array of genius comparable to that supported by the court of Louis XIV in his role of "patron of the arts" (Corneille, Racine, Molière, etc.). But no one will ever compute the still-born genius of those who perish under systems of that kind, unwilling to learn the art of bootlicking required by any political patron of the arts. (Read *Cyrano de Bergerac*.)

The fact is that motives do not alter facts. The paramount requirement of a nation's productivity and prosperity is freedom; men cannot—and, morally, will not—produce under compulsion and controls.

There is nothing new or mysterious about today's economic problems. Like Colbert, President Johnson is appealing to various economic groups, seeking advice on what he can do for them. And if he does not wish to go down in history with a record similar to Colbert's, he would do well to heed the voice of a modern Legendre, if such exists, who could give him the same immortal advice in a single word: "Decontrol!"

CURRENT STATE

14. THE ANATOMY OF COMPROMISE

BY AYN RAND

A major symptom of a man's—or a culture's—intellectual and moral disintegration is the shrinking of vision and goals to the concrete-bound range of the immediate moment. This means: the progressive disappearance of abstractions from a man's mental processes or from a society's concerns. The manifestation of a disintegrating consciousness is the inability to think and act in terms of *principles*.

A principle is "a fundamental, primary, or general truth, on which other truths depend." Thus a principle is an abstraction which subsumes a great number of concretes. It is only by means of principles that one can set one's long-range goals and evaluate the concrete alternatives of any given moment. It is only principles that enable a man to plan his future and to achieve it.

The present state of our culture may be gauged by the extent to which principles have vanished from public discussion, reducing our cultural atmosphere to the sordid, petty senselessness of a bickering family that haggles over trivial concretes, while betraying all its major values, selling out its future for some spurious advantage of the moment.

To make it more grotesque, that haggling is accompanied by an aura of hysterical self-righteousness, in the form of belligerent assertions that one must compromise with anybody on anything (except on the tenet that one must compromise) and by panicky appeals to "practicality."

But there is nothing as impractical as a so-called "practical" man. His view of practicality can best be illustrated as follows: if you want to drive from New York to Los Angeles, it is "impractical" and "idealistic" to consult a map and to select the best way to get there; you will get there much faster if you just start out driving at random, turning (or cutting) any corner, taking any road in any direction, following nothing but the mood and the weather of the moment.

The fact is, of course, that by this method you will never get there at all. But while most people do recognize this fact in regard to the course of a journey, they are not so perceptive in regard to the course of their life and of their country.

There is only one science that could produce blindness on so large a scale, the science whose job it was to provide men with sight: philosophy. Since modern philosophy, in essence, is a concerted attack against the conceptual level of man's consciousness—a sustained attempt to invalidate reason, abstractions, generalizations, and any integration of knowledge—men have been emerging from universities, for many decades past, with the helplessness of epistemological savages, with no inkling of the nature, function, or practical application of principles. These men have been groping blindly for some direction through the bewildering mass of (to them) incomprehensible concretes in the daily life of a complex industrial civilization—groping, struggling, failing, giving up, and perishing, unable to know in what manner they had acted as their own destroyers.

It is, therefore, important—for those who do not care to continue that suicidal process—to consider a few rules about the working of principles in practice and about the relationship of principles to goals.

The three rules listed below are by no means exhaustive; they are merely the first leads to the understanding of a vast subject.

> 1. In any *conflict* between two men (or two groups) who hold the *same* basic principles, it is the more consistent one who wins.
> 2. In any *collaboration* between two men (or two groups) who hold *different* basic principles, it is the more evil or irrational one who wins.
> 3. When opposite basic principles are clearly and openly defined, it works to the advantage of the rational side; when they are *not* clearly defined, but are hidden or evaded, it works to the advantage of the irrational side.

1. When two men (or groups) hold the same basic principles, yet oppose each other on a given issue, it means that at least one of them is inconsistent. Since basic principles determine the ultimate goal of any long-range process of action,

the person who holds a clearer, more consistent view of the end to be achieved, will be more consistently right in his choice of means; and the contradictions of his opponent will work to his advantage, psychologically and existentially.

Psychologically, the inconsistent person will endorse and propagate the same ideas as his adversary, but in a weaker, diluted form—and thus will sanction, assist, and hasten his adversary's victory, creating in the minds of their disputed following the impression of his adversary's greater honesty and courage, while discrediting himself by an aura of evasion and cowardice.

Existentially, every step or measure taken to achieve their common goal will necessitate further and more crucial steps or measures in the same direction (unless the goal is rejected and the basic principles reversed)—thus strengthening the leadership of the consistent person and reducing the inconsistent one to impotence.

The conflict will follow that course regardless of whether the basic principles shared by the two adversaries are right or wrong, true or false, rational or irrational.

For instance, consider the conflict between the Republicans and the Democrats (and, within each party, the same conflict between the "conservatives" and the "liberals"). Since both parties hold altruism as their basic moral principle, both advocate a welfare state or mixed economy as their ultimate goal. Every government control imposed on the economy (regardless in whose favor) necessitates the imposition of further controls, to alleviate—momentarily—the disasters caused by the first control. Since the Democrats are more consistently committed to the growth of government power, the Republicans are reduced to helpless "me-too'ing," to inept plagiarism of any program initiated by the Democrats, and to the disgraceful confession implied in their claim that they seek to achieve "the same ends" as the Democrats, but by different means.

It is precisely those ends (altruism-collectivism-statism) that ought to be rejected. But if neither party chooses to do it, the logic of the events created by their common basic principles will keep dragging them both further and further to the left. If and when the "conservatives" are kicked out of the game altogether, the same conflict will continue between the "liberals" and the avowed socialists; when the socialists win, the conflict will continue between the socialists and the communists; when the communists win, the ultimate goal of altruism will be achieved: universal immolation.

There is no way to stop or change that process except at

the root: by a change of basic principles.

The evidence of that process is mounting in every country on earth. And, observing it, the unthinking begin to whisper about some mysterious occult power called a "historical necessity" which, in some unspecified way, by some unknowable means, has preordained mankind to collapse into the abyss of communism. But there are no fatalistic "historical necessities": the "mysterious" power moving the events of the world is the awesome power of men's principles—which is mysterious only to the "practical" modern savages who were taught to discard it as "impotent."

But—it might be argued—since the advocates of a mixed economy are also advocating freedom, at least in part, why does the irrational part of their mixture have to win? This leads us to the fact that—

2. In any collaboration between two men (or groups) who hold different basic principles, it is the more evil or irrational one who wins.

The rational (principle, premise, idea, policy, or action) is that which is consonant with the facts of reality; the irrational is that which contradicts the facts and attempts to get away with it. A collaboration is a joint undertaking, a common course of action. The rational (the good) has nothing to gain from the irrational (the evil), except a share of its failures and crimes; the irrational has everything to gain from the rational: a share of its achievements and values. An industrialist does not need the help of a burglar in order to succeed; a burglar needs the industrialist's achievement in order to exist at all. What collaboration is possible between them and to what end?

If an individual holds mixed premises, his vices undercut, hamper, defeat, and ultimately destroy his virtues. What is the moral status of an honest man who steals once in a while? In the same way, if a group of men pursues mixed goals, its bad principles drive out the good. What is the political status of a free country whose government violates the citizens' rights once in a while?

Consider the case of a business partnership: if one partner is honest and the other is a swindler, the latter contributes nothing to the success of the business; but the reputation of the former disarms the victims and provides the swindler with a wide-scale opportunity which he could not have obtained on his own.

Now consider the collaboration of the semi-free countries with the communist dictatorships, in the United Nations. To identify that institution is to damn it, so that any criticism is superfluous. It is an institution allegedly dedicated to peace, freedom, and human rights, which includes Soviet Russia—the most brutal aggressor, the bloodiest dictatorship, the largest-scale mass-murderer and mass-enslaver in all history—among its charter members. Nothing can be added to that fact and nothing can mitigate it. It is so grotesquely evil an affront to reason, morality, and civilization that no further discussion is necessary, except for a glance at the consequences.

Psychologically, the U.N. has contributed a great deal to the gray swamp of demoralization—of cynicism, bitterness, hopelessness, fear and nameless guilt—which is swallowing the Western world. But the communist world has gained a moral sanction, a stamp of civilized respectability from the Western world—it has gained the West's assistance in deceiving its victims—it has gained the status and prestige of an equal partner, thus establishing the notion that the difference between human rights and mass slaughter is merely a difference of political opinion.

The declared goal of the communist countries is the conquest of the world. What they stand to gain from a collaboration with the (relatively) free countries is the latter's material, financial, scientific, and intellectual resources; the free countries have nothing to gain from the communist countries. Therefore, the only form of common policy or compromise possible between two such parties is the policy of property owners who make piecemeal concessions to an armed thug in exchange for his promise not to rob them.

The U.N. has delivered a larger part of the globe's surface and population into the power of Soviet Russia than Russia could ever hope to conquer by armed force. The treatment accorded to Katanga versus the treatment accorded to Hungary, is a sufficient example of U.N. policies. An institution allegedly formed for the purpose of using the united might of the world to stop an aggressor, has become the means of using the united might of the world to force the surrender of one helpless country after another into the aggressor's power.

Who, but a concrete-bound epistemological savage, could have expected any other results from such an "experiment in collaboration"? What would you expect from a crime-fighting committee whose board of directors included the leading gangsters of the community?

Only a total evasion of basic principles could make this possible. And this illustrates the reason why—

3. When opposite basic principles are clearly and openly

defined, it works to the advantage of the rational side; when they are *not* clearly defined, but are hidden or evaded, it works to the advantage of the irrational side.

In order to win, the rational side of any controversy requires that its goals be understood; it has nothing to hide, since reality is its ally. The irrational side has to deceive, to confuse, to evade, to hide its goals. Fog, murk, and blindness are not the tools of reason; they are the only tools of irrationality.

No thought, knowledge, or consistency is required in order to destroy; unremitting thought, enormous knowledge, and a ruthless consistency are required in order to achieve or create. Every error, evasion, or contradiction helps the goal of destruction; only reason and logic can advance the goal of construction. The *negative* requires an absence (ignorance, impotence, irrationality); the *positive* requires a presence, an existent (knowledge, efficacy, thought).

The spread of evil is the symptom of a vacuum. Whenever evil wins, it is only by default: by the moral failure of those who evade the fact that there can be no compromise on basic principles.

"In any compromise between food and poison, it is only death that can win. In any compromise between good and evil, it is only evil that can profit." (*Atlas Shrugged*)

15. IS ATLAS SHRUGGING?

BY AYN RAND

As the title of this discussion indicates, its theme is: the relationship of the events presented in my novel *Atlas Shrugged* to the actual events of today's world.

Or, to put the question in a form which has often been addressed to me: "Is *Atlas Shrugged* a prophetic novel—or a historical one?"

The second part of the question seems to answer the first: if some people believe that *Atlas Shrugged* is a *historical* novel, this means that it was a successful prophecy.

The truth of the matter can best be expressed as follows: although the political aspects of *Atlas Shrugged* are not its central theme nor its main purpose, my attitude toward these aspects—during the years of writing the novel—was contained in a brief rule I had set for myself: *"The purpose of this book is to prevent itself from becoming prophetic."*

The book was published in 1957. Since then, I have received many letters and heard many comments which amounted, in essence, to the following: "When I first read *Atlas Shrugged*, I thought that you were exaggerating, but then I realized suddenly—while reading the newspapers— that the things going on in the world today are exactly like the things in your book."

And so they are. Only more so.

The present state of the world, the political events, proposals, and ideas of today are so grotesquely irrational that neither I nor any other novelist could ever put them into fiction: no one would believe them. A novelist could not get away with it; only a politician might imagine that he can.

The political aspects of *Atlas Shrugged* are not its theme, but one of the consequences of its theme. The theme is: *the role of the mind in man's existence* and, as a corollary, the presentation of a new code of ethics—the morality of rational self-interest.

Lecture given at The Ford Hall Forum, Boston, on April 19, 1964. Published in *The Objectivist Newsletter,* August 1964.

The story of *Atlas Shrugged* shows what happens to the world when the men of the mind—the originators and innovators in every line of rational endeavor—go on strike and vanish, in protest against an altruist-collectivist society.

There are two key passages in *Atlas Shrugged* that give a brief summary of its meaning. The first is a statement of John Galt:

> There is only one kind of men who have never been on strike in human history. Every other kind and class have stopped, when they so wished, and have presented demands to the world, claiming to be indispensable—except the men who have carried the world on their shoulders, have kept it alive, have endured torture as sole payment, but have never walked out on the human race. Well, their turn has come. Let the world discover who they are, what they do and what happens when they refuse to function. This is the strike of the men of the mind, Miss Taggart. This is the mind on strike.

The second passage—which explains the title of the novel—is:

> "Mr. Rearden," said Francisco, his voice solemnly calm, "if you saw Atlas, the giant who holds the world on his shoulders, if you saw that he stood, blood running down his chest, his knees buckling, his arms trembling but still trying to hold the world aloft with the last of his strength, and the greater his effort the heavier the world bore down upon his shoulders—what would you tell him to do?"
>
> "I . . . don't know. What . . . could he do? What would *you* tell him?"
>
> "To shrug."

The story of *Atlas Shrugged* presents the conflict of two fundamental antagonists, two opposite schools of philosophy, or two opposite attitudes toward life. As a brief means of identification, I shall call them the "reason-individualism-capitalism axis" versus the "mysticism-altruism-collectivism axis." The story demonstrates that the basic conflict of our age is *not* merely political or economic, but moral and philosophical—that the dominant philosophy of our age is a virulent revolt against reason—that the so-called redistribution of wealth is only a superficial manifestation of the mysticism-altruism-collectivism axis—that the real nature and deepest, ultimate meaning of that axis is *anti-man, anti-mind, anti-life.*

Do you think that I was exaggerating?

During—and after—the writing of *Atlas Shrugged*, I kept a file which, formally, should be called a "Research or Documentation File." For myself, I called it "The Horror File." Let me give you a few samples from it.

Here is an example of modern ideology—from an Alumni-Faculty Seminar, entitled "The Distrust of Reason," at Wesleyan University, in June 1959.

> Perhaps in the future reason will cease to be important. Perhaps for guidance in time of trouble, people will turn not to human thought, but to the human capacity for suffering. Not the universities with their thinkers, but the places and people in distress, the inmates of asylums and concentration camps, the helpless decision-makers in bureaucracy and the helpless soldiers in foxholes—these will be the ones to lighten man's way, to refashion his knowledge of disaster into something creative. We may be entering a new age. Our heroes may not be intellectual giants like Isaac Newton or Albert Einstein, but victims like Anne Frank, who will show us a greater miracle than thought. They will teach us how to endure—how to create good in the midst of evil and how to nurture love in the presence of death. Should this happen, however, the university will still have its place. Even the intellectual man can be an example of creative suffering.

Do you think that this is a rare exception, a weird extreme? On January 4, 1963, *Time* published the following news story:

> "Ultimate performance in society"—not just brains and grades—should be the admissions criterion of top colleges, says Headmaster Leslie R. Severinghaus of the Haverford School near Philadelphia. In the *Journal of the Association of College Admissions Counselors,* he warns against the "highly intelligent, aggressive, personally ambitious, and socially indifferent and unconcerned egotist." Because these self-centered bright students have "little to offer, either now or later," colleges should be ready to welcome other good qualities. "Who says that brains and motivated performance represent the dimensions of excellence? Is not social concern a facet of excellence? Is it not exciting to find a candidate who believes that 'no man liveth unto himself?' What about leadership? Integrity? The ability to communicate both ideas and friendship? May we discount spiritual eager-

ness? And why should we pass over cooperation with others in good causes, even at some sacrifice of one's own scholastic achievement? What about graciousness and decency?" None of this shows up on college board scores, chides Severinghaus. "Colleges must themselves believe in the potential of young people of this sort."

Consider the meaning of this. If your husband, wife, or child were stricken with a deadly disease, of what use would the doctor's "social concern" or "graciousness" be to you, if that doctor had sacrificed his "own scholastic achievement"? If our country is threatened with nuclear destruction, will our lives depend on the *intelligence* and *ambition* of our scientists, or on their "spiritual eagerness" and "capacity to communicate friendship"?

I would not put a passage of that kind into the mouth of a character in the most exaggerated farce-satire—I would consider it too absurdly grotesque—and yet, this is said, heard, and discussed *seriously* in an allegedly civilized society.

Are you inclined to believe that theories of this kind will have no results in practice? I quote from the *Rochester Times Union,* of February 18, 1960, from an article entitled "Is Our Talent Running Out?"

Is this mighty nation running short of talent?

At this point in history, with Russia and the United States "in deadly competition," could this nation fall behind because of a lack of brainpower?

Dr. Harry Lionel Shapiro, chairman of the department of anthropology at the American Museum of Natural History in New York City, says, "There is a growing uneasiness, not yet fully expressed . . . that the supply of competence is running short."

The medical profession, he says, is "profoundly worried" about the matter. Studies have shown that today's medical students, on the basis of grades, are inferior to those of a decade ago.

Some spokesmen for the profession have been inclined to blame this on the dramatic and financial appeal of other professions in this space age—engineering and other technological fields.

But, Dr. Shapiro says, "This seems to be a universal complaint."

The anthropologist spoke before a group of science writers at Ardsley-on-Hudson. This same group listened to some 25 scientists over a 2-week period—and heard the same lament from engineers, physicists, a meteorologist and many others.

These scientists, outstanding spokesmen for their fields, found this subject of far greater importance than the need for more money.

Dr. William O. Baker, vice president in charge of research at Bell Telephone Laboratories in Murray Hill, N.J., one of the top scientists in the country, said more research is needed—but that it will come not as a result of more money.

"It all depends on ideas," he said, "not very many, but they have to be new ideas."

Dr. Baker argued that the National Institute of Health has continually increased its grants but the results of the work have remained on a level, "if they are not on the downgrade."

Eugene Kone, public relations director of the American Physical Society, said that in physics, "We are not getting anywhere near enough first-class people."

Dr. Sidney Ingram, vice president of the Engineering Manpower Commission, said the situation "is absolutely unique in the history of Western Civilization."

This news story was not given any prominence in our press. It reflects the first symptoms of anxiety over a situation which may still be hidden from the general public. But the same situation in Great Britain has become so obvious that it cannot be hidden any longer, and it is being discussed in terms of headlines. The British have coined a name for it: they call it "the brain drain."

Let me remind you, parenthetically, that in *Atlas Shrugged*, John Galt states, referring to the strike: "I have done by plan and intention what had been done throughout history by silent default." And he lists the various ways in which exceptional men had perished, in which intelligence had gone on strike against tyranny *psychologically*, deserting any mystic-altruist-collectivist society. You may also remember Dagny's description of Galt before she meets him, which he later repeats to her: "The man who's draining the brains of the world."

No, I do not mean to imply that the British have plagiarized my words. What is much more significant is that they *haven't*; most of them, undoubtedly, have never read *Atlas Shrugged*. What is significant is that they are facing—and groping to identify—the same phenomenon.

I quote from a news story in *The New York Times* of February 11, 1964:

The Labor party is calling for a Government study of the emigration of British scientists to the United States,

a problem known here as the "brain drain." Labor's
action . . . followed the disclosure that Prof. Ian Bush
and his research team are leaving Birmingham University for the Worcester Foundation for Experimental
Biology in Shrewsbury, Mass.

Professor Bush, who is 35 years old, heads the department of physiology at Birmingham. His team of
nine scientists has been investigating the treatment of
mental diseases with drugs.

Tonight it was learned that a leading physicist, Prof.
Maurice Pryce, and a top cancer research pathologist,
Dr. Leonard Weiss, would take posts in the United
States. . . .

Tom Dalyell, a Labor spokesman on science, will ask
if the Prime Minister, Sir Alec Douglas-Home, will
appoint a royal commission "to consider the whole
problem of the training, recruitment, and retention of
scientific manpower for service in Britain". . . .

Professor Bush's decision was termed "tragic" by Sir
George Pickering, president of the British Medical Association. He described the professor as the "most
brilliant pupil I ever had and one of the most brilliant
people I have ever met."

From *The New York Times* of February 12:

The furor over Britain's loss of scientific talent was
intensified today when a foremost theoretical physicist
said he was leaving for the United States.

Dr. John Anthony Pople, superintendent of the Basic
Physics Division at the National Physical Laboratory,
said he was going to the Carnegie Institute of Technology in Pittsburgh in about a month.

Afternoon newspapers used large headlines to report
the move, the 13th since the weekend. One paper's
front-page headline read: "Another One Down the
Brain Drain."

From *The New York Times* of February 13:

With the announcement today of the impending depar-
ture of at least five more scientists from Britain, the
nation began searching with new anxiety for root causes
of the exodus.

The story names two of the departing scientists: Dr. Ray
Guillery, 34-year-old associate professor of anatomy at University College, London, and also from University College,

Dr. Eric Shooter, 39, an assistant professor of biochemistry.

From *The New York Times* of February 16:

> With Britain in a furor over the steady departure of her scientists, the nation is again searching for the causes of the exodus and demanding remedies. . . .
>
> The "brain drain," as the departure of scientists is called here, is not new to Britain. For decades, foreign universities and other institutions of learning and research, especially in the United States, have been drawing scientific talent from Britain.
>
> In the last academic year Britain lost 160 senior university teachers, about 60 of them to the United States, according to a survey published by the Association of University Teachers. . . .
>
> British scientists with newly acquired Ph.D.'s have been leaving the country permanently at a rate of at least 140 a year, according to a report last year by the Royal Society. This would be about 12 per cent of the nation's output. . . .
>
> Most commonly, the scientists who depart permanently explain that funds available for research equipment and staff in the United States cannot be matched at home.
>
> Some say frankly that they are attracted by salaries two or three times higher than they get in Britain and also by what they consider a greater general regard in the United States for scientific effort and achievement.
>
> Others complain about the shortage of senior posts in universities, about the administrative jungle through which research grants must pass in Britain and about what they term the mean, controlling hand of the Treasury in all university grants.

What intellectual arguments are being offered to the scientists as an inducement to prevent them from leaving, and what practical remedies are being proposed? Quintin Hogg, Secretary of State for Education and Science, "appealed to the patriotism of scientists to stay at home. 'It is better to be British than anything else,' he said." An earlier story (*The New York Times,* October 31, 1963) stated that a "report, submitted by a committee headed by Sir Burke Trend, Secretary of the Cabinet, calls for reshaping Britain's civil science set-up and for giving *increased powers* to the Minister of Science." [Italics mine.]

There is, of course, a great deal of implicit and explicit

indignation against American wealth and big business, which the British seem to regard as chiefly to blame for the flight of their scientific talent.

Now I want to call your attention to two significant facts: the age and the professions of the scientists who were mentioned by name in these stories. Most of them are in their thirties; most of them are connected with theoretical medicine.

Socialized medicine is an established institution of Britain's political system. What future would brilliant young men be able to achieve under socialized medicine? Draw your own conclusions about the causes of the "brain drain"—about the future welfare of those left behind in the welfare state—and about the role of the mind in man's existence.

The next time you hear or read reports about the success of socialized medicine in Great Britain and in the other welfare states of Europe—the reports brought by the superficial, concrete-bound mentalities who cannot see beyond the range of the moment and who declare that they observe no change in the conscientious efficiency of the family doctors— remember that the source of the family doctors' efficiency, knowledge, and power lies in the laboratories of theoretical medicine, and that that source is drying up. *This* is the real price which a country pays for socialized medicine—a price which does not appear on the cost sheets of the state planners, but which will not take long to appear in reality.

At present, we lag behind Great Britain on the road to the collectivist abyss—but not very far behind. In recent years, our newspapers have been mentioning alarming reports on the state of the enrollment in our medical schools. There was a time when these schools had a much greater number of applicants than could be accepted—and only the ablest students, those with the highest academic grades and records, had a chance to be admitted. Today, the number of applicants is falling—and, according to some reports, will soon be *less* than the number of openings available in our medical schools.

Consider the growth of socialized medicine throughout the world—consider the Medicare plan in this country—consider the strike of the Canadian doctors in Saskatchewan, and the recent strike of the doctors in Belgium. Consider the fact that in every instance the overwhelming majority of the doctors fought against socialization and that the moral cannibalism of the welfare-statists did not hesitate to force them into slavery at the point of a gun. The picture was particularly eloquent in Belgium, with thousands of doctors fleeing blindly, escaping from the country—with the allegedly "humanitarian" government resorting to the crude, Nazi-like, militaristic measure of *drafting the doctors into the army* in order to force them back into practice.

Consider it—and then read the statement of Dr. Hendricks in *Atlas Shrugged,* the surgeon who went on strike in protest against socialized medicine: "I have often wondered at the smugness with which people assert their right to enslave me, to control my work, to force my will, to violate my conscience, to stifle my mind—yet what is it that they expect to depend on, when they lie on an operating table under my hands?"

That is the question that should be asked of the altruistic slave-drivers of Belgium.

The next time you hear a discussion of Medicare, give some thought to the future—particularly to the future of your children, who will live at a time when the best brains available will no longer choose to go into medicine.

Ragnar Danneskjöld, the pirate in *Atlas Shrugged,* said that he was fighting against "the idea that need is a sacred idol requiring human sacrifices—that the need of some men is the knife of a guillotine hanging over others and that the extent of our ability is the extent of our danger; so that success will bring our heads down on the block, while failure will give us the right to pull the cord." *This* is the essence of the morality of altruism: the greater a man's achievement and the greater society's need of him—the more vicious the treatment he receives and the closer he comes to the status of a sacrificial animal.

Businessmen—who provide us with the means of livelihood, with jobs, with labor-saving devices, with modern comforts, with an ever-rising standard of living—are the men most immediately and urgently needed by society. They have been the first victims, the hated, smeared, denounced, exploited scapegoats of the mystic-altruist-collectivist axis. Doctors come next; it is precisely because their services are so crucially important and so desperately needed that the doctors are now the targets of the altruists' attack, on a worldwide scale.

As to the present condition of businessmen, let me mention the following. After completing *Atlas Shrugged,* I submitted it, in galley-proofs, to a railroad expert, for a technical check-up. The first question he asked me, after he had read it, was: "Do you realize that all the laws and directives you invented are on our statute books already?" "Yes," I answered, "I realize it."

And *that* is what I want my readers to realize.

In my novel, I presented these issues in terms of abstractions which expressed the *essence* of government controls and of statist legislation at any time and in any country. But the principles of every edict and every directive presented in *Atlas Shrugged*—such as "The Equalization of Opportunity Bill" or "Directive 10–289"—can be found, and in cruder forms, in our *antitrust laws*.

In that accumulation of non-objective, undefinable, unjudicable statutes, you will find every variant of penalizing ability for being ability, of penalizing success for being success, of sacrificing productive genius to the demands of envious mediocrity. You will find such rulings as: the forced break-up of large companies or the "divorcement" of companies from their subsidiaries (which is my "Equalization of Opportunity Bill")—the forcing of established concerns to share with any newcomer the facilities it had taken them years to create—the compulsory licensing or the outright confiscation of patents—and, on top of this last, the order that the victims *teach* their own competitors how to use these patents.

The only thing that stands between us and the level of social disintegration presented in *Atlas Shrugged* is the fact that the statists do not dare as yet to enforce the antitrust laws to the full extent of their power. But the power is there—and you can observe the accelerating process of its widening application year by year.

Now you might think, however, that the "Railroad Unification Plan" and the "Steel Unification Plan," which I introduced toward the end of *Atlas Shrugged,* have no counterpart in real life. I thought so, too. I invented them—as a development dictated by the logic of events—to illustrate the last stages of a society's collapse. These two plans were typical collectivist devices for helping the weakest members of an industry at the expense of the strongest, by means of forcing them to "pool" their resources. I thought these plans were a bit ahead of our time.

I was wrong.

I quote from a news story of March 17, 1964:

The three television networks have been asked by the Federal Government to consider a tentative plan under which each would turn over a share of its programs to existing or new TV stations that might operate from a competitive disadvantage. . . .

A companion suggestion, also put forth for discussion by the [Federal Communications] Commission, would compel some stations now affiliated with one network to accept affiliation with an alternative chain.

The proposals, which in effect call upon the "haves" of the television industry to help the "have nots," drew strenuous objections over the weekend from the Columbia Broadcasting System. . . .

The thinking behind the F.C.C. proposals is to help sustain existing ultra-high frequency stations and encourage the start of additional such outlets by guaranteeing them program resources that would win audiences. Most advertisers normally prefer the more powerful very-high frequency stations. . . .

Under the controversial proposals, the total pool of network programming would be carved up among two V.H.F. stations and one U.H.F. station.

The alleged justification for these proposals is the desire to correct "competitive imbalance."

Now observe today's situation in the sphere of labor.

In *Atlas Shrugged*, I showed that at a time of desperate shortages of transportation, due to shortages of motive power, track, and fuel, the railroads of the country were ordered to run shorter trains at lower speeds. Today, at a time when the railroads are perishing, with most of them on the brink of bankruptcy, the railroad unions are demanding the preservation of "featherbedding" practices (that is, of useless, unneeded jobs) and of antiquated work and payment rules.

The press comments on this issue were mixed. But one editorial deserves a moment's special attention: it is from the *Star Herald* of Camden, New Jersey, of August 16, 1963, and it was sent to me by a fan.

The money-makers, the powerful business leaders of America, have failed to realize that prosperity can be inhuman. They have failed to understand that people take precedence over profits. . . .

Ambition and the drive for profit is a good thing. It spurs man to higher achievements. But it must be tempered by concern for society and its members. It must be slowed down in the light of human needs. . . .

These are the thoughts that trouble us when we ponder the railroad stalemate. Crying "featherbed!" like a war whoop, the managers of the railroads have insisted on eliminating tens of thousands of jobs . . . jobs that are the mainstays of homes . . . jobs that mean the difference between a man's feeling dignified or futile. . . . Before you vote yes for such painful progress, imagine your husband or brother or father as one of those destined to be sacrificed on the altar of progress. Far better, in our view, to have the government nationalize the railroads and prevent another human disaster on their one-way track of making profit at human expense.

This editorial had no byline, but my anonymous admirer had written on it in penciled block letters: "By Eugene Lawson???"

That kind of "humanitarian" attitude is not directed against profits, but against achievement; it is not directed against the rich, but against the *competent*. Do you think that the only victims of the mystic-altruist-collectivist axis are a few exceptional men on the top of the social pyramid, a few men of financial and intellectual genius?

Here is an old clipping from my "Horror File," a news story dating years back:

> Britain is currently stirred by the story of a young coal miner who has quit his job to prevent 2,000 miners from striking at Doncaster.
>
> Alan Bulmer, 31, got in trouble with his fellow workers when he finished a week's assignment three hours ahead of time. Instead of sitting down for three hours, he started on a new stint of work.
>
> More than 2,000 miners held a meeting last Sunday to object to his working too hard. They demanded that he be demoted for three months and his pay cut from $36 a week to $25.
>
> Bulmer quit his job to end the crisis, with the statement that it always has been his belief that "a man should do a full day's work for a full day's pay."
>
> Officials of the government-operated mines say the affair is up to the unions.

Ask yourself, what will become of that young man in the future? How long will he preserve his integrity and his ambition if he knows that they will bring him *punishments*, not rewards? Will he continue to exercise his ability if he is to be *demoted* for it? This is how a nation loses the best of its men.

Do you remember the scene in *Atlas Shrugged* when Hank Rearden finally decided to go on strike? The last straw, which made the situation clear to him, was James Taggart's statement that he, Rearden, would always find a way to "do something"—even in the face of the most irrational and impossible demands. Compare that with the following quotation in a news story of December 28, 1959—which is a statement by Michael J. Quill, head of the Transport Workers' Union, commenting on a threatened city transit strike: "A lot of people are thinking we are taking this to the brink. But it so happens that every time we went to the well before, there was something there."

In the closing chapters of *Atlas Shrugged,* I described the labor situation of the country as follows:

"Give us men!" The plea began to hammer progressively louder upon the desk of the Unification Board, from all parts of a country ravaged by unemployment, and neither the pleaders nor the Board dared to add the dangerous words which the cry was implying: "Give us men of ability!" There were waiting lines years' long for the jobs of janitors, greasers, porters, and bus boys; there was no one to apply for the jobs of executives, managers, superintendents, engineers.

An editorial in the July 29, 1963, issue of *Barron's* mentions:

the mounting scarcity of skilled labor including, as Dr. Arthur F. Burns noted in a recent critique of official unemployment statistics, "extensive shortages of scientists, teachers, engineers, doctors, nurses, typists, stenographers, automobile and TV mechanics, tailors and domestic servants."

Do you remember the story of the Minnesota harvest disaster in *Atlas Shrugged?* A bumper crop of wheat perished along the roadsides—around the overfilled silos and grain elevators—for lack of railroad freight cars which, by government order, had been sent to carry a harvest of soybeans.

The following news story is from the *Chicago Sun Times* of November 2, 1962:

Illinois farm officials and grain dealers met Thursday in an effort to relieve an acute freight car shortage which is threatening Midwest's bumper grain harvest. . . .

Farmers and grain dealers agreed that the shortage of railroad boxcars has become "critical," and saw little hope of relief for at least two weeks.

Some grain elevator operators showed the group photographs of corn piled on the ground near elevators plugged up with corn which can't be shipped. . . .

The boxcar shortage was blamed on the harvesting

of three major crops—corn, soybeans and milo—at the same time this year. In addition, there have been heavy movements of government-owned grain.

In *Atlas Shrugged*, Ragnar Danneskjöld denounced Robin Hood as the particular image of evil that he wanted to destroy in men's minds. "He is the man who became the symbol of the idea that need, not achievement, is the source of rights, that we don't have to produce, only to want, that the earned does not belong to us, but the unearned does."

I shall never know whether Ragnar was or was not the inspiration of an article denouncing Robin Hood, which appeared last year in a British journal called *Justice of the Peace and Local Government Review*, a magazine of law and police affairs. The occasion for the article was the revival of the Robin Hood festival.

Having regard to the fact [said the article] that the exploits of this legendary hero were chiefly concerned with robbing the rich under the specious motive of giving to the poor, a function which, in modern times, has been taken over by the welfare state, it is a question of some doubt whether a Robin Hood festival is not contrary to public policy.

But now we come to a composition that beats anything presented in *Atlas Shrugged*. I concede that I would have been unable to invent it and that no matter how low my estimate of the altruist-collectivist mentalities—and it is *very* low—I would not have believed this possible. It is not fiction. It is a *news story*, which appeared, on March 23, 1964, on the front page of *The New York Times*.

Every American should be guaranteed an adequate income as a matter of right whether he works or not, a 32-member group calling itself the Ad Hoc Committee on the Triple Revolution urged today. . . .

The three revolutions listed in their statement, which they sent to President Johnson, were "the cybernation revolution," "the weaponry revolution" and "the human rights revolution."

"The fundamental problem posed by the cybernation revolution in the United States is that it invalidates the general mechanism so far employed to undergird *people's rights as consumers*," the committee said.

"Up to this time," it continued, "economic resources have been distributed on the basis of contributions to production, with *machines and men competing for em-*

ployment on somewhat equal terms. In the developing cybernated system, potentially unlimited output can be achieved by systems of machines which will require little cooperation from human beings.

"The continuance of the income-through-jobs link as the only major mechanism for distributing effective demand—*for granting the right to consume*—now acts as the main brake on the almost unlimited capacity of a cybernated productive system."

The Committee urged that the link be broken by "an unqualified commitment" by society to provide, through its appropriate legal and governmental institutions, "every individual and every family *with an adequate income as a matter of right.*" [All italics mine.]

To be provided—by whom? Blank out.

One would expect a proclamation of this kind to be issued by a group of small-town crackpots dissociated from reality and from any knowledge of economics. Or one would expect it to be issued by a group of rabble-rousers, for the purpose of inciting the lowest elements of the population to violence against any business office that owns an electronic computer and thus deprives them of their "right to consume."

But such was not the case.

This proclamation was issued by a group of professors, economists, educators, writers, and other "intellectuals." What is frightening—as a symptom of the present state of our culture—is that it received front-page attention, and that apparently-civilized people are willing to regard it as within the bounds of civilized discussion.

What is the cultural atmosphere of our day? See whether the following description fits it. I quote from *Atlas Shrugged* —from a passage referring to a series of accelerating disasters and catastrophes:

The newspapers did not mention it. The editorials went on speaking of self-denial as the road to future progress, of self-sacrifice as the moral imperative, of greed as the enemy, of love as the solution—their threadbare phrases as sickeningly sweet as the odor of ether in a hospital.

Rumors went spreading through the country in whispers of cynical terror—yet people read the newspapers and acted as if they believed what they read, each competing with the others on who would keep most blindly silent, each pretending that he did not know what he knew, each striving to believe that the un-named was the unreal. It was as if a volcano were cracking open, yet the people at the foot of the mountain ignored the sudden fissures, the black fumes, the boiling trickles, and went on believing that their only danger was to acknowledge the reality of these signs.

The purpose of my discussing this today was, not to boast nor to leave you with the impression that I possess some mystical gift of prophecy, but to demonstrate the exact opposite: that that gift is *not* mystical. Contrary to the prevalent views of today's alleged scholars, history is *not* an unintelligible chaos ruled by chance and whim—historical trends *can* be predicted, and changed—men are *not* helpless, blind, doomed creatures carried to destruction by incomprehensible forces beyond their control.

There is only one power that determines the course of history, just as it determines the course of every individual life: the power of man's rational faculty—*the power of ideas*. If you know a man's convictions, you can predict his actions. If you understand the dominant philosophy of a society, you can predict its course. But convictions and philosophy are matters open to man's choice.

There is no fatalistic, predetermined historical necessity. *Atlas Shrugged* is not a prophecy of our unavoidable destruction, but a manifesto of our power to avoid it, if we choose to change our course.

It is the philosophy of the mysticism-altruism-collectivism axis that has brought us to our present state and is carrying us toward a finale such as that of the society presented in *Atlas Shrugged*. It is only the philosophy of the reason-individualism-capitalism axis that can save us and carry us, instead, toward the Atlantis projected in the last two pages of my novel.

Since men have free will, no one can predict with certainty the outcome of an *ideological* conflict nor how long such a conflict will last. It is too early to tell which choice this country will make. I can say only that if part of the purpose of *Atlas Shrugged* was to prevent itself from becoming prophetic, there are many, many signs to indicate that it is succeeding in that purpose.

(*Postscript.* Over a year after this article was written, there occurred an event worth noting here.

In the last chapter of *Atlas Shrugged*, which describes the collapse of the collectivists' rule, there is the following paragraph:

The plane was above the peaks of the skyscrapers when suddenly, with the abruptness of a shudder, as if the ground had parted to engulf it, the city disappeared from the face of the earth. It took them a moment to realize that the panic had reached the power stations—and that the lights of New York had gone out.

On November 9, 1965, the lights of New York and of the entire Eastern seaboard went out. The situation was not exactly parallel to that in my story, but a great many readers recognized the symbolic meaning of the event. I quote some of the letters and wires I received in the next few days:

A wire from Austin, Texas, signed by a number of names: "We thought you said the novel was not prophetic."

A wire from Marion, Wisconsin: "There is a John Galt."

From a letter from Indianapolis: "But it didn't even take a panic, did it, Miss Rand? Just that same old irresponsibility and incompetence. The train wrecks [etc.] have made us chuckle, but this fulfilled prophecy also brings a shudder."

A note from Dundee, Scotland: "I could not help but think of your book *Atlas Shrugged* when we saw on television New York without its lights—there on the screen the black canyons of the buildings and the low lights of the cars trying to find a way out."

From Memphis, Tennessee (a postcard sent by his mother to a reader who sent it to me): "I just had to pass this on: Last night in the blackout in the Northeast [a friend] called and asked if you were there. I said no, and she said 'Well, I'm sorry, I wanted to ask him if Atlas had shrugged!' "

A note from Chicago: "We waited expectantly for the one rational explanation for the 'blackout' of 11/9/65. 'This is John Galt Speaking.' ")

16. THE PULL PEDDLERS

BY AYN RAND

America's foreign policy is so grotesquely irrational that most people believe there must be some sensible purpose behind it. The extent of the irrationality acts as its own protection: like the technique of the "Big Lie," it makes people assume that so blatant an evil could not possibly be as evil as it appears to them and, therefore, that *somebody* must understand its meaning, even though they themselves do not.

The sickening generalities and contradictions cited in justification of the foreign aid program fall roughly into two categories which are offered to us simultaneously: the "idealistic" and the "practical," or mush and fear.

The "idealistic" arguments consist of appeals to altruism and swim out of focus in a fog of floating abstractions about our duty to support the "under-developed" nations of the entire globe, who are starving and will perish without our selfless help.

The "practical" arguments consist of appeals to fear and emit a different sort of fog, to the effect that our own selfish interest requires that we go bankrupt buying the favor of the "under-developed" nations, who, otherwise, will become a dangerous threat to us.

It is useless to point out to the advocates of our foreign policy that it's either-or: either the "under-developed" nations are so weak that they are doomed without our help, in which case they cannot become a threat to us—or they are so strong that with some other assistance they can develop to the point of endangering us, in which case we should not drain our economic power to help the growth of potential enemies who are that powerful.

It is useless to discuss the contradiction between these two assertions, because neither of them is true. Their proponents are impervious to facts, to logic, and to the mounting evidence that after two decades of global altruism, our foreign

policy is achieving the exact opposite of its alleged goals; it is
wrecking our economy—it is reducing us internationally to
the position of an impotent failure who has nothing but a
series of compromises, retreats, defeats, and betrayals on his
record—and, instead of bringing progress to the world, it is
bringing the bloody chaos of tribal warfare and delivering
one helpless nation after another into the power of communism.

When a society insists on pursuing a suicidal course, one
may be sure that the alleged reasons and proclaimed slogans
are mere rationalizations. The question is only: what is it that
these rationalizations are hiding?

Observe that there is no consistent pattern in the erratic
chaos of our foreign aid. And although in the long run it
leads to the benefit of Soviet Russia, Russia is not its direct,
immediate beneficiary. There is no consistent winner, only a
consistent loser: the United States.

In the face of such a spectacle, some people give up the
attempt to understand; others imagine that some omnipotent
conspiracy is destroying America, that the rationalizations
are hiding some malevolent, fantastically powerful giant.

The truth is worse than that: the truth is that the rationalizations are hiding nothing—that there is nothing at the bottom of the fog but a nest of scurrying cockroaches.

I submit in evidence excerpts from an article in the editorial section of *The New York Times,* of July 15, 1962, entitled: "Role of Foreign Lobbies."

A "non-diplomatic corps" of foreign agents [states the
article] has bloomed in recent years [in Washington]
. . .
  Lobbying in Congress to obtain—or prevent—the
passage of legislation of interest to their foreign clients,
seeking to pressure the Administration into adopting
certain political or economic policies, or attempting to
mold public opinion through a myriad of methods and
techniques, this legion of special agents has become an
elusive shadow for operating in Washington and the
width and the length of the land.

"Lobbying" is the activity of attempting to influence legislation by privately influencing the legislators. It is the result
and creation of a mixed economy—of government by pressure groups. Its methods range from mere social courtesies
and cocktail-party or luncheon "friendships" to favors,
threats, bribes, blackmail.

All lobbyists, whether serving foreign or domestic interests, are required—by laws passed in the last three decades—to register with the government. The registrations have been growing at such a rate—with the foreign lobbyists outnumbering the domestic ones—that legislators are beginning to be alarmed. The Senate Foreign Relations Committee has announced that it is preparing an investigation of these foreign agents' activities.

The *New York Times* article describes foreign lobbying as follows:

> The theory behind this whole enterprise is that for a fee or a retainer and often for hundreds of thousands of dollars in advertising, publicity and expense money, a foreign government or a foreign economic or political interest *can purchase a favorable legislation in the United States Congress, a friendly policy of the Administration* or a positive image in the eyes of the American public opinion, leading in turn to *profitable political or economic advantage.* [Italics mine.]

Who are these lobbyists? Men with political pull—with "access" to influential Washington figures—American men hired by foreign interests. The article mentions that most of these men are "Washington lawyers" or "New York public relations firms."

Russia is one of these foreign interests and is served by registered lobbyists in Washington; but she is merely cashing-in on the situation, like the others. The success of her conspiracy in this country is the result, not the cause, of our self-destruction; she is winning by default. The cause is much deeper than that.

The issue of lobbies has attracted attention recently through the struggle of foreign lobbyists to obtain sugar quotas from the American government.

> Their efforts [states the article] were centered on Representative Harold D. Cooley, Democrat of North Carolina, chairman of the House Committee on Agriculture, who at least until this year held almost the complete power in the distribution of quotas. It has never been too clear what criteria Mr. Cooley used in allocating these quotas, and, by the same token, it is impossible to determine what was the actual effect of the lobbyists' entreaties on him.
>
> But in offering their services to foreign governments or sugar growers' associations, these representatives were, in effect, offering for sale their real or alleged friendship with Mr. Cooley.

This is the core and essence of the issue of lobbying—and of our foreign aid—and of a mixed economy.

The trouble is not that "it has never been too clear what criteria Mr. Cooley used in allocating these quotas"—but that it has never been and never can be too clear what criteria he was expected to use by the legislation that granted him these powers. No criteria can ever be defined in this context; such is the nature of non-objective law and of all economic legislation.

So long as a concept such as "the public interest" (or the "social" or "national" or "international" interest) is regarded as a valid principle to guide legislation—lobbies and pressure groups will necessarily continue to exist. Since there is no such entity as *"the public,"* since the public is merely a number of individuals, the idea that "the public interest" supersedes private interests and rights, can have but one meaning: that the interests and rights of some individuals take precedence over the interests and rights of others.

If so, then all men and all private groups have to fight to the death for the privilege of being regarded as "the public." The government's policy has to swing like an erratic pendulum from group to group, hitting some and favoring others, at the whim of any given moment—and so grotesque a profession as lobbying (selling "influence") becomes a full-time job. If parasitism, favoritism, corruption, and greed for the unearned did not exist, a mixed economy would bring them into existence.

Since there is no rational justification for the sacrifice of some men to others, there is no objective criterion by which such a sacrifice can be guided in practice. All "public interest" legislation (and any distribution of money taken by force from some men for the unearned benefit of others) comes down ultimately to the grant of an undefined, undefinable, non-objective, arbitrary power to some government officials.

The worst aspect of it is not that such a power can be used dishonestly, but that *it cannot be used honestly.* The wisest man in the world, with the purest integrity, cannot find a criterion for the just, equitable, rational application of an unjust, inequitable, irrational principle. The best that an honest official can do is to accept no material bribe for his arbitrary decision; but this does not make his decision and its consequences more just or less calamitous.

A man of clear-cut convictions is impervious to anyone's influence. But when clear-cut convictions are impossible, personal influences take over. When a man's mind is trapped in the foggy labyrinth of the non-objective, that has no exits and no solutions, he will welcome any quasi-persuasive, semi-plausible argument. Lacking certainty, he will follow anyone's facsimile thereof. He is the natural prey of social "manipulators," of propaganda salesmen, of lobbyists.

When any argument is as inconclusive as any other, the subjective, emotional, or "human" element becomes decisive. A harried legislator may conclude, consciously or subconsciously, that the friendly man who smiled at him at the cocktail party last week was a good person who would not deceive him and whose opinion can be trusted safely. It is by considerations such as these that officials may dispose of your money, your effort, and your future.

Although cases of actual corruption do undoubtedly exist among legislators and government officials, they are not a major motivating factor in today's situation. It is significant that in such cases as have been publicly exposed, the bribes were almost pathetically small. Men who held the power to dispose of millions of dollars, sold their favors for a thousand-dollar rug or a fur coat or a refrigerator.

The truth, most likely, is that they did not regard it as bribery or as a betrayal of their public trust; they did not think that their particular decision could matter one way or another, in the kind of causeless choices they had to make, in the absence of any criteria, in the midst of the general orgy of tossing away an apparently ownerless wealth. Men who would not sell out their country for a million dollars, are selling it out for somebody's smile and a vacation trip to Florida. Paraphrasing John Galt: "It is of such pennies and smiles that the destruction of your country is made."

The general public is helplessly bewildered. The "intellectuals" do not care to look at our foreign policy too closely. They feel guilt; they sense that their own worn-out ideologies, which they dare not challenge, are the cause of the consequences which they dare not face. The more they evade, the greater their eagerness to grasp at any fashionable straw or rationalization and to uphold it with glassy-eyed aggressiveness. The threadbare cloak of altruism serves to cover it up and to sanction the evasions by a fading aura of moral righteousness. The exhausted cynicism of a bankrupt culture, of a society without values, principles, convictions, or intellectual standards, does the rest: it leaves a vacuum, for anyone to fill.

The motive power behind the suicidal bleeding of the greatest country in the world is not an altruistic fervor or a collectivist crusade any longer, but the manipulations of little lawyers and public relations men pulling the mental strings of lifeless automatons.

These—the lobbyists in the pay of foreign interests, the

men who could not hope to get, in any other circumstances, the money they are getting now—are the real and only profiteers on the global sacrifice, as their ilk has always been at the close of every altruistic movement in history. It is not the "under-developed" nations nor the "underprivileged" masses nor the starving children of jungle villages who benefit from America's self-immolation—it is only the men who are too small to start such movements and small enough to cash in at the end.

It is not any "lofty ideal" that the altruism-collectivism doctrine accomplishes or can ever accomplish. Its end-of-trail is as follows:

A local railroad had gone bankrupt in North Dakota, abandoning the region to the fate of a blighted area, the local banker had committed suicide, first killing his wife and children—a freight train had been taken off the schedule in Tennessee, leaving a local factory without transportation at a day's notice, the factory owner's son had quit college and was now in jail, awaiting execution for a murder committed with a gang of raiders—a way station had been closed in Kansas, and the station agent, who had wanted to be a scientist, had given up his studies and become a dishwasher—that he, James Taggart, might sit in a private barroom and pay for the alcohol pouring down Orren Boyle's throat, for the waiter who sponged Boyle's garments when he spilled his drink over his chest, for the carpet burned by the cigarettes of an ex-pimp from Chile who did not want to take the trouble of reaching for an ashtray across a distance of three feet. (*Atlas Shrugged*)

17. "EXTREMISM,"
OR THE ART OF SMEARING

BY AYN RAND

Among the many symptoms of today's moral bankruptcy, the performance of the so-called "moderates" at the Republican National Convention was the climax, at least to date. It was an attempt to institutionalize smears as an instrument of national policy—to raise those smears from the private gutters of yellow journalism to the public summit of a proposed inclusion in a political party platform. *The "moderates" were demanding a repudiation of "extremism" without any definition of that term.*

Ignoring repeated challenges to define what they meant by "extremism," substituting vituperation for identification, they kept the debate on the level of concretes and would not name the wider abstractions or principles involved. They poured abuse on a few specific groups and would not disclose the criteria by which these groups had been chosen. The only thing clearly perceivable to the public was a succession of snarling faces and hysterical voices screaming with violent hatred—while denouncing "purveyors of hate" and demanding "tolerance."

When men feel that strongly about an issue, yet refuse to name it, when they fight savagely for some seemingly incoherent, unintelligible goal—one may be sure that their actual goal would not stand public identification. Let us, therefore, proceed to identify it.

First, observe the peculiar incongruity of the concretes chosen as the objects of the "moderates'" hatred: "the Communist Party, the Ku Klux Klan, and the John Birch Society." If one attempts to abstract the common attribute, the *principle*, by which these three groups could be linked together, one finds none—or none more specific than "political group." Obviously, this is not what the "moderates" had in mind.

The Objectivist Newsletter, September 1964.

The common attribute—the "moderates" would snarl at this point—is "evil." Okay, what evil? The Communist Party is guilty of the wholesale slaughter of countless millions spread through every continent of the globe. The Ku Klux Klan is guilty of murdering innocent victims by the mob violence of lynchings. What is the John Birch Society guilty of? The only answer elicited from the "moderates" was: "They accused General Eisenhower of being a communist."

The worst category of crime in which this accusation could be placed is *libel*. Let us leave aside the fact that libel is what every anti-welfare-statist is chronically subjected to in public discussions. Let us agree that libel *is* a serious offense and ask only one question: does libel belong to the same category of evil as the actions of the Communist Party and the Ku Klux Klan?

Are we to regard wholesale slaughter, lynch-murders, and libel as equal evils?

If one heard a man declaring: "I am equally opposed to bubonic plague, to throwing acid in people's faces, and to my mother-in-law's nagging"—one would conclude that the mother-in-law was the only object of his hatred and that her elimination was his only goal. The same principle applies to both examples of the same technique.

No one truly opposed to the Communist Party and the Ku Klux Klan would take their evil so lightly as to equate it with the activities of a futile, befuddled organization whose alleged sin, at worst, might be irresponsible recklessness in making unproved or libelous assertions.

And more: the Communist Party as such is not a campaign issue, neither for the Republicans nor the Democrats nor the electorate at large; virtually everybody is denouncing the Communist Party these days and nobody needs the reassurance of a formal repudiation. The Ku Klux Klan is not a *Republican* issue or problem; its members, traditionally, are Democrats; for the Republicans to repudiate their vote would be like repudiating the vote of Tammany Hall, which is not theirs to repudiate.

This leaves only the John Birch Society as a real issue for a Republican convention. And it *was* the real issue—but in a deeper and more devious sense than might appear on the surface.

The real issue was not the John Birch Society as such: that Society was merely an artificial and somewhat unworthy straw man, picked by the "moderates" as a focal point for the intended destruction of much greater and much more important victims.

Observe that everyone at the Republican Convention seemed to understand the implicit purpose behind the issue of "extremism," but nobody would name it explicitly. The debate was conducted in terms of enormous, undefined "package-deals," as if words were merely approximations intended to *connote* an issue no one dared to *denote*. The result gave the impression of a life-and-death struggle conducted out of focus.

The same atmosphere dominates the public controversy now raging over this issue. People are arguing about "extremism" as if they knew what that word meant, yet no two statements use it in the same sense and no two speakers seem to be talking about the same subject. If there ever was a tower-of-Babel situation, this is surely it. Please note that *that* is an important part of the issue.

In fact, most people do not *know* the meaning of the word "extremism"; they merely sense it. They sense that something is being put over on them by some means which they cannot grasp.

In order to understand *what* is done and *how* it is being done, let us observe some earlier instances of the same technique.

A large-scale instance, in the 1930's, was the introduction of the world *"isolationism"* into our political vocabulary. It was a derogatory term, suggesting something evil, and it had no clear, explicit definition. It was used to convey two meanings: one alleged, the other real—and to damn both.

The alleged meaning was defined approximately like this: "Isolationism is the attitude of a person who is interested only in his own country and is not concerned with the rest of the world." The real meaning was: "Patriotism and national self-interest."

What, exactly, is *"concern* with the rest of the world"? Since nobody did or could maintain the position that the state of the world is of no *concern* to this country, the term "isolationism" was a straw man used to misrepresent the position of those who were concerned with this country's interests. The concept of patriotism was replaced by the term "isolationism" and vanished from public discussion.

The number of distinguished patriotic leaders smeared, silenced, and eliminated by that tag would be hard to compute. Then, by a gradual, imperceptible process, the real purpose of the tag took over: the concept of "concern" was switched into *"selfless* concern." The ultimate result was a view of foreign policy which is wrecking the United States to this day: the suicidal view that our foreign policy must be guided, not by considerations of national self-interest, but by concern for the interests and welfare of the world, that is, of all countries except our own.

In the late 1940's, another newly coined term was shot into our cultural arteries: *"McCarthyism."* Again, it was a derogatory term, suggesting some insidious evil, and without any clear definition. Its alleged meaning was: "Unjust accusations, persecutions, and character assassinations of innocent victims." Its real meaning was: "Anti-communism."

Senator McCarthy was never proved guilty of those allegations, but the effect of that term was to intimidate and silence public discussions. Any uncompromising denunciation of communism or communists was—and still is—smeared as "McCarthyism." As a consequence, opposition to and exposés of communist penetration have all but vanished from our intellectual scene. (I must mention that I am not an admirer of Senator McCarthy, but *not* for the reasons implied in that smear.)

Now consider the term *"extremism."* Its alleged meaning is: "Intolerance, hatred, racism, bigotry, crackpot theories, incitement to violence." Its real meaning is: "The advocacy of capitalism."

Observe the technique involved in these three examples. It consists of creating an artificial, unnecessary, and (rationally) unusable term, designed to replace and obliterate some legitimate concepts—a term which sounds like a concept, but stands for a "package-deal" of disparate, incongruous, contradictory elements taken out of any logical conceptual order or context, a "package-deal" whose (approximately) defining characteristic is always a non-essential. This last is the essence of the trick.

Let me remind you that the purpose of a definition is to distinguish the things subsumed under a single concept from all other things in existence; and, therefore, their defining characteristic must always be that essential characteristic which distinguishes them from everything else.

So long as men use language, *that* is the way they will use it. There is *no* other way to communicate. And if a man accepts a term with a definition by non-essentials, his mind will substitute for it the *essential* characteristic of the objects he is trying to designate.

For instance, "concern (or non-concern) with the rest of the world" is *not* an essential characteristic of any theory of foreign relations. If a man hears the term "isolationists" applied to a number of individuals, he will observe that the essential characteristic distinguishing them from other individuals is *patriotism*—and he will conclude that "isolationism" means "patriotism" and that patriotism is evil. Thus the real meaning of the term will automatically replace the alleged meaning.

If a man hears the term "McCarthyism," he will observe that the best-known characteristic distinguishing Senator McCarthy from other public figures is an *anti-communist* stand, and he will conclude that anti-communism is evil.

If a man hears the term "extremism" and is offered the innocuous figure of the John Birch Society as an example, he will observe that its best-known characteristic is *"conservatism,"* and he will conclude that "conservatism" is evil—as evil as the Communist Party and the Ku Klux Klan. ("Conservatism" is itself a loose, undefined, badly misleading term—but in today's popular usage it is taken to mean "pro-capitalism.")

Such is the function of modern smear-tags, and such is the process by which they destroy our public communications, making rational discussion of political issues impossible.

The same mentalities that create an "anti-hero" in order to destroy heroes, and an "anti-novel" in order to destroy novels, are creating *"anti-concepts"* in order to destroy concepts.

The purpose of "anti-concepts" is to obliterate certain concepts without public discussion; and, as a means to that end, to make public discussion unintelligible, and to induce the same disintegration in the mind of any man who accepts them, rendering him incapable of clear thinking or rational judgment. No mind is better than the precision of its concepts.

(I call this to the special attention of two particular classes of men who aid and abet the dissemination of "anti-concepts": the academic ivory-tower philosophers who claim that definitions are a matter of arbitrary social whim or convention, and that there can be no such thing as right or wrong definitions—and the "practical" men who believe that so abstract a science as epistemology can have no effect on the political events of the world.)

Of all the "anti-concepts" polluting our cultural atmosphere, "extremism" is the most ambitious in scale and implications; it goes much beyond politics. Let us now examine it in detail.

To begin with, "extremism" is a term which, standing by itself, has no meaning. The concept of "extreme" denotes a relation, a measurement, a degree. The dictionary gives the following definitions: "Extreme, *adj.*—1. of a character or kind farthest removed from the ordinary or average. 2. utmost or exceedingly great in degree."

It is obvious that the first question one has to ask, before using that term, is: a degree—of what?

To answer: "Of anything!" and to proclaim that any extreme is evil because it is an extreme—to hold the *degree* of a characteristic, regardless of its *nature*, as evil—is an absurdity (any garbled Aristotelianism to the contrary notwithstanding). Measurements, as such, have no value-significance—and acquire it only from the nature of that which is being measured.

Are an extreme of health and an extreme of disease equally undesirable? Are extreme intelligence and extreme stupidity—both equally far removed "from the ordinary or average"—equally unworthy? Are extreme honesty and extreme dishonesty equally immoral? Are a man of extreme virtue and a man of extreme depravity equally evil?

The examples of such absurdities can be multiplied indefinitely—particularly in the field of morality where only an *extreme* (*i.e.*, unbreached, uncompromised) degree of virtue can be properly called a virtue. (What is the moral status of a man of *"moderate"* integrity?)

But "don't bother to examine a folly—ask yourself only what it accomplishes." What is the "anti-concept" of "extremism" intended to accomplish in politics?

The basic and crucial political issue of our age is: *capitalism versus socialism*, or freedom versus statism. For decades, this issue has been silenced, suppressed, evaded, and hidden under the foggy, undefined rubber-terms of "conservatism" and "liberalism" which had lost their original meaning and could be stretched to mean all things to all men.

The goal of the "liberals"—as it emerges from the record of the past decades—was to smuggle this country into welfare statism by means of single, concrete, specific measures, enlarging the power of the government a step at a time, never permitting these steps to be summed up into principles, never permitting their direction to be identified or the basic issue to be named. Thus statism was to come, not by vote or by violence, but by slow rot—by a long process of evasion and epistemological corruption, leading to a *fait accompli*. (The goal of the "conservatives" was only to retard that process.)

The "liberals'" program required that the concept of *capitalism* be obliterated—not merely as if it could not exist any longer, but as if it had never existed. The actual nature, principles, and history of capitalism had to be smeared, distorted, misrepresented and thus kept out of public discussion—because socialism has not won and cannot win in open debate, in an uncorrupted marketplace of ideas, neither on the ground of logic nor economics nor morality nor historical performance. Socialism can win only by default—by the moral default of its alleged opponents.

That blackout seemed to work for a while. But "you can't fool all of the people all of the time." Today, the frayed, worn tags of "conservatism" and "liberalism" are cracking up—and what is showing underneath is: capitalism versus socialism.

The welfare-statists need a new cover. What we are witnessing now is a desperate, last-ditch attempt to put over two "anti-concepts": the *"extremists"* and the *"moderates."*

To put over an "anti-concept," one needs a straw man (or scarecrow or scapegoat) to serve as an example of its *alleged* meaning. That is the role for which the "liberals" have chosen the John Birch Society.

That Society was thrust into public prominence by the "liberal" press, a few years ago, and overpublicized out of all proportion to its actual importance. It has no clear, specific political philosophy (it is not *for* capitalism, but merely *against* communism), no real political program, no intellectual influence; it represents a confused, non-intellectual, "cracker-barrel" type of protest; it is certainly *not* the spokesman nor the rallying point of pro-capitalism or even of "conservatism." *These* precisely are the reasons why it was chosen by the "liberals."

The intended technique was: first, to ignore the existence of any serious, reputable, intellectual advocacy of capitalism and the growing body of literature on that subject, past and present—by literally pretending that it did not and does not exist; then, to publicize the John Birch Society as the only representative of the "right"; then to smear all "rightists" by equating them with the John Birch Society.

An explicit proof of this intention was given in a TV interview last year (September 15, 1963) by Governor Rockefeller, who later led the attack on "extremism" at the Republican Convention. Asked to define what he meant by "the radical right," he said:

The best illustration was what happened at the Young Republican Convention in San Francisco a number of months ago, where a man was elected, a Young Republican was elected on a platform to abolish the income tax, to withdraw from the United Nations, *I don't know whether he included* impeachment of Earl Warren, *but that is part of this whole concept,* and the idea that General Eisenhower was a crypto-communist. [Italics mine.]

Part of *what* concept?

The first two tenets listed are legitimate "rightist" positions, backed by many valid reasons; the third is a sample of purely Birchite foolishness; the fourth is a sample of the irresponsibility of just one Birchite. The total is a sample of the art of smearing.

Now consider the meaning ascribed to the term *"rightist"* within the "package-deal" of "extremism." In general usage, the terms "rightists" and "leftists" designate advocates of capitalism and socialism. But observe the abnormal, artificial stress of the attempt to associate *racism* and *violence* with "the extreme right"—two evils of which even the straw man, the Birch Society, is not guilty, and which can be much more plausibly associated with the Democratic Party (via the Ku Klux Klan). The purpose is to revive that old saw of pre-World War II vintage, the notion that the two political opposites confronting us, the two *"extremes,"* are: fascism versus communism.

The political origin of that notion is more shameful than the "moderates" would care publicly to admit. Mussolini came to power by claiming that that was the only choice confronting Italy. Hitler came to power by claiming that that was the only choice confronting Germany. It is a matter of record that in the German election of 1933, the Communist Party was ordered by its leaders to vote for the Nazis—with the explanation that they could later fight the Nazis for power, but first they had to help destroy their common enemy: capitalism and its parliamentary form of government.

It is obvious what the fraudulent issue of fascism versus communism accomplishes: it sets up, as opposites, two variants of the same political system; it eliminates the possibility of considering capitalism; it switches the choice of "Freedom or dictatorship?" into "Which kind of dictatorship?"—thus establishing dictatorship as an inevitable fact and offering only a choice of rulers. The choice—according to the proponents of that fraud—is: a dictatorship of the rich (fascism) or a dictatorship of the poor (communism).

That fraud collapsed in the 1940's, in the aftermath of World War II. It is too obvious, too easily demonstrable that fascism and communism are not two opposites, but two rival gangs fighting over the same territory—that both are variants of statism, based on the collectivist principle that man is the rightless slave of the state—that both are socialistic, in theory, in practice, and in the explicit statements of their leaders—that under both systems, the poor are enslaved and the rich are expropriated in favor of a ruling clique—that fascism is not the product of the political "right," but of the "left"—

that the basic issue is not "rich versus poor," but man versus the state, or: individual rights versus totalitarian government—which means: capitalism versus socialism.[1]

The smear of capitalism's advocates as "fascists" has failed in this country and, for over a decade, has been moldering in dark corners, seldom venturing to be heard openly, in public—coming only as an occasional miasma from under the ground, from the sewers of actual leftism. And *this* is the kind of notion that the "liberals" are unfastidious enough to attempt to revive. But it is obvious what vested interest that notion can serve.

If it were true that dictatorship is inevitable and that fascism and communism are the two "extremes" at the opposite ends of our course, then what is the safest place to choose? Why, the middle of the road. The safely undefined, indeterminate, mixed-economy, "moderate" middle—with a "moderate" amount of government favors and special privileges to the rich and a "moderate" amount of government handouts to the poor—with a "moderate" respect for rights and a "moderate" degree of brute force—with a "moderate" amount of freedom and a "moderate" amount of slavery—with a "moderate" degree of justice and a "moderate" degree of injustice—with a "moderate" amount of security and a "moderate" amount of terror—and with a moderate degree of tolerance for all, except those "extremists" who uphold principles, consistency, objectivity, morality and who refuse to compromise.

The notion of compromise as the supreme virtue superseding all else, is the moral imperative, the moral pre-condition of a mixed economy.[2] A mixed economy is an explosive, untenable mixture of two opposite elements, which cannot remain stable, but must ultimately go one way or the other; it is a mixture of freedom and controls, which means: not of fascism and communism, but of capitalism and statism (including all its variants). Those who wish to support the un-supportable, disintegrating *status quo*, are screaming in panic that it can be prolonged by eliminating the two *"extremes"* of its basic components; but the two extremes are: capitalism or total dictatorship.

Dictatorship feeds on the ideological chaos of bewildered, demoralized, cynically flexible, unresisting men. But capitalism requires an uncompromising stand. (Destruction can be

[1] See my lecture *The Fascist New Frontier*, published by Nathaniel Branden Institute, New York, 1963.
[2] See the chapter "The Cult of Moral Grayness" in *The Virtue of Selfishness*.

done blindly, at random; but construction requires strict adherence to specific principles.) The welfare-statists hope to eliminate capitalism by smear and silence—and to "avoid" dictatorship by "voluntary" compliance, by a policy of bargaining and compromise with the government's growing power.

This brings us to the deeper implications of the term "extremism." It is obvious that an uncompromising stand (on anything) is the actual characteristic which that "anti-concept" is designed to damn. It is also obvious that compromise is incompatible with morality. In the field of morality, compromise is surrender to evil.

There can be no compromise on basic principles. There can be no compromise on moral issues. There can be no compromise on matters of knowledge, of truth, of rational conviction.

If an uncompromising stand is to be smeared as "extremism," then that smear is directed at any devotion to values, any loyalty to principles, any profound conviction, any consistency, any steadfastness, any passion, any dedication to an unbreached, inviolate truth—*any man of integrity*.

And it is against all these that that "anti-concept" has been and is being used.

Here we can see the deeper roots, the source that has made the spread of "anti-concepts" possible. The mentally paralyzed, anxiety-ridden neurotics produced by the disintegration of modern philosophy—with its cult of uncertainty, its epistemological irrationalism and ethical subjectivism—come out of our colleges, broken by chronic dread, seeking escape from the absolutism of reality with which they feel themselves impotent to deal. Fear drives them to unite with slick political manipulators and pragmatist ward-heelers to make the world safe for mediocrity by raising to the status of a moral ideal that archetypical citizen of a mixed economy: the docile, pliable, moderate Milquetoast who never gets excited, never makes trouble, never cares too much, adjusts to anything and upholds nothing.

The best proof of an intellectual movement's collapse is the day when it has nothing to offer as an ultimate ideal but a plea for "moderation." Such is the final proof of collectivism's bankruptcy. The vision, the courage, the dedication, the moral fire are now on the barely awakening side of the crusaders for capitalism.

It will take more than an "anti-concept" to stop them.

18. THE OBLITERATION OF CAPITALISM

BY AYN RAND

In my article " 'Extremism,' or The Art of Smearing," I discussed the subject of "anti-concepts"—*i.e.*, artificial, unnecessary, undefined and (rationally) unusable terms intended to replace and obliterate certain legitimate concepts in people's minds.

I said that the "liberals" are coining and spreading "anti-concepts" in order to smuggle this country into statism by an imperceptible process—and that the primary target marked for obliteration is the concept of "capitalism," which, if lost, would carry away with it the knowledge that a free society can and did exist.

But there is something much less attractive (and, politically, much more disastrous) than capitalism's enemies: its alleged defenders—some of whom are muscling in on the game of manufacturing "anti-concepts" of their own.

Have you ever felt a peculiar kind of embarrassment when witnessing a grossly inappropriate human performance, such as the antics of an unfunny comedian? It is a depersonalized, almost metaphysical embarrassment at having to witness so undignified a behavior on the part of a member of the human species.

That is what I feel at having to hear the following statement of Governor Romney, which was his alleged answer to the communists' boast that they would bury capitalism:

"But what they do not understand—and what we have failed to tell the world—is that Americans buried capitalism long ago, and moved on to consumerism."

The implications of such a statement are too sickeningly obvious. The best comment on it came from *The Richardson Digest* (Richardson, Texas, April 28, 1965), from the column "Lively Comments" by Earl Lively, who wrote: "Afraid to stand alone, even on his knees, Romney then tells the rest of us that we do not know the definition of capitalism, we do not understand our economic principles, and we'd be better off if we quit going around defending such an unpopular concept as capitalism."

Mr. Lively is admirably precise in his description of the posture involved. But Mr. Romney is not alone in it. A number of intellectually more reputable men (including some distinguished free-enterprise economists) have adopted the same stance and the same line for the same psychological reasons.

There are the economists who proclaim that the essence (and the moral justification) of capitalism is "*service* to others—to the consumers," that the consumers' wishes are the absolute edicts ruling the free market, etc. (This is an example of what a definition by non-essentials accomplishes, and of why a half-truth is worse than a lie: what all such theorists fail to mention is the fact that capitalism grants economic recognition to only one kind of consumer: the producer—that only traders, *i.e.*, producers who have something to offer, are recognized on a free market, not "consumers" as such—that, in a capitalist economy, as in reason, in justice, and in reality, production is the pre-condition of consumption.)

There are the businessmen who spend fortunes on ideological ads, allegedly in defense of capitalism, which assure the public that all but a tiny fraction of an industry's income goes to labor (wages), to government (taxes), etc., with these shares represented as big chunks in full-color process, and, lost among them, an apologetic little sliver is marked "2½ percent" and labeled "profits."

There is the display of charts and models, in a hallway of the New York Stock Exchange, presenting the achievements of free enterprise and captioned: "The People's Capitalism."

Since none of these attempts can succeed in disguising the nature of capitalism nor in degrading it to the level of an altruistic stockyard, their sole result is to convince the public that capitalism hides some evil secret which imbues its alleged defenders with such an aura of abject guilt and hypocrisy. But, in fact, the secret they are struggling to hide is capitalism's essence and greatest virtue: that it is a system based on the recognition of individual rights—on man's right to exist (and to work) for his own sake—*not* on the altruistic view of man as a sacrificial animal. Thus it is capitalism's *virtue* that the public is urged—by such defenders—to regard as evil, and it is *altruism* that all their efforts help to reinforce and reaffirm as the standard of the good.

What they dare not allow into their minds is the fact that capitalism and altruism are incompatible; so they wonder why the more they propagandize, the more unpopular capitalism becomes. They blame it on people's stupidity (because people refuse to believe that a successful industrialist is an exponent of altruistic self-sacrifice)—and on people's greed for the unearned (because, after being battered with assurances that the industrialist's wealth is "morally" theirs, people do come to believe it).

No "anti-concept" launched by the "liberals" goes so far so crudely as the tag "consumerism." It implies loudly and clearly that the status of "consumer" is separate from and superior to the status of "producer"; it suggests a social system dedicated to the service of a new aristocracy which is distinguished by the ability to "consume" and vested with a special claim on the caste of serfs marked by the ability to produce. If taken seriously, such a tag would lead to the ultimate absurdity of the communists proclaiming: "Who does not toil, shall not eat"—and the alleged representatives of capitalism replying: "Oh yes, he shall!" And if the Ad Hoc Committee on the Triple Revolution propounds such a moral obscenity as *"the right to consume"*—who inspired it, Karl Marx or Governor Romney?

It is true that we are not a capitalist system any longer: we are a mixed economy, *i.e.*, a mixture of capitalism and statism, of freedom and controls. A mixed economy is a country in the process of disintegration, a civil war of pressure-groups looting and devouring one another. In this sense, "consumerism" might be the appropriate name for it.

Now to whom is it that the friends, the semi-friends, and even the acquaintances of capitalism are so anxiously apologizing?

As the clearest illustration of the psychological motives, the moral meaning and the intellectual technique involved in the manufacture of "anti-concepts," I offer you a column by C. L. Sulzberger, entitled "Should the Old Labels Be Changed," in the July 1964 issue of *The New York Times*.

A research report of the United States Information Agency [writes Mr. Sulzberger] has ruefully discovered that the more our propaganda advertises the virtues of "capitalism" and attacks "Socialism," the less the world likes us. . . . Confused semantics make bad public relations. . . . Having analyzed conclusions of its poll-takers in both hemispheres, the U.S.I.A. study observes: "Capitalism is evil. The United States is the leading capitalist country. Therefore, the United States is evil." It would be difficult to exaggerate the harm that this line of thinking has done. In the Soviet Union and

Communist China it sustains attitudes and actions that greatly increase the danger of thermonuclear war.

What is meant here by such a foggy expression as "sustains attitudes and actions"? The smear of capitalism as evil was originated and is constantly reiterated by the communists. Does the above mean that their own smear sustains their attitudes? And does it mean that the way to avoid thermonuclear war is for us to agree that the smear is true?

The report does not say. It merely goes on:

"In the non-Communist world it tends to poison the atmosphere in which we are trying to carry on our aid programs and other international cooperation."

This means that the harm, to us, lies in the danger that the recipients of our charity might refuse to take our money— and that in order to gain their "cooperation," we must spit in our own face and join in smearing the system which produced the wealth which is saving their lives.

"Capitalism" is a dirty word to millions of non-Marxists who see "Socialism" as vaguely benevolent. When the U.S.I.A. sampled foreign opinion it found that to the majority "Socialism" did not mean government ownership and was not necessarily related to communism. Rather it seemed to imply a system favoring welfare of common people.

If you have doubted that the philosophy of Pragmatism actually teaches that truth is to be established by public polls—here is a sample of it, in pure and naked form. Volumes of theory, a century of history, and the bloody practice of five continents to the contrary notwithstanding, "socialism" does not mean government ownership and is not related to communism—because a sampling of majority opinion said so. And what is meant by "a system favoring welfare of common people"? How does one "favor" the "common people"? At the expense of the uncommon? A "favor" means the unearned—since the earned is a right, not a favor. Whose rights and earnings are to be abrogated and expropriated— for whose benefit? The only variant of socialism that can distribute "favors" without government ownership, is fascism. Draw your own conclusions about the political inclinations of the moral cannibals involved in that poll.

Most foreigners apparently don't regard "capitalism" as

descriptive of an efficient economy or a safeguard of individual rights. To them it means little concern for the poor, unfair distribution of wealth, and undue influence of the rich.

How does one combine the safeguard of individual rights with a government-enforced "concern for the poor" and a government-distributed wealth and "influence"? No answer.

U.S.I.A. found an impressive percentage of British, West Germans, Italians, Japanese, Mexicans and Brazilians have a favorable opinion of "Socialism" and a strongly unfavorable opinion of "capitalism."

Consider the philosophical trends, the intellectual commitments, the moral records of these countries—and *their political results*. Germany, Italy, and Japan were fascist dictatorships; their claims to political wisdom consist of giving the world a demonstration of horror equaled only by their ideological brothers in Soviet Russia and Red China. Britain, Mexico, and Brazil are mixed economies which have long since gone over the borderline state of mixture into the category—and the economic bankruptcy—of socialistic countries. And *these* are the nations whose opinions we are asked to value, whose favor we are asked to court—these are the moral authorities to whom we must apologize for the noblest political system in history: ours—these are the judges whom we must placate by denying our system, dishonoring its record, and obliterating its name.

Is there any conceivable motive that could prompt a nation to so base a betrayal? Conceivable—no, if one refers to the realm of rational concepts. But—

"Capitalism" abroad is frequently a pejorative word. Efforts to purge it of negative connotations by phrases like "people's capitalism" have failed. . . . But "Socialism" is chic. [Yes, *chic*.] Even in Britain and West Germany, where private ownership is the mode, the majority expressed itself sympathetic to "Socialism," while abhorring Communism.

If the term "social metaphysics" occurs to you at this point, you would be right—except that even that term seems too clean, almost too innocent, to explain the following:

Leaders of underdeveloped nations, spurning "capitalism," boast of special brands of "Socialism." Leopold Senghor of Senegal says "Socialism is a sense of com-

munity which is a return to Africanism." Julius Nyerere
of Tanganyika insists "no underdeveloped country can
afford to be anything but 'Socialist.' " Tunisia's Habib
Bourguiba claims Mohammed's companions "were Socialists before the invention of the word." And Cambodia's Prince Norodom Sihanouk contends "our
Socialism is first and foremost an application of Buddhism."

The above is true, totally true, true all the way down to
the deepest philosophical, psychological, political, and moral
fundamentals. And *this* is the most damning indictment of
socialism that a rational person could need to see. Socialism *is*
a regression to primitive barbarism. But that is not the
appraisal or the conclusion of the U.S.I.A. report. It is to the
Mohammedans, the Buddhists, and the cannibals (the literal
cannibals, this time)—to the under-developed, the undeveloped, and the not-to-be-developed cultures—that the Capitalist United States of America is asked to apologize for her
skyscrapers, her automobiles, her plumbing, and her smiling,
confident, untortured, un-skinned-alive, un-eaten young men!
The column ends as follows:

The study concludes that foreigners attribute to the
U.S.A. "a high degree of capitalist exploitation and of
capitalist power over the society as a whole, as well as
*a great absence of those social welfare measures which,
to them, are the decisive criterion of Socialism."*
[U.S.I.A.'s own italics.]
There is surely no sense in proclaiming our philosophy in terms that are unsalable and peculiarly vulnerable to our opponents' attacks. . . .
Our system of capitalism has evolved immensely
from the outmoded economic doctrine to which the
label was originally applied by Marx and other 19th-
century thinkers. Might not the U.S.I.A. attempt another survey seeking ways of announcing our social and
political system in a manner more acceptable to those
abroad whose opinions we would influence?

Influence—how? In what direction? To what purpose? If,
for the sake of appeasement, we renounce our philosophy
and adopt theirs, if we discard the last remnants of capitalism
and proclaim ourselves to be a "National Socialist Welfare
State," who would have "influenced"—and buried—whom?
A great many things may be observed about this unusually
revealing column. It is true, of course, that if American
propagandists are defending capitalism abroad as they do at

home, the results would be precisely as described in that U.S.I.A. study, or worse. At home, it is the "conservatives" who are appeasing the "liberals" and losing the battle, because they dare not uphold the true nature of capitalism. Abroad, it is the "liberals" who are appeasing the communists and losing the battle, for the same reason: there is no way to defend capitalism without upholding man's right to exist, which means, without rejecting altruism.

Observe the appalling indifference to the issue of truth or falsehood, on the part of capitalism's alleged defenders. They attach no significance to such contradictions as sympathizing with socialism while abhorring communism—or to the fact that capitalism is the only opposite of and the only defense against communism. They attach no significance to the ignorance, the dishonesty, the injustice, the irrationality of capitalism's critics. In the face of a moral-philosophical issue, their response is an immediate, uncritical acceptance of the critics' terms, a surrender to ignorance, dishonesty, injustice, irrationality. In the face of the knowledge that capitalism is being smeared by the communists, by the very enemy they intend to fight, their policy is not to blast the smear, not to enlighten the world, not to defend the victim, not to speak out for justice—but to sanction the smear, to hide the truth, to sacrifice the victim, to join the lynching. What they feel is: Of what account is truth in the face of such a consideration as "people don't like us"? What they cry is: "But this is the way we'll make people like the victim!"—after we've helped them grind her to bits in the mud. Then they wonder why contempt is all they earn, from betrayed allies and sworn enemies alike. Moral cowardice is not an attractive nor an inspiring nor a very practical trait.

Observe the obscenity of those Europeans who—in this day and age, in the rising tide of global bloodshed, in the face of the unspeakable atrocities of the "newly emerging" nations—dare prattle about "little concern for the poor" and criticize the United States for *that*. Whatever their motives, concern for human suffering is not one of them.

We may observe all that, but it seems almost irrelevant beside the one central, overwhelming fact: the intellectual leaders of today's world are willing to condone and accept anything, they are willing to recognize the right of Buddhism and Africanism to their boastfully asserted traditions (remember the nature and record of those traditions)—but they make one exception. There is one country—the United States of America—who is not acceptable to them, who must renounce *her* tradition and, in atonement, must crawl on her knees, begging the savages of five continents to choose a new name for her system, which would obliterate the guilt of her past. What is her guilt? That for one brief moment in human history, she offered the world the vision of unsacrificed man in a non-sacrificial way of life.

When one grasps *this,* one knows that it is no use arguing over political trivia, or wondering about the nature of altruism and why the reign of the altruists is leading the world to an ever widening spread of horror. *This* is the nature of altruism, *this*—not any sort of benevolence, good will, or concern for human misfortune. Hatred of man, not the desire to help him—hatred of life, not the desire to further it— hatred of *the successful state of life*—and that ultimate, apocalyptic evil: *hatred of the good for being the good.*

What every successful man (successful at any human value, spiritual or material) has encountered, has sensed, has been bewildered by, but has seldom identified, can now be seen in the open, with nations, instead of individual men, re-enacting the same unspeakable evil on a world scale where it cannot be hidden any longer. It is not for her flaws that the United States of America is hated, but *for her virtues*—not for her weaknesses, but *for her achievements*—not for her failures, but *for her success*—her magnificent, shining, life-giving success.

> It is not your wealth that they're after. Theirs is a conspiracy against the mind, which means: against life and man. It is a conspiracy without leader or direction, and the random little thugs of the moment who cash in on the agony of one land or another are chance scum riding the torrent from the broken dam of the sewer of centuries, from the reservoir of hatred for reason, for logic, for ability, for achievement, for joy, stored by every whining anti-human who ever preached the superiority of the "heart" over the mind. (*Atlas Shrugged*)

With most of the world in ruins, with the voice of philosophy silent and the last remnants of civilization vanishing undefended, in an unholy alliance of savagery and decadence, bloody thugs are fighting over the spoils, while the cynical pragmatists left in charge and way out of their depth are trying to drown their panic at Europe's cocktail parties, where emasculated men and hysterical, white-lipped women determine the fate of the world by declaring that socialism is chic.

This is the face of our age. To attempt to fight it by means of compromise, conciliation, equivocation, and circumlocution is worse than grotesque. This is not a battle to be fought by joining the enemy in any manner—nor by borrowing any of his slogans or his bloody ideological equipment—nor by deluding the world about the nature of the battle—nor by pretending that one is "in" with that sort of crowd.

It is a battle only for those who know why it is necessary to be "out"—as far out of that stream as words will carry—why, when moral issues are at stake, one must begin by blasting the enemy's base and cutting off any link to it, any bridge, any toehold—and if one is to be misunderstood, let it be on the side of intransigence, not on the side of any resemblance to any part of so monstrous an evil.

It is a battle only for those who—paraphrasing a character in *Atlas Shrugged*—are prepared to say:

"Capitalism was the only system in history where wealth was not acquired by looting, but by production, not by force, but by trade, the only system that stood for man's right to his own mind, to his work, to his life, to his happiness, to himself. If this is evil, by the present standards of the world, if this is the reason for damning us, then we—we, the champions of man—accept it and choose to be damned by that world. We choose to wear the name 'Capitalism' printed on our foreheads, proudly, as our badge of nobility."

This is what the battle demands. Nothing less will do.

19. CONSERVATISM: AN OBITUARY

BY AYN RAND

Both the "conservatives" and the "liberals" stress a fact with which everybody seems to agree: that the world is facing a deadly conflict and that we must fight to save civilization.

But what is the nature of that conflict? Both groups answer: it is a conflict between communism and . . . and what?—blank out. It is a conflict between two ways of life, they answer, the communist way and . . . what?—blank out. It is a conflict between two ideologies, they answer. What is *our* ideology? Blank out.

The truth which both groups refuse to face and to admit is that, politically, the world conflict of today is the last stage of the struggle between *capitalism* and statism.

We stand for *freedom*, say both groups—and proceed to declare what kind of controls, regulations, coercions, taxes, and "sacrifices" they would impose, what arbitrary powers they would demand, what "social gains" they would hand out to various groups, without specifying from what other groups these "gains" would be expropriated. Neither of them cares to admit that government control of a country's economy—any kind or degree of such control, by any group, for any purpose whatsoever—rests on the basic principle of *statism*, the principle that man's life belongs to the state. A mixed economy is merely a semi-socialized economy—which means: a semi-enslaved society—which means: a country torn by irreconcilable contradictions, in the process of gradual disintegration.

Freedom, in a political context, means freedom from government coercion. It does *not* mean freedom from the landlord, or freedom from the employer, or freedom from the laws of nature which do not provide men with automatic prosperity. It means freedom from the coercive power of the state—and nothing else.

The world conflict of today is the conflict of the individual

Based on a lecture given at Princeton University on December 7, 1960.
Published by Nathaniel Branden Institute, New York, 1962.

against the state, the same conflict that has been fought throughout mankind's history. The names change, but the essence—and the results—remain the same, whether it is the individual against feudalism, or against absolute monarchy, or against communism or fascism or Nazism or socialism or the welfare state.

If one upholds freedom, one must uphold man's individual rights; if one upholds man's individual rights, one must uphold his right to his own life, to his own liberty, to the pursuit of his own happiness—which means: one must uphold a political system that guarantees and protects these rights—which means: the politico-economic system of *capitalism*.

Individual rights, freedom, justice, progress were the philosophical values, the theoretical goals, and the practical results of capitalism. No other system can create them or maintain them; no other system ever has or will. For proof, consider the nature and function of basic principles; for evidence, consult history—and the present state of the different countries of Europe.

The issue is *not* slavery for a "good" cause versus slavery for a "bad" cause; the issue is *not* dictatorship by a "good" gang versus dictatorship by a "bad" gang. The issue is freedom versus dictatorship. It is only *after* men have chosen slavery and dictatorship that they can begin the usual gang warfare of socialized countries—today, it is called pressure-group warfare—over whose gang will rule, who will enslave whom, whose property will be plundered for whose benefit, who will be sacrificed to whose "noble" purpose. All such arguments come later and are, in fact, of no consequence: the results will always be the same. The first choice—and the only one that matters—is: freedom or dictatorship, *capitalism or statism*.

That is the choice which today's political leaders are determined to evade. The "liberals" are trying to put statism over by stealth—statism of a semi-socialist, semi-fascist kind—without letting the country realize what road they are taking to what ultimate goal. And while such a policy is reprehensible, there is something more reprehensible still: the policy of the "conservatives," who are trying to defend *freedom* by stealth.

If the "liberals" are afraid to identify their program by its proper name, if they advocate every specific step, measure, policy, and principle of statism, but squirm and twist themselves into semantic pretzels with such euphemisms as the "Welfare State," the "New Deal," the "New Frontier," they still preserve a semblance of logic, if not of morality: it is the logic of a con man who cannot afford to let his victims discover his purpose. Besides, the majority of those who are loosely identified by the term "liberals" are afraid to let *themselves* discover that what they advocate *is* statism. They do not want to accept the full meaning of their goal; they want to keep all the advantages and effects of capitalism, while destroying the cause, and they want to establish statism without its necessary effects. They do not want to know or to admit that they are the champions of dictatorship and slavery. So they evade the issue, for fear of discovering that their goal is *evil*.

Immoral as this might be, what is one to think of men who evade the issue for fear of discovering that their goal is *good*? What is the moral stature of those who are afraid to proclaim that they are the champions of freedom? What is the integrity of those who outdo their enemies in smearing, misrepresenting, spitting at, and apologizing for their own ideal? What is the rationality of those who expect to trick people into freedom, cheat them into justice, fool them into progress, con them into preserving their rights, and, while indoctrinating them with statism, put one over on them and let them wake up in a perfect capitalist society some morning?

These are the "conservatives"—or most of their intellectual spokesmen.

One need not wonder *why* they are losing elections or why this country is stumbling anxiously, reluctantly toward statism. One need not wonder why any cause represented or upheld in such a manner, is doomed. One need not wonder why any group with such a policy does, in fact, declare its own bankruptcy, forfeiting any claim to moral, intellectual, or political leadership.

The meaning of the "liberals'" program is pretty clear by now. But *what are the "conservatives"?* What is it that they are seeking to *"conserve"*?

It is generally understood that those who support the "conservatives," expect them to uphold the system which has been camouflaged by the loose term of "the *American* way of life." The moral treason of the "conservative" leaders lies in the fact that they are hiding behind that camouflage: they do not have the courage to admit that the *American* way of life was *capitalism,* that *that* was the politico-economic system born and established in the United States, the system which, in one brief century, achieved a level of freedom, of progress, of prosperity, of human happiness, unmatched in all the other systems and centuries combined—and that *that* is the system which they are now allowing to perish by silent default.

If the "conservatives" do not stand for capitalism, they stand for and are nothing; they have no goal, no direction, no political principles, no social ideals, no intellectual values, no leadership to offer anyone.

Yet capitalism is what the "conservatives" dare not advocate or defend. They are paralyzed by the profound conflict between capitalism and the moral code which dominates our culture: the morality of altruism. Altruism holds that man has no right to exist for his own sake, that service to others is the only justification of his existence, and that *self-sacrifice* is his highest moral duty, virtue, and value. Capitalism and altruism are incompatible; they are philosophical opposites; they cannot co-exist in the same man or in the same society. The conflict between capitalism and altruism has been undercutting America from her start and, today, has reached its climax.

The American political system was based on a different moral principle: on the principle of man's inalienable right to his own life—which means: on the principle that man has the right to exist for his own sake, neither sacrificing himself to others nor sacrificing others to himself, and that men must deal with one another as *traders,* by voluntary choice to mutual benefit.

But this moral principle was merely implied in the American political system: it was not stated explicitly, it was not identified, it was not formulated into a full, philosophical code of ethics. *This* was the unfulfilled task which remained as a deadly flaw in our culture and which is destroying America today. Capitalism is perishing *for lack of a moral base* and of a full philosophical defense.

The social system based on and consonant with the altruist morality—with the code of self-sacrifice—is socialism, in all or any of its variants: fascism, Nazism, communism. All of them treat man as a sacrificial animal to be immolated for the benefit of the group, the tribe, the society, the state. Soviet Russia is the ultimate result, the final product, the full, consistent embodiment of the altruist morality in practice; it represents the only way that that morality can ever be practiced.

Not daring to challenge the morality of altruism, the "conservatives" have been struggling to evade the issue of morality or to bypass it. This has cost them their confidence, their courage, and their cause. Observe the guilty evasiveness, the apologetic timidity, the peculiarly non-intellectual, non-philosophical attitude projected by most "conservatives" in their speeches and in their writings. No man, and no movement, can succeed without *moral* certainty—without a full, rational conviction of the moral rightness of one's cause.

Just as the "conservatives" feel guilty, uncertain, morally disarmed in fighting the "liberals," so the "liberals" feel guilty, uncertain, morally disarmed in fighting the communists. When men share the same basic premise, it is the most consistent ones who win. So long as men accept the altruist morality, they will not be able to stop the advance of communism. The altruist morality is Soviet Russia's best and *only* weapon.

The hypocrisy of America's position in international affairs, the evasiveness, the self-effacing timidity, the apologies for her wealth, her power, her success, for all the greatest virtues of her system, the avoidance of any mention of *"capitalism,"* as if it were the skeleton in her closet—have done more for the prestige of Soviet Russia and for the growing spread of communism through the world than the Russians' own cheap, bombastic propaganda could ever accomplish. An attitude of *moral guilt* is not becoming to the leader of a world crusade and will not rouse men to follow us.

And what do we ask men to fight for? They would join a crusade for freedom versus slavery, which means: for capitalism versus communism. But who will care to fight in a crusade for socialism versus communism? Who will want to fight and die to defend a system under which he will have to do voluntarily—or rather, by public vote—what a dictator would accomplish faster and much more thoroughly: the sacrifice of everyone to everyone? Who will want to crusade against murder—for the privilege of committing suicide?

In recent years, the "conservatives" have gradually come to a dim realization of the weakness in their position, of the philosophical flaw that had to be corrected. But the means by which they are attempting to correct it are worse than the original weakness; the means are discrediting and destroying the last remnants of their claim to *intellectual* leadership.

There are three interrelated arguments used by today's "conservatives" to justify capitalism, which can best be designated as: the argument from *faith*—the argument from *tradition*—the argument from *depravity*.

Sensing their need of a moral base, many "conservatives" decided to choose *religion* as their moral justification; they claim that America and capitalism are based on faith in God.

Politically, such a claim contradicts the fundamental principles of the United States: in America, religion is a private matter which cannot and must not be brought into political issues.

Intellectually, to rest one's case on *faith* means to concede that reason is on the side of one's enemies—that one has no rational arguments to offer. The "conservatives'" claim that their case rests on faith, means that there are no rational arguments to support the American system, no rational justification for freedom, justice, property, individual rights, that these rest on a mystic revelation and can be accepted only *on faith*—that in reason and logic the enemy is right, but men must hold faith as superior to reason.

Consider the implications of that theory. While the communists claim that they are the representatives of reason and science, the "conservatives" concede it and retreat into the realm of mysticism, of faith, of the supernatural, into another world, surrendering *this* world to communism. It is the kind of victory that the communists' irrational ideology could never have won on its own merits.

Observe the results. On the occasion of Khrushchev's first visit to America, he declared, at a televised luncheon, that he had threatened to *bury* us because it has been *"scientifically"* proved that communism is the system of the future, destined to rule the world. What did *our* spokesman answer? Mr. Henry Cabot Lodge answered that our system is based on faith in God. Prior to Khrushchev's arrival, the "conservative" leaders—including senators and House members—were issuing indignant protests against his visit, but the only action they suggested to the American people, the only "practical" form of protest, was: prayer and the holding of religious services for Khrushchev's victims. To hear *prayer* offered as their only weapon by the representatives of the most powerful country on earth—a country allegedly dedicated to the fight for freedom—was enough to discredit America and capitalism in anyone's eyes, at home and abroad.

Now consider the second argument: the attempt to justify capitalism on the ground of *tradition*. Certain groups are trying to switch the word "conservative" into the exact opposite of its modern American usage, to switch it back to its nineteenth-century meaning, and to put this over on the public. These groups declare that to be a "conservative" means to uphold the *status quo*, the given, the established, regardless of what it might be, regardless of whether it is good or bad, right or wrong, defensible or indefensible. They declare that we must defend the American political system not because it is *right*, but because our ancestors chose it, not because it is *good*, but because it is *old*.

America was created by men who broke with all political traditions and who originated a system unprecedented in history, relying on nothing but the "unaided" power of their own intellect. But the "neo-conservatives" are now trying to tell us that America was the product of "faith in revealed truths" and of uncritical respect for the traditions of the past (!).

It is certainly irrational to use the *"new"* as a standard of value, to believe that an idea or a policy is good merely because it is new. But it is much more preposterously irrational to use the *"old"* as a standard of value, to claim that an idea or a policy is good merely because it is ancient. The "liberals" are constantly asserting that they represent the future, that they are "new," "progressive," "forward-looking," etc.—and they denounce the "conservatives" as old-fashioned representatives of a dead past. The "conservatives" concede it, and thus help the "liberals" to propagate one of today's most grotesque inversions: collectivism, the ancient, frozen, status society, is offered to us in the name of *progress*—while capitalism, the only free, dynamic, creative society ever devised, is defended in the name of *stagnation*.

The plea to preserve *"tradition"* as such, can appeal only to those who have given up or to those who never intended to achieve anything in life. It is a plea that appeals to the worst elements in men and rejects the best: it appeals to fear, sloth, cowardice, conformity, self-doubt—and rejects creativeness, originality, courage, independence, self-reliance. It is an outrageous plea to address to human beings anywhere, but particularly outrageous here, in America, the country based on the principle that man must stand on his own feet, live by his own judgment, and move constantly forward as a productive, creative innovator.

The argument that we must respect "tradition" as such, respect it *merely* because it is a "tradition," means that we must accept the values other men have chosen, *merely* because other men have chosen them—with the necessary implication of: who are *we* to change them? The affront to a man's self-esteem, in such an argument, and the profound contempt for man's nature are obvious.

This leads us to the third—and the worst—argument, used by some "conservatives": the attempt to defend capitalism on the ground of *man's depravity*.

This argument runs as follows: since men are weak, fallible, non-omniscient and innately depraved, no man may be entrusted with the responsibility of being a dictator and of ruling everybody else; therefore, a free society is the proper way of life for imperfect creatures. Please grasp fully the implications of this argument: since men are depraved, they are *not good enough for a dictatorship;* freedom is all that they deserve; if they were perfect, they would be worthy of a totalitarian state.

Dictatorship—this theory asserts—believe it or not, is the result of *faith in man* and in man's goodness; if people believed that man is depraved by nature, they would not entrust a dictator with power. This means that a belief in human depravity protects human freedom—that it is wrong to enslave the depraved, but would be right to enslave the virtuous. And more: dictatorships—this theory declares—and all the other disasters of the modern world are man's punishment for the sin of relying on his intellect and of attempting to improve his life on earth by seeking to devise a perfect political system and to establish a *rational* society. This means that humility, passivity, lethargic resignation and a belief in Original Sin are the bulwarks of capitalism. One could not go farther than this in historical, political, and psychological ignorance or subversion. This is truly the voice of the Dark Ages rising again—in the midst of our industrial civilization.

The cynical, man-hating advocates of this theory sneer at all ideals, scoff at all human aspirations and deride all attempts to improve men's existence. "You can't change human nature," is their stock answer to the socialists. Thus they concede that socialism *is* the ideal, but human nature is unworthy of it; after which, they invite men to crusade for capitalism—a crusade one would have to start by spitting in one's own face. Who will fight and die to defend his status as a miserable sinner? If, as a result of such theories, people become contemptuous of "conservatism," do not wonder and do not ascribe it to the cleverness of the socialists.

Such are capitalism's alleged defenders—and such are the arguments by which they propose to save it.

It is obvious that with this sort of theoretical equipment and with an unbroken record of defeats, concessions, compromises, and betrayals in practice, today's "conservatives" are futile, impotent and, culturally, dead. They have nothing to offer and can achieve nothing. They can only help to destroy intellectual standards, to disintegrate thought, to discredit capitalism, and to accelerate this country's uncontested collapse into despair and dictatorship.

But to those of you who do wish to contest it—particularly those of you who are young and are not ready to surrender—

I want to give a warning: nothing is as dead as the stillborn. Nothing is as futile as a movement without goals, or a crusade without ideals, or a battle without ammunition. A bad argument is worse than ineffectual: it lends credence to the arguments of your opponents. A half-battle is worse than none: it does not end in mere defeat—it helps and hastens the victory of your enemies.

At a time when the world is torn by a profound *ideological* conflict, do not join those who have no ideology—no ideas, no philosophy—to offer you. Do not go into battle armed with nothing but stale slogans, pious platitudes, and meaningless generalities. Do not join any so-called "conservative" group, organization, or person that advocates any variant of the arguments from "faith," from "tradition," or from "depravity." Any home-grown sophist in any village debate can refute those arguments and can drive you into evasions in about five minutes. What would happen to you, with such ammunition, on the philosophical battlefield of the world? But you would never reach that battlefield: you would not be heard on it, since you would have nothing to say.

It is not by means of evasions that one saves civilization. It is not by means of empty slogans that one saves a world perishing for lack of intellectual leadership. It is not by means of ignoring its causes that one cures a deadly disease.

So long as the "conservatives" ignore the issue of what destroyed capitalism, and merely plead with men to "go back," they cannot escape the question of: back to *what*? And none of their evasions can camouflage the fact that the implicit answer is: back to an earlier stage of the cancer which is devouring us today and which has almost reached its terminal stage. That cancer is the morality of altruism.

So long as the "conservatives" evade the issue of altruism, all of their pleas and arguments amount, in essence, to this: Why can't we just go back to the nineteenth century when capitalism and altruism seemed somehow to co-exist? Why do we have to go to extremes and think of surgery, when the early stages of the cancer were painless?

The answer is that the facts of reality—which includes history and philosophy—are not to be evaded. Capitalism was destroyed by the morality of altruism. Capitalism is based on individual rights—not on the sacrifice of the individual to the "public good" of the collective. Capitalism and altruism are incompatible. It's one or the other. It's too late for compromises, for platitudes, and for aspirin tablets. There is no way to save capitalism—or freedom, or civilization, or America—except by *intellectual* surgery, that is: by destroying the source of the destruction, by rejecting the morality of altruism.

If you want to fight for capitalism, there is only one type of argument that you should adopt, the only one that can ever win in a moral issue: *the argument from self-esteem*. This means: the argument from man's right to exist—from man's inalienable individual right to his own life.

I quote from my book *For the New Intellectual:*

> The world crisis of today is a *moral* crisis—and nothing less than a moral revolution can resolve it: a moral revolution to sanction and complete the political achievement of the American Revolution. . . . The New Intellectual must fight for capitalism, not as a "practical" issue, not as an economic issue, but, with the most righteous pride, as a *moral* issue. That is what capitalism deserves, and nothing less will save it.

Capitalism is not the system of the past; it is the system of the future—if mankind is to have a future. Those who wish to fight for it, must discard the title of "conservatives." "Conservatism" has always been a misleading name, inappropriate to America. Today, there is nothing left to "conserve": the established political philosophy, the intellectual orthodoxy, and the *status quo* are *collectivism*. Those who reject all the basic premises of collectivism are *radicals* in the proper sense of the word: "radical" means "fundamental." Today, the fighters for capitalism have to be, not bankrupt "conservatives," but new radicals, new intellectuals and, above all, new, dedicated moralists.

20. THE NEW FASCISM:
RULE BY CONSENSUS

BY AYN RAND

I shall begin by doing a very unpopular thing that does not fit today's intellectual fashions and is, therefore, "anti-consensus": I shall begin by defining my terms, so that you will know what I am talking about.

Let me give you the dictionary definitions of three political terms: socialism, fascism, and statism:

> *Socialism*—a theory or system of social organization which advocates the vesting of the ownership and control of the means of production, capital, land, etc. in the community as a whole.
>
> *Fascism*—a governmental system with strong centralized power, permitting no opposition or criticism, controlling all affairs of the nation (industrial, commercial, etc.) . . .
>
> *Statism*—the principle or policy of concentrating extensive economic, political, and related controls in the state at the cost of individual liberty.[1]

It is obvious that "statism" is the wider, generic term, of which the other two are specific variants. It is also obvious that statism is the dominant political trend of our day. But which of those two variants represents the specific direction of that trend?

Observe that both "socialism" and "fascism" involve the issue of property rights. The right to property is the right of use and disposal. Observe the difference in those two theories: socialism negates private property rights altogether, and advocates "the vesting of *ownership and control*" in the community as a whole, *i.e.*, in the state; fascism leaves *ownership* in the hands of private individuals, but transfers

---

Based on a lecture given at The Ford Hall Forum, Boston, on April 18, 1965. Published in *The Objectivist Newsletter*, May and June 1965.
[1] These definitions are from *The American College Dictionary*, New York: Random House, 1957.

control of the property to the government.

Ownership without control is a contradiction in terms: it means "property," without the right to use it or to dispose of it. It means that the citizens retain the responsibility of holding property, without any of its advantages, while the government acquires all the advantages without any of the responsibility.

In this respect, socialism is the more honest of the two theories. I say "more honest," *not* "better"—because, *in practice,* there is no difference between them: both come from the same collectivist-statist principle, both negate individual rights and subordinate the individual to the collective, both deliver the livelihood and the lives of the citizens into the power of an omnipotent government—and the differences between them are only a matter of time, degree, and superficial detail, such as the choice of slogans by which the rulers delude their enslaved subjects.

Which of these two variants of statism are we moving toward: socialism or fascism?

To answer this question, one must first ask: Which is the dominant ideological trend of today's culture?

The disgraceful and terrifying answer is: *there is no ideological trend today.* There is no ideology. There are no political principles, theories, ideals, or philosophy. There is no direction, no goal, no compass, no vision of the future, no intellectual element of leadership. Are there any *emotional* elements dominating today's culture? Yes. One. *Fear.*

A country without a political philosophy is like a ship drifting at random in mid-ocean, at the mercy of any chance wind, wave, or current, a ship whose passengers huddle in their cabins and cry: "Don't rock the boat!"—for fear of discovering that the captain's bridge is empty.

It is obvious that a boat which cannot stand rocking is doomed already and that it had better be rocked hard, if it is to regain its course—but this realization presupposes a grasp of facts, of reality, of principles and a long-range view, all of which are precisely the things that the "non-rockers" are frantically struggling to evade.

Just as a neurotic believes that the facts of reality will vanish if he refuses to recognize them—so, today, the neurosis of an entire culture leads men to believe that their desperate need of political principles and concepts will vanish if they succeed in obliterating all principles and concepts. But since, *in fact,* neither an individual nor a nation can exist without some form of ideology, this sort of *anti-ideology* is now the formal, explicit, dominant ideology of our bankrupt culture.

This anti-ideology has a new and very ugly name: it is called *"Government by Consensus."*

If some demagogue were to offer us, as a guiding creed, the following tenets: that statistics should be substituted for truth, vote-counting for principles, numbers for rights, and public polls for morality—that pragmatic, range-of-the-moment expediency should be the criterion of a country's interests, and that the number of its adherents should be the criterion of an idea's truth or falsehood—that any desire of any nature whatsoever should be accepted as a valid claim, provided it is held by a sufficient number of people—that a majority may do anything it pleases to a minority—in short, gang rule and mob rule—if a demagogue were to offer it, he would not get very far. Yet all of it is contained in—and camouflaged by—the notion of "Government by Consensus."

This notion is now being plugged, not as an ideology, but as an *anti-ideology;* not as a principle, but as a means of obliterating principles; not as reason, but as rationalization, as a verbal ritual or a magic formula to assuage the national anxiety neurosis—a kind of pep pill or goofball for the "non-boat-rockers," and a chance to play it deuces wild, for the others.

It is only today's lethargic contempt for the pronouncements of our political and intellectual leaders that blinds people to the meaning, implications, and consequences of the notion of "Government by Consensus." You have all heard it and, I suspect, dismissed it as politicians' oratory, giving no thought to its actual meaning. But *that* is what I urge you to consider.

A significant clue to that meaning was given in an article by Tom Wicker in *The New York Times* (October 11, 1964). Referring to "what Nelson Rockefeller used to call 'the mainstream of American thought,' " Mr. Wicker writes:

> That mainstream is what political theorists have been projecting for years as "the national consensus"—what Walter Lippmann has aptly called "the vital center." ... Political moderation, almost by definition, is at the heart of the consensus. That is, the consensus generally sprawls over all acceptable political views—all ideas that are not totally repugnant to and do not directly threaten some major segment of the population. Therefore, acceptable ideas must take the views of others into account and that is what is meant by moderation.

Now let us identify what this means. "The consensus generally sprawls over all *acceptable* political views ..." Acceptable—to whom? To the consensus. And since the government is to be ruled by the consensus, this means that political views are to be divided into those which are "acceptable" and those which are "unacceptable" to the government. What would be the criterion of "acceptability"? Mr. Wicker supplies it. Observe that the criterion is *not* intellectual, not a question of whether certain views are true or false; the criterion is *not* moral, not a question of whether the views are right or wrong; the criterion is *emotional:* whether the views are or are not "repugnant." To whom? "To some *major* segment of the population." There is also the additional proviso that those views must not "*directly* threaten" that major segment.

What about the *minor* segments of the population? Are the views that threaten *them* "acceptable"? What about the smallest segment: the individual? Obviously, the individual and the minority groups are not to be considered; no matter how repugnant an idea may be to a man and no matter how gravely it may threaten his life, his work, his future, he is to be ignored or sacrificed by the omnipotent consensus and its government—unless he has a gang, a *sizable* gang, to support him.

What exactly is a "direct threat" to any part of the population? In a mixed economy, every government action is a direct threat to some men and an indirect threat to all. Every government interference in the economy consists of giving an unearned benefit, extorted by force, to some men at the expense of others. By what criterion of justice is a consensus-government to be guided? By the size of the victim's gang.

Now note Mr. Wicker's last sentence: "Therefore, acceptable ideas must take the views of others into account and that is what is meant by moderation." And just *what* is meant here by "the views of others"? Of which others? Since it is not the views of individuals nor of minorities, the only discernible meaning is that every "major segment" must take into account the views of all the other "major segments." But suppose that a group of socialists wants to nationalize all factories, and a group of industrialists wants to keep its properties? What would it mean, for either group, to "take into account" the views of the other? And what would "moderation" consist of, in such a case? What would constitute "moderation" in a conflict between a group of men who want to be supported at public expense—and a group of taxpayers who have other uses for their money? What would constitute "moderation" in a conflict between the member of a smaller group, such as a Negro in the South, who believes that he has an inalienable right to a fair trial—and the larger group of Southern racists who believe that the "public good" of their community permits them to lynch him? What would constitute "moderation" in a conflict between *me* and a communist (or between our respective followers), when *my* views are that I have an inalienable right to my life, liberty, and happiness—and *his* views are that the "public good" of the state permits him to rob, enslave, or murder me?

There can be no meeting ground, no middle, no compromise between *opposite principles*. There can be no such thing as "moderation" in the realm of reason and of morality. But reason and morality are precisely the two concepts abrogated by the notion of "Government by Consensus."

The advocates of that notion would declare at this point that any idea which permits no compromise constitutes "extremism"—that any form of "extremism," any uncompromising stand, is evil—that the consensus "sprawls" only over those ideas which *are* amenable to "moderation"—and that "moderation" is the supreme virtue, superseding reason and morality.

This is the clue to the core, essence, motive, and real meaning of the doctrine of "Government by Consensus": the cult of *compromise*. Compromise is the pre-condition, the necessity, the imperative of a mixed economy. The "consensus" doctrine is an attempt to translate the brute facts of a mixed economy into an ideological—or anti-ideological—system and to provide them with a semblance of justification.

A mixed economy is a mixture of freedom and controls—with no principles, rules, or theories to define either. Since the introduction of controls necessitates and leads to further controls, it is an unstable, explosive mixture which, ultimately, has to repeal the controls or collapse into dictatorship. A mixed economy has no principles to define its policies, its goals, its laws—no principles to limit the power of its government. The *only* principle of a mixed economy—which, necessarily, has to remain unnamed and unacknowledged—is that no one's interests are safe, everyone's interests are on a public auction block, and anything goes for anyone who can get away with it. Such a system—or, more precisely, anti-system—breaks up a country into an ever-growing number of enemy camps, into economic groups fighting one another for self preservation in an indeterminate mixture of *defense* and *offense*, as the nature of such a jungle demands. While, *politically*, a mixed economy preserves the semblance of an organized society with a semblance of law and order, *economically* it is the equivalent of the chaos that had ruled China for centuries: a chaos of robber gangs looting—and draining—the productive elements of the country.

A mixed economy is rule by pressure groups. It is an amoral, institutionalized civil war of special interests and lobbies, all fighting to seize a momentary control of the legislative machinery, to extort some special privilege at one another's expense by an act of government—*i.e.*, by force. In the absence of individual rights, in the absence of any moral or legal principles, a mixed economy's only hope to preserve its precarious semblance of order, to restrain the savage, desperately rapacious groups it itself has created, and to prevent the legalized plunder from running over into plain, unlegalized looting of all by all—is *compromise;* compromise on everything and in every realm—material, spiritual, intellectual—so that no group would step over the line by demanding too much and topple the whole rotted structure. If the game is to continue, nothing can be permitted to remain firm, solid, absolute, untouchable; everything (and everyone) has to be fluid, flexible, indeterminate, approximate. By what standard are anyone's actions to be guided? By the expediency of any immediate moment.

The only danger, to a mixed economy, is any not-to-be-compromised value, virtue, or idea. The only threat is any uncompromising person, group, or movement. The only enemy is integrity.

It is unnecessary to point out who will be the steady winners and who the constant losers in a game of that kind.

It is also clear what sort of unity (of *consensus*) that game requires: the unity of a tacit agreement that anything goes, anything is for sale (or for "negotiation"), and the rest is up to the free-for-all of pressuring, lobbying, manipulating, favor-swapping, public-relation'ing, give-and-taking, double-crossing, begging, bribing, betraying—and chance, the blind chance of a war in which the prize is the privilege of using legal armed force against legally disarmed victims.

Observe that this type of prize establishes one basic interest held in common by all the players: the desire to have a strong government—a government of unlimited power, strong enough to let the winners and would-be winners get away with whatever they're seeking; a government uncommitted to any policy, unrestrained by any ideology, a government that hoards an ever-growing power, power for power's sake—which means: for the sake and use of any "major" gang who might seize it momentarily to ram their particular piece of legislation down the country's throat. Observe, therefore, that the doctrine of "compromise" and "moderation" applies to everything except one issue: any suggestion to limit the power of the government.

Observe the torrents of vilification, abuse, and hysterical hatred unleashed by the "moderates" against any advocate of freedom, *i.e.*, of capitalism. Observe that such designations as "extreme middle" or "militant middle" are being used by people seriously and self-righteously. Observe the inordinately vicious intensity of the smear-campaign against Senator Goldwater, which had the overtones of panic: the panic of the "moderates," the "vital-centrists," the "middle-of-the-roaders" in the face of the possibility that a real, pro-capitalism movement might put an end to their game. A movement, incidentally, which does not exist, as yet, since Senator Goldwater was not an advocate of capitalism—and since his meaningless, unphilosophical, unintellectual campaign has contributed to the entrenchment of the consensus-advocates. But what is significant here is the nature of their panic: it gave us a glimpse of their vaunted "moderation," their "democratic" respect for the people's choices and their tolerance of disagreements or opposition.

In a letter to *The New York Times* (June 23, 1964), an assistant professor of political science, fearing Goldwater's nomination, wrote as follows:

> The real danger lies in the divisive campaign which his nomination would provoke. . . . The result of a Goldwater candidacy would be a divided and embittered electorate. . . . To be effective, American government requires a high degree of consensus and bipartisanship on basic issues. . . .

When and *by whom* has statism been accepted as the basic principle of America—and as a principle which should now be placed beyond debate or dissension, so that no basic issues are to be raised any longer? Isn't that the formula of a one-party government? The professor did not specify.

Another letter-writer in *The New York Times* (June 24, 1964), identified in print as a "Liberal Democrat," went a little farther.

> Let the American people choose in November. If they choose overwhelmingly for Lyndon Johnson and the Democrats, then once and for all the Federal Government can get on, with no excuses, with the job millions of Negroes, unemployed, aged, sick and otherwise hand-

icapped persons expect it to do—to say nothing of our overseas commitments.

If the people choose Goldwater, then it would seem the nation was hardly worth saving after all.

Woodrow Wilson once said that there is such a thing as being too proud to fight; then he had to go to war. Once and for all let us have it out, while the battle yet can be fought with ballots instead of bullets.

Does this gentleman mean that if we don't vote his way, he will resort to bullets? Your guess is as good as mine.

The New York Times, which had been a conspicuous advocate of "Government by Consensus," said some curious things in its comment on President Johnson's victory. Its editorial of November 8, 1964, stated:

No matter how massive the electoral victory—and it was massive—the Administration cannot merely ride the crest of the popular wave rolling along on a sea of platitudinous generalizations and euphoric promises . . . now that it has a broad popular mandate, it has the moral as well as the political obligation not to try to be all things to all men but to settle down to a hard, concrete, purposeful course of action.

What kind of purposeful action? If the voters were offered nothing but "platitudinous generalizations and euphoric promises," how can their vote be taken as a "broad popular mandate"? A mandate for an *unnamed* purpose? A political blank check? And if Mr. Johnson did win a massive victory by trying "to be all things to all men," then which things is he now expected to be, which voters is he to disappoint or betray—and what becomes of the broad popular consensus?

Morally and philosophically, that editorial is highly dubious and contradictory. But it becomes clear and consistent in the context of a mixed economy's anti-ideology. The president of a mixed economy is not expected to have a specific program or policy. *A blank check on power* is all that he asks the voters to give him. Thereafter, it's up to the pressure-group game, which everybody is supposed to understand and endorse, but never mention. Which things he will be to which men depends on the chances of the game—and on the "major segments of the population." His job is only to hold the power—and to dispense the favors.

In the 1930's, the "liberals" had a program of broad social reforms and a crusading spirit, they advocated a planned society, they talked in terms of abstract principles, they propounded theories of a predominantly socialistic nature—and most of them were touchy about the accusation that they were enlarging the government's power; most of them were assuring their opponents that government power was only a temporary means to an end—a "noble end," the liberation of the individual from his bondage to material needs.

Today, nobody talks of a planned society in the "liberal" camp; long-range programs, theories, principles, abstractions, and "noble ends" are not fashionable any longer. Modern "liberals" deride any political concern with such large-scale matters as an entire society or an economy as a whole; they concern themselves with single, concrete-bound, range-of-the-moment projects and demands, without regard to cost, context, or consequences. "Pragmatic"—*not* "idealistic"—is their favorite adjective when they are called upon to justify their "stance," as they call it, not "stand." They are militantly opposed to political philosophy; they denounce political concepts as "tags," "labels," "myths," "illusions"—and resist any attempt to "label"—*i.e.*, to *identify*—their own views. They are belligerently anti-theoretical and—with a faded mantle of intellectuality still clinging to their shoulders—they are anti-intellectual. The only remnant of their former "idealism" is a tired, cynical, ritualistic quoting of shopworn "humanitarian" slogans, when the occasion demands it.

Cynicism, uncertainty, and fear are the insignia of the culture which they are still dominating by default. And the only thing that has not rusted in their ideological equipment, but has grown savagely brighter and clearer through the years, is their lust for power—for an autocratic, statist, totalitarian government power. It is not a crusading brightness, it is not the lust of a fanatic with a mission—it is more like the glassy-eyed brightness of a somnambulist whose stuporous despair has long since swallowed the memory of his purpose, but who still clings to his mystic weapon in the stubborn belief that "there ought to be a law," that everything will be all right if only somebody will pass a law, that every problem can be solved by the magic power of brute force. . . .

Such is the present intellectual state and ideological trend of our culture.

Now I shall ask you to consider the question I raised at the beginning of this discussion: Which of these two variants of statism are we moving toward: socialism or fascism?

Let me submit in evidence, as part of the answer, a quotation from an editorial that appeared in the *Washington Star* (October 1964). It is an eloquent mixture of truth and

misinformation, and a typical example of the state of today's
political knowledge:

> Socialism is quite simply the state ownership of the
> means of production. This has never been proposed by
> a major party candidate for the Presidency and is not
> now proposed by Lyndon Johnson. [*True.*]
>
> There is, however, a whole series of American legis-
> lative acts that increase either government regulation of
> private business or government responsibility for indi-
> vidual welfare. [*True.*] It is to such legislation that
> warning cries of "socialism!" refer.
>
> Besides the Constitutional provision for Federal reg-
> ulation of interstate commerce, such "intrusion" of
> government into the market-place begins with the anti-
> trust laws. [*Very true.*] To them we owe the continued
> existence of competitive capitalism and the non-arrival
> of cartel capitalism. [*Untrue.*] Inasmuch as socialism is
> the product, one way or another, of cartel capitalism
> [*untrue*], it may reasonably be said that such govern-
> ment interference with business has in fact prevented
> socialism. [*Worse than untrue.*]
>
> As to welfare legislation, it is still light years away
> from the "cradle to grave" security sponsored by con-
> temporary socialism. [*Not quite true.*] It seems much
> more like ordinary human concern for human distress
> than like an ideological program of any kind. [*The last
> part of this sentence is true: it is not an ideological
> program. As to the first part, ordinary human concern
> for human distress does not manifest itself ordinarily in
> the form of a gun aimed at the wallets and earnings of
> one's neighbors.*]

This editorial did not mention, of course, that a system in
which the government does *not* nationalize the means of
production, but assumes total control over the economy is
fascism.

It is true that the welfare-statists are not socialists, that
they never advocated or intended the socialization of private
property, that they want to "preserve" private property—
with government control of its use and disposal. But *that* is
the fundamental characteristic of fascism.

Here is another piece of evidence. This one is less crudely
naive than the first and much more insidiously wrong. This is
from a letter to *The New York Times* (November 1, 1964),
written by an assistant professor of economics:

> Viewed by almost every yardstick, the United States

today is more committed to private enterprise than probably any other industrial country and is not even remotely approaching a socialist system. As the term is understood by students of comparative economic systems and others who do not use it loosely, socialism is identified with extensive nationalization, a dominant public sector, a strong cooperative movement, egalitarian income distribution, a total welfare state and central planning.

In the United States not only has there been no nationalization, but Government concerns have been turned over to private enterprise. . . .

Income distribution in this country is one of the most unequal among the developed nations, and tax cuts and tax loopholes have blunted the moderate progressivity of our tax structure. Thirty years after the New Deal, the United States has a very limited welfare state, compared with the comprehensive social security and public housing schemes in many European countries.

By no stretch of the imagination is the real issue in this campaign a choice between capitalism and socialism or between a free and a planned economy. The issue is about two differing concepts of the role of government within the framework of an essentially private enterprise system.

The role of government in a private enterprise system is that of a policeman who protects man's individual rights (including property rights) by protecting men from physical force; in a free economy, the government does not control, regulate, coerce, or interfere with men's economic activities.

I do not know the political views of the writer of that letter; he may be a "liberal" or he may be an alleged defender of capitalism. But if he is this last, then I must point out that such views as his—which are shared by many "conservatives"—are more damaging and derogatory to capitalism than the ideas of its avowed enemies.

Such "conservatives" regard capitalism as a system compatible with government controls, and thus help to spread the most dangerous misconceptions. While full, laissez-faire capitalism has not yet existed anywhere, while some (unnecessary) government controls were allowed to dilute and undercut the original American system (more through error than through theoretical intention)—such controls were minor impediments, the mixed economies of the nineteenth century were predominantly free, and it is this unprecedented freedom that brought about mankind's unprecedented progress. The principles, the theory, and the actual practice of capitalism rest on a free, unregulated market, as the history of the last two centuries has amply demonstrated. No defender of capitalism can permit himself to ignore the exact meaning of the term "laissez-faire"—and of the term "mixed economy," which clearly indicates the two opposite elements involved in the mixture: the element of economic freedom, which is capitalism, and the element of government controls, which is statism.

An insistent campaign has been going on for years to make us accept the Marxist view that all governments are tools of economic class interests and that capitalism is not a free economy, but a system of government controls serving some privileged class. The purpose of that campaign is to distort economics, rewrite history, and obliterate the existence and the possibility of a free country and an uncontrolled economy. Since a system of nominal private property ruled by government controls is *not* capitalism, but *fascism,* the only choice this obliteration would leave us is the choice between fascism and socialism (or communism)—which all the statists in the world, of all varieties, degrees, and denominations, are struggling frantically to make us believe. (The destruction of freedom is their common goal, after which they hope to fight one another for power.)

It is thus that the views of that professor and of many "conservatives" lend credence and support to the vicious leftist propaganda which equates capitalism with fascism.

But there is a bitter kind of justice in the logic of events. That propaganda is having an effect which may be advantageous to the communists, but which is the opposite of the effect intended by the "liberals," the welfare-statists, the socialists, who share the guilt of spreading it: instead of smearing capitalism, that propaganda has succeeded in whitewashing and disguising fascism.

In this country, few people care to advocate, to defend, or even to understand capitalism; yet fewer still wish to give up its advantages. So if they are told that capitalism is compatible with controls, with the particular controls which further their particular interests—be it government handouts, or minimum wages, or price-supports, or subsidies, or antitrust laws, or censorship of dirty movies—they will go along with such programs, in the comforting belief that the results will be nothing worse than a "modified" capitalism. And thus a country which does abhor fascism is moving by imperceptible degrees—through ignorance, confusion, evasion, moral cowardice, and intellectual default—not toward socialism or any mawkish altruistic ideal, but toward a plain, brutal, predatory, power-grubbing, *de facto* fascism.

No, we have not reached that stage. But we are certainly *not* "an essentially private enterprise system" any longer. At present, we are a disintegrating, unsound, precariously unstable mixed economy—a random, mongrel mixture of socialistic schemes, communistic influences, fascist controls, and shrinking remnants of capitalism still paying the costs of it all—the total of it rolling in the direction of a fascist state.

Consider our present Administration. I don't think I'll be accused of unfairness if I say that President Johnson is *not* a philosophical thinker. No, he is not a fascist, he is not a socialist, he is not a pro-capitalist. Ideologically, he is not anything in particular. Judging by his past record and by the consensus of his own supporters, the concept of an *ideology* is not applicable in his case. He is a *politician*—a very dangerous, yet very appropriate phenomenon in our present state. He is an almost fiction-like, archetypical embodiment of the perfect leader of a mixed economy: a man who enjoys power for power's sake, who is expert at the game of manipulating pressure groups, of playing them all against one another, who loves the process of dispensing smiles, frowns, and favors, particularly *sudden* favors, and whose vision does not extend beyond the range of the next election.

Neither President Johnson nor any of today's prominent groups would advocate the socialization of industry. Like his modern predecessors in office, Mr. Johnson knows that businessmen are the milch-cows of a mixed economy, and he does not want to destroy them, he wants them to prosper and to feed his welfare projects (which the next election requires), while they, the businessmen, are eating out of his hand, as they seem to be anxiously eager to do. The business lobby is certain to get its fair share of influence and of recognition—just like the labor lobby or the farm lobby or the lobby of any "major segment"—on his own terms. He will be particularly adept at the task of creating and encouraging the type of businessmen whom I call "the aristocracy of pull." This is not a socialistic pattern; it is the typical pattern of fascism.

The political, intellectual, and *moral* meaning of Mr. Johnson's policy toward businessmen was summed up eloquently in an article in *The New York Times* of January 4, 1965:

> Mr. Johnson is an out-and-out Keynesian in his assiduous wooing of the business community. Unlike President Roosevelt, who delighted in attacking businessmen until World War II forced him into a reluctant truce, and President Kennedy, who also incurred busi-

ness hostility, President Johnson has worked long and hard to get businessmen to join ranks in a national consensus for his programs.

This campaign may perturb many Keynesians, but it is pure Keynes. Indeed, Lord Keynes, who once was regarded as a dangerous and Machiavellian figure by American businessmen, made specific suggestions for improving relations between the President and the business community.

He set down his views in 1938 in a letter to President Roosevelt, who was running into renewed criticism from businessmen following the recession that took place the previous year. Lord Keynes, who always sought to transform capitalism in order to save it, recognized the importance of business confidence and tried to convince Mr. Roosevelt to repair the damage that had been done.

He advised the President that businessmen were not politicians and did not respond to the same treatment. They are, he wrote "much milder than politicians, at the same time allured and terrified by the glare of publicity, easily persuaded to be 'patriots,' perplexed, bemused, indeed terrified, yet only too anxious to take a cheerful view, vain perhaps but very unsure of themselves, pathetically responsive to a kind word. . . ."

He was confident that Mr. Roosevelt could tame them and make them do his bidding, provided he followed some simple Keynesian rules.

"You could do anything you liked with them," the letter continued, "if you would treat them (even the big ones), not as wolves and tigers, but as domestic animals by nature, even though they have been badly brought up and not trained as you would wish."

President Roosevelt ignored his advice. So, apparently, did President Kennedy. But President Johnson seems to have got the message. . . . By kind words and frequent pats on the head, he had had the business community eating out of his hand.

Mr. Johnson appears to agree with Lord Keynes's view that there is little to be gained by carrying on a feud with businessmen. As he put it, "If you work them into the surly, obstinate, terrified mood of which domestic animals, wrongly handled, are capable, the nation's burden will not get carried to market; and in the end, public opinion will veer their way."

The view of businessmen as *"domestic animals"* who carry "the nation's burden" and who must be "trained" by the President "to do his bidding" is certainly not a view compatible with capitalism. It is not a view applicable to socialism, since there are no businessmen in a socialist state. It is a view that expresses the economic essence of fascism, of the relationship between business and government in a fascist state.

No matter what the verbal camouflage, such is the actual meaning of any variant of *"transformed"* (or "modified" or "modernized" or "humanized") capitalism. In all such doctrines, the "humanization" consists of turning some members of society (the most productive ones) into beasts of burden.

The formula by which the sacrificial animals are to be fooled and tamed is being repeated today with growing insistence and frequency: businessmen, it is said, must regard the government, not as an enemy, but as a "partner." The notion of a "partnership" between a private group and public officials, between business and government, between production and force, is a linguistic corruption (an "anti-concept") typical of a fascist ideology—an ideology that regards force as the basic element and ultimate arbiter in all human relationships.

"Partnership" is an indecent euphemism for "government control." There can be no partnership between armed bureaucrats and defenseless private citizens who have no choice but to obey. What chance would you have against a "partner" whose *arbitrary* word is law, who may give you a hearing (if your pressure group is big enough), but who will play favorites and bargain your interests away, who will always have the last word and the legal "right" to enforce it on you at the point of a gun, holding your property, your work, your future, your life in his power? Is *that* the meaning of "partnership"?[2]

But there are men who may find such a prospect attractive; they exist among businessmen as among every other group or profession: the men who dread the competition of a free market and would welcome an armed "partner" to extort special advantages over their abler competitors; men who seek to rise, not by merit but by pull, men who are willing and eager to live not by right, but by favor. Among businessmen, this type of mentality was responsible for the passage of the antitrust laws and is still supporting them today.

[2] Ayn Rand, *The Fascist New Frontier,* New York: Nathaniel Branden Institute, 1963, p. 8.

A substantial number of Republican businessmen switched to the side of Mr. Johnson in the last election. Here are some interesting observations on this subject, from a survey by *The New York Times* (September 16, 1964):

> Interviews in five cities in the industrial Northeast and Midwest disclose striking differences in political outlook between officials of large corporations and men who operate smaller businesses. . . . The business executives who expect to cast the first Democratic Presidential vote of their lives are nearly all affiliated with large companies. . . . There is more support for President Johnson among business executives who are in their 40's and 50's than there is among either older or younger businessmen. . . . Many businessmen in their 40's and 50's say they find relatively little shifting toward support of Mr. Johnson on the part of younger business executives. Interviews with those in their 30's confirm this. . . . The younger executives themselves speak with pride of their generation as the one that interrupted and reversed the trend toward more liberalism in younger persons. . . . It is on the issue of Government deficits that the division of opinion between small and large businessmen emerges most dramatically. Officials of giant corporations have a far greater tendency to accept the idea that budget deficits are sometimes necessary and even desirable. The typical small businessman, however, reserves a very special scorn for deficit spending. . . .

This gives us an indication of who are the vested interests in a mixed economy—and what such an economy does to the beginners or the young.

An essential aspect of the socialistically inclined mentality is the desire to obliterate the difference between the earned and the unearned, and, therefore, to permit no differentiation between such businessmen as Hank Rearden and Orren Boyle. To a concrete-bound, range-of-the-moment, primitive socialist mentality—a mentality that clamors for a "redistribution of wealth" without any concern for the origin of wealth—the enemy is all those who are rich, regardless of the source of their riches. Such mentalities, those aging, graying "liberals," who had been the "idealists" of the 30's, are clinging desperately to the illusion that we are moving toward some sort of socialist state inimical to the rich and beneficial to the poor—while frantically evading the spectacle of *what kind of rich* are being destroyed and what kind are flourish-

ing under the system they, the "liberals," have established.
The grim joke is on them: their alleged "ideals" have paved
the way, not toward socialism, but toward fascism. The
collector of their efforts is not the helplessly, brainlessly
virtuous "little man" of their flat-footed imagination and
shopworn fiction, but the worst type of predatory rich, the
rich-by-force, the rich-by-political-privilege, the type who has
no chance under capitalism, but who is always there to cash
in on every collectivist "noble experiment."

It is the creators of wealth, the Hank Reardens, who are
destroyed under any form of statism—socialist, communist,
or fascist; it is the parasites, the Orren Boyles, who are the
privileged "elite" and the profiteers of statism, particularly of
fascism. (The special profiteers of socialism are the James
Taggarts; of communism—the Floyd Ferrises.) The same is
true of their psychological counterparts among the poor and
among the men of all the economic levels in-between.

The particular form of economic organization, which is
becoming more and more apparent in this country, as an
outgrowth of the power of pressure groups, is one of the
worst variants of statism: *guild socialism.* Guild socialism
robs the talented young of their future—by freezing men into
professional castes under rigid rules. It represents an open
embodiment of the basic motive of most statists, though they
usually prefer not to confess it: the entrenchment and protection of mediocrity from abler competitors, the shackling of
the men of superior ability down to the mean average of
their professions. That theory is not too popular among
socialists (though it has its advocates)—but the most famous
instance of its large-scale practice was Fascist Italy.

In the 1930's, a few perceptive men said that Roosevelt's
New Deal was a form of guild socialism and that it was
closer to Mussolini's system than to any other. They were
ignored. Today, the evidence is unmistakable.

It was also said that if fascism ever came to the United
States, it would come disguised as socialism. In this connection, I recommend that you read or re-read Sinclair
Lewis' *It Can't Happen Here*—with special reference to the
character, style, and ideology of Berzelius Windrip, the fascist leader.

Now let me mention, and answer, some of the standard
objections by which today's "liberals" attempt to camouflage
(to differentiate from fascism) the nature of the system they
are supporting.

"Fascism requires one-party rule." What will the notion of "Government by Consensus" amount to in practice?

"Fascism's goal is the conquest of the world." What is the goal of those global-minded, bipartisan champions of the United Nations? And, if they reach it, what positions do they expect to acquire in the power-structure of "One World"?

"Fascism preaches racism." Not necessarily. Hitler's Germany did; Mussolini's Italy did not.

"Fascism is opposed to the welfare state." Check your premises and your history books. The father and originator of the welfare state, the man who put into practice the notion of buying the loyalty of some groups with money extorted from others, was Bismarck—the political ancestor of Hitler. Let me remind you that the full title of the Nazi Party was: the National Socialist Workers Party of Germany.

Let me remind you also of some excerpts from the political program of that party, adopted in Munich, on February 24, 1920:

We ask that the government undertake the obligation above all of providing citizens with adequate opportunity for employment and earning a living.

The activities of the individual must not be allowed to clash with the interests of the community, but must take place within its confines and be for the good of all. Therefore, we demand: . . . *an end to the power of the financial interests.*

We demand profit sharing in big business.

We demand a broad extension of care for the aged.

We demand . . . the greatest possible consideration of small business in the purchases of the national, state, and municipal governments.

In order to make possible to every capable and industrious [citizen] the attainment of higher education and thus the achievement of a post of leadership, the government must provide an all-around enlargement of our entire system of public education. . . . We demand the education at government expense of gifted children of poor parents. . . .

The government must undertake the improvement of public health—by protecting mother and child, by prohibiting child labor . . . by the greatest possible support for all clubs concerned with the physical education of youth.

[We] combat the ... materialistic spirit within and without us, and are convinced that a permanent recovery of our people can only proceed from within on the foundation of *The Common Good Before the Individual Good*.[3]

There is, however, one difference between the type of fascism toward which we are drifting, and the type that ravaged European countries: ours is not a militant kind of fascism, not an organized movement of shrill demagogues, bloody thugs, hysterical third-rate intellectuals, and juvenile delinquents—ours is a tired, worn, cynical fascism, fascism by default, not like a flaming disaster, but more like the quiet collapse of a lethargic body slowly eaten by internal corruption.

Did it have to happen? No. Can it still be averted? Yes.

If you doubt the power of philosophy to set the course and shape the destiny of human societies, observe that our mixed economy is the literal, faithfully carried-out product of *Pragmatism*—and of the generation brought up under its influence. Pragmatism is the philosophy which holds that there is no objective reality or permanent truth, that there are no absolute principles, no valid abstractions, no firm concepts, that anything may be tried by rule-of-thumb, that objectivity consists of collective subjectivism, that whatever people wish to be true, *is* true, whatever people wish to exist, *does* exist—provided a *consensus* says so.

If you want to avert the final disaster, it is this type of thinking—every one of those propositions and all of them—that you must face, grasp, and reject. Then you will have grasped the connection of philosophy to politics and to the daily events of your life. Then you will have learned that no society is better than its philosophical foundation. And then—to paraphrase John Galt—you will be ready, not to *return* to capitalism, but to *discover* it.

---

[3] *Der Nationalsozialismus Dokumente 1933–1945*, edited by Walther Hofer, Frankfurt am Main: Fischer Bucherei, 1957, pp. 29–31.

For many more quotations of this kind, revealing the altruist-collectivist base of the Nazi and fascist ideology, I refer you to *The Fascist New Frontier*.

21. THE WRECKAGE OF THE CONSENSUS

BY AYN RAND

Two years ago, on April 18, 1965, I spoke at this Forum on the subject of "The New Fascism: Rule by Consensus." I said: "The clue to the core, essence, motive, and real meaning of the doctrine of 'Government by Consensus' [is] the cult of *compromise*. Compromise is the pre-condition, the necessity, the imperative of a mixed economy. The 'consensus' doctrine is an attempt to translate the brute facts of a mixed economy into an ideological—or anti-ideological—system and to provide them with a semblance of justification." The brute facts of a mixed economy are gang-rule, *i.e.*, a scramble for power by various pressure groups—without any moral or political principles, without any program, direction, purpose, or long-range goal—with the tacit belief in rule by force, as their only common denominator, and, unless the trend is changed, a fascist state as the ultimate result.

In September of 1965, writing in *The Objectivist Newsletter,* I said: "Contrary to the fanatical belief of its advocates, compromise does not satisfy, but *dissatisfies* everyone; it does not lead to general fulfillment, but to general frustration; those who try to be all things to all men, end up by not being anything to anyone."

It is startling to observe how rapidly this principle took effect—in an age that takes no cognizance of principles.

Where is President Johnson's consensus today? And where, politically, is President Johnson? To descend—in two years, in an era of seeming prosperity, without the push of any obvious national disaster—to descend from the height of a popular landslide to the status of a liability to his own party in the elections of 1966, is a feat that should give pause to anyone concerned with modern politics.

Lecture given at The Ford Hall Forum, Boston, on April 16, 1967. Published in *The Objectivist,* April and May, 1967.

If there were any way to make compromise work, President Johnson is the man who would have done it. He was an expert at the game of manipulating pressure groups—a game that consists of making promises and friends, and keeping the second, but not the first. His skill as a manipulator was the one characteristic that his "public-image builders" were selling us at the height of his popularity. If *he* could not make it, no amateur can.

The practical efficacy of compromise is the first premise that Johnson's history should prompt people to check. And, I believe, a great many people *are* checking it. People, but not Republicans—or, at least, not all of them. Not those who are now pushing an unformed, soft-shelled thing like Romney to succeed where a pro has failed.

What are we left with, now that the consensus has collapsed? Nothing but the open spectacle of a mixed economy's intellectual and moral bankruptcy, the random wreckage of its naked mechanism, with the screeching of its gears as the only sound in our public silence—the sound of crude, range-of-the-moment demands by pressure groups who have abandoned even the pretense at any political ideals or moral justification.

The consensus-doctrine was a disguise, a shoddy, cheese-cloth one, but still a disguise to give a semblance of theoretical status to the practice of plain gang warfare. Today, even the cheesecloth is gone, leaving the anti-ideology to function in the open, more brazenly than ever.

A political ideology is a set of principles aimed at establishing or maintaining a certain social system; it is a program of long-range action, with the principles serving to unify and integrate particular steps into a consistent course. It is only by means of principles that men can project the future and choose their actions accordingly.

Anti-ideology consists of the attempts to shrink men's minds down to the range of the immediate moment, without regard to past or future, without context or memory—above all, without memory, so that contradictions cannot be detected, and errors or disasters can be blamed on the victims.

In anti-ideological practice, principles are used implicitly and are relied upon to disarm the opposition, but are never acknowledged, and are switched at will, when it suits the purpose of the moment. Whose purpose? The gang's. Thus men's moral criterion becomes, not "my view of the good—or of the right—or of the truth," but "my *gang*, right or wrong."

This is what makes today's public issues and discussions so sickeningly false and futile. Most issues rest on so many wrong premises and carry so many contradictions that instead of the question: "Who is right?" one is constantly and tacitly confronted with the question: "Which gang do you want to support?"

For example, consider the issue of the war in Vietnam.

Everything is wrong about that hideous mess (but not for the reasons which are shouted most loudly), starting from its designation. A "cold war" is a brazen contradiction in terms. It is not very "cold" for the American soldiers killed on battlefields, nor for their families, nor for any of us.

A "cold war" is a typically Hegelian term. It rests on the premise that A is non-A, that things are not what they are, so long as we don't name them; or, practically speaking, things are what our leaders tell us they are—and, unless they tell us, we have no way of knowing. This sort of epistemology is not working too well even in regard to the ignorant hordes of Russian peasants. That this should be attempted in regard to American citizens is, perhaps, the most disgraceful symptom of our cultural disintegration.

When men are being killed by a foreign army in military action, it is a *war*, a whole war and nothing but a war—regardless of what temperature anyone chooses to ascribe to it.

But observe what advantages the Hegelian terminology offers to the leaders of a mixed economy. When a country is at war, it has to use all of its power to fight and win as fast as possible. It cannot fight and non-fight at the same time. It cannot send its soldiers to die as cannon fodder, forbidding them to win. When a country is at war, its leaders cannot prattle about "cultural exchanges" and about "building bridges" to the enemy, as our leaders are doing—*trade* bridges to bolster the enemy's economy and enable it to produce the planes and guns which are killing our own soldiers.

A country at war often resorts to smearing its enemy by spreading atrocity stories—a practice which a free, civilized country need not and should not resort to. A civilized country, with a free press, can let the facts speak for themselves. But what is the moral-intellectual state of a country that spreads smears and atrocity stories about *itself* and ignores or suppresses the facts known about the enemy's atrocities? What is the moral-intellectual state of a country that permits its citizens to stage parades carrying the enemy's—the Vietcong's—flag? Or to collect funds for the enemy on university campuses? What makes this possible? The claim that we are not, allegedly, at war—only at "cold war."

A country's morale is crucially important, in wartime. In World War II, the British Lord Haw-Haw was, properly, regarded as a traitor—for the crime of trying to undercut the British soldiers' morale by broadcasting scare stories about Nazi Germany's invincible power. In a "cold war," such as we have today, Lord Haw-Haw's job is performed by our own public leaders. The sickening scare stories about "escalation," about our fear of war with China, would be morally shameful if indulged in by the leaders of Monaco or Luxemburg. When they come from the leaders of the most powerful country on earth, "shameful" is not an adequate word to describe their moral meaning.

If a country knows that it cannot fight another country, *it does not undertake to fight*. If a country is actually weak, it does not go into battle screaming: "Please don't take me seriously—I won't go very far!" It does not proclaim its fear as proof of its desire for peace.

There is only one sense in which that ghastly phenomenon has to be classified as a non-war: the United States has nothing to gain from it. Wars are the second greatest evil that human societies can perpetrate. (The first is dictatorship, the enslavement of their own citizens, which is the cause of wars.) When a nation resorts to war, it has some purpose, rightly or wrongly, something to fight for—and the only justifiable purpose is self-defense. If you want to see the ultimate, suicidal extreme of altruism, on an international scale, observe the war in Vietnam—a war in which American soldiers are dying for no purpose whatever.

This is the ugliest evil of the Vietnam war, that *it does not serve any national interest of the United States*—that it is a pure instance of blind, senseless, altruistic, self-sacrificial slaughter. *This* is the evil—not the revolting stuff that the Vietniks are howling about.

None of us knows *why* we are in that war, *how* we got in, or *what* will take us out. Whenever our public leaders attempt to explain it to us, they make the mystery greater. They tell us simultaneously that we are fighting for the interests of the United States—and that the United States has no "selfish" interests in that war. They tell us that communism is the enemy—and they attack, denounce, and smear any anti-communists in this country. They tell us that the spread of communism must be contained in Asia—but not in Africa. They tell us that communist aggression must be resisted in Vietnam—but not in Europe. They tell us that we must defend the freedom of South Vietnam—but not the freedom of East Germany, Poland, Hungary, Latvia, Czechoslovakia, Yugoslavia, Katanga, etc. They tell us that North Vietnam is a threat to our national security—but Cuba is not. They tell us that we must defend South Vietnam's right to hold a "democratic" election, and to vote itself into communism, if it wishes, provided it does so by vote—which means that we are not fighting for any political ideal or any principle of justice, but only for unlimited majority rule, and that the goal for which American soldiers are dying is to be determined by somebody else's vote. They tell us also that we must force South Vietnam to accept communists into a coalition government—a process by which we delivered China to the communists, which fact we must not mention. They tell us that we must defend South Vietnam's right to "national self-determination"—and that anyone upholding the national sovereignty of the United States is an isolationist, that nationalism is evil, that the globe is our homeland and we must be prepared to die for any part of it, except the continent of North America.

Is it any wonder that no one believes the pronouncements of our public leaders any longer, neither the American people nor foreign nations? Our anti-ideologists are beginning to worry about this problem. But—in their typical style—they do not say that somebody is lying, they say that there exists a "credibility gap."

Observe the terms in which the war in Vietnam is discussed. There are no stated goals, no intellectual issues. But there are, apparently, two opposing sides which are designated, not by any specific ideological concepts, but by *images,* which is appropriate to the primitive epistemology of savages: the "hawks" and the "doves." But the "hawks" are cooing apologetically, and the "doves" are snarling their heads off.

The same groups that coined the term "isolationist" in World War II—to designate anyone who held that the internal affairs of other countries are not the responsibility of the United States—these same groups are screaming that the United States has no right to interfere in the internal affairs of Vietnam.

Nobody has proposed a goal which, if achieved, would terminate that war—except President Johnson, who has offered a billion dollars as the price of peace; *not* a billion dollars paid *to* us, but a billion dollars paid *by* us for the economic development of Vietnam; which means that we are fighting for the privilege of turning every American taxpayer into a serf laboring part of his time for the benefit of his Vietnamese masters. But, demonstrating that irrationality is not a monopoly of the United States, North Vietnam has rejected that offer.

No, there is no proper solution for the war in Vietnam: it is a war we should never have entered. To continue it, is senseless—to withdraw from it, would be one more act of appeasement on our long, shameful record. The ultimate result of appeasement is a world war, as demonstrated by World War II; in today's context, it may mean a nuclear world war.

That we let ourselves be trapped into a situation of that kind, is the consequence of fifty years of a suicidal foreign policy. One cannot correct a consequence without correcting its cause; if such disasters could be solved "pragmatically," *i.e.*, out of context, on the spur and range of the moment, a nation would not need any foreign policy. And *this* is an example of why we do need a policy based on long-range principles, *i.e.*, an *ideology*. But a revision of our foreign policy, from its basic premises on up, is what today's anti-ideologists dare not contemplate. The worse is its results, the louder our public leaders proclaim that our foreign policy is *bipartisan*.

A proper solution would be to elect statesmen—if such appeared—with a radically different foreign policy, a policy explicitly and proudly dedicated to the defense of America's rights and national self-interests, repudiating foreign aid and all forms of international self-immolation. On such a policy, we could withdraw from Vietnam at once—and the withdrawal would not be misunderstood by anyone, and the world would have a chance to achieve peace. But such statesmen do not exist at present. In today's conditions, the only alternative is to fight that war and win it as fast as possible—and thus gain time to develop new statesmen with a new foreign policy, before the old one pushes us into another "cold war," just as the "cold war" in Korea pushed us into Vietnam.

The institution that enables our leaders to indulge in such recklessly irresponsible ventures is the military draft.

The question of the draft is, perhaps, the most important single issue debated today. But the terms in which it is being debated are a sorry manifestation of our anti-ideological "mainstream."

Of all the statist violations of individual rights in a mixed economy, the military draft is the worst. It is an abrogation of rights. It negates man's fundamental right—the right to life—and establishes the fundamental principle of statism: that a man's life belongs to the state, and the state may claim it by compelling him to sacrifice it in battle. Once that principle is accepted, the rest is only a matter of time.

If the state may force a man to risk death or hideous maiming and crippling, in a war declared at the state's discretion, for a cause he may neither approve of nor even understand, if his consent is not required to send him into unspeakable martyrdom—then, in principle, *all* rights are negated in that state, and its government is not man's protector any longer. What else is there left to protect?

The most immoral contradiction—in the chaos of today's anti-ideological groups—is that of the so-called "conservatives," who posture as defenders of individual rights, particularly *property* rights, but uphold and advocate the draft. By what infernal evasion can they hope to justify the proposition that creatures who have no right to life, have the right to a bank account? A slightly higher—though not much higher—rung of hell should be reserved for those "liberals" who claim that man has the "right" to economic security, public housing, medical care, education, recreation, but no right to life, or: that man has the right to *livelihood*, but not to *life*.

One of the notions used by all sides to justify the draft, is that "rights impose obligations." Obligations, to whom?—and imposed, by whom? Ideologically, that notion is worse than the evil it attempts to justify: it implies that rights are a gift from the state, and that a man has to buy them by offering something (his life) in return. Logically, that notion is a contradiction: since the only proper function of a government is to protect man's rights, it cannot claim title to his life in exchange for that protection.

The only "obligation" involved in individual rights is an obligation imposed, not by the state, but by the nature of reality (*i.e.*, by the law of identity): *consistency*, which, in this case, means the obligation to respect the rights of others, if one wishes one's own rights to be recognized and protected.

Politically, the draft is clearly unconstitutional. No amount of rationalization, neither by the Supreme Court nor by private individuals, can alter the fact that it represents "involuntary servitude."

A *volunteer* army is the only proper, moral—and practical—way to defend a free country. Should a man volunteer to fight, if his country is attacked? Yes—if he values his own rights and freedom. A free (or even semi-free) country has never lacked volunteers in the face of foreign aggression. Many military authorities have testified that a volunteer army—an army of men who know what they are fighting for and why—is the best, most effective army, and that a drafted one is the least effective.

It is often asked: "But what if a country cannot find a sufficient number of volunteers?" Even so, this would not give the rest of the population a right to the lives of the country's young men. But, in fact, the lack of volunteers occurs for one of two reason: (1) If a country is demoralized by a corrupt, authoritarian government, its citizens will not volunteer to defend it. But neither will they fight for long, if drafted. For example, observe the literal disintegration of the Czarist Russian army in World War I. (2) If a country's government undertakes to fight a war for some reason other than self-defense, for a purpose which the citizens neither share nor understand, it will not find many volunteers. Thus a volunteer army is one of the best protectors of peace, not only against foreign aggression, but also against any warlike ideologies or projects on the part of a country's own government.

Not many men would volunteer for such wars as Korea or Vietnam. Without the power to draft, the makers of our foreign policy would not be able to embark on adventures of that kind. This is one of the best practical reasons for the abolition of the draft.

Consider another practical reason. The age of large, mass armies is past. A modern war is a war of *technology;* it requires a highly trained, scientific personnel, not hordes of passive, unthinking, bewildered men; it requires brains, not brawn—intelligence, not blind obedience. One can force men to die; one cannot force them to think. Observe that the more technological branches of our armed services—such as the Navy and the Air Force—do not accept draftees and are made up of volunteers. The draft, therefore, applies only to the least efficacious and—in today's conditions—the least essential part of our armed forces: the infantry. If so, then is national defense the main consideration of those who advocate and uphold the draft?

The practical question of the country's military protection is *not* the issue at stake; it is not the chief concern of the draft's supporters. Some of them may be motivated by routine, traditional notions and fears; but, on a national scale, there is a deeper motive involved.

When a vicious principle is accepted implicitly, it does not take long to become explicit: pressure groups are quick to find practical advantages in its logical implications. For instance, in World War II, the military draft was used as a justification for proposals to establish labor conscription—*i.e.,* compulsory labor service for the entire population, with the government empowered to assign anyone to any job of its choice. "If men can be drafted to die for their country," it was argued, "why can't they be drafted to work for their country?" Two bills embodying such proposals were introduced in Congress, but, fortunately, were defeated. The second of those bills had an interesting quirk: drafted labor, it proposed, would be paid a union scale of wages—in order not to undercut union scales—but, in "fairness" to the military draftees, the labor draftees would be given only the equivalent of army pay, and the rest of their wages would go to the government (!).

What political group, do you suppose, came up with a notion of this kind? Both bills were introduced by Republicans—and were defeated by organized labor, which was the only large economic group standing between us and a totalitarian state.

Now observe the terms in which the draft is being debated today. The main reason advanced for the continuation of the draft is not military, but financial (!). It is generally conceded that the draft is unnecessary, but, it is argued, a volunteer army would cost too much.

As matters stand, the army is one of the lowest paid groups in the country; a drafted soldier's pay, in cash or equivalent (*i.e.*, including room and board), amounts to about *one dollar* an hour. To attract volunteers, it would be necessary to offer higher pay and better conditions, thus making an army career comparable to the standards of the civilian labor market.

No exact estimates of the cost of a volunteer army have been offered, but the approximate estimates place it at about four billion dollars a year.

Hold this figure in mind. Hold it while you read about our national budget in the daily papers—and while you hold also, clearly and specifically, the image of what this figure would buy.

The years from about fifteen to twenty-five are the crucial formative years of a man's life. This is the time when he confirms his impressions of the world, of other men, of the society in which he is to live, when he acquires conscious convictions, defines his moral values, chooses his goals, and plans his future, developing or renouncing ambition. These are the years that mark him for life. And it is *these* years that an allegedly humanitarian society forces him to spend in terror—the terror of knowing that he can plan nothing and count on nothing, that any road he takes can be blocked at any moment by an unpredictable power, that, barring his vision of the future, there stands the gray shape of the barracks, and, perhaps, beyond it, death for some unknown reason in some alien jungle.

A pressure of that kind is devastating to a young man's psychology, if he grasps the issue consciously—and still worse, if he doesn't.

The first thing he is likely to give up, in either case, is his intellect: an intellect does not function on the premise of its own impotence. If he acquires the conviction that existence is hopeless, that his life is in the hands of some enormous, incomprehensible evil, if he develops a helpless, searing contempt for the hypocrisy of his elders, and a profound hatred for all mankind—if he seeks to escape from that inhuman psychological pressure by turning to the beatnik cult of the immediate moment, by screaming: "Now, now, now!" (he has nothing else but that *"now"*), or by dulling his terror and killing the last of his mind with LSD—don't blame him. Brothers, you asked for it!

. . *This* is what four billion dollars would buy—*this* is what it would spare him and every other young man in the country and every person who loves them. Remember down what drains our money is being poured today: according to the Federal budget for fiscal year 1968, we will spend 4.5 billion on foreign aid and allied projects, 5.3 billion on space programs, 11.3 billion on just one of the many, many departments dealing with public welfare—yet we claim that we cannot afford four billion dollars to save our youth from the agony of a mangling, brutalizing psychological torture.

But, of course, the real motive behind that social crime is not financial; the issue of costs is merely a rationalization. The real motive may be detected in the following statement made by Lieutenant General Lewis B. Hershey, Director of the Selective Service System, on June 24, 1966: "I am not concerned with the uncertainty involved in keeping our citizenry believing that they owe something to their country. There are too many, too many people that think individualism has to be completely recognized, even if the group rights go to the devil."

The same motive was made fully clear in a proposal which was advanced by Secretary of Defense Robert S. McNamara and is now being plugged with growing insistence by the press.

On May 18, 1966, Mr. McNamara said the following: "As matters stand, our present Selective system draws on only a minority of eligible young men. That is an inequity. It seems to me that we could move toward remedying that inequity by asking every young person in the United States to give two years of service to his country—whether in one of the military services, in the Peace Corps or in some other volunteer developmental work at home or abroad."

"Developmental" work—devoted to *whose* development?

Apparently, planting rice or digging ditches in Asia, Africa, and South America, constitutes service to the United States—but preparing oneself for a productive career, does not. Teaching our own illiterates in hillbilly regions or city slums, constitutes service to the United States—but going to college does not. Teaching retarded children to weave baskets, constitutes service to the United States—but acquiring a Ph.D. does not.

Isn't the unnamed principle clear? Developing yourself into a productive, ambitious, *independent* person, is not regarded as a value to the United States; turning yourself into an abject sacrificial animal, is.

This, I submit, is a moral obscenity.

Whatever country such a principle could apply to, it is *not* the United States. It is not even Soviet Russia—where they do destroy the minds of their youth, but not in so mawkishly, wantonly senseless a manner.

That proposal represents the naked essence of *altruism* in its pure and fully consistent form. It does not seek to sacrifice men for the alleged benefit of the state—it seeks to sacrifice them *for the sake of sacrifice.* It seeks to break man's spirit—to destroy his mind, his ambition, his self-esteem, his self-confidence, his *self,* during the very years when he is in the process of acquiring them.

Mr. McNamara's trial balloon did not go over too well, at first. There were outcries of protest and indignation, which compelled the government to issue a hasty disclaimer. "The Johnson Administration," said *The New York Times* of May 20, 1966, "quickly made it plain today that it had no plans to draft young Americans for civilian duty or to let such duty become an alternative to military service." The same news story said that "officials called upon to interpret his [McNamara's] words stressed that he had suggested 'asking' rather than 'compelling' young people to serve." Well, *I* want to stress that if a government intends to "ask" rather than "compel," it does not choose the Secretary of Defense to do the "asking," and he does not "ask" it in the context of a passage dealing with the military draft.

The suggestion of "voluntary service" under a threat to one's life, is *blackmail*—blackmail directed at the entire American youth—blackmail demanding their surrender into explicit serfdom.

After that initial suggestion—obviously, as an intermediary step, to "condition" the sacrificial animals—the statist-altruist gangs began to plug the notion of "voluntary" social service.

On September 14, 1966, James Reston of *The New York Times* quoted President Johnson as saying: "I hope to see a day when some form of voluntary service to the community and the nation and the world is as common in America as going to school; when no man has truly lived who only served himself."

The motivation of all this is obvious. The draft is not needed for military purposes, it is not needed for the protection of this country, but the statists are struggling not to relinquish the power it gave them and the unnamed principle (and precedent) it established—above all, not to relinquish the principle: that man's life belongs to the state.

This is the real issue—and the only issue—and there is no way to fight it or to achieve the abolition of the draft except by upholding the principle of man's right to his own life. There is no way to uphold that right without a full, consistent, moral-political ideology. But that is not the way the issue is now debated by the frantic anti-ideologists of all sides.

It is the "conservatives," the alleged defenders of freedom and capitalism, who should be opposing the draft. They are not; they are supporting it. Early in the presidential election campaign of 1964, Barry Goldwater made a vague suggestion favoring the abolition of the draft, which aroused the public's hopeful attention; he promptly dropped it, and devoted his campaign to denouncing the morals of Bobby Baker. Who brought the issue of the draft into public focus and debate, demanding its repeal? The extreme *left*—the Vietniks and Peaceniks.

In line with the anti-ideological methods of all other groups, the Vietniks—whose sympathies are on the side of Russia, China, and North Vietnam—are screaming against the draft in the name of their "individual rights"—*individual rights,* believe it or not. They are proclaiming their right to choose which war they'll fight in—while sympathizing with countries where the individual does not even have the right to choose and utter a thought of his own. What is still worse is the fact that they are the only group that even mentions individual rights (if newspaper reports are to be trusted).

But of all this anti-ideological mess, I would pick one small incident as, morally, the worst. I quote from *The New York Times* of February 6, 1967:

Leaders of 15 student organizations representing both political extremes as well as the center called today for the abolition of the draft and the encouragement of voluntary service in humanitarian pursuits. In a resolution ending a two-day conference on the draft and national service at the Shoreham Hotel [Washington, D.C.], the student leaders declared: "The present draft system with its inherent injustices is incompatible with traditional American principles of individual freedom within a democratic society, and for this reason the draft should be eliminated. An urgent need exists within our society for young people to become involved in the elimination of such social ills as ignorance, poverty, racial discrimination and war." Among those who signed the resolution were leading members of the leftwing Students for a Democratic Society, the rightwing Young Americans for Freedom, and the moderate Youth and College Division of the National Association for the Advancement of Colored People. . . . Although no unanimity on concrete recommendations was arrived at, Mr. Chickering [the sponsor of the conference] said he believed that most of the student leaders favored his proposal for the creation of a system of voluntary national service. Under this proposal . . . students at campuses throughout the country will be asked to fill out cards expressing their willingness to serve in humanitarian work.

(Observe the formulation "traditional American principles of individual freedom within a democratic society"—instead of "individual *right* to life." What is "individual freedom within a democratic society"? What is a "democratic society"? "Individual freedom" is not a primary political principle and cannot be defined, defended, or practiced without the primary principle of individual rights. And a "democratic society," *traditionally,* means: unlimited majority rule. This is an example of the method by which today's anti-ideologists are obliterating the concept of rights. Observe also that the leaders of the "conservative" Young Americans for Freedom signed a document of that kind.)

These are not men who are being whipped: these are men who take the lash obediently and whip themselves.

Politically, that proposal is much worse than the draft. The draft, at least, offers the excuse that one is serving one's own country in time of danger—and its political implications are diluted by a long historical tradition associated with patriotism. But if young men accept the belief that it is their duty to spend their irreplaceable formative years on growing rice and carrying bedpans—they're done for psychologically, and so is this country.

The same news story carried some shocking statistics on the attitude of college students at large. It quoted a poll conducted by the National Students Association at twenty-three campuses throughout the country. If that poll is to be trusted, "Approximately 75 per cent said they preferred the establishment of some means to allow work in the Peace Corps, the Teacher Corps or Volunteers in Service to America as an alternative to military service. About 90 per cent, however, said they believed that the Government has a right to conscript its citizens, and 68 per cent thought such conscription was necessary in periods other than those of a declared national emergency."

This is an example, on a grand scale, of what I call "the sanction of the victim." It is also an example of the fact that men cannot be enslaved politically until they have been disarmed *ideologically*. When they are so disarmed, it is the victims who take the lead in the process of their own destruction.

Such is the swamp of contradictions swallowing the two most immediately prominent issues of today—Vietnam and the draft. The same is true of all the other issues and pseudo-issues now clogging all the avenues of public communication. And, adding insult to injury, the anti-ideologists, who are responsible for it, are complaining about the public's lethargy.

Lethargy is only a precarious psychological cover for confusion, disgust, and despair.

The country at large is bitterly dissatisfied with the *status quo*, disillusioned with the stale slogans of welfare statism, and desperately seeking an alternative, *i.e.*, an intelligible program and course. The intensity of that need may be gauged by the fact that a single good speech raised a man, who had never held public office, to the governorship of California. The statists of both parties, who are now busy smearing Governor Reagan, are anxious not to see and not to let others discover the real lesson and meaning of his election: that the country is starved for a voice of consistency, clarity, and moral self-confidence—which were the outstanding qualities of his famous speech, and which cannot be achieved or projected by consensus-seeking anti-ideologists.

As of this date, Governor Reagan seems to be a promising public figure—I do not know him and cannot speak for the future. It is difficult to avoid a certain degree of skepticism: we have been disappointed too often. But whether he lives up to the promise or not, the people's need, quest for, and response to clear-cut ideas remain a fact—and will become a tragic fact if the intellectual leaders of this country continue to ignore it.

Since the elections of 1966, some commentators have been talking about the country's "swing to the right." There was no swing to the right (except, perhaps, in California)—there was only a swing against the left (if by "right," we mean capitalism—and by "left," statism). Without a firm, consistent *ideological* program and leadership, the people's desperate protest will be dissipated in the blind alleys of the same statism that they are opposing. It is futile to fight *against,* if one does not know what one is fighting *for.* A merely negative trend or movement cannot win and, historically, has never won: it leads nowhere.

The consensus-doctrine has achieved the exact opposite of its alleged goal: instead of creating unity or agreement, it has disintegrated and atomized the country to such an extent that no communication, let alone agreement, is possible. It is not unity, but intellectual coherence that a country needs. That coherence can be achieved only by fundamental principles, not by compromises among groups of men—by the primacy of ideas, not of gangs.

The task of defining ideas and goals is not the province of politicians and is not accomplished at election time: elections are merely consequences. The task belongs to the intellectuals. The need is more urgent than ever.

(*Postscript.* Once in a while, I receive letters from young men asking me for personal advice on problems connected with the draft. Morally, no one can give advice in any issue where choices and decisions are not voluntary: "Morality ends where a gun begins." As to the practical alternatives available, the best thing to do is to consult a good lawyer.

There is, however, one moral aspect of the issue that needs clarification. Some young men seem to labor under the misapprehension that since the draft is a violation of their rights, compliance with the draft law would constitute a moral sanction of that violation. This is a serious error. A forced compliance is not a sanction. All of us are forced to comply with many laws that violate our rights, but so long as we advocate the repeal of such laws, our compliance does not constitute a sanction. Unjust laws have to be fought ideologically; they cannot be fought or corrected by means of mere disobedience and futile martyrdom. To quote from an editorial on this subject in the April 1967 issue of *Persuasion:* "One does not stop the juggernaut by throwing oneself in front of it. . . .")

22. THE CASHING-IN:

THE STUDENT "REBELLION"

BY AYN RAND

The so-called student "rebellion," which was started and keynoted at the University of California at Berkeley, has profound significance, but not of the kind that most commentators have ascribed to it. And the nature of the misrepresentations is part of its significance.

The events at Berkeley began, in the fall of 1964, ostensibly as a student protest against the University administration's order forbidding political activity—specifically, the recruiting, fund-raising, and organizing of students for political action off-campus—on a certain strip of ground adjoining the campus, which was owned by the University. Claiming that their rights had been violated, a small group of "rebels" rallied thousands of students of all political views, including many "conservatives," and assumed the title of the "Free Speech Movement." The Movement staged "sit-in" protests in the administration building, and committed other acts of physical force, such as assaults on the police and the seizure of a police car for use as a rostrum.

The spirit, style, and tactics of the rebellion are best illustrated by one particular incident. The University administration called a mass meeting, which was attended by eighteen thousand students and faculty members, to hear an address on the situation by the University President, Clark Kerr; it had been expressly announced that no student speakers would be allowed to address the meeting. Kerr attempted to end the rebellion by capitulating: he promised to grant most of the rebels' demands; it looked as if he had won the audience to his side. Whereupon, Mario Savio, the rebel leader, seized the microphone, in an attempt to take over the meeting, ignoring the rules and the fact that the meeting had been adjourned. When he was—properly—dragged off the platform, the leaders of the F.S.M. admitted, openly and

---

The Objectivist Newsletter, July, August, and September 1965.

jubilantly, that they had almost lost their battle, but had saved it by provoking the administration to an act of "violence" (thus admitting that the victory of their publicly proclaimed goals was not the goal of their battle).

What followed was nation-wide publicity, of a peculiar kind. It was a sudden and, seemingly, spontaneous outpouring of articles, studies, surveys, revealing a strange unanimity of approach in several basic aspects: in ascribing to the F.S.M. the importance of a national movement, unwarranted by the facts—in blurring the facts by means of unintelligible generalities—in granting to the rebels the status of spokesmen for American youth, acclaiming their "idealism" and "commitment" to political action, hailing them as a symptom of the "awakening" of college students from "political apathy." If ever a "puff-job" was done by a major part of the press, this was it.

In the meantime, what followed at Berkeley was a fierce, three-cornered struggle among the University administration, its Board of Regents, and its faculty, a struggle so sketchily reported in the press that its exact nature remains fogbound. One can gather only that the Regents were, apparently, demanding a "tough" policy toward the rebels, that the majority of the faculty were on the rebels' side and that the administration was caught in the "moderate" middle of the road.

The struggle led to the permanent resignation of the University's Chancellor (as the rebels had demanded)—the temporary resignation, and later reinstatement, of President Kerr —and, ultimately, an almost complete capitulation to the F.S.M., with the administration granting most of the rebels' demands. (These included the right to advocate illegal acts and the right to an unrestricted freedom of speech *on campus*.)

To the astonishment of the naive, this did not end the rebellion: the more demands were granted, the more were made. As the administration intensified its efforts to appease the F.S.M., the F.S.M. intensified its provocations. The unrestricted freedom of speech took the form of a "Filthy Language Movement," which consisted of students carrying placards with four-letter words, and broadcasting obscenities over the University loudspeakers (which Movement was dismissed with mild reproof by most of the press, as a mere "adolescent prank").

This, apparently, was too much even for those who sympathized with the rebellion. The F.S.M. began to lose its following—and was, eventually, dissolved. Mario Savio quit the

University, declaring that he "could not keep up with the *undemocratic* procedures that the administration is following" [italics mine]—and departed, reportedly to organize a nation-wide revolutionary student movement.

This is a bare summary of the events as they were reported by the press. But some revealing information was provided by volunteers, outside the regular news channels, such as in the letters-to-the-editor columns.

An eloquent account was given in a letter to *The New York Times* (March 31, 1965) by Alexander Grendon, a biophysicist in the Donner Laboratory, University of California:

> The F.S.M. has always applied coercion to insure victory. One-party "democracy," as in the Communist countries or the lily-white portions of the South, corrects opponents of the party line by punishment. The punishment of the recalcitrant university administration (and more than 20,000 students who avoided participation in the conflict) was to "bring the university to a grinding halt" by physical force.
>
> To capitulate to such corruption of democracy is to teach students that these methods are right. President Kerr capitulated repeatedly. . . .
>
> Kerr agreed the university would not control "advocacy of illegal acts," an abstraction until illustrated by examples: In a university lecture hall, a self-proclaimed anarchist advises students how to cheat to escape military service; a nationally known Communist uses the university facilities to condemn our Government in vicious terms for its action in Vietnam, while funds to support the Vietcong are illegally solicited; propaganda for the use of marijuana, with instructions where to buy it, is openly distributed on campus.
>
> Even the abstraction "obscenity" is better understood when one hears a speaker, using the university's amplifying equipment, describe in vulgar words his experiences in group sexual intercourse and homosexuality and recommend these practices, while another suggests students should have the same sexual freedom on campus as dogs. . . .
>
> Clark Kerr's "negotiation"—a euphemism for surrender—on each deliberate defiance of orderly university processes contributes not to a liberal university but to a lawless one.

David S. Landes, Professor of History, Harvard University, made an interesting observation in a letter to *The New*

York Times (December 29, 1964). Stating that the Berkeley revolt represents potentially one of the most serious assaults on academic freedom in America, he wrote:

> In conclusion, I should like to point out the deleterious implications of this dispute for the University of California. I know personally of five or six faculty members who are leaving, not because of lack of sympathy with "free speech" or "political action," but because, as one put it, who wants to teach at the University of Saigon?

The clearest account and most perceptive evaluation were offered in an article in the *Columbia University Forum* (Spring 1965), entitled "What's left at Berkeley," by William Petersen, Professor of Sociology at the University of California at Berkeley. He writes:

> The first fact one must know about the Free Speech Movement is that it has little or nothing to do with free speech. . . . If not free speech, what then is the issue? In fact, preposterous as this may seem, the real issue is the seizure of power. . . .
>
> That a tiny number, a few hundred out of a student body of more than 27,000, was able to disrupt the campus is the consequence of more than vigor and skill in agitation. This minuscule group could not have succeeded in getting so many students into motion without three other, at times unwitting, sources of support: off-campus assistance of various kinds, the University administration, and the faculty.
>
> Everyone who has seen the efficient, almost military organization of the agitators' program has a reasonable basis for believing that skilled personnel and money are being dispatched into the Berkeley battle. . . . Around the Berkeley community a dozen *"ad hoc* committees to support" this or that element of the student revolt sprang up spontaneously, as though out of nowhere.
>
> The course followed by the University administration . . . could hardly have better fostered a rebellious student body if it had been devised to do so. To establish dubious regulations and when they are attacked to defend them by unreasonable argument is bad enough; worse still, the University did not impose on the students any sanctions that did not finally evaporate. . . . Obedience to norms is developed when it is suitably rewarded, and when noncompliance is suitably punished. That professional educators should need to be

reminded of this axiom indicates how deep the roots of
the Berkeley crisis lie.

But the most important reason that the extremists
won so many supporters among the students was the
attitude of the faculty. Perhaps their most notorious
capitulation to the F.S.M. was a resolution passed by
the Academic Senate on December 8, by which the
faculty notified the campus not only that they supported all of the radicals' demands but also that, in effect,
they were willing to fight for them against the Board of
Regents, should that become necessary. When that
resolution passed by an overwhelming majority—824 to
115 votes—it effectively silenced the anti-F.S.M. student
organizations. . . .

The Free Speech Movement is reminiscent of the
Communist fronts of the 1930's, but there are several
important differences. The key feature, that a radical
core uses legitimate issues ambiguously in order to
manipulate a large mass, is identical. The core in this
case, however, is not the disciplined Communist party,
but a heterogeneous group of radical sects.

Professor Petersen lists the various socialist, Trotskyist,
communist, and other groups involved. His conclusion is:

The radical leaders on the Berkeley campus, like those
in Latin American or Asian universities, are not the less
radical for being, in many cases, outside the discipline
of a formal political party. They are defined not by
whether they pay dues to a party, but by their actions,
their vocabulary, their way of thinking. The best term
to describe them, in my opinion, is Castroite. [This
term, he explains, applies primarily to their choice of
tactics, to the fact that] in critical respects all of them
imitate the Castro movement. . . .

At Berkeley, provocative tactics applied not against a
dictatorship but against the liberal, divided, and vacillat-
ing University administration proved to be enormously
effective. Each provocation and subsequent victory led
to the next.

Professor Petersen ends his article on a note of warning:

By my diagnosis . . . not only has the patient [the
University] not recovered but he is sicker than ever.
The fever has gone down temporarily, but the infection
is spreading and becoming more virulent.

Now let us consider the ideology of the rebels, from such indications as were given in the press reports. The general tone of the reports was best expressed by a headline in *The New York Times* (March 15, 1965): "The New Student Left: Movement Represents Serious Activists in Drive for Changes."

What kind of changes? No specific answer was given in the almost full-page story. Just "changes."

Some of these activists "who liken their movement to a 'revolution,' want to be called radicals. Most of them, however, prefer to be called 'organizers.' "

Organizers—of what? Of "deprived people." For what? No answer. Just "organizers."

> Most express contempt for any specific labels, and they don't mind being called cynics. . . . The great majority of those questioned said they were as skeptical of Communism as they were of any other form of political control. . . . "You might say we're a-Communist," said one of them, "just as you might say we're amoral and a-almost everything else."

There are exceptions, however. A girl from the University of California, one of the leaders of the Berkeley revolt, is quoted as saying: "At present the socialist world, even with all its problems, is moving closer than any other countries toward the sort of society I think should exist. In the Soviet Union, it has almost been achieved."

Another student, from the City College of New York, is quoted as concurring: " 'The Soviet Union and the whole Socialist bloc are on the right track,' he said."

In view of the fact that most of the young activists were active in the civil rights movement, and that the Berkeley rebels had started by hiding behind the issue of civil rights (attempting, unsuccessfully, to smear all opposition as of "racist" origin), it is interesting to read that: "There is little talk among the activists about racial integration. Some of them consider the subject passé. They declare that integration will be almost as evil as segregation if it results in a complacent, middle-class interracial society."

The central theme and basic ideology of all the activists is: *anti-ideology*. They are militantly opposed to all "labels," definitions, and theories; they proclaim the supremacy of the immediate moment and commitment to action—to subjectively, emotionally motivated action. Their anti-intellectual attitude runs like a stressed leitmotif through all the press reports.

An article in *The New York Times Magazine* (February 14, 1965) declares:

> The Berkeley mutineers did not seem political in the sense of those student rebels in the Turbulent Thirties. They are too suspicious of all adult institutions to embrace wholeheartedly even those ideologies with a stake in smashing the system. An anarchist or I.W.W. strain seems as pronounced as any Marxist doctrine. "Theirs is a sort of political existentialism," says Paul Jacobs, a research associate at the university's Center for the Study of Law and Society, who is one of the F.S.M.'s applauders. "All the old labels are out. . . ."
>
> The proudly immoderate zealots of the F.S.M. pursue an activist creed—that only commitment can strip life of its emptiness, its absence of meaning in a great "knowledge factory" like Berkeley.

An article in *The Saturday Evening Post* (May 8, 1965), discussing the various youth groups on the left, quotes a leader of Students for a Democratic Society:

> "We began by rejecting the old sectarian left and its ancient quarrels, and with a contempt for American society, which we saw as depraved. We are interested in direct action and specific issues. We do not spend endless hours debating the nature of Soviet Russia or whether Yugoslavia is a degenerate workers' state." [And]: "With sit-ins we saw for the first time the chance for direct participation in meaningful social revolution."
>
> In their off-picket-line hours, [states the same article] the P.L. [Progressive Labor] youngsters hang out at the experimental theaters and coffee shops of Manhattan's East Village. Their taste in reading runs more to Sartre than to Marx.

With an interesting touch of unanimity, a survey in *Newsweek* (March 22, 1965) quotes a young man on the other side of the continent: " 'These students don't read Marx,' said one Berkeley Free Student Movement leader. 'They read Camus.' "

"If they are rebels," the survey continues, "they are rebels without an ideology, and without long-range revolutionary programs. They rally over issues, not philosophies, and seem unable to formulate or sustain a systematized political theory of society, either from the left or right."

"Today's student seeks to find himself through what he

does, not what he thinks," the survey declares explicitly—and quotes some adult authorities in sympathetic confirmation. " 'What you have now, as in the 30's,' says New York Post editor James A. Wechsler, 'are groups of activists who really want to function in life.' But not ideologically. 'We used to sit around and debate Marxism, but students now are working for civil-rights and peace.' " Richard Unsworth, chaplain at Dartmouth, is quoted as saying: "In the world of today's campus 'the avenue now is doing and then reflecting on your doing, instead of reflecting, then deciding, and then doing, the way it was a few years ago.' " Paul Goodman, described as writer, educator and "one of the students' current heroes," is quoted as hailing the Berkeley movement because: "The leaders of the insurrection, he says, 'didn't play it cool, they took risks, *they were willing to be confused*, they didn't know whether it all would be a success or a failure. Now they don't want to be cool any more, they want to take over.' " [Italics mine. The same tribute could be paid to any drunken driver.]

The theme of "taking over" is repeated again and again. The immediate target, apparently, is the take-over of the universities. *The New York Times Magazine* article quotes one of the F.S.M. leaders: "Our idea is that the university is composed of faculty, students, books, and ideas. In a literal sense, the administration is merely there to make sure the sidewalks are kept clean. It should be the servant of the faculty and the students."

The climax of this particular line was a news story in *The New York Times* (March 29, 1965) under the heading: "Collegians Adopt a 'Bill of Rights.' "

> A group of Eastern college students declared here [in Philadelphia] this weekend that college administrators should be no more than housekeepers in the educational community.
>
> "The modern college or university," they said, "should be run by the students and the professors; administrators would be maintenance, clerical and safety personnel whose purpose is to enforce the will of faculty and students."

A manifesto to this effect was adopted at a meeting held at the University of Pennsylvania and attended by two hundred youths

> from 39 colleges in the Philadelphia and New York areas, Harvard, Yale, the University of California at

Berkeley, and from schools in the Midwest.

A recurring theme in the meeting was that colleges and universities had become servants of the "financial, industrial, and military establishment," and that students and faculty were being "sold down the river" by administrators.

Among the provisions of the manifesto were declarations of freedom to join, organize or hold meetings of any organization . . . abolition of tuition fees; control of law enforcement by the students and faculty; an end to the Reserve Officer Training Corps; abolition of loyalty oaths; student-faculty control over curriculum. . . .

The method used to adopt that manifesto is illuminating: "About 200 students attended the meeting, 45 remaining until the end when the 'Student Bill of Rights' was adopted." So much for "democratic procedures" and for the activists' right to the title of spokesmen for American youth.

What significance is ascribed to the student rebellion by all these reports and by the authorities they choose to quote? Moral courage is not a characteristic of today's culture, but in no other contemporary issue has moral cowardice been revealed to such a naked, ugly extent. Not only do most of the commentators lack an independent evaluation of the events, not only do they take their cue from the rebels, but of all the rebels' complaints, it is the most superficial, irrelevant and, therefore, the *safest,* that they choose to support and to accept as the cause of the rebellion: the complaint that the universities have grown "too big."

As if they had mushroomed overnight, the "bigness" of the universities is suddenly decried by the consensus as a national problem and blamed for the "unrest" of the students, whose motives are hailed as youthful "idealism." In today's culture, it has always been safe to attack "bigness." And since the meaningless issue of mere *size* has long served as a means of evading real issues, on all sides of all political fences, a new catch-phrase has been added to the list of "Big Business," "Big Labor," "Big Government," etc.: "Big University."

For a more sophisticated audience, the socialist magazine *The New Leader* (December 21, 1964) offers a Marxist-Freudian appraisal, ascribing the rebellion primarily to "alienation" (quoting Savio: "Somehow people are being separated off from something") and to "generational revolt" ("Spontaneously the natural idiom of the student political protest was that of sexual protest against the forbidding university administrator who ruled *in loco parentis*").

But the prize for expressing the moral-intellectual essence

of today's culture should go to Governor Brown of California. Remember that the University of California is a state institution, that its Regents are appointed by the Governor and that he, therefore, was the ultimate target of the revolt, including all its manifestations, from physical violence to filthy language.

> Have we made our society safe for students with ideas? [said Governor Brown at a campus dinner] We have not. Students have changed but the structure of the university and its attitudes towards its students have not kept pace with that change.
> Therefore, some students felt they had the right to go outside the law to force the change. But in so doing, they displayed the height of *idealistic hypocrisy*. [Italics mine.] On the one hand, they held up the Federal Constitution, demanding their rights of political advocacy. But at the same time, they threw away the principle of due process in favor of direct action.
> In doing so, they were as wrong as the university. This, then, is the great challenge that faces us, the challenge of change.[1]

Consider the fact that Governor Brown is generally regarded as a powerful chief executive and, by California Republicans, as a formidable opponent. Consider the fact that "according to the California Public Opinion Poll, 74 percent of the people disapprove of the student protest movement in Berkeley."[2] Then observe that Governor Brown did not dare denounce a movement led or manipulated by a group of forty-five students—and that he felt obliged to qualify the term "hypocrisy" by the adjective "idealistic," thus creating one of the weirdest combinations in today's vocabulary of evasion.

Now observe that in all that mass of comments, appraisals, and interpretations (including the ponderous survey in *Newsweek* which offered statistics on every imaginable aspect of college life), not one word was said about the *content* of modern education, about *the nature of the ideas* that are being inculcated by today's universities. Every possible question was raised and considered, except: *What are the students taught to think?* This, apparently, was what no one dared discuss.

This is what we shall now proceed to discuss.

If a dramatist had the power to convert philosophical ideas

[1] *The New York Times,* May 22, 1965.
[2] *The New Leader,* April 12, 1965.

into real, flesh-and-blood people, and attempted to create the walking embodiments of modern philosophy—the result would be the Berkeley rebels.

These "activists" are so fully, literally, loyally, devastatingly the products of modern philosophy that someone should cry to all the university administrations and faculties: "Brothers, you asked for it!"

Mankind could not expect to remain unscathed after decades of exposure to the radiation of intellectual fission-debris, such as: "Reason is impotent to know things as they are—reality is unknowable—certainty is impossible—knowledge is mere probability—truth is that which works—mind is a superstition—logic is a social convention—ethics is a matter of subjective commitment to an arbitrary postulate." And the consequent mutations are those contorted young creatures who scream, in chronic terror, that they know nothing and want to rule everything.

If that dramatist were writing a movie, he could justifiably entitle it "Mario Savio, Son of Immanuel Kant."

With rare and academically neglected exceptions, the philosophical "mainstream" that seeps into every classroom, subject, and brain in today's universities, is: epistemological agnosticism, avowed irrationalism, ethical subjectivism. Our age is witnessing the ultimate climax, the cashing-in on a long process of destruction, at the end of the road laid out by Kant.

Ever since Kant divorced reason from reality, his intellectual descendants have been diligently widening the breach. In the name of reason, Pragmatism established a range-of-the-moment view as an enlightened perspective on life, context-dropping as a rule of epistemology, expediency as a principle of morality, and collective subjectivism as a substitute for metaphysics. Logical Positivism carried it farther and, in the name of reason, elevated the immemorial psycho-epistemology of shyster-lawyers to the status of a scientific epistemological system—by proclaiming that knowledge consists of linguistic manipulations. Taking this seriously, Linguistic Analysis declared that the task of philosophy is, not to identify universal principles, but to tell people what they mean when they speak, which they are otherwise unable to know (which last, by that time, was true—in philosophical circles). This was the final stroke of philosophy breaking its moorings and floating off, like a lighter-than-air balloon, losing any semblance of connection to reality, any relevance to the problems of man's existence.

No matter how cautiously the proponents of such theories skirted any reference to the relationship between theory and practice, no matter how coyly they struggled to treat philosophy as a parlor or classroom game—the fact remained that young people went to college for the purpose of acquiring *theoretical* knowledge to guide them in *practical* action. Philosophy teachers evaded questions about the application of their ideas to reality, by such means as declaring that "reality is a meaningless term," or by asserting that philosophy has no purpose other than the amusement of manufacturing arbitrary "constructs," or by urging students to temper every theory with "common sense"—the common sense they had spent countless hours trying to invalidate.

As a result, a student came out of a modern university with the following sediment left in his brain by his four to eight years of study: existence is an uncharted, unknowable jungle, fear and uncertainty are man's permanent state, skepticism is the mark of maturity, cynicism is the mark of realism, and, above all, the hallmark of an intellectual is the denial of the intellect.

When and if academic commentators gave any thought to the practical results of their theories, they were predominantly united in claiming that uncertainty and skepticism are socially valuable traits which would lead to tolerance of differences, flexibility, social "adjustment," and willingness to compromise. Some went so far as to maintain explicitly that intellectual certainty is the mark of a dictatorial mentality, and that chronic *doubt*—the absence of firm convictions, the lack of absolutes—is the guarantee of a peaceful, "democratic" society.

They miscalculated.

It has been said that Kant's dichotomy led to two lines of Kantian philosophers, both accepting his basic premises, but choosing opposite sides: those who chose reason, abandoning reality—and those who chose reality, abandoning reason. The first delivered the world to the second.

The collector of the Kantian rationalizers' efforts—the receiver of the bankrupt shambles of sophistry, casuistry, sterility, and abysmal triviality to which they had reduced philosophy—was *Existentialism.*

Existentialism, in essence, consists of pointing to modern philosophy and declaring: "Since *this* is reason, to hell with it!"

In spite of the fact that the pragmatists-positivists-analysts had obliterated reason, the existentialists accepted them as reason's advocates, held them up to the world as examples of rationality and proceeded to reject reason altogether, proclaiming its impotence, rebelling against its "failure," calling for a return to reality, to the problems of human existence, to values, to action—to subjective values and mindless action. In the name of reality, they proclaimed the moral supremacy of "instincts," urges, feelings—and the cognitive powers of stomachs, muscles, kidneys, hearts, blood. It was a rebellion of headless bodies.

The battle is not over. The philosophy departments of today's universities are the battleground of a struggle which, in fact, is only a family quarrel between the analysts and the existentialists. Their progeny are the activists of the student rebellion.

If these activists choose the policy of "doing and then reflecting on your doing"—hasn't Pragmatism taught them that truth is to be judged by consequences? If they "seem unable to formulate or sustain a systematized political theory of society," yet shriek with moral righteousness that they propose to achieve their social goals by physical force—hasn't Logical Positivism taught them that ethical propositions have no cognitive meaning and are merely a report on one's feelings or the equivalent of emotional ejaculations? If they are savagely blind to everything but the immediate moment—hasn't Logical Positivism taught them that nothing else can be claimed with certainty to exist? And while the linguistic analysts are busy demonstrating that "The cat is on the mat" does *not* mean that "the mat" is an attribute of "the cat," nor that "on-the-mat" is the genus to which "the cat" belongs, nor yet that "the-cat" equals "on-the-mat"—is it any wonder that students storm the Berkeley campus with placards inscribed "Strike now, analyze later"? (This slogan is quoted by Professor Petersen in the *Columbia University Forum*.)

On June 14, CBS televised a jumbled, incoherent, unintelligible—and for these very reasons, authentic and significant—documentary entitled *The Berkeley Story*. There is method in every kind of madness—and for those acquainted with modern philosophy, that documentary was like a display of sideshow mirrors throwing off twisted reflections and random echoes of the carnage perpetrated in the academic torture-chambers of the mind.

"Our generation has no ideology," declared the first boy interviewed, in the tone of defiance and hatred once reserved for saying: "Down with Wall Street!"—clearly projecting that the enemy now is not the so-called Robber Barons, but *the mind*. The older generation, he explained scornfully, had "a neat little pill" to solve everything, but the pill didn't work and they merely "got their hearts busted." "We don't believe in pills," he said.

"We've learned that there are no absolute rules," said a

young girl, hastily and defensively, as if uttering an axiom—and proceeded to explain inarticulately, with the help of gestures pointing inward, that "we make rules for ourselves" and that what is right for *her* may not be right for others.

A girl described her classes as "words, words, words, paper, paper, paper"—and quietly, in a tone of authentic despair, said that she stopped at times to wonder: "What am I doing here? I'm not learning anything."

An intense young girl who talked volubly, never quite finishing a sentence nor making a point, was denouncing society in general, trying to say that since people are social products, society has done a bad job. In the middle of a sentence, she stopped and threw in, as a casual aside: "Whatever way I turn out, I still am a product," then went on. She said it with the simple earnestness of a conscientious child acknowledging a self-evident fact of nature. It was not an act: the poor little creature meant it.

The helpless bewilderment on the face of Harry Reasoner, the commentator, when he tried to sum up what he had presented, was an eloquent indication of why the press is unable properly to handle the student rebellion. "Now—immediacy—any situation must be solved *now*," he said incredulously, describing the rebels' attitude, neither praising nor blaming, in the faintly astonished, faintly helpless tone of a man unable to believe that he is seeing savages running loose on the campus of one of America's great universities.

Such are the products of modern philosophy. They are the type of students who are too intelligent not to see the logical consequences of the theories they have been taught—but not intelligent nor independent enough to see through the theories and reject them.

So they scream their defiance against "The System," not realizing that they are its most consistently docile pupils, that theirs is a rebellion against the *status quo* by its archetypes, against the intellectual "Establishment" by its robots who have swallowed every shopworn premise of the "liberals" of the 1930's, including the catch-phrases of altruism, the dedication to "deprived people," to such a safely *conventional* cause as "the war on poverty." A rebellion that brandishes banners inscribed with bromides is not a very convincing nor very inspiring sight.

As in any movement, there is obviously a mixture of motives involved: there are the little shysters of the intellect, who have found a gold mine in modern philosophy, who delight in arguing for argument's sake and stumping opponents by means of ready-to-wear paradoxes—there are the little role-players, who fancy themselves as heroes and enjoy defiance for the sake of defiance—there are the nihilists, who, moved by a profound hatred, seek nothing but destruction for the sake of destruction—there are the hopeless dependents, who seek to "belong" to any crowd that would have them—and there are the plain hooligans, who are always there, on the fringes of any mob action that smells of trouble. Whatever the combination of motives, *neurosis* is stamped in capital letters across the whole movement, since there is no such thing as rejecting reason through an innocent error of knowledge. But whether the theories of modern philosophy serve merely as a screen, a defense-mechanism, a rationalization of neurosis or are, in part, its cause—the fact remains that modern philosophy has destroyed the best in these students and fostered the worst.

Young people do seek a comprehensive view of life, *i.e.*, a philosophy, they do seek meaning, purpose, ideals—and most of them take what they get. It is in their teens and early twenties that most people seek philosophical answers and set their premises, for good or evil, for the rest of their lives. Some never reach that stage; some never give up the quest; but the majority are open to the voice of philosophy for a few brief years. These last are the permanent, if not innocent, victims of modern philosophy.

They are not independent thinkers nor intellectual originators; they are unable to answer or withstand the flood of modern sophistries. So some of them give up, after one or two unintelligible courses, convinced that thinking is a waste of time—and turn into lethargic cynics or stultified Babbitts by the time they reach twenty-five. Others accept what they hear; they accept it blindly and *literally;* these are today's activists. And no matter what tangle of motives now moves them, every teacher of modern philosophy should cringe in their presence, if he is still open to the realization that it is by means of the best within them, by means of their twisted, precarious groping for ideas, that he has turned them into grotesque little monstrosities.

Now what happens to the better minds in modern universities, to the students of above average intelligence who are actually eager to learn? What they find and have to endure is a long, slow process of psycho-epistemological torture.

Directly or indirectly, the influence of philosophy sets the epistemological standards and methods of teaching for all departments, in the physical sciences as well as in the humanities. The consequence, today, is a chaos of subjective whims setting the criteria of logic, of communication, demonstration, evidence, proof, which differ from class to class, from teacher to teacher. I am not speaking of a difference in viewpoint or content, but of the absence of *basic epistemolog-*

ical principles and the consequent difference in the method of functioning required of a student's mind. It is as if each course were given in a different language, each requiring that one *think* exclusively in that language, none providing a dictionary. The result—to the extent that one would attempt to comply—is intellectual disintegration.

Add to this: the opposition to "system-building," *i.e.*, to the integration of knowledge, with the result that the material taught in one class contradicts the material taught in the others, each subject hanging in a vacuum and to be accepted out of context, while any questions on how to integrate it are rejected, discredited, and discouraged.

Add to this: the arbitrary, senseless, haphazard conglomeration of most curricula, the absence of any hierarchical structure of knowledge, any order, continuity or rationale—the jumble of courses on out-of-context minutiae and out-of-focus surveys—the all-pervading unintelligibility—the arrogantly self-confessed irrationality—and, consequently, the necessity to memorize, rather than learn, to recite, rather than understand, to hold in one's mind a cacophony of undefined jargon long enough to pass the next exam.

Add to this: the professors who refuse to answer questions—the professors who answer by evasion and ridicule—the professors who turn their classes into bull-sessions on the premise that "we're here to mull things over together"—the professors who *do* lecture, but, in the name of "anti-dogmatism," take no stand, express no viewpoint and leave the students in a maze of contradictions with no lead to a solution—the professors who *do* take a stand and invite the students' comments, then penalize dissenters by mean of lower grades (particularly in political courses).

Add to this: the moral cowardice of most university administrations, the policy of permanent moral neutrality, of compromising on anything, of evading any conflict at any price—and the students' knowledge that the worst classroom injustice will remain uncorrected, that no appeal is practicable and no justice is to be found anywhere.

Yes, of course, there are exceptions—there *are* competent educators, brilliant minds, and rational men on the university staffs—but they are swallowed in the rampaging "mainstream" of irrationality and, too often, defeated by the hopeless pessimism of bitter, long-repressed frustration.

And further: most professors and administrators are much more competent and rational as individuals than they are in their collective performance. Most of them realize and, privately, complain about the evils of today's educational world. But each of them feels individually impotent before the enormity of the problem. So they blame it on some nameless, disembodied, almost mystical power, which they designate as "The System"—and too many of them take it to be a *political* system, specifically *capitalism*. They do not realize that there is only one human discipline which enables men to deal with large-scale problems, which has the power to integrate and unify human activities—and that that discipline is *philosophy,* which they have set, instead, to the task of disintegrating and destroying their work.

What does all this do to the best minds among the students? Most of them endure their college years with the teeth-clenched determination of serving out a jail sentence. The psychological scars they acquire in the process are incalculable. But they struggle as best they can to preserve their capacity to think, sensing dimly that the essence of the torture is an assault on their mind. And what they feel toward their schools ranges from mistrust to resentment to contempt to hatred—intertwined with a sense of exhaustion and excruciating boredom.

To various extents and various degrees of conscious awareness, these feelings are shared by the entire pyramid of the student body, from intellectual top to bottom. *This* is the reason why the handful of Berkeley rebels was able to attract thousands of students who did not realize, at first, the nature of what they were joining and who withdrew when it became apparent. Those students were moved by a desperate, incoherent frustration, by a need to protest, not knowing fully against what, by a blind desire to strike out at the university somehow.

I asked a small group of intelligent students at one of New York's best universities—who were ideologically opposed to the rebels—whether they would fight for the university administration, if the rebellion came to their campus. All of them shook their heads, with faint, wise, bitter smiles.

The philosophical impotence of the older generation is the reason why the adult authorities—from the Berkeley administration to the social commentators to the press to Governor Brown—were unable to take a firm stand and had no rational answer to the Berkeley rebellion. Granting the premises of modern philosophy, logic was on the side of the rebels. To answer them would require a *total* philosophical re-evaluation, down to basic premises—which none of those adults would dare attempt.

Hence the incredible spectacle of brute force, hoodlum tactics, and militantly explicit irrationality being brought to a university campus—and being met by the vague, uncertain, apologetic concessions, the stale generalities, the evasive platitudes of the alleged defenders of academic law and order.

In a civilized society, a student's declaration that he rejects reason and proposes to act outside the bounds of rationality, would be taken as sufficient grounds for immediate expulsion—let alone if he proceeded to engage in mob action and physical violence on a university campus. But modern universities have long since lost the moral right to oppose the first—and are, therefore, impotent against the second.

The student rebellion is an eloquent demonstration of the fact that when men abandon reason, they open the door to physical force as the only alternative and the inevitable consequence.

The rebellion is also one of the clearest refutations of the argument of those intellectuals who claimed that skepticism and chronic doubt would lead to social harmony.

When men reduce their virtues to the approximate, then evil acquires the force of an absolute, when loyalty to an unyielding purpose is dropped by the virtuous, it's picked up by scoundrels—and you get the indecent spectacle of a cringing, bargaining, traitorous good and a self-righteously uncompromising evil. (*Atlas Shrugged*)

Who stands to profit by that rebellion? The answer lies in the nature and goals of its leadership.

If the rank-and-file of the college rebels are victims, at least in part, this cannot be said of their leaders. Who are their leaders? Any and all of the statist-collectivist groups that hover, like vultures, over the remnants of capitalism, hoping to pounce on the carcass—and to accelerate the end, whenever possible. Their minimal goal is just "to make trouble"—to undercut, to confuse, to demoralize, to destroy. Their ultimate goal is to take over.

To such leadership, the college rebels are merely cannon-fodder, intended to stick their headless necks out, to fight on campuses, to go to jail, to lose their careers and their future—and eventually, if the leadership succeeds, to fight in the streets and lose their "non-absolute" lives, paving the way for the absolute dictatorship of whoever is the bloodiest among the thugs scrambling for power. Young fools who refuse to look beyond the immediate *"now,"* have no way of knowing whose long-range goals they are serving.

The communists are involved, among others; but, like the others, they are merely the manipulators, not the cause, of the student rebellion. This is an example of the fact that whenever they win, they win by default—like germs feeding on the sores of a disintegrating body. They did not create the conditions that are destroying American universities—they did not create the hordes of embittered, aimless, neurotic teen-agers—but they *do* know how to attack through the sores which their opponents insist on evading. They are professional ideologists, and it is not difficult for them to move into an intellectual vacuum and to hang the cringing advocates of "anti-ideology" by their own contradictions.

For its motley leftist leadership, the student rebellion is a trial balloon, a kind of cultural temperature-taking. It is a test of how much they can get away with and what sort of opposition they will encounter.

For the rest of us, it is a miniature preview—in the microcosm of the academic world—of what is to happen to the country at large, if the present cultural trend remains unchallenged.

The country at large is a mirror of its universities. The practical result of modern philosophy is today's mixed economy with its moral nihilism, its range-of-the-moment pragmatism, its anti-ideological ideology, and its truly shameful recourse to the notion of "Government by Consensus."

Rule by pressure groups is merely the prelude, the social conditioning for mob rule. Once a country has accepted the obliteration of moral principles, of individual rights, of objectivity, of justice, of reason, and has submitted to the rule of legalized brute force—the elimination of the concept "legalized" does not take long to follow. Who is to resist it—and in the name of what?

When numbers are substituted for morality, and no individual can claim a right, but any gang can assert any desire whatever, when *compromise* is the only policy expected of those in power, and the preservation of the moment's "stability," of peace at any price, is their only goal—the winner, necessarily, is whoever presents the most unjust and irrational demands; the system serves as an open invitation to do so. If there were no communists or other thugs in the world, such a system would create them.

The more an official is committed to the policy of compromise, the less able he is to resist anything: to give in, is his "instinctive" response in any emergency, his basic principle of conduct, which makes him an easy mark.

In this connection, the extreme of naive superficiality was reached by those commentators who expressed astonishment that the student rebellion had chosen Berkeley as its first battleground and President Kerr as its first target *in spite of* his record as a "liberal" and as a renowned mediator and arbitrator. "Ironically, some of the least mature student spokesmen . . . tried to depict Mr. Kerr as the illiberal administrator," said an editorial in *The New York Times* (March 11, 1965). "This was, of course, absurd in view of Mr. Kerr's long and courageous battle to uphold academic freedom and students' rights in the face of those right-wing pressures that abound in California." Other commentators pictured Mr. Kerr as an innocent victim caught between the conflicting pressures of the "conservatives" on the Board of Regents and the "liberals" on the faculty. But, in fact and in logic, the middle of the road can lead to no other final destination—and it is clear that the rebels chose Clark Kerr as their first target, not *in spite of*, but *because of* his record.

Now project what would happen if the technique of the Berkeley rebellion were repeated on a national scale. Contrary to the fanatical belief of its advocates, compromise does not satisfy, but *dissatisfies* everybody; it does not lead to general fulfillment, but to general frustration; those who try to be all things to all men, end up by not being anything to anyone. And more: the partial victory of an unjust claim, encourages the claimant to try further; the partial defeat of a just claim, discourages and paralyzes the victim. If a determined, disciplined gang of statists were to make an assault on the crumbling remnants of a mixed economy, boldly and explicitly proclaiming the collectivist tenets which the country had accepted by tacit default—what resistance would they encounter? The dispirited, demoralized, embittered majority would remain lethargically indifferent to any public event. And many would support the gang, at first, moved by a desperate, incoherent frustration, by a need to protest, not knowing fully against what, by a blind desire to strike out somehow at the suffocating hopelessness of the *status quo*.

Who would feel morally inspired to fight for Johnson's "consensus"? Who fought for the aimless platitudes of the Kerensky government in Russia—of the Weimar Republic in Germany—of the Nationalist government in China?

But no matter how badly demoralized and philosophically disarmed a country might be, it has to reach a certain psychological turning point before it can be pushed from a state of semi-freedom into surrender to full-fledged dictatorship. And *this* was the main ideological purpose of the student rebellion's leaders, whoever they were: *to condition the country to accept force as the means of settling political controversies.*

Observe the ideological precedents which the Berkeley

rebels were striving to establish: all of them involved the abrogation of rights and the advocacy of force. These notions have been publicized, yet their meaning has been largely ignored and left unanswered.

1. The main issue was the attempt to make the country accept *mass civil disobedience* as a proper and valid tool of political action. This attempt has been made repeatedly in connection with the civil rights movement. But there the issue was confused by the fact that the Negroes *were* the victims of legalized injustice and, therefore, the matter of breaching legality did not become unequivocally clear. The country took it as a fight for justice, not as an assault on the law.

Civil disobedience may be justifiable, in some cases, when and if an individual disobeys a law in order to bring an issue to court, as a test case. Such an action involves respect for legality and a protest directed only at a particular law which the individual seeks an opportunity to prove to be unjust. The same is true of a group of individuals when and if the risks involved are their own.

But there is no justification, in a civilized society, for the kind of mass civil disobedience that involves the violation of the rights of others—regardless of whether the demonstrators' goal is good or evil. The end does *not* justify the means. No one's rights can be secured by the violation of the rights of others. Mass disobedience is an assault on the concept of rights: it is a mob's defiance of legality as such.

The forcible occupation of another man's property or the obstruction of a public thoroughfare is so blatant a violation of rights that an attempt to justify it becomes an abrogation of morality. An individual has no right to do a "sit-in" in the home or office of a person he disagrees with—and he does not acquire such a right by joining a gang. Rights are not a matter of numbers—and there can be no such thing, in law or in morality, as actions forbidden to an individual, but permitted to a mob.

The only power of a mob, as against an individual, is greater muscular strength—*i.e.*, plain, brute physical force. The attempt to solve social problems by means of physical force is what a civilized society is established to prevent. The advocates of mass civil disobedience admit that their purpose is intimidation. A society that tolerates intimidation as a means of settling disputes—the *physical* intimidation of some men or groups by others—loses its moral right to exist as a social system, and its collapse does not take long to follow.

Politically, mass civil disobedience is appropriate only as a prelude to civil war—as the declaration of a total break with a country's political institutions. And the degree of today's intellectual chaos and context-dropping was best illustrated by some "conservative" California official who rushed to declare that he objects to the Berkeley rebellion, but respects civil disobedience as a valid American tradition. "Don't forget the Boston Tea Party," he said, forgetting it.

If the meaning of civil disobedience is somewhat obscured in the civil rights movement—and, therefore, the attitude of the country is inconclusive—that meaning becomes blatantly obvious when a sit-in is staged on a university campus. If the universities—the supposed citadels of reason, knowledge, scholarship, civilization—can be made to surrender to the rule of brute force, the rest of the country is cooked.

2. To facilitate the acceptance of force, the Berkeley rebels attempted to establish a special distinction between *force* and *violence:* force, they claimed explicitly, is a proper form of social action, but violence is not. Their definition of the terms was as follows: coercion by means of a *literal* physical contact is "violence" and is reprehensible; any other way of violating rights is merely "force" and is a legitimate, peaceful method of dealing with opponents.

For instance, if the rebels occupy the administration building, that is "force"; if policemen drag them out, that is "violence." If Savio seizes a microphone he has no right to use, that is "force"; if a policeman drags him away from it, that is "violence."

Consider the implications of that distinction as a rule of social conduct: if you come home one evening, find a stranger occupying your house and throw him out bodily, he has merely committed a peaceful act of "force," but *you* are guilty of "violence," and *you* are to be punished.

The theoretical purpose of that grotesque absurdity is to establish a moral inversion: to make the *initiation* of force moral, and *resistance* to force immoral—and thus to obliterate *the right of self-defense.* The immediate practical purpose is to foster the activities of the lowest political breed: the provocateurs, who commit acts of force and place the blame on their victims.

3. To justify that fraudulent distinction, the Berkeley rebels attempted to obliterate a legitimate one: the distinction between *ideas* and *actions.* They claimed that freedom of speech means freedom of action and that no clear line of demarcation can be drawn between them.

For instance, if they have the right to advocate any political viewpoint—they claimed—they have the right to organize, on campus, any off-campus activities, even those forbidden by law. As Professor Petersen put it, they were claiming the right "to use the University as a sanctuary from which to make illegal raids on the general community."

The difference between an exchange of ideas and an exchange of blows is self-evident. The line of demarcation between freedom of speech and freedom of action is established by the ban on the initiation of physical force. It is only when that ban is abrogated that such a problem can arise—but when that ban is abrogated, no political freedom of any kind can remain in existence.

At a superficial glance, the rebels' "package-deal" may seem to imply a sort of anarchistic extension of freedom; but, in fact and in logic, it implies the exact opposite—which is a grim joke on those unthinking youths who joined the rebellion in the name of "free speech." If the freedom to express ideas were equated with the freedom to commit crimes, it would not take long to demonstrate that no organized society can exist on such terms and, therefore, that the expression of ideas has to be curtailed and some ideas have to be forbidden, just as criminal acts are forbidden. Thus the gullible would be brought to concede that the right of free speech is undefinable and "impracticable."

4. An indication of such a motive was given by the rebels' demand for unrestricted freedom of speech on campus—with the consequent "Filthy Language Movement."

There can be no such thing as the right to an unrestricted freedom of speech (or of action) *on someone else's property.* The fact that the University at Berkeley is owned by the state, merely complicates the issue, but does not alter it. The owners of a state university are the voters and taxpayers of that state. The University administration, appointed (directly or indirectly) by an elected official, is, theoretically, the agent of the owners—and has to act as such, so long as state universities exist. (Whether they *should* exist, is a different question.)

In any undertaking or establishment involving more than one man, it is the owner or owners who set the rules and terms of appropriate conduct; the rest of the participants are free to go elsewhere and seek different terms, if they do not agree. There can be no such thing as the right to act on whim, to be exercised by some participants at the expense of others.

Students who attend a university have the right to expect that they will not be subjected to hearing the kind of obscenities for which the owner of a semi-decent barroom would bounce hoodlums out on the street. The right to determine what sort of language is permissible, belongs to the administration of a university—fully as much as to the owner of a barroom.

The technique of the rebels, as of all statists, was to take advantage of the principles of a free society in order to undercut them by an alleged demonstration of their "impracticability"—in this case, the "impracticability" of the right of free speech. But, in fact, what they have demonstrated is a point farthest removed from their goals: that *no rights of any kind can be exercised without property rights.*

It is only on the basis of property rights that the sphere and application of individual rights can be defined in any given social situation. Without property rights, there is no way to solve or to avoid a hopeless chaos of clashing views, interests, demands, desires, and whims.

There was no way for the Berkeley administration to answer the rebels except by invoking property rights. It is obvious why neither modern "liberals" nor "conservatives" would care to do so. It is not the contradictions of a free society that the rebels were exposing and cashing-in on, but the contradictions of a mixed economy.

As to the question of what ideological policy should properly be adopted by the administration of a state university, it is a question that has no answer. There are no solutions for the many contradictions inherent in the concept of "public property," particularly when the property is directly concerned with the dissemination of ideas. This is one of the reasons why the rebels would choose a state university as their first battleground.

A good case could be made for the claim that a state university has no right to forbid the teaching or advocacy of any political viewpoint whatever, as, for instance, of communism, since some of the taxpaying owners may be communists. An equally good case could be made for the claim that a state university has no right to permit the teaching and advocacy of any political viewpoint which (as, for instance, communism) is a direct threat to the property, freedom, and lives of the majority of the taxpaying owners. Majority rule is not applicable in the realm of ideas; an individual's convictions are not subject to a majority vote; but neither an individual nor a minority nor a majority should be forced to support their own destroyers.

On the one hand, a government institution has no right to forbid the expression of any ideas. On the other hand, a government institution has no right to harbor, assist, and finance the country's enemies (as, for instance, the collectors of funds for the Vietcong).

The source of these contradictions does not lie in the principle of individual rights, but in their violation by the collectivist institution of "public property."

This issue, however, has to be fought in the field of constitutional law, not on campus. As students, the rebels have no greater rights in a state university than in a private one. As taxpayers, they have no greater rights than the millions of other California taxpayers involved. If they object to the policies of the Board of Regents, they have no recourse except at the polls at the next election—if they can persuade a sufficient number of voters. This is a pretty slim chance—and this is a good argument *against* any type of "public property." But it is not an issue to be solved by physical force.

What is significant here is the fact that the rebels—who, to put it mildly, are *not* champions of private property—refused to abide by the kind of majority rule which is inherent in public ownership. *That* is what they were opposing when they complained that universities have become servants of the "financial, industrial, and military establishment." It is the rights of these particular groups of taxpayers (the right to a voice in the management of state universities) that they were seeking to abrogate.

If anyone needs proof of the fact that the advocates of public ownership are not seeking "democratic" control of property by majority rule, but control by dictatorship—this is one eloquent piece of evidence.

5. As part of the ideological conditioning for that ultimate goal, the rebels attempted to introduce a new variant on an old theme that has been the object of an intense drive by all statist-collectivists for many years past: the obliteration of the difference between private action and government action.

This has always been attempted by means of a "package-deal" ascribing to private citizens the specific violations constitutionally forbidden to the government, and thus destroying individual rights while freeing the government from any restrictions. The most frequent example of this technique consists of accusing private citizens of practicing "censorship" (a concept applicable only to the government) and thus negating their right to disagree.[3]

The new variant provided by the rebels was their protest against alleged "double jeopardy." It went as follows: if the

---

[3] See my article "Man's Rights" in the appendix.

students commit illegal acts, they will be punished by the courts and must not, therefore, be penalized by the university for the same offense.

"Double jeopardy" is a concept applicable only to the government, and only to *one* branch of the government, the judiciary, and only to a specific judiciary action: it means that a man must not be put on trial twice for the same offense.

To equate private judgment and action (or, in this context, a government official's judgment and action) with a court trial, is worse than absurd. It is an outrageous attempt to obliterate the right to moral judgment and moral action. It is a demand that a lawbreaker suffer no *civil* consequences of his crime.

If such a notion were accepted, individuals would have no right to evaluate the conduct of others nor to act according to their evaluation. They would have to wait until a court had decreed whether a given man was guilty or innocent—and even after he was pronounced guilty, they would have no right to change their behavior toward him and would have to leave the task of penalizing him exclusively to the government.

For instance, if a bank employee were found guilty of embezzlement and had served his sentence, the bank would have no right to refuse to give him back his former job—since a refusal would constitute "double jeopardy."

Or: a government official would have no right to watch the legality of the actions of his department's employees, nor to lay down rules for their strict observance of the law, but would have to wait until a court had found them guilty of law-breaking—and would have to reinstate them in their jobs, after they had served their sentences for influence-peddling or bribe-taking or treason.

The notion of *morality as a monopoly of the government* (and of a single branch or group within the government) is so blatantly a part of the ideology of a dictatorship that the rebels' attempt to get away with it is truly shocking.

6. The rebels' notion that universities should be run by students and faculties was an open, explicit assault on the right attacked implicitly by all their other notions: the right of private property. And of all the various statist-collectivist systems, the one they chose as their goal is, politico-economically, the least practical; intellectually, the least defensible; morally, the most shameful: *guild socialism*.

Guild socialism is a system that abolishes the exercise of individual ability by chaining men into groups according to their line of work, and delivering the work into the group's power, as its exclusive domain, with the group dictating the rules, standards, and practices of how the work is to be done and who shall or shall not do it.

Guild socialism is the concrete-bound, routine-bound mentality of a savage, elevated into a social theory. Just as a tribe of savages seizes a piece of jungle territory and claims it as a monopoly by reason of the fact of being there—so guild socialism grants a monopoly, not on a jungle forest or water-hole, but on a factory or a university—not by reason of a man's ability, achievement, or even "public service," but by reason of the fact that he is there.

Just as savages have no concept of causes or consequences, of past or future, and no concept of efficacy beyond the muscular power of their tribe—so guild socialists, finding themselves in the midst of an industrial civilization, regard its institutions as phenomena of nature and see no reason why the gang should not seize them.

If there is any one proof of a man's incompetence, it is the stagnant mentality of a worker (or of a professor) who, doing some small, routine job in a vast undertaking, does not care to look beyond the lever of a machine (or the lectern of a classroom), does not choose to know how the machine (or the classroom) got there or what makes his job possible, and proclaims that the management of the undertaking is parasitical and unnecessary. Managerial work—the organization and integration of human effort into purposeful, large-scale, long-range activities—is, in the realm of action, what man's conceptual faculty is in the realm of cognition. It is beyond the grasp and, therefore, is the first target of the self-arrested, sensory-perceptual mentality.

If there is any one way to confess one's own mediocrity, it is the willingness to place one's work in the absolute power of a group, particularly a group of one's *professional colleagues*. Of any forms of tyranny, this is the worst; it is directed against a single human attribute: the mind—and against a single enemy: the innovator. The innovator, by definition, is the man who challenges the established practices of his profession. To grant a professional monopoly to any group, is to sacrifice human ability and abolish progress; to advocate such a monopoly, is to confess that one has nothing to sacrifice.

Guild socialism is the rule of, by, and for mediocrity. Its cause is a society's intellectual collapse; its consequence is a quagmire of stagnation; its historical example is the guild system of the Middle Ages (or, in modern times, the fascist system of Italy under Mussolini).

The rebels' notion that students (along with faculties) should run universities and determine their curricula is a crude absurdity. If an ignorant youth comes to an institution of learning in order to acquire knowledge of a certain science, by what means is he to determine what is relevant and how he should be taught? (In the process of learning, he can judge only whether his teacher's presentation is clear or unclear, logical or contradictory; he cannot determine the proper course and method of teaching, ahead of any knowledge of the subject.) It is obvious that a student who demands the right to run a university (or to decide who should run it) has no knowledge of the concept of knowledge, that his demand is self-contradictory and disqualifies him automatically. The same is true—with a much heavier burden of moral guilt—of the professor who taught him to make such demands and who supports them.

Would you care to be treated in a hospital where the methods of therapy were determined by a vote of doctors and patients?

Yet the absurdity of these examples is merely more obvious—not more irrational nor more vicious—than the standard collectivist claim that workers should take over the factories created by men whose achievement they can neither grasp nor equal. The basic epistemological-moral premise and pattern are the same: the obliteration of reason obliterates the concept of reality, which obliterates the concept of achievement, which obliterates the concept of the distinction between *the earned* and *the unearned*. Then the incompetent can seize factories, the ignorant can seize universities, the brutes can seize scientific research laboratories—and nothing is left in a human society but the power of whim and fist.

What makes guild socialism cruder than (but not different from) most statist-collectivist theories is the fact that it represents the other, the usually unmentioned, side of altruism: it is the voice, not of the givers, but of the receivers. While most altruistic theorists proclaim "the common good" as their justification, advocate self-sacrificial service to the "community," and keep silent about the exact nature or identity of the recipients of sacrifices—guild socialists brazenly declare themselves to be the recipients and present their claims to the community, demanding its services. If they want a monopoly on a given profession, they claim, the rest of the community must give up the right to practice it. If they want a university, they claim, the community must provide it.

And if "selfishness" is taken, by the altruists, to mean the sacrifice of others to self, I challenge them to name an uglier example of it than the pronouncement of the little Berkeley collectivist who declared: "Our idea is that the university is composed of faculty, students, books, and ideas. In a literal sense, the administration is merely there to make sure the sidewalks are kept clean. It should be the servant of the faculty and the students."

What did that little disembodied mystic omit from his idea of a university? Who pays the salaries of the faculty? Who provides the livelihood of the students? Who publishes the books? Who builds the classrooms, the libraries, the dormitories—and the sidewalks? Leave it to a modern "mystic of *muscle*" to display the kind of contempt for "vulgar material concerns". that an old-fashioned mystic would not quite dare permit himself.

Who—besides the university administration—is to be the voiceless, rightless "servant" and sidewalk-sweeper of the faculty and students? No, not only the men of productive genius who create the material wealth that makes universities possible, not only the "tycoons of big business," not only the "financial, industrial, and military establishment"—but every taxpayer of the state of California, every man who works for a living, high or low, every human being who earns his sustenance, struggles with his budget, pays for what he gets, and does not permit himself to evade the reality of "vulgar material concerns."

Such is the soul revealed by the ideology of the Berkeley rebellion. Such is the meaning of the rebels' demands and of the ideological precedents they were trying to establish.

Observe the complexity, the equivocations, the tricks, the twists, the intellectual acrobatics performed by these avowed advocates of unbridled feelings—and the ideological consistency of these activists who claim to possess no ideology.

The first round of the student rebellion has not gone over too well. In spite of the gratuitous "puff-job" done by the press, the attitude of the public is a mixture of bewilderment, indifference, and antagonism. Indifference—because the evasive vagueness of the press reports was self-defeating: people do not understand what it is all about and see no reason to care. Antagonism—because the American public still holds a profound respect for universities (as they might be and ought to be, but are not any longer), and the commentators' half-laudatory, half-humorous platitudes about the "idealism of youth" have not succeeded in white-washing the fact that brute physical force was brought to a university campus. That fact has aroused a vague sense of uneasiness in people, a sense of undefined, apprehensive condemnation.

The rebellion's attempt to invade other campuses did not get very far. There were some disgraceful proclamations of appeasement by some university administrators and commencement orators this spring, but no discernible public sympathy.

There were a few instances of a proper attitude on the part of university administrations—an attitude of firmness, dignity and uncompromising severity—notably at Columbia University. A commencement address by Dr. Meng, President of Hunter College, is also worth noting. Declaring that the violation of the rights of others "is intolerable" in an academic community and that any student or teacher guilty of it deserves "instant expulsion," he said: "Yesterday's ivory tower has become today's foxhole. The leisure of the theory class is increasingly occupied in the organization of picket lines, teach-ins, think-ins, and stake-outs of one sort or another."[4]

But even though the student rebellion has not aroused much public sympathy, the most ominous aspect of the situation is the fact that it has not met any *ideological opposition*, that the implications of the rebels' stand have neither been answered nor rejected, that such criticism as it did evoke was, with rare exceptions, evasively superficial.

As a trial balloon, the rebellion has accomplished its leaders' purpose: it has demonstrated that they may have gone a bit too far, bared their teeth and claws a bit too soon, and antagonized many potential sympathizers, even among the "liberals"—but that the road ahead is empty, with no intellectual barricades in sight.

The battle is to continue. The long-range intentions of the student rebellion have been proclaimed repeatedly by the same activists who proclaim their exclusive dedication to the immediate moment. The remnants of the "Free Speech Movement" at Berkeley have been reorganized into a "Free Student Union," which is making militant noises in preparation for another assault. No matter how absurd their notions, the rebels' assaults are directed at the most important philosophical-political issues of our age. These issues cannot be ignored, evaded, or bribed away by compromise. When brute force is on the march, compromise is the red carpet. When reason is attacked, common sense is not enough.

Neither a man nor a nation can exist without some form of philosophy. A man has the free will to think or not; if he does not, he takes what he gets. The free will of a nation is its intellectuals; the rest of the country takes what they offer; they set the terms, the values, the course, the goal.

In the absence of intellectual opposition, the rebels' notions will gradually come to be absorbed into the culture. The uncontested absurdities of today are the accepted slogans of tomorrow. They come to be accepted by degrees, by precedent, by implication, by erosion, by default, by dint of constant pressure on one side and constant retreat on the other— until the day when they are suddenly declared to be the country's official ideology. That is the way welfare statism came to be accepted in this country.

What we are witnessing today is an acceleration of the attempts to cash-in on the ideological implications of welfare statism and to push beyond it. The college rebels are merely the commandos, charged with the task of establishing ideological beachheads for a full-scale advance of all the statist-collectivist forces against the remnants of capitalism in America; and part of their task is the take-over of the ideological control of America's universities.

If the collectivists succeed, the terrible historical irony will lie in the fact that what looks like a noisy, reckless, belligerent confidence is, in fact, a hysterical bluff. The acceleration of collectivism's advance is not the march of winners, but the blind stampede of losers. Collectivism has lost the battle for men's minds; its advocates know it; their last chance consists of the fact that no one else knows it. If they are to cash-in on decades of philosophical corruption, on all the gnawing, scrapping, scratching, burrowing to dig a maze of philosophical rat-holes which is about to cave in, it's now or never.

As a cultural-intellectual power and a moral ideal, collectivism died in World War II. If we are still rolling in its direction, it is only by the inertia of a void and the momentum of disintegration. A social movement that began with the ponderous, brain-cracking, dialectical constructs of Hegel and Marx, and ends up with a horde of morally unwashed children stamping their foot and shrieking: "I want it *now!*"—is through.

All over the world, while mowing down one helpless nation after another, collectivism has been steadily losing the two elements that hold the key to the future: the brains of mankind and its youth. In regard to the first, observe Britain's "brain drain." In regard to the second, consider the fact (which was not mentioned in the press comments on the student rebellion) that in a predominant number of American universities, the political views of the faculty are perceptibly more "liberal" than those of the student body. (The same is true of the youth of the country at large—as against the older generation, the thirty-five to fifty age bracket, who were reared under the New Deal and who hold the country's leadership, at present.) That is one of the facts which the student rebellion was intended to disguise.

This is not to say that the anti-collectivists represent a *numerical* majority among college students. The passive supporters of the *status quo* are always the majority in any group, culture, society, or age. But it is not by passive majorities that the trends of a nation are set. Who sets them? Anyone who cares to do so, if he has the intellectual ammunition to win on the battlefield of ideas, which belongs to those who *do* care. Those who don't, are merely social ballast by their own choice and predilection.

The fact that the "non-liberals" among college students (and among the youth of the world) can be identified at present only as "anti-collectivists" is the dangerous element and the question mark in today's situation. They are the young people who are not ready to give up, who want to fight againt a swamp of evil, but do not know what is the good. They have rejected the sick, worn platitudes of collectivism (along with all of its cultural manifestations, including the cult of despair and depravity—the studied mindlessness of jerk-and-moan dancing, singing or acting—the worship of anti-heroes—the experience of looking up to the dissection of a psychotic's brain, for inspiration, and to the bare feet of an inarticulate brute, for guidance—the stupor of reduction to sensory stimuli—the sense of life of a movie such as *Tom Jones*). But they have found, as yet, no direction, no consistent philosophy, no rational values, no long-range goals. Until and unless they do, their incoherent striving for a better future will collapse before the final thrust of the collectivists.

Historically, we are now in a kind of intellectual no man's land—and the future will be determined by those who venture out of the trenches of the *status quo*. Our direction will depend on whether the venturers are crusaders fighting for a new Renaissance or scavengers pouncing upon the wreckage left of yesterday's battles. The crusaders are not yet ready; the scavengers are.

That is why—in a deeper sense than the little zombies of college campuses will ever grasp—"Now, now, now!" is the last slogan and cry of the ragged, bearded stragglers who had once been an army rallied by the promise of a *scientifically* (!) planned society.

The two most accurate characterizations of the student rebellion, given in the press, were: "Political Existentialism" and "Castroite." Both are concepts pertaining to intellectual bankruptcy: the first stands for the abdication of reason—the second, for that state of hysterical panic which brandishes a fist as its sole recourse.

In preparation for its published survey (March 22, 1965), *Newsweek* conducted a number of polls among college students at large, on various subjects, one of which was the question of who are the students' heroes. The editors of *Newsweek* informed me that my name appeared on the resultant list, and sent an interviewer to question me about my views on the state of modern universities. For reasons best known to themselves, they chose not to publish any part of that interview. What I said (in briefer form) was what I am now saying in this article—with the exception of the concluding remarks which follow and which I want to address most particularly to those college students who chose me as one of their heroes.

Young people are constantly asking what they can do to fight today's disastrous trends; they are seeking some form of action, and wrecking their hopes in blind alleys, particularly every four years, at election time. Those who do not realize that the battle is ideological, had better give up, because they have no chance. Those who do realize it, should grasp that the student rebellion offers them a chance to train themselves for the kind of battle they will have to fight in the world, when they leave the university; a chance, not only to train themselves, but to win the first rounds of that wider battle.

If they seek an important cause, they have the opportunity to fight the rebels, to fight *ideologically*, on *moral-intellectual* grounds—by identifying and exposing the meaning of the rebels' demands, by naming and answering the basic principles which the rebels dare not admit. The battle consists, above all, of providing the country (or all those within hearing) with *ideological answers*—a field of action from which the older generation has deserted under fire.

Ideas cannot be fought except by means of better ideas. The battle consists, not of opposing, but of exposing; not of denouncing, but of disproving; not of evading, but of boldly proclaiming a full, consistent, and radical alternative.

This does not mean that rational students should enter debates with the rebels or attempt to convert them: one cannot argue with self-confessed irrationalists. The goal of an ideological battle is to enlighten the vast, helpless, bewildered majority in the universities—and in the country at large—or, rather, the minds of those among the majority who are struggling to find answers or those who, having heard nothing but collectivist sophistries for years, have withdrawn in revulsion and given up.

The first goal of such a battle is to wrest from a handful of beatniks the title of "spokesmen for American youth," which the press is so anxious to grant them. The first step is to make oneself heard, on the campus and outside. There are many civilized ways to do it: protest meetings, public petitions, speeches, pamphlets, letters-to-editors. It is a much more important issue than picketing the United Nations or parading in support of the House Un-American Activities Committee. And while such futile groups as Young Americans for Freedom are engaged in such undertakings, they are letting the collectivist vanguard speak in their name—in the name of American college students—without any audible sound of protest.

But in order to be heard, one must have something to say. To have that, one must know one's case. One must know it fully, logically, consistently, all the way down to philosophical fundamentals. One cannot hope to fight nuclear experts with Republican pea-shooters. And the leaders behind the student rebellion *are* experts at their particular game.

But they are dangerous only to those who stare at the issues out of focus and hope to fight ideas by means of faith, feelings, and fund-raising. You would be surprised how quickly the ideologists of collectivism retreat when they encounter a confident, *intellectual* adversary. Their case rests on appealing to human confusion, ignorance, dishonesty, cowardice, despair. Take the side they dare not approach: appeal to human intelligence.

Collectivism has lost the two crucial weapons that raised it to world power and made all of its victories possible: intellectuality and idealism, or reason and morality. It had to lose them precisely at the height of its success, since its claim to both was a fraud: the full, actual reality of socialist-communist-fascist states has demonstrated the brute irrationality of collectivist systems and the inhumanity of altruism as a moral code.

Yet reason and morality are the only weapons that determine the course of history. The collectivists dropped them because they had no right to carry them. Pick them up; you have.

23. ALIENATION

BY NATHANIEL BRANDEN

> And how am I to face the odds
> of man's bedevilment and God's?
> I, a stranger and afraid
> in a world I never made.

In the writings of contemporary psychologists and sociologists, one encounters these lines from A. E. Housman's poem more and more often today—quoted as an eloquent summation of the sense of life and psychological plight of twentieth-century man.

In book after book of social commentary, one finds the same message: modern man is overwhelmed by anxiety, modern man suffers from an "identity crisis," modern man is *alienated.* " 'Who am I?' 'Where am I going?' 'Do I belong?': these are the crucial questions man asks himself in modern mass society," declares the sociologist and psychoanalyst Hendrik M. Ruitenbeek, in *The Individual and the Crowd— A Study of Identity in America.*[1]

The concept of *alienation,* in its original psychiatric usage, denoted the mentally ill, the severely mentally ill—often, particularly in legal contexts, the insane. It conveyed the notion of the breakdown of rationality and self-determination, the notion of a person driven by forces which he cannot grasp or control, which are experienced by him as compelling and alien, so that he feels estranged from himself.

Centuries earlier, medieval theologians had spoken with distress of man's alienation from God—of an over-concern with the world of the senses that caused man to become lost to himself, estranged from his proper spiritual estate.

It was the philosopher Hegel who introduced the concept

The Objectivist Newsletter, July, August, and September 1965.

[1] New York: The New American Library (Mentor), 1965, p. 15.

of alienation (outside of its psychiatric context) to the modern world. The history of man, maintained Hegel, is the history of man's self-alienation: man is blind to his true essence, he is lost in the "dead world" of social institutions and of property, which he himself has created, he is estranged from the Universal Being of which he is a part—and human progress consists of man's motion toward that Whole, as he transcends the limitations of his individual perceptions.

"Alienation" was taken over by Karl Marx and given a narrower, less cosmic meaning. He applied the concept primarily to the worker. The worker's alienation was inevitable, he asserted, with the development of the division of labor, specialization, exchange, and private property. The worker must sell his services; thus he comes to view himself as a "commodity," he becomes alienated from the product of his own labor, and his work is no longer the expression of his powers, of his inner self. The worker, who is alive, is ruled by that which is "dead" (*i.e.*, capital, machinery). The consequence, says Marx, is spiritual impoverishment and mutilation: the worker is alienated from himself, from nature and from his fellow-men; he exists only as an animated *object*, not as a human being.

Since the time of Marx, the idea of alienation has been used more and more extensively by psychologists, sociologists, and philosophers—gathering to itself a wide variety of usages and meanings. But from Hegel and Marx onward, there appears to be an almost universal reluctance, on the part of those who employ the term, to define it precisely; it is as if one were expected to *feel* its meaning, rather than to grasp it conceptually. In a two-volume collection of essays entitled *Alienation*, the editor, Gerald Sykes, specifically scorns those who are too eager for a definition of the term; haste for a definition, he declares, reveals that one suffers from "an advanced case of—alienation."[2]

Certain writers—notably those of a Freudian or Jungian orientation—declare that the complexity of modern industrial society has caused man to become "over-civilized," to have lost touch with the deeper roots of his being, to have become alienated from his "instinctual nature." Others—notably those of an existentialist or Zen Buddhist orientation—complain that our advanced technological society compels man to live too intellectually, to be ruled by abstractions, thus alienating him from the real world which can be experienced in its "wholeness" only via his emotions. Others—notably those of

---

[2] New York: George Braziller, 1964, Vol. I, p. xiii.

a petulant mediocrity orientation—decry specifically the alienation of the artist; they assert that, with the vanishing of the age of patrons, with the artist thrown on his own resources to struggle in the marketplace—which is ruled by "philistines"—the artist is condemned to fight a losing battle for the preservation of his spiritual integrity: he is too besieged by material temptations.

Most of these writers declare that the problem of alienation—and of man's search for identity—is not new, but has been a source of anguish to man in every age and culture. But they insist that today, in Western civilization—above all, in America—the problem has reached an unprecedented severity. It has become a crisis.

What is responsible for this crisis? What has alienated man and deprived him of identity? The answer given by most writers on alienation is not always stated explicitly, but—in their countless disparaging references to "the dehumanizing effects of industrialism," "soul-destroying commercialism," "the arid rationalism of a technological culture," "the vulgar materialism of the West," etc.—the villain in their view of things, the destroyer whom they hold chiefly responsible, is not hard to identify. It is *capitalism*.

This should not be startling. Since its birth, capitalism has been made the scapegoat responsible for almost every real or imagined evil denounced by anyone. As the distinguished economist Ludwig von Mises observes:

> Nothing is more unpopular today than the free market economy, *i.e.*, capitalism. Everything that is considered unsatisfactory in present-day conditions is charged to capitalism. The atheists make capitalism responsible for the survival of Christianity. But the papal encyclicals blame capitalism for the spread of irreligion and the sins of our contemporaries, and the Protestant churches and sects are no less vigorous in their indictment of capitalist greed. Friends of peace consider our wars as an offshoot of capitalist imperialism. But the adamant nationalist warmongers of Germany and Italy indicted capitalism for its "bourgeois" pacifism, contrary to human nature and to the inescapable laws of history. Sermonizers accuse capitalism of disrupting the family and fostering licentiousness. But the "progressives" blame capitalism for the preservation of allegedly outdated rules of sexual restraint. Almost all men agree that poverty is an outcome of capitalism. On the other hand many deplore the fact that capitalism, in catering lavishly to the wishes of people intent upon getting

more amenities and a better living, promotes a crass materialism. These contradictory accusations of capitalism cancel one another. But the fact remains that there are few people left who would not condemn capitalism altogether.[8]

It is true that a great many men suffer from a chronic feeling of inner emptiness, of spiritual impoverishment, the sense of lacking personal identity. It is true that a great many men feel alienated—*from something*—even if they cannot say from what—from themselves or other men or the universe. And it is profoundly significant that capitalism should be blamed for this. Not because there is any justification for the charge, but because, by analyzing the reasons given for the accusation, one can learn a good deal about the nature and meaning of men's sense of alienation and non-identity—and, simultaneously, about the psychological motives that give rise to hostility toward capitalism.

The writers on alienation, as I have indicated, are not an intellectually homogeneous group. They differ in many areas: in their view of what the problem of alienation exactly consists of, in the aspects of modern industrial society and a free-market economy which they find most objectionable, in the explicitness with which they identify capitalism as the villain, and in the details of their own political inclinations. Some of these writers are socialists, some are fascists, some are medievalists, some are supporters of the welfare state, some scorn politics altogether. Some believe that the problem of alienation is largely or entirely solvable by a new system of social organization; others believe that the problem, at bottom, is metaphysical and that no entirely satisfactory solution can be found.

Fortunately for the purposes of this analysis, however, there is one contemporary writer who manages to combine in his books virtually all of the major errors perpetrated by commentators in this field: psychologist and sociologist Erich Fromm. Let us, therefore, consider Fromm's view of man and his theory of alienation in some detail.

Man, declares Erich Fromm, is "the freak of the universe."

This theme is crucial and central throughout his writings: man is radically different from all other living species, he is "estranged" and "alienated" from nature, he is overwhelmed by a feeling of "isolation" and "separateness"—he has lost, in the process of evolution, the undisturbed tranquillity of other

---

[8] Ludwig von Mises, *Socialism*, New Haven, Connecticut: Yale University Press, 1951, p. 527.

organisms, he has lost the "pre-human harmony" with nature which is enjoyed by an animal, a bird, or a worm. The *source* of his curse is the fact that he possesses a mind.

"Self-awareness, reason, and imagination," Fromm writes in *Man for Himself*, "have disrupted the 'harmony' which characterizes animal existence. Their emergence has made man into an anomaly, into the freak of the universe." Man cannot live as an animal: he is not equipped to adapt himself automatically and unthinkingly to his environment. An animal blindly "repeats the pattern of the species," its behavior is biologically prescribed and stereotyped, it "either fits in or it dies out"—but it does not have to *solve* the problem of survival, *it is not conscious of life and death as an issue.* Man does and is; this is his tragedy. "Reason, man's blessing, is also his curse. . . ."[4]

In *The Art of Loving,* he writes:

> What is essential in the existence of man is the fact that he has emerged from the animal kingdom, from instinctive adaptation, that he has transcended nature—although he never leaves it; he is part of it—and yet once torn away from nature, he cannot return to it; once thrown out of paradise—a state of original oneness with nature—cherubim with flaming swords block his way, if he should try to return.[5]

That man's rational faculty deprives man of "paradise," alienating and estranging him from nature, is clearly revealed, says Fromm, in the "existential dichotomies" which his mind dooms man to confront—"contradictions" inherent in life itself. What are these tragic "dichotomies"? He names three as central and basic. Man's mind permits him to "visualize his own end: death"—yet "his body makes him want to be alive."[6] Man's nature contains innumerable potentialities—yet "the short span of his life does not permit their full realization under even the most favorable circumstances."[7] Man "must be alone when he has to judge or to make decisions solely by the power of his reason"—yet "he cannot bear to be alone, to be unrelated to his fellow men."[8]

These "contradictions," says Fromm, constitute the dilem-

[4] Erich Fromm, *Man for Himself,* New York: Rinehart & Co., 1947, pp. 39, 40.
[5] Erich Fromm, *The Art of Loving,* New York: Harper & Brothers, 1956, p. 7.
[6] *Man for Himself,* p. 40.
[7] *Ibid.,* p. 42.
[8] *Ibid.,* p. 43.

ma of the "human situation"—contradictions with which man is compelled to struggle, but which he can never resolve or annul, *and which alienate man from himself, from his fellow men, and from nature.*

If the logic of the foregoing is not readily perceivable, the reason does not lie in the brevity of the synopsis. It lies in the unmitigated arbitrariness of Fromm's manner of presenting his ideas; he writes, not like a scientist, but like an oracle who is not obliged to give reasons or proof.

It is true that man differs fundamentally from all other living species, by virtue of possessing a rational, conceptual faculty. It is true that, for man, survival is a problem to be solved—by the exercise of his intelligence. It is true that no man lives long enough to exhaust his every potentiality. It is true that every man is alone, separate, and unique. It is true that thinking requires independence. These are the facts that grant glory to man's existence. Why would one choose to regard these facts as a terrifying cosmic paradox and to see in them the evidence of monumentally tragic human problems?

There *are* men who resent the fact that their life is their responsibility and that the task of their reason is to discover how to maintain it. Large numbers of such men—men who prefer the state of animals—may be found (or used to be found) sleeping on the benches of any public park; they are called tramps. There *are* men who find thought abnormal and unnatural. Large numbers of such men may be found in mental institutions; they are called morons. There *are* men who suffer a chronic preoccupation with death; who bitterly resent the fact that they cannot simultaneously be a concert pianist, a business tycoon, a railroad engineer, a baseball player, and a deep-sea diver; who find their existence as separate, independent entities an unendurable burden. Large numbers of such men may be found in the offices of psychotherapists; they are called neurotics. But why does Fromm choose tramps, morons, and neurotics as his symbols of humanity, as his image of man—and why does he choose to claim that *theirs* is the state in which all men are destined to start, and out of which they must struggle to rise?

Fromm does not tell us. Nowhere does he establish any logical connection between the facts he observes and the conclusions he announces.

If we are *not* to regard his conclusions as arbitrary—as mystical revelations, in effect—then we must assume that he does not bother to give reasons for his position because he regards his conclusions as virtually self-evident, as irresistibly conveyed by the facts he cites, easily available to everyone's experience and introspection. But if he feels it is readily apparent, by introspection, that the facts he cites constitute an agonizing problem for man—the most appropriate answer one can give is: "Speak for yourself, brother!"

Reason, Fromm insists, and the self-awareness which reason makes possible, turns man's "separate, disunited existence" into an "unbearable prison"—and man "would become insane could he not liberate himself from this prison and reach out, unite himself in some form or other with men, with the world outside."[9]

The following paragraph is typical of what Fromm considers an explanation:

> The experience of separateness arouses anxiety; it is, indeed, the source of all anxiety. Being separate means being cut off, without any capacity to use my human powers. Hence to be separate means to be helpless, unable to grasp the world—things and people—actively; it means that the world can invade me without my ability to react. Thus, separateness is the source of intense anxiety. Beyond that, it arouses shame and the feeling of guilt. This experience of guilt and shame in separateness is expressed in the Biblical story of Adam and Eve. After Adam and Eve have eaten of the "tree of knowledge of good and evil," after they have disobeyed . . . after they have become human by having emancipated themselves from the original animal harmony with nature, *i.e.*, after their birth as human beings—they saw "that they were naked—and they were ashamed." Should we assume that a myth as old and elementary as this has the prudish morals of the nineteenth-century outlook, and that the important point the story wants to convey to us is the embarrassment that their genitals were visible? This can hardly be so, and by understanding the story in a Victorian spirit, we miss the main point, which seems to be the following: after man and woman have become aware of themselves and of each other, they are aware of their separateness, and of their difference, inasmuch as they belong to different sexes. But while recognizing their separateness they remain strangers, because they have not yet learned to love each other (as is also made very clear by the fact that Adam defends himself by blaming Eve, rather than by trying to defend her). *The awareness of human separation, without reunion*

> *by love—is the source of shame. It is at the same time*
> *the source of guilt and anxiety.*[10]

All social institutions, all cultures, all religions and philoso-phies, all progress, asserts Fromm, are motivated by man's need to escape the terrifying sense of helplessness and aloneness to which his reason condemns him.

> *The necessity to find ever-new solutions for the contra-*
> *dictions in his existence, to find ever-higher forms of*
> *unity with nature, his fellowmen and himself, is the*
> *source of all psychic forces which motivate man. . . .*[11]

In *Man for Himself,* Fromm states that only through "reason, productiveness and love" can man solve the problem of his "separateness" and achieve a "new union" with the world around him. Fromm's claim to be an advocate of *reason* is disingenuous, to say the least. He speaks of reason and love as being "only two different forms of comprehend-ing the world."[12] As if this were not an unequivocal proof of his mysticism, he goes on to speak, in *The Art of Loving,* of the "paradoxical logic" of Eastern religions, which, he tells us approvingly, is not encumbered by the Aristotelian law of contradiction and which teaches that "man can perceive reality only in contradictions."[13] (Hegel and Marx, he asserts—correctly—belong to his "paradoxical" epistemologi-cal line.) His discussion of what he means by "produc-tiveness" is scarcely more gratifying.

In *The Art of Loving,* written some years after *Man for Himself,* he declares that reason and productive work, though certainly important, provide only partial and, by themselves, very unsatisfactory solutions: the "unity" they achieve is "not interpersonal," and the "desire for interpersonal fusion is the most powerful striving in man."[14] Fromm pulls an unex-plained switch at this point. What began as a problem be-tween man and nature is now to be solved (in some un-specified manner) by human "togetherness." One is not sur-prised; in reading Fromm, this is the sort of pronouncement for which one is waiting—there is a sense of inevitability

---

[10] *Ibid.,* pp. 8–9.
[11] Erich Fromm, *The Sane Society,* New York: Rinehart & Co., 1955, p. 25.
[12] *Man for Himself,* p. 97.
[13] *The Art of Loving,* p. 77.
[14] *Ibid.,* p. 18.

about it. Love and love alone, he tells us with wonderful originality, can allay man's terror—"Love is the only sane and satisfactory answer to the problem of human existence."[15]

Only through "relating" oneself positively to others, only through feeling "care and responsibility" for them—while preserving one's personal integrity, he adds somewhat mysteriously—can man establish new ties, a new union, that will release him from alienated aloneness.

The cat is now ready to be let fully out of the bag. The preceding is Fromm's view of alienation as a *metaphysical* problem; its full meaning and implication become clear when one turns to his *social-political* analysis of alienation. In the context of the latter, one can see clearly what sort of "ties," what sort of "union" and what sort of "love" Fromm has in mind.

Every society, as a system of human relationships, may be evaluated by how well it satisfies man's basic psychological needs, says Fromm—*i.e.*, he explains, by the possibilities for love, relatedness, and the experience of personal identity which it offers man.

Capitalism, Fromm declares, has been disastrous in this regard: far from solving the problem of man's alienation, it worsens it immeasurably in many respects. In liberating man from medieval regulation and authority, in breaking the chains of ecclesiastical, economic and social tyranny, in destroying the "stability" of the feudal order, capitalism and individualism thrust upon man an unprecedented freedom that was "bound to create a deep feeling of insecurity, powerlessness, doubt, aloneness, and anxiety."[16]

Scratch a collectivist and you will usually find a medievalist. Fromm is not an exception. Like so many socialists, he is a glamorizer of the Middle Ages. He perfunctorily acknowledges the faults of that historical period—but in contrasting it with the capitalism that succeeded it, he is enchanted by what he regards as its virtues.

What characterizes medieval in contrast to modern society is its lack of individual freedom. . . . But although a person was not free in the modern sense, neither was he alone and isolated. In having a distinct,

[15] *Ibid.*, p. 133.
[16] Erich Fromm, *Escape from Freedom*, New York: Rinehart & Co., 1941, p. 63.

unchangeable, and unquestionable place in the social world from the moment of birth, man was rooted in a structuralized whole, and thus life had a meaning which left no place, and no need, for doubt. A person was identical with his role in society; he *was* a peasant, an artisan, a knight, and not *an individual* who *happened* to have this or that occupation. The social order was conceived as a natural order, and being a definite part of it gave man a feeling of security and of belonging. There was comparatively little competition. One was born into a certain economic position which guaranteed a livelihood determined by tradition, just as it carried economic obligations to those higher in the social hierarchy. But within the limits of his social sphere the individual actually had much freedom to express his self in his work and in his emotional life. Although there was no individualism in the modern sense of the unrestricted choice between many possible ways of life (a freedom of choice which is largely abstract), there was a great deal of *concrete individualism in real life.*[17]

It is not uncommon to encounter this sort of perspective on the Middle Ages, among writers on alienation. But what makes the above passage especially shocking and offensive, in the case of Fromm, is that he repeatedly professes to be a lover of freedom and a valuer of human life.

The complete lack of control over any aspect of one's existence, the ruthless suppression of intellectual freedom, the paralyzing restrictions on any form of individual initiative and independence—these are cardinal characteristics of the Middle Ages. But all of this is swept aside by Fromm—along with the famines, the plagues, the exhausting labor from sunrise to sunset, the suffocating routine, the superstitious terror, the attacks of mass hysteria afflicting entire towns, the nightmare brutality of men's dealings with one another, the use of legalized torture as a normal way of life—all of this is swept aside, so entranced is Fromm by the vision of a world in which men did not have to invent and compete, they had only to submit and obey.

Nowhere does he tell us what specifically the medieval man's *"concrete individualism"* consisted of. One is morbidly curious to know what he would say.

With the collapse of medievalism and the emergence of a free-market society, Fromm declares, man was compelled to

[17] *Ibid.,* pp. 41–42.

assume total responsibility for his own survival: he had to produce and to trade—he had to think and to judge—he had no authority to guide him, and nothing but his own ability to keep him in existence. No longer could he, by virtue of the class into which he was born, *inherit* his sense of personal identity: henceforward, he had to *achieve* it. This posed a devastating psychological problem for man, intensifying his basic feeling of isolation and separateness.

"It is true," Fromm remarks, "that the capitalistic mode of production is conducive to political freedom, while any centrally planned social order is in danger of leading to political regimentation and eventually to dictatorship."[18] Capitalism, he further concedes, has proven itself superlatively capable of producing goods and of raising men's material standard of living to undreamed-of heights. But a "sane society" must have more to offer man than political freedom and material well-being. Capitalism, Fromm insists, is destructive of man's *spirit*. He offers several reasons for this charge, which are very revealing.

(1) Like Marx, Fromm decries the humiliating predicament of the worker who has to *sell* his *services*. Capitalism condemns the worker to experience himself, not as a man, but as a commodity, as a thing to be traded. Furthermore, since he is only a tiny part of a vast production process, since, for example, he does not build an entire automobile himself (and then drive home in it), but builds only a small part of it (the total being subsequently sold to some unknown, distant party), the worker feels alienated from the product of his own labor and, therefore, feels alienated from his own labor as such—unlike the artisan of the Middle Ages, whose labor could express the "full richness" of his personality.

It is an elementary fact of economics that specialization and exchange, under a division of labor, make a level of productivity possible which otherwise would not be remotely attainable. In pre-capitalist centuries, when a man's economic well-being was limited by the goods he himself could produce with his own primitive tools, an unconscionable amount of labor was required to make or acquire the simplest necessities—and the general standard of living was appallingly low: human existence was a continual, exhausting struggle against imminent starvation. About half of the children born, perished before the age of ten. But with the development of the wages system under capitalism, the introduction of machinery

[18] *The Sane Society,* p. 138.

and the opportunity for a man to sell his labor, life (to say nothing of an ever-increasing standard of material well-being) was made possible for millions who could have had no chance at survival in pre-capitalist economies. However, for Fromm and those who share his viewpoint, these considerations are, doubtless, too "materialistic." To offer men a chance to enjoy an unprecedented material well-being, is, evidently, to sentence them to alienation; whereas to hold them down to the stagnant level of a medieval serf or guildsman, is to offer them spiritual fulfillment.

(2) Fromm decries the "anonymity of the social forces . . . inherent in the structure of the capitalistic mode of production."[19] The laws of the market, of supply and demand, of economic cause and effect, are ominously impersonal: no single individual's *wishes* control them. Is it the worker who determines how much he is to be paid? No. It is not even the employer. It is that faceless monster, the market. *It* determines the wage level in some manner beyond the worker's power to grasp. As for the capitalist, his position is scarcely better: he, too, is helpless. "The individual capitalist expands his enterprise not primarily because he *wants* to, but because he *has* to, because . . . postponement of further expansion would mean regression."[20] If he attempts to stagnate, he will go out of business. Under such a system, asks Fromm, how can man *not* feel alienated?

Consider what Fromm is denouncing. Under capitalism, the wages paid to a man for his work are determined *objectively*—by the law of supply and demand. The market—reflecting the voluntary judgments of all those who participate in it, all those who buy and sell, produce and consume, offer or seek employment—establishes the general price level of goods and services. This is the context which men are obliged to consider in setting the prices they will ask for their work or offer for the work of others; if a man demands more than the market value of his work, he will remain unemployed; if a particular employer offers him less than the market value of his work, the man will seek—and find—employment elsewhere. The same principle applies to the capitalist who offers his goods for sale. If the prices and quality of his goods are comparable or preferable to those of other men in the same field of production, he will be able to compete; if others can do better than he can, if they can offer superior goods and/or lower prices, he will be obliged to improve, to grow, to equal their achievement, or else he will lose his customers.

[19] *Ibid.*
[20] *Ibid.*, p. 86.

The standard determining a producer's success or failure is the *objective* value of his product—as judged, within the context of the market (and of their knowledge), by those to whom he offers his product. This is the only rational and just principle of exchange. But *this* is what Fromm considers evil.

What he rebels against is *objectivity*. How—he demands—can a man not feel alienated in a system where his wishes are not omnipotent, where the unearned is not to be had, where growth is rewarded and stagnation is penalized?

It is clear from the foregoing that Fromm's basic quarrel is with *reality*—since nature confronts man with the identical conditions, which a free economy merely reflects: nature, too, holds man to the law of cause and effect; nature, too, makes constant growth a condition of successful life.

There are writers on alienation who recognize this and do not bother to center their attacks on capitalism: they damn nature outright. They declare that man's life is intrinsically and inescapably *tragic*—since reality is "tyrannical," since contradictory desires cannot be satisfied, since objectivity is a "prison," since time is a "net" that no one can elude, etc. Existentialists, in particular, specialize in this sort of pronouncement.

(3) As *consumer* in a capitalist economy, Fromm contends, man is subject to further alienating pressures. He is overwhelmed with innumerable products among which he must choose. He is bewildered and brainwashed by the blandishments of advertisers, forever urging him to buy their wares. This staggering multiplicity of possible choices is threatening to his sanity. Moreover, he is "conditioned" to consume for the sake of consuming—to long for an ever-higher standard of living—merely in order to keep the "system" going. With automatic washing machines, automatic cameras, and automatic can openers, modern man's relationship to nature becomes more and more remote. He is increasingly condemned to the nightmare of an *artificial* world.

No such problem confronted the feudal serf.

This much is true: sleeping on an earthen floor, the medieval serf—to say nothing of the caveman—was much *closer* to nature, in one uncomfortable and unhygienic sense of the word.

The above criticism of capitalism has become very fashionable among social commentators. What is remarkable is that almost invariably, as in the case of Fromm, the criticism is made by the same writers who are loudest in crying that man needs more *leisure*. Yet the purpose of the "gadgets" they condemn is, specifically, to liberate man's time. Thus they wish to provide man with more leisure, while damning the material means that make leisure possible.

As for the charge—equally popular—that the multiplicity of choices offered to man in capitalistic society is threatening to his mental equilibrium, it should be remembered that *fear* of choices and decisions is a basic symptom of mental illness. To whose mentality, then, do these critics of capitalism demand that society be adjusted?

(4) The development of a complex, highly industrialized society requires an extreme degree of quantification and abstraction in men's method of thinking, observes Fromm—and this, in still another way, estranges man from the world around him: he loses the ability to relate to things in "their concreteness and uniqueness."[21]

One can agree with Fromm in part: an industrial technological society demands the fullest development and exercise of man's *conceptual* faculty, *i.e.*, of his distinctively *human* form of cognition. The *sensory-perceptual* level of consciousness— the level of an animal's cognition—will not do.

Those who assert that the conceptual level of consciousness alienates man from the real world, merely confess that their concepts bear no relation to reality—or that they do not understand the relation of concepts to reality. But it should be remembered that the capacity to abstract and conceptualize offers man—to the extent that he is rational—a means of "relating" to the world around him immeasurably superior to that enjoyed by any other species. It does not "alienate" man from nature, it makes him nature's master: an animal obeys nature *blindly;* man obeys her *intelligently*—and thereby acquires the power to command her.

(5) Finally, most alienating of all, perhaps, are the sort of relationships that exist among men under capitalism, says Fromm.

What is the modern man's *relationship to his fellow man?* It is one between two abstractions, two living machines, who use each other. The employer uses the ones whom he employs; the salesman uses his customers. ... There is not much love or hate to be found in human relations of our day. There is, rather, a superficial friendliness, and a more than superficial fairness, but behind that surface is distance and indifference. ... The alienation between man and man results in the loss

[21] *Ibid.*, p. 114.

of those general and social bonds which characterize medieval as well as most other precapitalist societies.[22]

Fromm is claiming that there existed, in pre-capitalist societies, a mutual good will among men, an attitude of respect and benevolent solidarity, a regard for the value of the human person, that vanished with the rise of a free-market society. This is worse than false. The claim is absurd historically and disgraceful morally.

It is notorious that, in the Middle Ages, human relationships were characterized by mutual suspiciousness, hostility, and cruelty: everyone regarded his neighbor as a potential threat, and nothing was held more cheaply than human life. Such invariably is the case in *any* society where men are ruled by brute force. In putting an end to slavery and serfdom, capitalism introduced a social benevolence that would have been impossible under earlier systems. Capitalism valued a man's life as it had never been valued before. Capitalism is the politico-economic expression of the principle that a man's life, freedom, and happiness are his by moral right.

There is a passage in *The Fountainhead* that bears on this issue. "Civilization is the progress toward a society of privacy. The savage's whole existence is public, ruled by the laws of his tribe. Civilization is the process of setting man free from men."

Under capitalism, men are free to *choose* their "social bonds"—meaning: to choose whom they will associate with. Men are not trapped within the prison of their family, tribe, caste, class, or neighborhood. They choose whom they will value, whom they will befriend, whom they will deal with, what kind of relationships they will enter. This implies and entails man's responsibility to form independent value-judgments. It implies and entails, also, that a man must *earn* the social relationships he desires. But this, clearly, is anathema to Fromm.

"Love," he has told us, "is the only sane and satisfactory answer to the problem of human existence"—but, he asserts, love and capitalism are *inimical.* "The *principle* underlying capitalistic society and the *principle* of love are incompatible."[23] The principle of capitalism, says Fromm, is that of "fairness ethics," of *trade,* of the exchange of values, without recourse to force or fraud; individuals deal with one another only on the premise of mutual self-interest; they

[22] *Ibid.,* p. 139.
[23] *The Art of Loving,* p. 131.

engage only in those transactions from which they expect a profit, reward, or gain. "It may even be said that the development of fairness ethics is the particular ethical contribution of capitalist society."[24]

But to approach love with any concern for one's self-interest is—he asserts—to negate the very essence of love. To love an individual is to feel care and responsibility for him; it is not to appraise his character or personality as a "commodity" from which one expects pleasure. To love "ideally" is to love "unconditionally"—it is to love a human being, not for the fact of *what* he is, but for the fact *that* he is—it is to love without reference to values or standards or judgment. "In essence, all human beings are identical. We are all part of One; we are One. This being so, it should not make any difference whom we love."[25]

It should not, in other words, make any difference whether the person we love is a being of stature or a total nonentity, a genius or a fool, a hero or a scoundrel. "We are all part of One." Is it necessary to point out who stands to gain and who to lose by this view of love?

The desire to be loved "unconditionally," the desire to be loved with no concern for his objective personal worth, is one of man's "deepest longings," Fromm insists; whereas to be loved on the basis of *merit*, "because one deserves it," invokes doubt and uncertainty, since merit has to be struggled for and since such love can be withdrawn should the merit cease to exist. "Furthermore, 'deserved' love easily leaves a bitter feeling that one is not loved for oneself, that one is loved *only* because one pleases . . ."[26]

It is typical of Fromm that he should deliver what is in fact (though not in Fromm's estimate) a deadly insult to human nature, without offering any justification for his charge. He assumes that all men, by nature, are so profoundly lacking in self-esteem that they crave a love which bears no relation to their actions, achievements, or character, a love not to be earned but to be received only as a free gift.

What does it mean to be loved "for oneself"? In reason, it can mean only: to be loved for the values one has achieved in one's character and person. The highest compliment one can be paid by another human being is to be told: "Because of what you are, you are essential to my happiness." But this

[24] *Ibid.,* p. 129.
[25] *Ibid.,* p. 55.
[26] *Ibid.,* p. 42.

is the love that, according to Fromm, leaves one with "a bitter feeling."

It is the capitalistic culture, he declares, that inculcates such concepts as the "deserved" and the "undeserved"—the earned and the unearned—and thus poisons the growth of proper love. Proper love, Fromm tells us, should be given solely out of the richness of the spirit of the giver, in demonstration of the giver's "potency." Fromm nowhere reveals the exact nature of this "potency," of course. "Love is an act of faith . . ."[27] Proper love should raise no questions about the virtue or character of its object; it should desire no joy from such virtue as the object might possess—for, if it does, it is not proper love, it is only capitalistic selfishness.

But, Fromm asks, "how can one act within the framework of existing society and at the same time practice love?"[28] He does not declare that love is *impossible* under capitalism—merely that it is exceptionally difficult.

Commenting, in *Who Is Ayn Rand?*, on Fromm's theory of love, I wrote:

> To love . . . is to *value;* love, properly, is the consequence and expression of admiration—"the emotional price paid by one man for the joy he receives from the virtues of another." [*Atlas Shrugged*] Love is not alms, but a moral tribute.
>
> If love did *not* imply admiration, if it did not imply an acknowledgment of moral qualities that the recipient of love possessed—what meaning or significance would love have, and why would Fromm or anyone consider it desirable? Only one answer is possible, and it is not an attractive one: when love is divorced from values, then "love" becomes, not a tribute, but a moral blank check: a promise that one will be forgiven anything, that one will not be abandoned, that one will be taken care of.[29]

This view of love is not, of course, peculiar to Fromm; it is a central component of the mystic-altruist tradition—and is as prevalent among psychologists, sociologists, and philosophers as it is among religionists. Perhaps the simplest and most eloquent answer to this view of love is one sentence of

[27] *Ibid.*, p. 128.
[28] *Ibid.*, pp. 130–131.
[29] Nathaniel Branden, *Who Is Ayn Rand?*, New York: Random House, 1962, pp. 38–39; Paperback Library, 1964.

John Galt in *Atlas Shrugged:* "A morality that professes the belief that the values of the spirit are more precious than matter, a morality that teaches you to scorn a whore who gives her body indiscriminately to all men—this same morality demands that you surrender your soul to promiscuous love for all comers."

To divorce love from values (and value-judgments), is to confess one's longing for the unearned. The idealization of this longing as a proper moral goal is a constant theme running through Fromm's writing.

That the underlying motive is the desire to be taken care of, the desire to be spared the responsibility of independence, is revealed explicitly in Fromm's socio-political "solution" to the problem of alienation.

In order that man may be enabled to conquer his feeling of aloneness and alienation, to practice love and to achieve a full sense of personal identity, a new social system must be established, Fromm declares.

Private ownership of the means of production must be abolished. The profit motive must be forbidden. Industry must be decentralized. Society should be divided into self-governing industrial guilds; factories should be owned and run by all those who work in them.

Why—according to Fromm's social philosophy—should a janitor in an industrial plant not have the same right to determine its management as the man who happened to create the plant? Does not the janitor's personality require as much self-expression as anyone else's?

Under capitalism, says Fromm, men are overwhelmed by and are the pawns of a complex industrial machine whose omnipotent forces and laws are beyond their comprehension or control. Under the decentralized, "democratic" system he proposes—which is some sort of blend of guild socialism and syndicalism—industrial establishments will be broken down into units whose function is within everyone's easy comprehension, with no "alienating" demands made on anyone's abstract capacity.

Under this system, he explains, every person will be provided with his minimum subsistence, whether the person wishes to work or not. This is necessary if man is to develop healthily and happily. However, to discourage parasitism, Fromm suggests that this support should not extend beyond two years. Who is to provide this support, whether they will be willing to do so, and what will happen if they are not willing, are questions Fromm does not discuss.

So long as men are occupied with the problem of survival, Fromm feels, their spiritual concerns—the concerns that really *matter*—are almost inevitably neglected. How can the worker's personality not be impoverished, if he must face daily the necessity of earning a livelihood? How can the businessman develop his creative potentialities, if he is in bondage to his obsession with production? How can the artist preserve his soul's integrity, if he is plagued with temptations by Hollywood and Madison Avenue? How can the consumer cultivate individual tastes and preferences, if he is surrounded by the standardized commodities begotten by mass production?

If one wishes to understand the relevance of epistemology to politics, one should observe what is gained for Fromm by that "paradoxical logic" of which he writes so approvingly. If, as it it teaches, "man can perceive reality only in contradictions," then Fromm does not have to be troubled by the conflict between his claim to be an advocate of reason and his enthusiasm for Eastern mysticism—nor does he have to be troubled by the conflict between his claim to be a defender of individualism and his advocacy of political collectivism. His disdain for the law of contradiction permits him to announce that true individualism is possible only in the collectivized community—that true freedom is possible only when production is taken out of the hands of private individuals and placed under the absolute control of the group—that men will cease to be objects of "use" by others, only when they are willing to renounce personal profit and make *social usefulness* the goal of their lives.[30]

Fromm calls his proposed system "Humanistic Communitarian Socialism." Under it, he maintains, man will achieve "a new harmony with nature" to replace the one he has lost—man will enjoy the tranquillity and self-fulfillment of the animals whose state Fromm finds so enviable.

If, often, Fromm is more than a little disingenuous in the presentation of his views, he is, nonetheless, extremely *explicit*. This is what is unusual about him. Most writers of his persuasion twist themselves for pages and pages in order to obscure their advocacy of the ideas—and contradictions—which he announces openly. With rare exceptions, one will find comparable candor only among the existentialists and Zen Buddhists, many of whose premises Fromm shares.

His explicitness notwithstanding, he is very representative culturally and should be recognized as such. The recurrent themes running through the literature on alienation—and

---

[30] For the most detailed presentation of these doctrines, see Fromm's *The Sane Society*.

through today's social commentary generally—are the themes which Fromm brings into naked focus: that reason is "unnatural," that a non-contradictory, objective reality "restricts" one's individuality, that the necessity of *choice* is an awesome burden, that it is "tragic" not to be able to eat one's cake and have it, too, that self-responsibility is frightening, that the achievement of personal identity is a *social* problem—that "love" is the omnipotent solution—and that the political implementation of this solution is socialism.

The transparent absurdity or the unintelligibility of most discussions of alienation might tempt one to believe that the issue is entirely illusory. But this would be an error. Although the explanations offered for it are spurious, the problem of alienation is real. A great many men do recognize the painful emotional state which writers on alienation describe. A great many men do lack a sense of personal identity. A great many men do feel themselves to be strangers and afraid in a world they never made.

But *why?* What *is* the problem of alienation? What *is* personal identity? Why should so many men experience the task of achieving it as a dreaded burden? And what is the significance of the attacks on capitalism in connection with this issue?

These are the questions we must now proceed to answer.

The problem of alienation and the problem of personal identity are inseparable. The man who lacks a firm sense of personal identity feels alienated; the man who feels alienated lacks a firm sense of personal identity.

Pain is an organism's alarm-signal, warning of danger; the particular species of pain which is the feeling of alienation announces to a man that he is existing in a psychological state improper to him—*that his relationship to reality is wrong.*

No animal faces such questions as: What should I make of myself? What manner of life is proper to my nature? Such questions are possible only to a rational being, *i.e.*, a being whose characteristic method of cognitive functioning (of apprehending reality) is conceptual, who is not only conscious but also self-conscious, and whose power of abstraction enables him to project many alternative courses of action. Further, such questions are possible only to a being w ose cognitive faculty is exercised *volitionally* (thinking is not automatic)—a being who is self-directing and self-regulating in thought and in action, and whose existence, therefore, entails a constant process of *choice.*

As a living entity, man is born with specific needs and capacities; these constitute his *species* identity, so to speak—

i.e., they constitute his human nature. How he exercises his capacities to satisfy his needs—*i.e.*, how he deals with the facts of reality, how he chooses to function, in thought and in action—constitutes his *personal* or *individual* identity. His sense of himself—his implicit concept or image of the kind of person he is (including his self-esteem or lack of it)—is the cumulative product of the choices he makes. This is the meaning of Ayn Rand's statement that "man is a being of self-made soul."

A man's "I," his ego, his deepest self, is his faculty of awareness, his capacity to think. To choose to think, to identify the facts of reality—to assume the responsibility of judging what is true or false, right or wrong—is man's basic form of *self-assertiveness*. It is his acceptance of his own nature as a rational being, his acceptance of the responsibility of intellectual independence, his commitment to the efficacy of his own mind.

The essence of *selflessness* is the suspension of one's consciousness. When and to the extent that a man chooses to evade the effort and responsibility of thinking, of seeking knowledge, of passing judgment, his action is one of *self-abdication*. To relinquish thought, is to relinquish one's ego—and to pronounce oneself unfit for existence, incompetent to deal with the facts of reality.

To the extent that a man chooses to think, his premises and values are acquired first-hand and they are not a mystery to him; he experiences himself as the *active cause* of his character, behavior, and goals. To the extent that a man attempts to live without thinking, he experiences himself as *passive*, his person and actions are the accidental products of forces he does not understand, of his range-of-the-moment feelings and random environmental influences. When a man defaults on the responsibility of thought, he is left at the mercy of his involuntary, subconscious reactions—and *these* will be at the mercy of the outside forces impinging upon him, at the mercy of whoever and whatever is around him. By his default, such a person turns himself into the social determinists' view of man: into an empty mold waiting to be filled, into a will-less robot waiting to be taken over by any environment and any conditioners.

A strong sense of personal identity is the product of two things: a policy of independent thinking—and, as a consequence, the possession of an integrated set of values. Since it is his values that determine a man's emotions and goals, and give direction and meaning to his life, a man experiences his values as an extension of himself, as an integral part of his identity, as crucial to that which makes him himself.

"Values," in this context, refers to fundamental and abstract values, not to concrete value-judgments. For example, a man holding rationality as his abstract value may choose a friend who appears to embody this value; if, subsequently, he decides that he was mistaken in his judgment, that his friend is not rational and that their relationship should be ended, this does not alter his personal identity; but if, instead, he decides that he no longer values rationality, his personal identity *is* altered.

If a man holds contradictory values, these necessarily do violence to his sense of personal identity. They result in a splintered sense of self, a self broken into unintegratable fragments. To avoid this painful experience of a splintered identity, a man whose values are contradictory will commonly seek to escape knowledge of his contradictions by means of evasion, repression, rationalization, etc. Thus, to escape a problem created by a failure of thought, he suspends thinking. To escape a threat to his sense of personal identity, *he suspends his ego*—he suspends his self *qua* thinking, judging entity.

Thus, he displaces his sense of self *downward,* so to speak, from his reason, which is the active, initiating element in man, to his emotions, which are the passive, reactive element. Moved by feelings whose source he does not understand, and by contradictions whose existence he does not acknowledge, he suffers a progressive sense of self-estrangement, of self-alienation. A man's emotions are the product of his premises and values, of the thinking he has done or has failed to do. But the man who is run by his emotions, attempting to make them a substitute for rational judgment, experiences them as alien forces. The paradox of his position is this: his emotions become his only source of personal identity, but his experience of identity becomes: *a being ruled by demons*.

It is important to observe that the experience of self-alienation and the feeling of being alienated from reality, from the world around one, proceed from the same cause: one's default on the responsibility of thinking. The suspension of proper cognitive contact with reality and the suspension of one's ego, are a single act. A flight from reality is a flight from self.

One of the consequences is a feeling of alienation from other men, the sense that one is not part of the human race—that one is, in effect, a freak. In betraying one's status as a human being, one makes oneself a metaphysical outcast. This is not altered by the knowledge that many other human beings have committed the same betrayal. One feels alone and cut off—cut off by the unreality of one's own existence, by one's desolate inner sense of spiritual impoverishment.

The same failure of rationality and independence by which men rob themselves of personal identity leads them, most commonly, to the self-destructive policy of seeking a *substitute* for identity—or, more precisely, seeking a *second-hand* identity—through mindless conformity to the values of others. This is the psychological phenomenon which I have designated as social metaphysics. In my article "Rogues Gallery,"[31] dealing with different types of social metaphysicians, I commented on the type most relevant to the present context, the "Conventional" social metaphysician:

> This is the person who accepts the world and its prevailing values ready-made; his is not to reason why. What is true? What others say is true. What is right? What others believe is right. How should one live? As others live. . . . [This is] the person whose sense of identity and personal worth is *explicitly* a function of his ability to satisfy the values, terms and expectations of those omniscient and omnipresent "others." . . . In a culture such as the present one, with its disintegrating values, its intellectual chaos, its moral bankruptcy— where the familiar guideposts and rules are vanishing, where the authoritative mirrors reflecting "reality" are splintering into a thousand unintelligible subcults, where "adjustment" is becoming harder and harder—the Conventional social metaphysician is the first to run to a psychiatrist, crying that he has lost his identity, because he no longer knows unequivocally what he is supposed to do and be.

It would never occur to a person of self-esteem and independent judgment that one's "identity" is a thing to be gained from or determined by others. To a person untouched by self-doubt, the wails heard today about the anguish of modern man as he confronts the question "Who am I?" are incomprehensible. But in the light of the above, the wailing becomes more intelligible. It is the cry of social metaphysicians who no longer know which authorities to obey—and who are moaning that it is *someone's* duty to herd them to a sense of self, that "The System" must provide them with self-esteem.

[31] *The Objectivist Newsletter*, February 1965.

This is the psychological root of the modern intellectuals' mystique of the Middle Ages, of the dazed longing for that style of life—and of the massive evasion concerning the actual conditions of existence during that period. The Middle Ages represents the social metaphysician's unconfessed dream: a system in which his dread of independence and self-responsibility is proclaimed to be a virtue and is made a social imperative.

When—in any age—a man attempts to evade the responsibility of intellectual independence, and to derive his sense of identity from "belonging," he pays a deadly price in terms of the sabotaging of his mental processes thereafter. The degree to which a man substitutes the judgment of others for his own, failing to look at reality directly, is the degree to which his mental processes are alienated from reality. He functions not by means of concepts, but by means of memorized cue-words, *i.e.*, learned *sounds* associated with certain contexts and situations, but lacking authentic cognitive content for their user. This is the unidentified, unrecognized phenomenon that prompts unthinking people today to grant validity to the charge that modern man lives "too abstractly," "too intellectually," and that he needs to "get back to nature." They sense dimly that they are out of contact with reality, that something is wrong with their grasp of the world around them. But they accept an entirely fallacious interpretation of their problem The truth is not that they are lost among "abstractions," but that they have failed to discover the nature and proper use of abstractions; they are not lost among concepts, they are lost among *cue-words.* They are cut off from reality not because they attempt to grasp it too intellectually, but because they attempt to grasp it *only as seen by others;* they attempt to grasp it *second-hand.* And they move through an unreal world of verbal rituals, mouthing the slogans and phrases they hear repeated by others, falsely imagining that those empty words are concepts, and never apprehending the proper use of their conceptual faculty, never learning what first-hand, conceptual knowledge consists of. Then they are ready for the Zen Buddhist who tells them that the solution to their alienation from reality is to empty their mind of all thought and sit for an hour, cross-legged, contemplating the pattern of veins on a leaf.

It is a well-known psychological fact that when men are neurotically anxious, when they suffer from feelings of dread for which they cannot account, they often attempt to make their plight more tolerable by directing their fear at some external object: they seek to persuade themselves that their fear is a rational response to the threat of germs, or the possible appearance of burglars, or the danger of lightning, or the brain-controlling radiations of Martians. The process by which men decide that the cause of their alienation is capitalism, is not dissimilar.

There are reasons, however, why capitalism is the target for their projection and rationalization.

The alienated man is fleeing from the responsibility of a volitional (*i.e.*, self-directing) consciousness: the freedom to think or not to think, to initiate a process of reason or to evade it, is a burden he longs to escape. But since this freedom is inherent in his nature as man, there is no escape from it; hence his guilt and anxiety when he abandons reason and sight in favor of feelings and blindness. But there is another level on which man confronts the issue of freedom: the existential or social level—and here escape *is* possible. *Political* freedom is not a metaphysical given: it has to be *achieved*—hence it can be rejected. The psychological root of the revolt against freedom in one's existence, is the revolt against freedom in one's consciousness. *The root of the revolt against self-responsibility in action is the revolt against self-direction in thought.* The man who does not want to think, does not want to bear responsibility for the consequences of his actions nor for his own life.

It is appropriate, in this connection, to quote a passage from *Who Is Ayn Rand?* in which I discuss the similarity of the attacks against capitalism launched by nineteenth-century medievalists and socialists:

> In the writings of both medievalists and socialists, one can observe the unmistakable longing for a society in which man's existence will be automatically guaranteed to him—that is, in which man will not have to bear responsibility for his own survival. Both camps project their ideal society as one characterized by that which they call "harmony," by freedom from rapid change or challenge or the exacting demands of competition; a society in which each must do his prescribed part to contribute to the well-being of the whole, but in which no one will face the necessity of making choices and decisions that will crucially affect his life and future; in which the question of what one has or has not earned, and does or does not deserve, will not come up; in which rewards will not be tied to achievement and in which someone's benevolence will guarantee that one need never bear the consequences of one's errors. The failure of capitalism to conform to what may be

termed this *pastoral* view of existence, is essential to the medievalists' and socialists' indictment of a free society. It is not a Garden of Eden that capitalism offers men.[32]

Today, of course, capitalism has largely been abandoned in favor of a mixed economy, *i.e.*, a mixture of freedom and statism—moving steadily in the direction of increasing statism. Today, we are far closer to the "ideal society" of the socialists than when Marx first wrote of the worker's "alienation." Yet with every advance of collectivism, the cries concerning man's alienation grow louder. The problem, we are told, is getting worse. In communist countries, when such criticisms are allowed to be voiced, some commentators are beginning to complain that the Marxist solution to the worker's alienation has failed, that man under communism is still alienated, that the "new harmony" with nature and one's fellow men has not come.

It didn't come to the medieval serf or guildsman, either—the propaganda of commentators such as Erich Fromm notwithstanding.

Man cannot escape from his nature, and if he establishes a social system which is inimical to the requirements of his nature—a system which forbids him to function as a rational, independent being—psychological and physical disaster is the result.

A free society, of course, cannot automatically guarantee the mental well-being of all its members. Freedom is not a *sufficient* condition to assure man's proper fulfillment, but it is a *necessary* condition. And capitalism—laissez-faire capitalism—is the only system which provides that condition.

The problem of alienation is not metaphysical; it is not man's natural fate, never to be escaped, like some sort of Original Sin; it is a *disease*. It is not the consequence of capitalism or industrialism or "bigness"—and it cannot be legislated out of existence by the abolition of property rights. The problem of alienation is *psycho-epistemological*: it pertains to how man chooses to use his own consciousness. It is the product of man's revolt against thinking—which means: against reality.

If a man defaults on the responsibility of seeking knowledge, choosing values and setting goals—if this is the sphere he surrenders to the authority of others—*how is he to escape the feeling that the universe is closed to him?* It is. By his own choice.

---

[32] Branden, *Who Is Ayn Rand?*, pp. 15–16.

The proper answer to the question—

> And how am I to face the odds
> of man's bedevilment and God's?
> I, a stranger and afraid
> in a world I never made

—is: *Why didn't you?*

24. REQUIEM FOR MAN

BY AYN RAND

In advocating capitalism, I have said and stressed for years that capitalism is incompatible with altruism and mysticism. Those who chose to doubt that the issue is "either-or," have now heard it from the highest authority of the opposite side: Pope Paul VI.

The encyclical *"Populorum Progressio"* ("On the Development of Peoples") is an unusual document: it reads as if a long-repressed emotion broke out into the open, past the barrier of carefully measured, cautiously calculated sentences, with the hissing pressure of centuries of silence. The sentences are full of contradictions; the emotion is consistent.

The encyclical is the manifesto of an impassioned hatred for capitalism; but its evil is much more profound and its target is more than mere politics. It is written in terms of a mystic-altruist "sense of life." A sense of life is the subconscious equivalent of metaphysics: a pre-conceptual, emotionally integrated appraisal of man's nature and of his relationship to existence. To a mystic-altruist sense of life, words are mere approximations; hence the encyclical's tone of evasion. But what is eloquently revealing is the nature of that which is being evaded.

On the question of capitalism, the encyclical's position is explicit and unequivocal. Referring to the industrial revolution, the encyclical declares: "But it is unfortunate that on these new conditions of society a system has been constructed which considers profit as the key motive for economic progress, competition as the supreme law of economics, and private ownership of the means of production as an absolute right that has no limits and carries no corresponding social obligation. . . . But if it is true that a type of capitalism has been the source of excessive suffering, injustices and fratricidal conflicts whose effects still persist, it would also be wrong to attribute to industrialization itself evils that belong to the woeful system which accompanied it." (Paragraph 26)

The Vatican is not the city room of a third-rate Marxist tabloid. It is an institution geared to a perspective of centuries, to scholarship and timeless philosophical deliberation. Ignorance, therefore, cannot be the explanation of the above. Even the leftists know that the advent of capitalism and industrialization was not an "unfortunate" coincidence, and that the first made the second possible.

What are the "excessive suffering, injustices and fratricidal conflicts" caused by capitalism? The encyclical gives no answer. What social system, past or present, has a better record in respect to *any* social evil that anyone might choose to ascribe to capitalism? Has the feudalism of the Middle Ages? Has absolute monarchy? Has socialism or fascism? No answer. If one is to consider "excessive suffering, injustices and fratricidal conflicts," what aspect of capitalism can be placed in the same category with the terror and wholesale slaughter of Nazi Germany or Soviet Russia? No answer. If there is no causal connection between capitalism and the people's progress, welfare, and standard of living, why are these highest in the countries whose systems have the largest element of capitalistic economic freedom? No answer.

Since the encyclical is concerned with history and with fundamental political principles, yet does not discuss or condemn any social system other than capitalism, one must conclude that all other systems are compatible with the encyclical's political philosophy. This is supported by the fact that capitalism is condemned, not for some lesser characteristics, but *for its essentials,* which are not the base of any other system: the profit motive, competition, and private ownership of the means of production.

By what moral standard does the encyclical judge a social system? Its most specific accusation directed at capitalism reads as follows: "The desire for necessities is legitimate, and work undertaken to obtain them is a duty: 'If any man will not work, neither let him eat.' But the acquiring of temporal goods can lead to greed, to the insatiable desire for more, and can make increased power a tempting objective. Individuals, families and nations can be overcome by avarice, be they poor or rich, and all can fall victim to a stifling materialism." (18)

Since time immemorial and pre-industrial, "greed" has been the accusation hurled at the rich by the concrete-bound illiterates who were unable to conceive of the source of wealth or of the motivation of those who produce it. But the above was not written by an illiterate.

Terms such as "greed" and "avarice" connote the carica-ture image of two individuals, one fat, the other lean, one indulging in mindless gluttony, the other starving over chests of hoarded gold—both symbols of the acquisition of riches for the sake of riches. Is that the motive-power of capital-ism?

If all the wealth spent on personal consumption by all the rich of the United States were expropriated and distributed among our population, it would amount to less than a dollar per person. (Try to figure out the amount, if distributed to the entire population of the globe.) The rest of American wealth is invested in production—and it is this constantly growing investment that raises America's standard of living by raising the productivity of its labor. This is primer economics which Pope Paul VI cannot fail to know.

To observe the technique of epistemological manipulation, read that quoted paragraph again—and look past the images invoked by the window-dressing of "greed" and "avarice." You will observe that the evil being denounced is: "the insatiable desire for more." Of what? Of "increased power." What sort of power? No direct answer is given in that paragraph, but the entire encyclical provides the answer by means of a significant omission: no distinction is drawn between *economic* power and *political* power (between production and force), they are used interchangeably in some passages and equated explicitly in others. If you look at the facts of reality, you will observe that the "increased power" which men of wealth seek under capitalism is the power of *indepen-dent* production, the power of an "insatiable" ambition to expand their productive capacity—and that *this* is what the encyclical damns. The evil is not work, but *ambitious* work.

These implications are supported and gently stressed in a subsequent paragraph, which lists the encyclical's view of "less human" conditions of social existence: "The lack of material necessities for those who are without the minimum essential for life, the moral deficiencies of those who are mutilated by selfishness. . . . Oppressive social structures, whether due to the abuses of ownership or to the abuses of power . . ."And, as "more human" conditions: "the passage from misery toward the possession of necessities. . . ." (21)

What "necessities" are the "minimum essential for life"? For what kind of life? Is it for mere physical survival? If so, for how long a survival? No answer is given. But the encycli-cal's principle is clear: only those who rise no higher than the barest minimum of subsistence have the *right* to material possessions—and this right supersedes all the rights of all other men, including their right to life. This is stated explicitly:

"The Bible, from the first page on, teaches us that the whole of creation is for man, that it is his responsibility to develop it by intelligent effort and by means of his labor to perfect it, so to speak, for his use. If the world is made to furnish each individual with the means of livelihood and the instruments for his growth and progress, each man has therefore the right to find in the world what is necessary for himself. The recent Council reminded us of this: 'God intended the earth and all that it contains for the use of every human being and people. Thus, as all men follow justice and charity, created goods should abound for them on a reasonable basis.' All other rights whatsoever, including those of property and of free commerce, are to be subordinated to this principle." (22)

Observe what element is missing from this view of the world, what human faculty is regarded as inessential or non-existent. I shall discuss this aspect later in more detail. For the moment, I shall merely call your attention to the use of the word "man" in the above paragraph (*which* man?)— and to the term "created goods." Created—by whom? Blank out.

That missing element becomes blatant in the encyclical's next paragraph: "It is well known how strong were the words used by the fathers of the church to describe the proper attitude of persons who possess anything toward persons in need. To quote St. Ambrose: 'You are not making a gift of your possessions to the poor person. You are handing over to him what is his. For what has been given in common for the use of all, you have arrogated to yourself. The world is given to all, and not only to the rich.' That is, private property does not constitute for anyone an absolute and unconditional right. No one is justified in keeping for his exclusive use what he does not need, when others lack necessities." (23)

St. Ambrose lived in the fourth century, when such views of property could conceivably have been explicable, if not justifiable. From the nineteenth century on, they can be neither.

What solution does the encyclical offer to the problems of today's world? "Individual initiative alone and the mere free play of competition could never assure successful development. One must avoid the risk of increasing still more the wealth of the rich and the dominion of the strong, while leaving the poor in their misery and adding to the servitude of the oppressed. Hence programs are necessary in order 'to encourage, stimulate, coordinate, supplement and integrate' the activity of individuals and of intermediary bodies. It pertains to the public authorities to choose, even to lay down, the objectives to be pursued, the ends to be achieved, and the means for attaining these, and it is for them to stimulate all the forces engaged in this common activity." (33)

A society in which the government ("the public authorities") chooses and lays down the objectives to be pursued, the ends to be achieved, and the means for achieving them, is a totalitarian state. It is, therefore, morally shocking to read the very next sentence:

"But let them take care to associate private initiative and intermediary bodies with this work. They will thus avoid the danger of complete collectivization or of arbitrary planning, which, by denying liberty, would prevent the exercise of the fundamental rights of the human person." (33)

What are "the fundamental rights of the human person" (which are never defined in the encyclical) in a state where "all other rights whatsoever . . . are to be subordinated to this principle [the "right" to minimum sustenance]"? (22) What is "liberty" or "private initiative" in a state where the government lays down the ends and commandeers the means? What is *incomplete* collectivization?

It is difficult to believe that modern compromisers, to whom that paragraph is addressed, could stretch their capacity for evasion far enough to take it to mean the advocacy of a mixed economy. A mixed economy is a mixture of capitalism and statism; when the principles and practices of capitalism are damned and annihilated at the root, what is to prevent the statist collectivization from becoming *complete*?

(The moral shock comes from the realization that the encyclical regards some men's capacity for evasion as infinitely elastic. Judging by the reactions it received, the encyclical did not miscalculate.)

I have always maintained that every political theory is based on some code of ethics. Here again, the encyclical confirms my statement, though from the viewpoint of a moral code which is the opposite of mine. "The same duty of solidarity that rests on individuals exists also for nations: 'Advanced nations have a very heavy obligation to help the developing peoples.' It is necessary to put this teaching of the council into effect. Although it is normal that a nation should be the first to benefit from the gifts that Providence has bestowed on it as the fruit of the labors of its people, still no country can claim on that account to keep its wealth for itself alone." (48)

This seems clear enough, but the encyclical takes pains not to be misunderstood. "In other words, the rule of free trade, taken by itself, is no longer able to govern international relations. . . . One must recognize that it is the fundamental principle of liberalism, as the rule for commercial exchange, which is questioned here." (58)

"We must repeat once more that the superfluous wealth of rich countries should be placed at the service of poor nations, the rule which up to now held good for the benefit of those nearest to us, must today be applied to all the needy of this world." (49)

If need—*global* need—is the criterion of morality, if minimum subsistence (the standard of living of the least developed savages) is the criterion of property rights, then every new shirt or dress, every ice cream cone, every automobile, refrigerator, or television set becomes "superfluous wealth."

Remember that "rich" is a relative concept and that the share-croppers of the United States are fabulously rich compared to the laborers of Asia or Africa. Yet the encyclical denounces, as "unjust," free trade among unequally developed countries, on the grounds that "highly industrialized nations export for the most part manufactured goods, while countries with less developed economies have only food, fibers, and other raw materials to sell." (57) Alleging that this perpetuates the poverty of the undeveloped countries, the encyclical demands that international trade be ruled, not by the laws of the free market, but by the *need* of its neediest participants.

How this would work in practice is made explicitly clear: "This demands great generosity, much sacrifice and unceasing effort on the part of the rich man. Let each one examine his conscience, a conscience that conveys a new message for our times. . . . Is he ready to pay higher taxes so that the public authorities can intensify their efforts in favor of development? Is he ready to pay a higher price for imported goods so that the producer may be more justly rewarded?" (47)

It is not only the rich who pay taxes; the major share of the tax burden in the United States is carried by the middle and lower income classes. It is not for the exclusive personal consumption of the rich that foreign goods or raw materials are imported. The price of food is not a major concern to the rich; it is a crucial concern to the poor. And since *food* is listed as one of the chief products of the undeveloped countries, project what the encyclical's proposal would mean: it would mean that an American housewife would have to buy food produced by men who scratch the soil with bare hands or hand-plows, and would pay prices which, if paid to America's mechanized farmers, would have given her a hundred or a thousand times more. Which items of her family budget would she have to sacrifice so that those undeveloped producers "may be more justly rewarded"? Would she sacrifice some purchases of clothing? But her clothing budget would have shrunk in the same manner and proportion—since she would have to provide the "just rewards" of the producers of "fibers and other raw materials." And so on. What, then, would happen to her standard of living? And what would happen to the American farmers and producers of raw materials? Forced to compete, not in terms of productive competence, but of *need*, they would have to arrest their "development" and revert to the methods of the hand-plow. What, then, would happen to the standard of living of the whole world?

No, it is not possible that Pope Paul VI was so ignorant of economics and so lacking in the capacity to concretize his theories that he offered such proposals in the name of "humanism" without realizing the unspeakably inhuman cruelty they entail.

It seems inexplicable. But there is a certain basic premise that would explain it. It would integrate the encyclical's clashing elements—the contradictions, the equivocations, the omissions, the unanswered questions—into a consistent pattern. To discover it, one must ask: What is the encyclical's view of man's nature?

That particular view is seldom admitted or fully identified by those who hold it. It is less a matter of conscious philosophy than of a feeling dictated by a sense of life. The conscious philosophy of those who hold it, consists predominantly of attempts to rationalize it.

To identify that view, let us go to its roots, to the kind of phenomena which give rise to it, in sense-of-life terms.

I will ask you to project the look on a child's face when he grasps the answer to some problem he has been striving to understand. It is a radiant look of joy, of liberation, almost of triumph, which is unself-conscious, yet self-assertive, and its radiance seems to spread in two directions: outward, as an illumination of the world—inward, as the first spark of what is to become the fire of an earned pride. If you have seen this look, or experienced it, you know that if there is such a concept as "sacred"—meaning: the best, the highest possible to man—this look is the sacred, the not-to-be-

betrayed, the not-to-be-sacrificed for anything or anyone.

This look is not confined to children. Comic-strip artists are in the habit of representing it by means of a light-bulb flashing on, above the head of a character who has suddenly grasped an idea. In simple, primitive terms, this is an appropriate symbol: an idea is a light turned on in a man's soul.

It is the steady, confident reflection of that light that you look for in the faces of adults—particularly of those to whom you entrust your most precious values. You look for it in the eyes of a surgeon performing an operation on the body of a loved one; you look for it in the face of a pilot at the controls of the plane in which you are flying; and, if you are consistent, you look for it in the person of the man or woman you marry.

That light-bulb look is the flash of a human intelligence in action; it is the outward manifestation of man's rational faculty; it is the signal and symbol of man's *mind*. And, to the extent of your humanity, it is involved in everything you seek, enjoy, value, or love.

But suppose that admiration is *not* your response to that look on the face of a child or adult? Suppose that your response is a nameless fear? Then you will spend your life and your philosophical capacity on the struggle never to let that fear be named. You will find rationalizations to hide it, and you will call that child's look a look of "selfishness" or "arrogance" or "intransigence" or "pride"—all of which will be true, but not in the way you will struggle to suggest. You will feel that that look in man's eyes is your greatest, most dangerous enemy—and the desire to vanquish that look will become your only absolute, taking precedence over reason, logic, consistency, existence, reality. The desire to vanquish that look is the desire to break man's spirit.

Thus you will acquire the kind of sense of life that produced the encyclical *"Populorum Progressio."* It was not produced by the sense of life of any one person, but by the sense of life of an institution.

The dominant chord of the encyclical's sense of life is hatred for man's *mind*—hence hatred for man—hence hatred for life and for this earth—hence hatred for man's enjoyment of his life on earth—and hence, as a last and least consequence, hatred for the only social system that makes all these values possible in practice: capitalism.

I could maintain this on the grounds of a single example. Consider the proposal to condemn Americans to a lifetime of unrewarded drudgery at forced labor, making them work as hard as they do or harder, with nothing to gain but the barest subsistence—while savages collect the products of their effort. When you hear a proposal of this sort, what image leaps into your mind? What *I* see is the young people who start out in life with self-confident eagerness, who work their way through school, their eyes fixed on their future with a joyous, uncomplaining dedication—and what meaning a new coat, a new rug, an old car bought second-hand, or a ticket to the movies has in their lives, as the fuel of their courage. Anyone who evades that image while he plans to dispose of "the fruit of the labors of people" and declares that human effort is not a sufficient reason for a man to keep his own product—may claim any motive but love of humanity.

I could rest my case on this alone, but I shan't. The encyclical offers more than a sense of life: it contains specific, conscious, philosophical corroboration.

Observe that it is not aimed at destroying man's mind, but at a slower, more agonizing equivalent: at enslaving it.

The key to understanding the encyclical's social theories is contained in a statement of John Galt: "I am the man whose existence your blank-outs were intended to permit you to ignore. I am the man whom you did not want either to live or to die. You did not want me to live, because you were afraid of knowing that I carried the responsibility you dropped and that your lives depended upon me; you did not want me to die, because you knew it." (*Atlas Shrugged*)

The encyclical neither denies nor acknowledges the existence of human intelligence: it merely treats it as an inconsequential human attribute requiring no consideration. The main, and virtually only, reference to the role of intelligence in man's existence reads as follows: "The introduction of industry is a necessity for economic growth and human progress; it is also a sign of development and contributes to it. By persistent work and use of his intelligence, man gradually wrests nature's secrets from her and finds a better application for her riches. As his self-mastery increases, he develops a taste for research and discovery, an ability to take a calculated risk, boldness in enterprises, generosity in what he does and a sense of responsibility." (25)

Observe that the creative power of man's mind (of his basic means of survival, of the faculty that distinguishes him from animals) is described as an acquired *"taste"*—like a taste for olives or for ladies' fashions. Observe that even this paltry acknowledgment is not allowed to stand by itself: lest "research and discovery" be taken as a value, they are enmeshed in such irrelevancies as "generosity."

The same pattern is repeated in discussing the subject of *work*. The encyclical warns that "it [work] can sometimes be given exaggerated significance," but admits that work is a creative process, then adds that "when work is done in common, when hope, hardship, ambition and joy are shared . . . men find themselves to be brothers." (27) And then: "Work, of course, can have contrary effects, for it promises money, pleasure and power, invites some to selfishness, others to revolt . . ." (28)

This means that *pleasure* (the kind of pleasure which is earned by productive work) is evil—*power* (economic power, the kind earned by productive work) is evil—and *money* (the thing which the entire encyclical begs for passionately) is evil if kept in the hands of those who earned it.

Do you see John Galt doing work "in common," sharing "hope, hardship, ambition and joy" with James Taggart, Wesley Mouch, and Dr. Floyd Ferris? But these are only fiction characters, you say? Okay. Do you see Pasteur? Do you see Columbus? Do you see Galileo—and what happened to him when he tried to share his "hope, hardship, ambition and joy" with the Catholic Church?

No, the encyclical does not deny the existence of men of genius; if it did, it would not have to plead so hard for global *sharing*. If all men were interchangeable, if degrees of ability were of no consequence, everyone would produce the same amount and there would be no benefits for anyone to derive from sharing. The encyclical assumes that the unnamed, unrecognized, unacknowledged fountainheads of wealth would somehow continue to function—and proceeds to set up conditions of existence which would make their functioning impossible.

Remember that intelligence is not an exclusive monopoly of genius; it is an attribute of all men, and the differences are only a matter of degree. If conditions of existence are destructive to genius, they are destructive to every man, each in proportion to his intelligence. If genius is penalized, so is the faculty of intelligence in every other man. There is only this difference: the average man does not possess the genius's power of self-confident resistance, and will break much faster; he will give up his mind, in hopeless bewilderment, under the first touch of pressure.

There is no place for the mind in the world proposed by the encyclical, and no place for man. The entities populating it are insentient robots geared to perform prescribed tasks in a gigantic tribal machine, robots deprived of choice, judgment, values, convictions and self-esteem—above all, of self-esteem.

"You are not making a gift of your possessions to the poor person. You are handing over to him what is his." (23) Does the wealth created by Thomas A. Edison belong to the bushmen who did not create it? Does the paycheck you earned this week belong to the hippies next door who did not earn it? A man would not accept that notion; a robot would. A man would take pride in his achievement; it is the pride of achievement that has to be burned out of the robots of the future.

"For what has been given in common for the use of all, you have arrogated to yourself." (23) "God intended the earth and all that it contains for the use of every human being and people." (22) *You* are one of the things that the earth contains; are you, therefore, intended "for the use of every human being and people"? The encyclical's answer is apparently "Yes"—since the world it proposes is based on that premise in every essential respect.

A man would not accept that premise. A man, such as John Galt, would say: "You have never discovered the industrial age—and you cling to the morality of the barbarian eras when a miserable form of human subsistence was produced by the muscular labor of slaves. Every mystic had always longed for slaves, to protect him from the material reality he dreaded. But *you*, you grotesque little atavists, stare blindly at the skyscrapers and smokestacks around you and dream of enslaving the material providers who are scientists, inventors, industrialists. When you clamor for public ownership of the means of production, you are clamoring for public ownership of the mind." (*Atlas Shrugged*)

But a robot would not say it. A robot would be programmed not to question the source of wealth—and would never discover that the source of wealth is man's mind.

On hearing such notions as "The whole of creation is for man" (22) and "The world is given to all" (23), a man would grasp that these are equivocations which evade the question of what is necessary to *make use* of natural resources. He would know that nothing is *given* to him, that the transformation of raw materials into human goods requires a process of thought and labor, which some men will perform and others will not—and that, *in justice*, no man can have a primary *right* to the goods created by the thought and labor of others. A robot would not protest; it would see no difference between itself and raw materials; it would take its own motions as the *given*.

A man who loves his work and knows what enormous virtue—what discipline of thought, of energy, of purpose, of devotion—it requires, would rebel at the prospect of letting it serve those who scorn it. And scorn for material production is splattered all over the encyclical. "Less well off peoples can never be sufficiently on their guard against this temptation, which comes to them from wealthy nations." This temptation is "a way of acting that is principally aimed at the conquest of material prosperity." (41) Advocating a "dialogue" between different civilizations for the purpose of founding "world solidarity," the encyclical stresses that it must be: "A dialogue based on man and not on commodities or technical skills. . . ." (73) Which means that technical skills are a negligible characteristic, that no virtue was needed to acquire them, that the ability to produce commodities deserves no acknowledgment and is not part of the concept "man."

Thus, while the entire encyclical is a plea for the *products* of industrial wealth, it is scornfully indifferent to their source; it asserts a right to the effects, but ignores the cause; it purports to speak on a lofty moral plane, but leaves the *process* of material production outside the realm of morality—as if that process were an activity of a low order that neither involved nor required any moral principles.

I quote from *Atlas Shrugged:* "An industrialist—blank-out—there is no such person. A factory is a 'natural resource,' like a tree, a rock or a mud puddle. . . . Who solved the problem of production? Humanity, they answer. What was the solution? The goods are here. How did they get here? Somehow. What caused it? Nothing has causes." (The last sentence is inapplicable; the encyclical's answer would be: "Providence.")

The process of production is directed by man's mind. Man's mind is not an indeterminate faculty; it requires certain conditions in order to function—and the cardinal one among them is *freedom*. The encyclical is singularly, eloquently devoid of any consideration of the mind's requirements, as if it expected human thought to keep on gushing forth anywhere, under any conditions, from under any pressures—*or as if it intended that gusher to stop*.

If concern for human poverty and suffering were one's primary motive, one would seek to discover their cause. One would not fail to ask: Why did some nations develop, while others did not? Why have some nations achieved material abundance, while others have remained stagnant in sub-human misery? History and, specifically, the unprecedented prosperity-explosion of the nineteenth century, would give an immediate answer: capitalism is the only system that enables men to produce abundance—and the key to capitalism is individual freedom.

It is obvious that a political system affects a society's economics, by protecting or impeding men's productive activities. But *this* is what the encyclical will neither admit nor permit. The relationship of politics and economics is the thing it most emphatically ignores or evades and denies. It declares that no such relationship exists.

In projecting its world of the future, where the civilized countries are to assume the burden of helping and developing the uncivilized ones, the encyclical states: "And the receiving countries could demand that there be no interference in their political life or subversion of their social structures. As sovereign states they have the right to conduct their own affairs, to decide on their policies and to move freely toward the kind of society they choose." (54)

What if the kind of society they choose makes production, development, and progress impossible? What if it practices communism, like Soviet Russia?—or exterminates minorities, like Nazi Germany?—or establishes a religious caste system, like India?—or clings to a nomadic, anti-industrial form of existence, like the Arab countries?—or simply consists of tribal gangs ruled by brute force, like some of the new countries of Africa? The encyclical's tacit answer is that these are the prerogatives of sovereign states—that we must respect different "cultures"—and that the civilized nations of the world must make up for these deficits, *somehow*.

Some of the answer is not tacit. "Given the increasing needs of the underdeveloped countries, it should be considered quite normal for an advanced country to devote a part of its production to meet their needs, and to train teachers, engineers, technicians and scholars prepared to put their knowledge and their skill at the disposal of less fortunate peoples." (48)

The encyclical gives severely explicit instructions to such emissaries. "They ought not to conduct themselves in a lordly fashion, but as helpers and co-workers. A people quickly perceives whether those who come to help them do so with or without affection . . . Their message is in danger of being rejected if it is not presented in the context of brotherly love." (71) They should be free of "all nationalistic pride"; they should "realize that their competence does not confer on them a superiority in every field." They should realize that theirs "is not the only civilization, nor does it enjoy a monopoly of valuable elements." They should "be intent on discovering, along with its history, the component elements of the

cultural riches of the country receiving them. Mutual understanding will be established which will enrich both cultures."
(72)

This is said to civilized men who are to venture into
countries where sacred cows are fed, while children are left
to starve—where female infants are killed or abandoned by
the roadside—where men go blind, medical help being forbidden by their religion—where women are mutilated, to insure
their fidelity—where unspeakable tortures are ceremonially
inflicted on prisoners—where cannibalism is practiced. Are
these the "cultural riches" which a Western man is to greet
with "brotherly love"? Are these the "valuable elements"
which he is to admire and adopt? Are these the "fields" in
which he is not to regard himself as superior? And when he
discovers entire populations rotting alive in such conditions, is
he not to acknowledge, with a burning stab of pride—of
pride and gratitude—the achievements of *his* nation and *his*
culture, of the men who created them and left him a nobler
heritage to carry forward?

The encyclical's implicit answer is "No." He is not to
judge, not to question, not to condemn—only to love; to love
without cause, indiscriminately, unconditionally, in violation
of any values, standards, or convictions of his own.

(The only valuable assistance that Western men could, in
fact, offer to undeveloped countries is to enlighten them on
the nature of capitalism and help them to establish it. But
this would clash with the natives' "cultural traditions"; industrialization cannot be grafted onto superstitious irrationality;
the choice is either-or. Besides, it is a knowledge which the
West itself has lost; and it is *the* specific element which the encyclical damns.)

While the encyclical demands a kind of unfastidious rela-
tivism in regard to cultural values and stressedly urges respect for the right of primitive cultures to hold any values
whatever, it does not extend this tolerance to Western civilization. Speaking of Western businessmen who deal with
countries "recently opened to industrialization," the encyclical states: "Why, then, do they return to the inhuman principles of individualism when they operate in less developed
countries?" (70)

Observe that the horrors of tribal existence in those undeveloped countries evoke no condemnation from the encyclical; only individualism—the principle that raised mankind
out of the primordial swamps—is branded as "inhuman."

In the light of that statement, observe the encyclical's
contempt for conceptual integrity, when it advocates "the

construction of a better world, one which shows deeper respect for the rights and the vocation of the individual." (65) What are the rights of the individual in a world that regards individualism as "inhuman"? No answer.

There is another remark pertaining to Western nations, which is worth noting. The encyclical states: "We are pleased to learn that in certain nations 'military service' can be partially accomplished by doing 'social service,' a 'service pure and simple.' " (74)

It is interesting to discover the probable source of the notion of substituting social work for military service, of the claim that American youths owe their country some years of *servitude* pure and simple—a vicious notion, more evil than the draft, a singularly un-American notion in that it contradicts every fundamental principle of the United States.

The philosophy that created the United States is the encyclical's target, the enemy it seeks to obliterate. A casual reference that seems aimed at Latin America is a bit of window-dressing, a booby-trap for compromisers, upon which they did pounce eagerly. That reference states: "If certain landed estates impede the general prosperity because they are extensive, unused or poorly used . . . the common good sometimes demands their expropriation." (24)

But whatever the sins of Latin America, capitalism is not one of them. Capitalism—a system based on the recognition and protection of individual rights—has never existed in Latin America. In the past and at present, Latin America was and is ruled by a primitive form of fascism: an unorganized, unstructured rule by *coup d'état*, by militaristic gangs, *i.e.*, by physical force, which tolerates a nominal pretense at private property subject to expropriation by any gang in power (which is the cause of Latin America's economic stagnation).

The encyclical is concerned with help to the undeveloped nations of the world. Latin America is high on the list of the undeveloped; it is unable to feed its own people. Can anyone imagine Latin America in the role of global provider, supplying the needs of the entire world? It is only the United States—the country created by the principles of individualism, the freest example of capitalism in history, the first and last exponent of the Rights of Man—that could attempt such a role and would thereby be induced to commit suicide.

Now observe that the encyclical is not concerned with man, with the individual; the "unit" of its thinking is *the tribe*: nations, countries, peoples—and it discusses them as if they had a totalitarian power to dispose of their citizens, as if such entities as individuals were of no significance any longer. This is indicative of the encyclical's strategy: the United States is the highest achievement of the millennia of Western civilization's struggle toward individualism, and its last, precarious remnant. With the obliteration of the United States— *i.e.,* of capitalism—there will be nothing left to deal with on the face of the globe but collectivized tribes. To hasten that day, the encyclical treats it as a *fait accompli* and addresses itself to the relationships among tribes.

Observe that the same morality—*altruism,* the morality of self-immolation—which, for centuries, has been preached against the individual, is now preached against the *civilized nations.* The creed of self-sacrifice—the primordial weapon used to penalize man's success on earth, to undercut his self-confidence, to cripple his independence, to poison his enjoyment of life, to emasculate his pride, to stunt his self-esteem and paralyze his mind—is now counted upon to wreak the same destruction on civilized nations and on civilization as such.

I quote John Galt: "You have reached the blind alley of the treason you committed when you agreed that you had no right to exist. Once, you believed it was 'only a compromise': you conceded it was evil to live for yourself, but moral to live for the sake of your children. Then you conceded that it was selfish to live for your children, but moral to live for your community. Then you conceded that it was selfish to live for your community, but moral to live for your country. *Now,* you are letting this greatest of countries be devoured by any scum from any corner of the earth, while you concede that it is selfish to live for your country and that your moral duty is to live for the globe. A man who has no right to life, has no right to values and will not keep them." (*Atlas Shrugged*)

Rights are conditions of existence required by man's nature for his proper survival qua man—*i.e.,* qua *rational* being. They are not compatible with altruism.

Man's soul or spirit is his consciousness; the motor of his consciousness is reason; deprive him of freedom, *i.e.,* of the right to use his mind—and what is left of him is only a physical body, ready to be manipulated by the strings of any tribe.

Ask yourself whether you have ever read a document as body-oriented as that encyclical. The inhabitants of the world it proposes to establish are robots tuned to respond to a single stimulus: *need*—the lowest, grossest, physical, *physicalistic* need of any other robots anywhere: the minimum necessities, the barely sufficient to keep all robots in working order, eating, sleeping, eliminating, and procreating, to produce more robots to work, eat, sleep, eliminate, and procreate. The most dehumanizing level of poverty is the level on which bare animal necessities become one's only concern and goal; this is the level which the encyclical proposes to institutionalize and on which it proposes to immobilize all of mankind forever, with the animal needs of all as the only motivation of all ("all other rights whatsoever ... are to be subordinated to this principle").

If the encyclical charges that in a capitalist society men fall victim to "a stifling materialism," what is the atmosphere of that proposed world?

The survivor of one such plan described it as follows: "We had no way of knowing their ability [the ability of others], we had no way of controlling their needs—all we knew was that we were beasts of burden struggling blindly in some sort of place that was half-hospital, half-stockyards—a place geared to nothing but disability, disaster, disease—beasts put there for the relief of whatever whoever chose to say was whichever's need: ... To work—with no chance for an extra ration, till the Cambodians have been fed and the Patagonians have been sent through college. To work—on a blank check held by every creature born, by men whom you'll never see, whose needs you'll never know, whose ability or laziness or sloppiness or fraud you have no way to learn and no right to question—just to work and work and work—and leave it up to the Ivys and the Geralds of the world to decide whose stomach will consume the effort, the dreams and the days of your life." (*Atlas Shrugged*)

Do you think that I was exaggerating and that no one preaches ideals of that kind?

But, you say, the encyclical's ideal will not work? It is not intended to work.

It is not intended to relieve suffering or to abolish poverty; it is intended to induce guilt. It is not intended to be accepted and practiced; it is intended to be accepted and broken—broken by man's "selfish" desire to live, which will thus be turned into a shameful weakness. Men who accept as an ideal an irrational goal which they cannot achieve, never lift their heads thereafter—and never discover that their bowed heads were the only goal to be achieved.

The relief of suffering is not altruism's motive, it is only its rationalization. Self-sacrifice is not altruism's means to a happier end, it is its end—self-sacrifice as man's permanent state, as a way of life and joyless toil in the muck of a desolate earth where no "Why?" is ever to flash on in the veiled, extinguished eyes of children.

The encyclical comes close to admitting this prospect, and does not attempt to offer any *earthly* justification for altruistic martyrdom. It declares: "Far from being the ultimate measure of all things, man can only realize himself by reaching beyond himself." (42) (Beyond the grave?) And: "This road toward a greater humanity requires effort and sacrifice, but suffering itself, accepted for the love of our brethren, favors the progress of the entire human family." (79) And: "We are all united in this progress toward God." (80)

As to the attitude toward man's mind, the clearest admission is to be found outside the encyclical. In a speech to a national conference of Italian bishops, on April 7, 1967, Pope Paul VI denounced the questioning of "any dogma that does not please and that demands the humble homage of the mind to be received." And he urged the bishops to combat the "cult of one's own person." (*The New York Times*, April 8, 1967.)

On the question of what political system it advocates, the encyclical is scornfully indifferent: it would, apparently, find any political system acceptable provided it is a version of statism. The vague allusions to some nominal form of private property make it probable that the encyclical favors fascism. On the other hand, the tone, style, and vulgarity of argumentation suggest a shopworn Marxism. But this very vulgarity seems to indicate a profound indifference to intellectual discourse—as if, contemptuous of its audience, the encyclical picked whatever clichés were deemed to be safely fashionable today.

The encyclical insists emphatically on only two political demands: that the nations of the future embrace statism, with a totalitarian control of their citizens' economic activities—and that these nations unite into a global state, with a totalitarian power over global planning. "This international collaboration on a worldwide scale requires institutions that will prepare, coordinate and direct it . . . Who does not see the necessity of thus establishing progressively a world authority, capable of acting effectively in the juridical and political sectors?" (78)

Is there any difference between the encyclical's philosophy and communism? I am perfectly willing, on this matter, to take the word of an eminent Catholic authority. Under the headline: "Encyclical Termed Rebuff to Marxism," *The New*

York Times of March 31, 1967, reports: "The Rev. John Courtney Murray, the prominent Jesuit theologian, described Pope Paul's newest encyclical yesterday as 'the church's definitive answer to Marxism.' . . . 'The Marxists have proposed one way, and in pursuing their program they rely on man alone,' Father Murray said. 'Now Pope Paul VI has issued a detailed plan to accomplish the same goal on the basis of true humanism—humanism that recognizes man's religious nature.' "

Amen.

So much for those American "conservatives" who claim that religion is the base of capitalism—and who believe that they can have capitalism and eat it, too, as the moral cannibalism of the altruist ethics demands.

And so much for those modern "liberals" who pride themselves on being the champions of reason, science, and progress—and who smear the advocates of capitalism as superstitious, reactionary representatives of a dark past. Move over, comrades, and make room for your latest fellow-travelers, who had always belonged on *your* side—then take a look, if you dare, at the kind of past *they* represent.

This is the spectacle of religion climbing on the bandwagon of statism, in a desperate attempt to recapture the power it lost at the time of the Renaissance.

The Catholic Church has never given up the hope to re-establish the medieval union of church and state, with a global state and a global *theocracy* as its ultimate goal. Since the Renaissance, it has always been cautiously last to join that political movement which could serve its purpose at the time. This time, it is too late: collectivism is dead intellectually; the band-wagon on which the Church has climbed is a hearse. But, counting on that vehicle, the Catholic Church is deserting Western civilization and calling upon the barbarian hordes to devour the achievements of man's mind.

There is an element of sadness in this spectacle. Catholicism had once been the most philosophical of all religions. Its long, illustrious philosophical history was illuminated by a giant: Thomas Aquinas. He brought an Aristotelian view of reason (an Aristotelian *epistemology*) back into European culture, and lighted the way to the Renaissance. For the brief span of the nineteenth century, when his was the dominant influence among Catholic philosophers, the grandeur of his thought almost lifted the Church close to the realm of reason (though at the price of a basic contradiction). Now, we are witnessing the end of the Aquinas line—with the Church turning again to his primordial antagonist, who fits it better, to the mind-hating, life-hating St. Augustine. One could only wish they had given St. Thomas a more dignified requiem.

The encyclical is the voice of the Dark Ages, rising again in today's intellectual vacuum, like a cold wind whistling through the empty streets of an abandoned civilization.

Unable to resolve a lethal contradiction, the conflict between individualism and altruism, the West is giving up. When men give up reason and freedom, the vacuum is filled by faith and force.

No social system can stand for long without a moral base. Project a magnificent skyscraper being built on quicksands: while men are struggling upward to add the hundredth and two-hundredth stories, the tenth and twentieth are vanishing, sucked under by the muck. That is the history of capitalism, of its swaying, tottering attempt to stand erect on the foundation of the altruist morality.

It's either-or. If capitalism's befuddled, guilt-ridden apologists do not know it, two fully consistent representatives of altruism do know it: Catholicism and communism.

Their rapprochement, therefore, is not astonishing. Their differences pertain only to the supernatural, but here, in reality, on earth, they have three cardinal elements in common: the same morality, altruism—the same goal, global rule by force—the same enemy, man's mind.

There is a precedent for their strategy. In the German election of 1933, the communists supported the Nazis, on the premise that they could fight each other for power later, but must first destroy their common enemy, capitalism. Today, Catholicism and communism may well cooperate, on the premise that they will fight each other for power later, but must first destroy their common enemy, the individual, by forcing mankind to unite to form one neck ready for one leash.

The encyclical was endorsed with enthusiasm by the communist press the world over. "The French Communist party newspaper, L'Humanité, said the encyclical was 'often moving' and constructive for highlighting the evils of capitalism long emphasized by Marxists," reports *The New York Times* (March 30, 1967).

Those who do not understand the role of moral self-confidence in human affairs, will not appreciate the sardonically ludicrous quality of the following item from the same report: "The French Communists, however, deplored the failure of the Pope to make a distinction between rich Communist countries and rich capitalist countries in his general strictures against imbalance between the 'have' and 'have-not' nations."

Thus, wealth acquired by force, is rightful property, but wealth earned by production, is not; looting is moral, but producing is not. And while the looters' spokesmen object to the encyclical's damnation of wealth, the producers' spokesmen crawl, evading the issues, accepting the insults, promising to give their wealth away. If capitalism does not survive, *this* is the spectacle that will have made it unworthy of survival.

The New York Times (March 30, 1967) declared editorially that the encyclical "is remarkably advanced in its economic philosophy. It is sophisticated, comprehensive and penetrating . . ." If, by "advanced," the editorial meant that the encyclical's philosophy has caught up with that of modern "liberals," one would have to agree—except that the *Times* is mistaken about the *direction* of the motion involved: it is not that the encyclical has progressed to the twentieth century, it is that the "liberals" have reverted to the fourth.

The Wall Street Journal (May 10, 1967) went further. It declared, in effect, that the Pope didn't mean it. The encyclical, it alleged, was just a misunderstanding caused by some mysterious conspiracy of the Vatican translators who misinterpreted the Pope's ideas in transferring them from the original Latin into English. "His Holiness may not be showering compliments on the free market system. But he is not at all saying what the Vatican's English version appeared to make him say."

Through minute comparisons of Latin paragraphs with their official and unofficial translations, and columns of casuistic hair-splitting, *The Wall Street Journal* reached the conclusion that it was not capitalism that the Pope was denouncing, but only *"some opinions"* of capitalism. Which opinions? According to the unofficial translation, the encyclical's paragraph 26 reads as follows: "But out of these new conditions, we know not how, some opinions have crept into human society according to which profit was regarded (in these opinions) as the foremost incentive to encourage economic progress, free competition as the supreme rule of economics, private ownership of the means of production as an absolute right which would accept neither limits nor a social duty related to it. . . ."

"In the Latin," said the article, "Pope Paul is acknowledging the hardships . . . in the development of 'some kinds of capitalism.' But he puts the blame for that not on 'the whole woeful system'—*i.e.*, the whole capitalistic system—but on some corrupt views of it."

If the views advocating the profit motive, free competition, and private property are "corrupt," just *what* is capitalism? Blank out. What is *The Wall Street Journal*'s definition of capitalism? Blank out. What are we to designate as "capitalism" once all of its essential characteristics are removed? Blank out.

This last question indicates the unstated meaning of that article: since the Pope does not attack capitalism, but only its fundamental principles, we don't have to worry.

And for what, do you suppose, did that article find courage to reproach the encyclical? "What might have been wished for in the encyclical was an acknowledgment that capitalism can accept, and in the United States as well as other places does accept, a great many social responsibilities."

Sic transit gloria viae Wall.

A similar attitude, with a similar range of vision, is taken by *Time* magazine (April 7, 1967). "Although Pope Paul had probably tried to give a Christian message relevant to the world's contemporary economic situation, his encyclical virtually ignored the fact that old-style laissez-faire capitalism is about as dead as *Das Kapital*. Quite clearly, the Pope's condemnation of capitalism was addressed to the unreconstructed variety that persists, for example, in Latin America."

If this were a competition, the prize would go to *Fortune,* the businessmen's magazine (May 1967). Its attitude is aggressively amoral and a-philosophical; it is proudly determined to maintain the separation of economics and ethics. "Capitalism is only an economic system," it says.

First acknowledging the Pope's "praiseworthy purpose," *Fortune* declares: "But despite its modern and global vision, *Populorum Progressio* may be a self-defeating document. It takes a dated and suspicious view of the workings of economic enterprise. . . . The Pope has set up a straw man that has few defenders—if this passage [paragraph 26] is taken literally. Unalloyed laissez-faire in fact governs no significant part of the world's commerce. . . . 'Ownership,' in advanced countries, has evolved in a way that subsumes 'social obligations.'. . . 'Absolute' private rights are irrelevant in advanced industrial societies."

After conceding all that, *Fortune* seems to be astonished and hurt that the Pope did not find it necessary to include businessmen among the "men of good will" whom he calls upon to combat global poverty. "In omitting any specific reference to the businessman, he slights a natural and necessary ally, who, indeed is already deeply committed in many parts of the world to the kind of effort that Paul urges. Perhaps the businessman is taken for granted, as a kind of primordial force that can be counted upon to provide motive power, and that needs only to be tamed and harnessed and carefully watched. [And isn't that *Fortune*'s own view of businessmen in their "unalloyed" state?]

"The Vatican has seldom seemed able to look at capitalism as other than a necessary evil, at best, and *Populorum Progressio* suggests that a better understanding still comes hard. This is not to suggest that capitalism is a complete formula for social enlightenment and progress; it is only an economic system that men of good will can use—more successfully than any other system yet conceived—to attain the social goals that politics and religion help to define."

Observe the indecency of trying to justify capitalism on the grounds of altruistic service. Observe also the naiveté of the cynical: it is not their wealth nor the relief of poverty that the encyclical is after.

Militantly concrete-bound, equating cynicism with "practicality," modern pragmatists are unable to see beyond the range of the moment or to grasp what moves the world and determines its direction. Men who are willing to swim with any current, to compromise on anything, to serve as means to anyone's ends, lose the ability to understand the power of ideas. And while two hordes of man-haters, who do understand it, are converging on civilization, they sit in the middle, declaring that principles are straw men.

I have heard the same accusation directed at Objectivism: we are fighting a straw man, they say, nobody preaches the kind of ideas we are opposing.

Well, as a friend of mine observed, only the Vatican, the Kremlin, and the Empire State Building* know the real issues of the modern world.

---

*This publication moved its offices to the Empire State Building in September.

APPENDIX: MAN'S RIGHTS

BY AYN RAND

If one wishes to advocate a free society—that is, capitalism—one must realize that its indispensable foundation is the principle of individual rights. If one wishes to uphold individual rights, one must realize that capitalism is the only system that can uphold and protect them. And if one wishes to gauge the relationship of freedom to the goals of today's intellectuals, one may gauge it by the fact that the concept of individual rights is evaded, distorted, perverted and seldom discussed, most conspicuously seldom by the so-called "conservatives."

"Rights" are a moral concept—the concept that provides a logical transition from the principles guiding an individual's actions to the principles guiding his relationship with others—the concept that preserves and protects individual morality in a social context—the link between the moral code of a man and the legal code of a society, between ethics and politics. *Individual rights are the means of subordinating society to moral law.*

Every political system is based on some code of ethics. The dominant ethics of mankind's history were variants of the altruist-collectivist doctrine which subordinated the individual to some higher authority, either mystical or social. Consequently, most political systems were variants of the same statist tyranny, differing only in degree, not in basic principle, limited only by the accidents of tradition, of chaos, of bloody strife and periodic collapse. Under all such systems, morality was a code applicable to the individual, but not to society. Society was placed *outside* the moral law, as its embodiment or source or exclusive interpreter—and the inculcation of self-sacrificial devotion to social duty was regarded as the main purpose of ethics in man's earthly existence.

Since there is no such entity as "society," since society is only a number of individual men, this meant, in practice, that

Reprinted from *The Virtue of Selfishness*.

the rulers of society were exempt from moral law; subject only to traditional rituals, they held total power and exacted blind obedience—on the implicit principle of: "The good is that which is good for society (or for the tribe, the race, the nation), and the ruler's edicts are its voice on earth."

This was true of all statist systems, under all variants of the altruist-collectivist ethics, mystical or social. "The Divine Right of Kings" summarizes the political theory of the first—"*Vox populi, vox dei*" of the second. As witness: the theocracy of Egypt, with the Pharoah as an embodied god—the unlimited majority rule or *democracy* of Athens—the welfare state run by the Emperors of Rome—the Inquisition of the late Middle Ages—the absolute monarchy of France—the welfare state of Bismarck's Prussia—the gas chambers of Nazi Germany—the slaughterhouse of the Soviet Union.

All these political systems were expressions of the altruist-collectivist ethics—and their common characteristic is the fact that society stood above the moral law, as an omnipotent, sovereign whim worshiper. Thus, politically, all these systems were variants of an *amoral* society.

The most profoundly revolutionary achievement of the United States of America was *the subordination of society to moral law*.

The principle of man's individual rights represented the extension of morality into the social system—as a limitation on the power of the state, as man's protection against the brute force of the collective, as the subordination of *might* to *right*. The United States was the first *moral* society in history.

All previous systems had regarded man as a sacrificial means to the ends of others, and society as an end in itself. The United States regarded man as an end in himself, and society as a means to the peaceful, orderly, *voluntary* co-existence of individuals. All previous systems had held that man's life belongs to society, that society can dispose of him in any way it pleases, and that any freedom he enjoys is his only by favor, by the *permission* of society, which may be revoked at any time. The United States held that man's life is his by *right* (which means: by moral principle and by his nature), that a right is the property of an individual, that society as such has no rights, and that the only moral purpose of a government is the protection of individual rights.

A "right" is a moral principle defining and sanctioning a man's freedom of action in a social context. There is only *one* fundamental right (all the others are its consequences or corollaries): a man's right to his own life. Life is a process of self-sustaining and self-generated action; the right to life means the right to engage in self-sustaining and self-generated action—which means: the freedom to take all the actions required by the nature of a rational being for the support, the furtherance, the fulfillment and the enjoyment of his own life. (Such is the meaning of the right to life, liberty, and the pursuit of happiness.)

The concept of a "right" pertains only to action—specifically, to freedom of action. It means freedom from physical compulsion, coercion or interference by other men.

Thus, for every individual, a right is the moral sanction of a *positive*—of his freedom to act on his own judgment, for his own goals, by his own *voluntary, uncoerced* choice. As to his neighbors, his rights impose no obligations on them except of a *negative* kind: to abstain from violating his rights.

The right to life is the source of all rights—and the right to property is their only implementation. Without property rights, no other rights are possible. Since man has to sustain his life by his own effort, the man who has no right to the product of his effort has no means to sustain his life. The man who produces while others dispose of his product, is a slave.

Bear in mind that the right to property is a right to action, like all the others: it is not the right *to an object,* but to the action and the consequences of producing or earning that object. It is not a guarantee that a man *will* earn any property, but only a guarantee that he will own it if he earns it. It is the right to gain, to keep, to use and to dispose of material values.

The concept of individual rights is so new in human history that most men have not grasped it fully to this day. In accordance with the two theories of ethics, the mystical or the social, some men assert that rights are a gift of God—others, that rights are a gift of society. But, in fact, the source of rights is man's nature.

The Declaration of Independence stated that men "are endowed by their Creator with certain unalienable rights." Whether one believes that man is the product of a Creator or of nature, the issue of man's origin does not alter the fact that he is an entity of a specific kind—a rational being—that he cannot function successfully under coercion, and that rights are a necessary condition of his particular mode of survival.

"The source of man's rights is not divine law or congressional law, but the law of identity. A is A—and Man is Man.

Rights are conditions of existence required by man's nature for his proper survival. If man is to live on earth, it is *right* for him to use his mind, it is *right* to act on his own free judgment, it is *right* to work for his values and to keep the product of his work. If life on earth is his purpose, he has a *right* to live as a rational being: nature forbids him the irrational." (*Atlas Shrugged*)

To violate man's rights means to compel him to act against his own judgment, or to expropriate his values. Basically, there is only one way to do it: by the use of physical force. There are two potential violators of man's rights: the criminals and the government. The great achievement of the United States was to draw a distinction between these two—by forbidding to the second the legalized version of the activities of the first.

The Declaration of Independence laid down the principle that "to secure these rights, governments are instituted among men." This provided the only valid justification of a government and defined its only proper purpose: to protect man's rights by protecting him from physical violence.

Thus the government's function was changed from the role of ruler to the role of servant. The government was set to protect man from criminals—and the Constitution was written to protect man from the government. The Bill of Rights was not directed against private citizens, but against the government—as an explicit declaration that individual rights supersede any public or social power.

The result was the pattern of a civilized society which—for the brief span of some hundred and fifty years—America came close to achieving. A civilized society is one in which physical force is banned from human relationships—in which the government, acting as a policeman, may use force *only* in retaliation and *only* against those who initiate its use.

This was the essential meaning and intent of America's political philosophy, implicit in the principle of individual rights. But it was not formulated explicitly, nor fully accepted nor consistently practiced.

America's inner contradiction was the altruist-collectivist ethics. Altruism is incompatible with freedom, with capitalism and with individual rights. One cannot combine the pursuit of happiness with the moral status of a sacrificial animal.

It was the concept of individual rights that had given birth to a free society. It was with the destruction of individual rights that the destruction of freedom had to begin.

A collectivist tyranny dare not enslave a country by an

outright confiscation of its values, material or moral. It has to be done by a process of internal corruption. Just as in the material realm the plundering of a country's wealth is accomplished by inflating the currency—so today one may witness the process of inflation being applied to the realm of rights. The process entails such a growth of newly promulgated "rights" that people do not notice the fact that the meaning of the concept is being reversed. Just as bad money drives out good money, so these "printing-press rights" negate authentic rights.

Consider the curious fact that never has there been such a proliferation, all over the world, of two contradictory phenomena: of alleged new "rights" and of slave-labor camps.

The "gimmick" was the switch of the concept of rights from the political to the economic realm.

The Democratic Party platform of 1960 summarizes the switch boldly and explicitly. It declares that a Democratic Administration "will reaffirm the economic bill of rights which Franklin Roosevelt wrote into our national conscience sixteen years ago."

Bear clearly in mind the meaning of the concept of *"rights"* when you read the list which that platform offers:

"1. The right to a useful and remunerative job in the industries or shops or farms or mines of the nation.

"2. The right to earn enough to provide adequate food and clothing and recreation.

"3. The right of every farmer to raise and sell his products at a return which will give him and his family a decent living.

"4. The right of every businessman, large and small, to trade in an atmosphere of freedom from unfair competition and domination by monopolies at home and abroad.

"5. The right of every family to a decent home.

"6. The right to adequate medical care and the opportunity to achieve and enjoy good health.

"7. The right to adequate protection from the economic fears of old age, sickness, accidents and unemployment.

"8. The right to a good education."

A single question added to each of the above eight clauses would make the issue clear: *At whose expense?*

Jobs, food, clothing, recreation (!), homes, medical care, education, etc., do not grow in nature. These are man-made values—goods and services produced by men. *Who* is to provide them?

If some men are entitled *by right* to the products of the work of others, it means that those others are deprived of rights and condemned to slave labor.

Any alleged "right" of one man, which necessitates the violation of the rights of another, is not and cannot be a right.

No man can have a right to impose an unchosen obligation, an unrewarded duty or an involuntary servitude on another man. There can be no such thing as *"the right to enslave."*

A right does not include the material implementation of that right by other men; it includes only the freedom to earn that implementation by one's own effort.

Observe, in this context, the intellectual precision of the Founding Fathers: they spoke of the right to *the pursuit* of happiness—*not* of the right to happiness. It means that a man has the right to take the actions he deems necessary to achieve his happiness; it does *not* mean that others must make him happy.

The right to life means that a man has the right to support his life by his own work (on any economic level, as high as his ability will carry him); it does *not* mean that others must provide him with the necessities of life.

The right to property means that a man has the right to take the economic actions necessary to earn property, to use it and to dispose of it; it does *not* mean that others must provide him with property.

The right of free speech means that a man has the right to express his ideas without danger of suppression, interference or punitive action by the government. It does *not* mean that others must provide him with a lecture hall, a radio station or a printing press through which to express his ideas.

Any undertaking that involves more than one man, requires the *voluntary* consent of every participant. Every one of them has the *right* to make his own decision, but none has the right to force his decision on the others.

There is no such thing as "a right to a job"—there is only the right of free trade, that is: a man's right to take a job if another man chooses to hire him. There is no "right to a home," only the right of free trade: the right to build a home or to buy it. There are no "rights to a 'fair' wage or a 'fair' price" if no one chooses to pay it, to hire a man or to buy his product. There are no "rights of consumers" to milk, shoes, movies or champagne if no producers choose to manufacture such items (there is only the right to manufacture them oneself). There are no "rights" of special groups, there are no "rights of farmers, of workers, of businessmen, of employees, of employers, of the old, of the young, of the unborn."

There are only *the Rights of Man*—rights possessed by every individual man and by *all* men as individuals.

Property rights and the right of free trade are man's only "economic rights" (they are, in fact, *political* rights)—and there can be no such thing as "an *economic* bill of rights." But observe that the advocates of the latter have all but destroyed the former.

Remember that rights are moral principles which define and protect a man's freedom of action, but impose no obligations on other men. Private citizens are not a threat to one another's rights or freedom. A private citizen who resorts to physical force and violates the rights of others is a criminal—and men have legal protection against him.

Criminals are a small minority in any age or country. And the harm they have done to mankind is infinitesimal when compared to the horrors—the bloodshed, the wars, the persecutions, the confiscations, the famines, the enslavements, the wholesale destructions—perpetrated by mankind's governments. Potentially, a government is the most dangerous threat to man's rights: it holds a legal monopoly on the use of physical force against legally disarmed victims. When unlimited and unrestricted by individual rights, a government is man's deadliest enemy. It is not as protection against *private* actions, but against governmental actions that the Bill of Rights was written.

Now observe the process by which that protection is being destroyed.

The process consists of ascribing to private citizens the specific violations constitutionally forbidden to the government (which private citizens have no power to commit) and thus freeing the government from all restrictions. The switch is becoming progressively more obvious in the field of free speech. For years, the collectivists have been propagating the notion that a private individual's refusal to finance an opponent is a violation of the opponent's right of free speech and an act of "censorship."

It is "censorship," they claim, if a newspaper refuses to employ or publish writers whose ideas are diametrically opposed to its policy.

It is "censorship," they claim, if businessmen refuse to advertise in a magazine that denounces, insults and smears them.

It is "censorship," they claim, if a TV sponsor objects to some outrage perpetrated on a program he is financing—such as the incident of Alger Hiss being invited to denounce former Vice-President Nixon.

And then there is Newton N. Minow who declares: "There is censorship by ratings, by advertisers, by networks, by affiliates which reject programming offered to their areas." It is the same Mr. Minow who threatens to revoke the license of any station that does not comply with his views on programming—and who claims that *that* is not censorship.

Consider the implications of such a trend.

"Censorship" is a term pertaining only to governmental action. No private action is censorship. No private individual or agency can silence a man or suppress a publication; only the government can do so. The freedom of speech of private individuals includes the right not to agree, not to listen and not to finance one's own antagonists.

But according to such doctrines as the "economic bill of rights," an individual has no right to dispose of his own material means by the guidance of his own convictions—and must hand over his money indiscriminately to any speakers or propagandists, who have a "right" to his property.

This means that the ability to provide the material tools for the expression of ideas deprives a man of the right to hold any ideas. It means that a publisher has to publish books he considers worthless, false or evil—that a TV sponsor has to finance commentators who choose to affront his convictions— that the owner of a newspaper must turn his editorial pages over to any young hooligan who clamors for the enslavement of the press. It means that one group of men acquires the "right" to unlimited license—while another group is reduced to helpless irresponsibility.

But since it is obviously impossible to provide every claimant with a job, a microphone or a newspaper column, *who* will determine the "distribution" of "economic rights" and select the recipients, when the owners' right to choose has been abolished? Well, Mr. Minow has indicated *that* quite clearly.

And if you make the mistake of thinking that this applies only to big property owners, you had better realize that the theory of "economic rights" includes the "right" of every would-be playwright, every beatnik poet, every noise-composer and every non-objective artist (who have political pull) to the financial support you did not give them when you did not attend their shows. What else is the meaning of the project to spend your tax money on subsidized art?

And while people are clamoring about "economic rights," the concept of political rights is vanishing. It is forgotten that the right of free speech means the freedom to advocate one's views and to bear the possible consequences, including disagreement with others, opposition, unpopularity and lack of support. The political function of "the right of free speech" is to protect dissenters and unpopular minorities from forcible suppression—*not* to guarantee them the support, advantages and rewards of a popularity they have not gained.

The Bill of Rights reads: "Congress shall make no law . . . abridging the freedom of speech, or of the press . . ." It does not demand that private citizens provide a microphone for the man who advocates their destruction, or a passkey for the burglar who seeks to rob them, or a knife for the murderer who wants to cut their throats.

Such is the state of one of today's most crucial issues: *political* rights versus *"economic* rights." It's either-or. One destroys the other. But there are, in fact, no "economic rights," no "collective rights," no "public-interest rights." The term "individual rights" is a redundancy: there is no other kind of rights and no one else to possess them.

Those who advocate laissez-faire capitalism are the only advocates of man's rights.

APPENDIX: THE NATURE OF GOVERNMENT

BY AYN RAND

A government is an institution that holds the exclusive power to *enforce* certain rules of social conduct in a given geographical area.

Do men need such an institution—and why?

Since man's mind is his basic tool of survival, his means of gaining knowledge to guide his actions—the basic condition he requires is the freedom to think and to act according to his rational judgment. This does not mean that a man must live alone and that a desert island is the environment best suited to his needs. Men can derive enormous benefits from dealing with one another. A social environment is most conducive to their successful survival—*but only on certain conditions...*

"The two great values to be gained from social existence are: knowledge and trade. Man is the only species that can transmit and expand his store of knowledge from generation to generation; the knowledge potentially available to man is greater than any one man could begin to acquire in his own lifespan; every man gains an incalculable benefit from the knowledge discovered by others. The second great benefit is the division of labor: it enables a man to devote his effort to a particular field of work and to trade with others who specialize in other fields. This form of cooperation allows all men who take part in it to achieve a greater knowledge, skill and productive return on their effort than they could achieve if each had to produce everything he needs, on a desert island or on a self-sustaining farm.

"But these very benefits indicate, delimit and define what kind of men can be of value to one another and in what kind of society: only rational, productive, independent men in a rational, productive, free society." ("The Objectivist Ethics" in *The Virtue of Selfishness.*)

A society that robs an individual of the product of his effort, or enslaves him, or attempts to limit the freedom of

Reprinted from *The Virtue of Selfishness.*

his mind, or compels him to act against his own rational judgment—a society that sets up a conflict between its edicts and the requirements of man's nature—is not, strictly speaking, a society, but a mob held together by institutionalized gang-rule. Such a society destroys all the values of human coexistence, has no possible justification and represents, not a source of benefits, but the deadliest threat to man's survival. Life on a desert island is safer than and incomparably preferable to existence in Soviet Russia or Nazi Germany.

If men are to live together in a peaceful, productive, rational society and deal with one another to mutual benefit, they must accept the basic social principle without which no moral or civilized society is possible: the principle of individual rights.

To recognize individual rights means to recognize and accept the conditions required by man's nature for his proper survival.

Man's rights can be violated only by the use of physical force. It is only by means of physical force that one man can deprive another of his life, or enslave him, or rob him, or prevent him from pursuing his own goals, or compel him to act against his own rational judgment.

The precondition of a civilized society is the barring of physical force from social relationships—thus establishing the principle that if men wish to deal with one another, they may do so only by means of *reason:* by discussion, persuasion and voluntary, uncoerced agreement.

The necessary consequence of man's right to life is his right to self-defense. In a civilized society, force may be used only in retaliation and only against those who initiate its use. All the reasons which make the initiation of physical force an evil, make the retaliatory use of physical force a moral imperative.

If some "pacifist" society renounced the retaliatory use of force, it would be left helplessly at the mercy of the first thug who decided to be immoral. Such a society would achieve the opposite of its intention: instead of abolishing evil, it would encourage and reward it.

If a society provided no organized protection against force, it would compel every citizen to go about armed, to turn his home into a fortress, to shoot any strangers approaching his door—or to join a protective gang of citizens who would fight other gangs, formed for the same purpose, and thus bring about the degeneration of that society into the chaos of gang-rule, *i.e.,* rule by brute force, into the perpetual tribal warfare of prehistorical savages.

The use of physical force—even its retaliatory use—cannot be left at the discretion of individual citizens. Peaceful coexistence is impossible if a man has to live under the constant threat of force to be unleashed against him by any of his neighbors at any moment. Whether his neighbors' intentions are good or bad, whether their judgment is rational or irrational, whether they are motivated by a sense of justice or by ignorance or by prejudice or by malice—the use of force against one man cannot be left to the arbitrary decision of another.

Visualize, for example, what would happen if a man missed his wallet, concluded that he had been robbed, broke into every house in the neighborhood to search it, and shot the first man who gave him a dirty look, taking the look to be a proof of guilt.

The retaliatory use of force requires *objective* rules of evidence to establish that a crime has been committed and to *prove* who committed it, as well as *objective* rules to define punishments and enforcement procedures. Men who attempt to prosecute crimes, without such rules, are a lynch mob. If a society left the retaliatory use of force in the hands of individual citizens, it would degenerate into mob rule, lynch law and an endless series of bloody private feuds or vendettas.

If physical force is to be barred from social relationships, men need an institution charged with the task of protecting their rights under an *objective* code of rules.

This is the task of a government—of a *proper* government —its basic task, its only moral justification and the reason why men do need a government.

A government is the means of placing the retaliatory use of physical force under objective control—i.e., under objectively defined laws.

The fundamental difference between private action and governmental action—a difference thoroughly ignored and evaded today—lies in the fact that a government holds a monopoly on the legal use of physical force. It has to hold such a monopoly, since it is the agent of restraining and combating the use of force; and for that very same reason, its actions have to be rigidly defined, delimited and circumscribed; no touch of whim or caprice should be permitted in its performance; it should be an impersonal robot, with the laws as its only motive power. If a society is to be free, its government has to be controlled.

Under a proper social system, a private individual is legally free to take any action he pleases (so long as he does not violate the rights of others), while a government official is bound by law in his every official act. A private individual may do anything except that which is legally *forbidden;* a government official may do nothing except that which is legally *permitted.*

This is the means of subordinating "might" to "right." This is the American concept of "a government of laws and not of men."

The nature of the laws proper to a free society and the source of its government's authority are both to be derived from the nature and purpose of a proper government. The basic principle of both is indicated in The Declaration of Independence: "to secure these [individual] rights, governments are instituted among men, deriving their just powers from the consent of the governed . . ."

Since the protection of individual rights is the only proper purpose of a government, it is the only proper subject of legislation: all laws must be based on individual rights and aimed at their protection. All laws must be *objective* (and objectively justifiable): men must know clearly, and in advance of taking an action, what the law forbids them to do (and why), what constitutes a crime and what penalty they will incur if they commit it.

The source of the government's authority is "the consent of the governed." This means that the government is not the *ruler,* but the servant or *agent* of the citizens; it means that the government as such has no rights except the rights *delegated* to it by the citizens for a specific purpose.

There is only one basic principle to which an individual must consent if he wishes to live in a free, civilized society: the principle of renouncing the use of physical force and delegating to the government his right of physical self-defense, for the purpose of an orderly, objective, legally defined enforcement. Or, to put it another way, he must accept *the separation of force and whim* (any whim, including his own).

Now what happens in case of a disagreement between two men about an undertaking in which both are involved?

In a free society, men are not forced to deal with one another. They do so only by voluntary agreement and, when a time element is involved, by *contract.* If a contract is broken by the arbitrary decision of one man, it may cause a disastrous financial injury to the other—and the victim would have no recourse except to seize the offender's property as compensation. But here again, the use of force cannot be left to the decision of private individuals. And this leads to one of the most important and most complex functions of the government: to the function of an arbiter who settles disputes among men according to objective laws.

Criminals are a small minority in any semi-civilized society. But the protection and enforcement of contracts through courts of civil law is the most crucial need of a peaceful society; without such protection, no civilization could be developed or maintained.

Man cannot survive, as animals do, by acting on the range of the immediate moment. Man has to project his goals and achieve them across a span of time; he has to calculate his actions and plan his life long-range. The better a man's mind and the greater his knowledge, the longer the range of his planning. The higher or more complex a civilization, the longer the range of activity it requires—and, therefore, the longer the range of contractual agreements among men, and the more urgent their need of protection for the security of such agreements.

Even a primitive barter society could not function if a man agreed to trade a bushel of potatoes for a basket of eggs and, having received the eggs, refused to deliver the potatoes. Visualize what this sort of whim-directed action would mean in an industrial society where men deliver a billion dollars' worth of goods on credit, or contract to build multimillion-dollar structures, or sign ninety-nine-year leases.

A unilateral breach of contract involves an indirect use of physical force: it consists, in essence, of one man receiving the material values, goods or services of another, then refusing to pay for them and thus keeping them by force (by mere physical possession), not by right—*i.e.*, keeping them without the consent of their owner. Fraud involves a similarly indirect use of force: it consists of obtaining material values without their owner's consent, under false pretenses or false promises. Extortion is another variant of an indirect use of force: it consists of obtaining material values, not in exchange for values, but by the threat of force, violence or injury.

Some of these actions are obviously criminal. Others, such as a unilateral breach of contract, may not be criminally motivated, but may be caused by irresponsibility and irrationality. Still others may be complex issues with some claim to justice on both sides. But whatever the case may be, all such issues have to be made subject to objectively defined laws and have to be resolved by an impartial arbiter, administering the laws, *i.e.*, by a judge (and a jury, when appropriate).

Observe the basic principle governing justice in all these cases: it is the principle that no man may obtain any values from others without the owners' consent—and, as a corollary, that a man's rights may not be left at the mercy of the unilateral decision, the arbitrary choice, the irrationality, *the whim* of another man.

Such, in essence, is the proper purpose of a government, to make social existence possible to men, by protecting the benefits and combating the evils which men can cause to one another.

The proper functions of a government fall into three broad categories, all of them involving the issues of physical force and the protection of men's rights: *the police,* to protect men from criminals—*the armed services,* to protect men from foreign invaders—*the law courts,* to settle disputes among men according to objective laws.

These three categories involve many corollary and derivative issues—and their implementation in practice, in the form of specific legislation, is enormously complex. It belongs to the field of a special science: the philosophy of law. Many errors and many disagreements are possible in the field of implementation, but what is essential here is the principle to be implemented: the principle that the purpose of law and of government is the protection of individual rights.

Today, this principle is forgotten, ignored and evaded. The result is the present state of the world, with mankind's retrogression to the lawlessness of absolutist tyranny, to the primitive savagery of rule by brute force.

In unthinking protest against this trend, some people are raising the question of whether government as such is evil by nature and whether anarchy is the ideal social system. Anarchy, as a political concept, is a naive floating abstraction: for all the reasons discussed above, a society without an organized government would be at the mercy of the first criminal who came along and who would precipitate it into the chaos of gang warfare. But the possibility of human immorality is not the only objection to anarchy: even a society whose every member were fully rational and faultlessly moral, could not function in a state of anarchy; it is the need of *objective* laws and of an arbiter for honest disagreements among men that necessitates the establishment of a government.

A recent variant of anarchistic theory, which is befuddling some of the younger advocates of freedom, is a weird absurdity called "competing governments." Accepting the basic premise of the modern statists—who see no difference between the functions of government and the functions of industry, between force and production, and who advocate government ownership of business—the proponents of "competing governments" take the other side of the same coin and declare that since competition is so beneficial to business, it should also be applied to government. Instead of a single, monopolistic government, they declare, there should be a number of different governments in the same geographical area, competing for the allegiance of individual citizens, with every citizen free to "shop" and to patronize whatever government he chooses.

Remember that forcible restraint of men is the only service a government has to offer. Ask yourself what a competition in forcible restraint would have to mean.

One cannot call this theory a contradiction in terms, since it is obviously devoid of any understanding of the terms "competition" and "government." Nor can one call it a floating abstraction, since it is devoid of any contact with or reference to reality and cannot be concretized at all, not even roughly or approximately. One illustration will be sufficient: suppose Mr. Smith, a customer of Government A, suspects that his next-door neighbor, Mr. Jones, a customer of Government B, has robbed him; a squad of Police A proceeds to Mr. Jones's house and is met at the door by a squad of Police B, who declare that they do not accept the validity of Mr. Smith's complaint and do not recognize the authority of Government A. What happens then? You take it from there.

The evolution of the concept of "government" has had a long, tortuous history. Some glimmer of the government's proper function seems to have existed in every organized society, manifesting itself in such phenomena as the recognition of some implicit (if often non-existent) difference between a government and a robber gang—the aura of respect and of moral authority granted to the government as the guardian of "law and order"—the fact that even the most evil types of government found it necessary to maintain some semblance of order and some pretense at justice, if only by routine and tradition, and to claim some sort of moral justification for their power, of a mystical or social nature. Just as the absolute monarchs of France had to invoke "The Divine Right of Kings," so the modern dictators of Soviet Russia have to spend fortunes on propaganda to justify their rule in the eyes of their enslaved subjects.

In mankind's history, the understanding of the government's proper function is a very recent achievement: it is only two hundred years old and it dates from the Founding Fathers of the American Revolution. Not only did they identify the nature and the needs of a free society, but they devised the means to translate it into practice. A free society—like any other human product—cannot be achieved by random means, by mere wishing or by the leaders' "good intentions." A complex legal system, based on *objectively* valid principles, is required to make a society free and *to keep it free*—a system that does not depend on the motives, the moral character or the intentions of any given official, a system that leaves no opportunity, no legal loophole for the development of tyranny.

. The American system of checks and balances was just such an achievement. And although certain contradictions in the Constitution did leave a loophole for the growth of statism, the incomparable achievement was the concept of a constitution as a means of limiting and restricting the power of the government.

Today, when a concerted effort is made to obliterate this point, it cannot be repeated too often that the Constitution is a limitation on the government, not on private individuals— that it does not prescribe the conduct of private individuals, only the conduct of the government—that it is not a charter *for* government power, but a charter of the citizens' protection *against* the government.

Now consider the extent of the moral and political inversion in today's prevalent view of government. Instead of being a protector of man's rights, the government is becoming their most dangerous violator; instead of guarding freedom, the government is establishing slavery; instead of protecting men from the initiators of physical force, the government is initiating physical force and coercion in any manner and issue it pleases; instead of serving as the instrument of *objectivity* in human relationships, the government is creating a deadly, subterranean reign of uncertainty and fear, by means of non-objective laws whose interpretation is left to the arbitrary decisions of random bureaucrats; instead of protecting men from injury by whim, the government is arrogating to itself the power of unlimited whim—so that we are fast approaching the stage of the ultimate inversion: the stage where the government is *free* to do anything it pleases, while the citizens may act only by *permission;* which is the stage of the darkest periods of human history, the stage of rule by brute force.

It has often been remarked that in spite of its material progress, mankind has not achieved any comparable degree of moral progress. That remark is usually followed by some pessimistic conclusion about human nature. It is true that the moral state of mankind is disgracefully low. But if one considers the monstrous moral inversions of the governments (made possible by the altruist-collectivist morality) under which mankind has had to live through most of its history, one begins to wonder how men have managed to preserve

even a semblance of civilization, and what indestructible
vestige of self-esteem has kept them walking upright on two
feet.

One also begins to see more clearly the nature of the
political principles that have to be accepted and advocated, as
part of the battle for man's intellectual Renaissance.

RECOMMENDED BIBLIOGRAPHY

For a study of Objectivism:

Branden, Nathaniel, Who Is Ayn Rand?, *New York: Random House, 1962; Paperback Library, 1964.*

The Objectivist, *a monthly journal published by The Objectivist, Inc., The Empire State Building, 350 Fifth Avenue, New York City.* (Formerly The Objectivist Newsletter.)

Rand, Ayn, Anthem, *Caldwell, Idaho: The Caxton Printers, 1953; New York: The New American Library (Signet), 1961.*

———, Atlas Shrugged, *New York: Random House, 1957; New York: The New American Library (Signet), 1959.*

———, For the New Intellectual, *New York: Random House, 1961; New York: The New American Library (Signet), 1963.*

———, The Fountainhead, *New York: The Bobbs-Merrill Company, 1943; New York: The New American Library (Signet), 1952.*

———, The Virtue of Selfishness, *New York: The New American Library (Signet), 1964; New York: The New American Library, 1965.*

———, We the Living, *New York: Random House, 1959; New York: The New American Library (Signet), 1960.*

The following authors are not exponents of Objectivism, and these recommendations should not be understood as an unqualified endorsement of their total intellectual positions.

Anderson, Benjamin M., Economics and the Public Welfare: Financial and Economic History of the United States, 1914–1946, *Princeton, New Jersey: D. Van Nostrand Co., 1949.*

Anderson, Martin, The Federal Bulldozer: A Critical Analysis of Urban Renewal, 1949–1962, *Cambridge, Massachusetts: The M.I.T. Press, 1964.*

Ashton, T. S., An Economic History of England: The Eighteenth Century, *New York: Barnes and Noble, 1955.*

———, The Industrial Revolution, 1760–1830, *London: Oxford University Press, 1948.*

Ballvé, Faustino, Essentials of Economics, *Princeton, New Jersey: D. Van Nostrand Co., 1963.*

Bastiat, Frédéric, Economic Sophisms, *Princeton, New Jersey: D. Van Nostrand Co., 1964.*

——, Selected Essays on Political Economy, *Princeton, New Jersey: D. Van Nostrand Co., 1964.*

Boehm-Bawerk, Eugen von, The Exploitation Theory, *South Holland, Illinois: Libertarian Press, 1960.*

Buer, Mabel C., Health, Wealth and Population in the Early Days of the Industrial Revolution, 1760–1815, *London: George Routledge & Sons, 1926.*

Chu, Valentin, Ta Ta, Tan Tan (Fight fight, talk talk); The Inside Story of Communist China, *New York: W. W. Norton & Co., 1963.*

Crocker, George N., Roosevelt's Road to Russia, *Chicago: Henry Regnery Co., 1959.*

Dallin, David J., and Nicolaevsky, Boris I., Forced Labor in Soviet Russia, *New Haven, Connecticut: Yale University Press, 1947.*

Ekirch, Arthur A., Jr., The Decline of American Liberalism, *New York: Longmans, Green & Co., 1955.*

Fertig, Lawrence, Prosperity Through Freedom, *Chicago: Henry Regnery Co., 1961.*

Fleming, Harold, Ten Thousand Commandments: A Story of the Antitrust Laws, *New York: Prentice-Hall, 1951.*

Flynn, John T., The Roosevelt Myth, *revised edition, New York: The Devin-Adair Co., 1956.*

George, M. Dorothy, England in Transition: Life and Work in the Eighteenth Century, *London: Penguin, 1953.*

——, London Life in the Eighteenth Century, *3rd edition, London: reprinted by The London School of Economics and Political Science, 1951; New York: Harper and Row (Harper Torchbooks), 1964.*

Hazlitt, Henry, ed., The Critics of Keynesian Economics, *Princeton, New Jersey: D. Van Nostrand Co., 1960.*

——, Economics in One Lesson, *New York: Harper and Brothers, 1946.*

——, The Failure of the "New Economics": An Analysis of the Keynesian Fallacies, *Princeton, New Jersey: D. Van Nostrand Co., 1959.*

——, What You Should Know About Inflation, *2nd edition, Princeton, New Jersey: D. Van Nostrand Co., 1965.*

Hewitt, Margaret, Wives and Mothers in Victorian Industry, *London: Rockliff, 1958.*

Keller, Werner, East Minus West = Zero: Russia's Debt to the Western World. 862–1962, *New York: G. P. Putnam's Sons, 1962. (Published in Great Britain as Are the Russians Ten Feet Tall?, London: Thames and Hudson, 1961.)*

Kubek, Anthony, How the Far East Was Lost: American Policy and the Creation of Communist China, 1941–1949, *Chicago: Henry Regnery Co., 1963.*

Lynch, Matthew J., and Raphael, Stanley S., Medicine and the State, *Springfield, Illinois: Charles C. Thomas, 1963.*

Mason, Lowell B., The Language of Dissent, *New Canaan, Connecticut: The Long House. (Originally published Cleveland, Ohio: The World Publishing Co., 1959.)*

Neale, A. D., The Antitrust Laws of the United States of America: A Study of Competition Enforced by Law, *Cambridge, England: Cambridge University Press, 1960.*

Paterson, Isabel, The God of the Machine, *Caldwell, Idaho: The Caxton Printers, 1964. (Originally published New York: G. P. Putnam's Sons, 1943.)*

Snyder, Carl, Capitalism the Creator: The Economic Foundations of Modern Industrial Society, *New York: The Macmillan Company, 1940.*

von Mises, Ludwig, The Anti-Capitalistic Mentality, *Princeton, New Jersey: D. Van Nostrand Co., 1956*

——, Bureaucracy, *New Haven, Connecticut, and London: Yale University Press, 1944.*

——, Human Action: A Treatise on Economics, *New Haven, Connecticut: Yale University Press, 1949.*

——, Omnipotent Government, *New Haven, Connecticut: Yale University Press, 1944.*

——, Planned Chaos, *Irvington-on-Hudson, New York: The Foundation for Economic Education, 1947.*

——, Planning for Freedom, *2nd edition, South Holland, Illinois: Libertarian Press, 1962.*

——, Socialism: An Economic and Sociological Analysis, *New Haven, Connecticut: Yale University Press, 1951.*

——, The Theory of Money and Credit, *new edition, New Haven, Connecticut, and London: Yale University Press, 1953.*

INDEX

INDEX

Prepared by *Allan Gotthelf,*

Department of Philosophy, Wesleyan University

THE VIRTUE OF SELFISHNESS:

A New Concept of Egoism

by Ayn Rand

Ayn Rand here sets forth the moral principles of Objectivism, the philosophy that holds man's life—the life proper to a rational being—as the standard of moral values and regards altruism as incompatible with man's nature, with the creative requirements of his survival, and with a free society.

Her unique philosophy is the underlying theme of Ayn Rand's famous novels.

Signet E8645—$1.75

ATLAS SHRUGGED
by *Ayn Rand*

Tremendous in scope, breath-taking in its suspense, this is the story of a man who said that he would stop the motor of the world—and did.

Is he a destroyer or a liberator? Why does he have to fight his battle not against his enemies but against those who need him most—including the woman he loves?

Ayn Rand says about this book, "To all the readers who discovered *The Fountainhead* and asked me many questions about the wider application of its ideas, I want to say that I am answering these questions in the present novel, and that *The Fountainhead* was only an overture to *Atlas Shrugged*. I trust that no one will tell me that men such as I write about don't exist. That this book has been written—and published—is my proof that they do."

(#E9135—$3.50)